To Nancy, Jackie, Miles, Margot, and Blair

Microtrends

▲

The Small Forces

Behind Today's Big Changes

Mark J. Penn
with E. Kinney Zalesne

ALLEN LANE
an imprint of
PENGUIN BOOKS

ALLEN LANE

Published by the Penguin Group
Penguin Books Ltd, 80 Strand, London WC2R ORL, England
Penguin Group (USA) Inc., 375 Hudson Street, New York, New York 10014, USA
Penguin Group (Canada), 90 Eglinton Avenue East, Suite 700, Toronto, Ontario, Canada M4P 2Y3
(a division of Pearson Penguin Canada Inc.)
Penguin Ireland, 25 St Stephen's Green, Dublin 2, Ireland (a division of Penguin Books Ltd)
Penguin Group (Australia), 250 Camberwell Road, Camberwell, Victoria 3124, Australia
(a division of Pearson Australia Group Pty Ltd)
Penguin Books India Pvt Ltd, 11 Community Centre, Panchsheel Park, New Delhi – 110 017, India
Penguin Group (NZ), 67 Apollo Drive, Rosedale, North Shore 0632, New Zealand
(a division of Pearson New Zealand Ltd)
Penguin Books (South Africa) (Pty) Ltd, 24 Sturdee Avenue, Rosebank, Johannesburg 2196, South Africa

Penguin Books Ltd, Registered Offices: 80 Strand, London WC2R ORL, England

www.penguin.com

First published in the United States of America by Twelve, an imprint of Grand Central Publishing 2007
First published in Great Britain by Allen Lane 2007

1

Copyright © Mark Penn, 2007

Printed in Great Britain by Clays Ltd, St Ives plc

A CIP catalogue record for this book is available from the British Library

HARDBACK
978–1–846–14042–6

TRADE PAPERBACK
978–1–846–14062–4

www.greenpenguin.co.uk

Contents

Introduction

▲

In 1960, Volkswagen shook up the car world with a full-page ad that had just two words on it: *Think Small.* It was a revolutionary idea—a call for the shrinking of perspective, ambition, and scale in an era when success was all about accumulation and territorial gain, even when you were just driving down the street.

At the same time that America was becoming the world's superpower, growing the dominant economy and setting the pace for global markets, the Beetle took off as a counterculture phenomenon—representing individuality in reaction to the conformity of the 1950s.

America never quite got used to small when it came to cars. But ask two-thirds of America, and they will tell you they work for a small business. Americans are willing to make big changes only when they first see the small, concrete steps that will lead to those changes. And they yearn for the lifestyles of small-town America. Many of the biggest movements in America today are small—generally hidden from all but the most careful observer.

Microtrends is based on the idea that the most powerful forces in our society are the emerging, counterintuitive trends that are shaping tomorrow right before us. With so much of a spotlight on teen crime, it is hard to see the young people who are succeeding as never before. With so much focus on poverty as the cause of terrorism, it is hard to see that it is richer, educated terrorists who have been behind many of the attacks. With so much attention to big organized religion, it is hard to see that it is newer, small sects that are the fastest-growing.

The power of individual choice has never been greater, and the reasons and patterns for those choices never harder to understand and analyze. The skill of microtargeting—identifying small, intense subgroups and communicating with them about their individual needs and wants—has never been more critical in marketing or in political campaigns. The one-size-fits-all approach to the world is dead.

Thirty years ago sitting in Harvard's Lamont Library, I read a book that started out, "The perverse and unorthodox thesis of this little book is that the voters are not fools." Its author, V.O. Key, Jr., made an argument that, since that day, has guided how I think not just about voters but consumers, corporations, governments and the world at large. If you use the right tools and look at the facts, it turns out that the average Joe is actually pretty smart, making some very rational choices.

Yet almost every day, I hear experts say that voters and consumers are misguided scatterbrains, making decisions on the basis of the color of a tie. That's why politicians pay consultants to tell them to wear earth-tone suits, or get their facial lines removed. That's why many commercials feature pointless stories with no relation to the products. Too often, candidates and marketers don't believe the facts or the issues matter that much. Oftentimes, it is they who are the fools. I bet at least two-thirds of all communications are wasted with messages and images that only their creators understood.

The perspective of this book is that, thirty years later, V.O Key, Jr.'s, observation is not only sound, but should be the guiding principle of understanding the trends we see in America and around the world. People have never been more sophisticated, more individualistic, or more knowledgeable about the choices they make in their daily lives. Yet, as Key observed, it takes intensive, scientific study to find the logical patterns that underlie those choices. When faced with people's seemingly contradictory choices, it can be a lot easier to chalk them up to brown suits and Botox.

And indeed, the contradictions today are striking. While people are eating more healthful foods than ever, Big Mac sales have never been higher. While Fox News is number one in the ratings, the antiwar movement dominates most news coverage. While America is growing older, most of what we see in advertising and entertainment has been created with youth in mind. While people are dating as never before, they have never been more interested in deeper, longer-lasting relationships. While more people than ever before are drinking clear, natural water, more people are also drinking "monster" energy drinks loaded with chemicals and caffeine.

In fact, the whole idea that there are a few huge trends that determine how America and the world work is breaking down. There are no longer a couple of megaforces sweeping us all along. Instead, America and the world are being pulled apart by an intricate maze of choices, accumulating in "microtrends"—small, under-the-radar forces that can involve as little as 1 percent of the population, but which are powerfully shaping our society. It's not just that small is the new big. It's that in order to truly know what's going on, we need better tools than just the naked eye and an eloquent tongue. We need the equivalent of magnifying glasses and microscopes, which in sociological terms are polls, surveys, and statistics. They take a slice of the matter being studied and lay it open—bigger and clearer—for examination. And inside, you will find yourself, your friends, your clients, your customers, and your competition, clearer than you ever thought you might.

Working for President Clinton in 1996, I identified the under-the-radar group that became known as the Soccer Moms. (I like to think I did something for the youth soccer movement, although I really didn't mean to. The phrase was just meant to get at busy suburban women devoted to their jobs and their kids, who had real concerns about real presidential policies.) Until that campaign, it was generally thought that politics was dominated by men, who decided how their households would vote. But the truth was, in 1996, most male voters had already made up their minds by the campaign. The people left to influence were the new group of independent Moms, devoted to both work and their kids, who had not yet firmly decided which party would be good for their families. They, not their husbands, were the critical swing voters. To win them over, President Clinton initiated a campaign to give them a helping hand in raising their kids—drug-testing in schools, measures against teen smoking, limits on violence in the media, and school uniforms. These Moms did not want more government in their lives, but they were quite happy to have a little more government in their kids' lives to keep them on the straight and narrow.

In retrospect, a profound political change was spawned by this bit of trend-spotting. Previously, almost all Democrats had targeted downscale, noncollege workers, particularly in the manufacturing sector. But union membership and manufacturing jobs were shrinking, more people were going to college, and almost the entire electorate in the U.S. was calling itself middle class. If Democrats missed the key trends, they would miss the boat.

Now candidates enthusiastically target Soccer Moms—although someone may want to let them know that trends move fast, and Soccer Moms, too, have moved on. Now, a decade later, their kids are getting ready for college, many of them have been through a divorce, and their own financial security has become as big an issue for them as raising their children was ten years ago.

And with all of the attention being paid to those Moms, Dads— suburban-based, family-focused, office-park-working Dads—are all but neglected in politics, advertising, and the media. In the twenty-first century, Dads spend more time with their children then ever in history. Has Madison Avenue adjusted? Are Dads *ever* the target of back-to-school campaigns?

There could be as big a shift ahead in marketing as 1996 saw in Democratic politics.

The art of trend-spotting, through polls, is to find groups that are pursuing common activities and desires, and that have either started to come together or can be brought together by the right appeal that crystallizes their needs. Soccer Moms had been there for a decade or more—but they became a political class only when they were recognized as a remarkably powerful voting bloc in America.

Today, changing lifestyles, the Internet, the balkanization of communications, and the global economy are all coming together to create a new sense of individualism that is powerfully transforming our society. The world may be getting flatter, in terms of globalization, but it is occupied by 6 billion little bumps who do not *have* to follow the herd to be heard. No matter how offbeat their choices, they can now find 100,000 people or more who share their taste for deep fried yak on a stick.

In fact, by the time a trend hits 1 percent, it is ready to spawn a hit movie, best-selling book, or new political movement. The power of individual choice is increasingly influencing politics, religion, entertainment, and even war. In today's mass societies, it takes only 1 percent of people making a dedicated choice—contrary to the mainstream's choice—to create a movement that can change the world.

Just look at what has happened in the U.S. to illegal immigrants. A few years ago, they were the forgotten Americans, hiding from daylight and the authorities. Today they are holding political rallies, and given where they and their legal, voting relatives live, they may turn out to be the new Soccer Moms. Militant immigrants fed up with a broken immigration system just may be the most important voters in the next presidential election, distributed in the key Southwest states that are becoming the new battleground areas.

It's the same in business, too, since the Internet has made it so easy to link people together. In the past, it was almost impossible to market to small groups who were spread around the country. Now it's a virtual piece of cake to find 1 million people who want to try your grapefruit diet, or who can't get their kids to sleep at night.

The math can be not just strategic, but also catastrophic. If Islamic terrorists were to convince even just *one-tenth* of 1 percent of America's population that they were right, they would have 300,000 soldiers of terror, more than enough to destabilize our society. If they could convert just *1 percent* of the world's 1 billion Muslims to take up violence, that would be 10 million terrorists, a group that could dwarf even the largest armies and police forces on earth. This is the power of small groups that come together today.

The power of choice is especially evident as more and more Americans make decisions about their own lives. For example, the population growth in America has slowed to .9 percent, but the number of households has exploded. Between people getting divorced, staying single longer, living longer, and never marrying at all, we are experiencing an explosion in the number of people who are heads of households—almost 115 million in 2006 compared to about 80 million in 1980. The percentage of households consisting of one person living alone increased from 17 percent in 1970 to 26 percent in 2003. The proportion of married-with-kids households has fallen to less than 25 percent.

All these people out there living a more single, independent life are slivering America into hundreds of small niches. Single people, and people without kids at home, have more time to follow their interests, pick up hobbies, get on the Internet, have a political debate, or go out to movies. By all rights, no one should even go to the movies anymore—you can get movies practically as fast by downloading them or using pay-per-view—but for people with a free Saturday night, movies are such a solid preference that theaters are *raising* their prices, not lowering them. More people have more disposable resources (including money, time, and energy) than ever before. They are deploying them in pursuit of personal satisfaction like never before. And as a result, we're getting a clearer picture of who people are and what they want. And in business, politics, and social-problem-solving, having that information can make all the difference.

This book is all about the niching of America. How there is no One America anymore, or Two, or Three, or Eight. In fact, there are hundreds of Americas, hundreds of new niches made up of people drawn together by common interests.

Nor is niching confined just to America. It is a global phenomenon that is making it extremely difficult to unify people in the twenty-first century. Just when we thought that, thanks to the Internet, the world would be not only connected but ultimately unified around shared values favoring democracy, peace and security, exactly the opposite is happening. We are flying apart at a record pace.

I recently went bowling and, contrary to another popular but misguided idea, no one was there alone. But actually, the people hurling the balls down the lanes weren't the clichéd pot-bellied, beer-drinking bowlers, either. In fact, there appeared to be no similarity at all from one group to another. In one lane was a family of Indian immigrants, including the grandparents. In another lane was a black Mom with two adolescent kids. In a third lane were four white teens, some with tattoos, some with polo shirts. And two lanes down, a Spanish-speaking man and woman were clearly on a bowling date, smooching between spares.

With the rise in freedom of choice has come a rise in individuality. And with the rise of individuality has come a rise in the power of choice. The more choices people have, the more they segregate themselves into smaller and smaller niches in society.

The Explosion of Choice

At the Boston Tea Party in 1773, there was probably only one kind of tea hurled overboard—English Breakfast. Today, if Americans staged that rebellion, there would be hundreds of different teas flying into the harbor, from caffeine-free jasmine rose to Moroccan mint to sweet Thai delight.

You can't even buy potato chips anymore without having to pick from among baked, fried, rippled, fat-reduced, salted, or flavored—with flavor sub-categories including barbeque, sweet potato, onion and chive, and Monterey Pepper Jack.

We live in a world with a deluge of choices. In almost every area of life, Americans have wider freedom of choice today than ever in history, including new kinds of jobs, new foods, new religions, new technologies, and new forms of communication and interaction.

In some sense, it's the triumph of the Starbucks economy over the Ford economy. In the early 1900s, Henry Ford created the assembly line so that mass consumerism could take place—uniformly. Thousands of workers turned out one black car, millions and millions of times.

Today, few products still exist like that. (One that does, ironically, is the personal computer, which has made it to every desk in every home in essentially the same form. There is some customization around the edges, but if you go to a typical CompUSA to buy a computer, you'll have fewer options than you do choosing lettuce in the supermarket.)

By contrast, Starbucks is governed by the idea that people make choices—in their coffee, their milk, their sweetener—and that the more choices people have, the greater satisfaction they feel. (And in just those simple choices, you can see the unpredictability of the consumers—some are avoiding caffeine, fat, or sugar, and others are happily ordering them all.) Starbucks is successful because it can be all things to all people—it makes no bets on one set of choices over another.

Whereas in the Ford economy, the masses were served by many people working to make one, uniform product, in the Starbucks economy, the masses are served by a few people working to make thousands of customized, personalized products.

The Starbucks model seems to be winning. iPods are popular not because we can carry around music—we could do that with the Walkman in the 1980s. They are popular because they let us pick and choose our own songs. Personal technology has become *personalized* technology, and now we can have exactly what we want in almost every consumer area. You can even have a made-to-order car delivered in less than a month—longer than it takes to get a pizza, but still an amazing feat made possible by technology.

The triumph of personalization and choice is a boon for coffee-drinkers and car-buyers, but it's a nightmare for trend-spotters. As choices get more and more finely sliced, you have to look all the harder to see how choices change.

But remember the terrorists, or realize that the best-selling car in America is bought by barely 300,000 people. Unlike any other time in history, small trends can make a big difference. So while it is harder than ever to spot trends, it is also more important.

Small groups, drawn together by shared needs, habits, and preferences, are on the rise. They are powerful, and they are hard to find. This book aims to pin some of them down.

The Power of Numbers

There have been some very good books in recent years that claim that America is moving in a couple of big directions. This book contends the opposite. America is moving in hundreds of small directions. At once. Quickly. It's part of our great energy and part of our looming challenge.

Because small trends pay very little deference to one another. For every high-profile group of young, urban chic in America, there is another group of older, old-fashioned churchgoers. For every group of Gadget Geeks, there are the people who say turn the technology off. Americans are dieting more than ever, but the steak houses have never been more full. Politics is split to the extremes with "red states" and "blue states," but there have never been more voters who call themselves Independent.

For thirty years since reading V. O. Key, I have used the most reliable device I know of to spot trends, or the shifts and evolutions in these groups: numbers. Americans claim to be a "gut" nation—which is kind of a bodily metaphor for what we roughly term our "values." How many times do you hear that the right thing to do is to follow your gut?

Most of the time, though, that advice is pretty lousy. If you want the safest form of transportation, get on a plane; don't go near a car. If you want to lose weight, count calories; forget the cranberry juice and flaxseed. Numbers will almost always take you where you want to go if you know how to read them.

In general we love numbers—a hit TV show these days is even called Numb3rs. But we also fear them. In part because we're less well trained in math and science than we are in language and literature. As a country, we suspect we're not that good at numbers. They scare us, almost as much as public speaking. At the same time they fascinate us.

Many of us have a healthy mistrust of numbers, because some people, in an effort to advance an agenda, misuse them. Do you remember the Y2K scare? Every computer-user on earth worried that their files were in jeopardy as the millennium turned over. In fact, only one-third of the world's computers were ever even susceptible to Y2K errors—and in those, hardly any problems materialized. Or avian flu. In late 2005, it sped around the world that out of 140 or so human cases of avian flu reported in Southeast Asia, more than half had resulted in death. Reporters somberly concluded that the mortality rate for avian flu is more than 50 percent. Terrifying! But in fact the sample those numbers came from was only the very sickest people. People who contracted the flu and never went to the hospital never even made it into the calculations. I call these reported numbers "scaretistics."

My job, in thirty years as a pollster, has been to separate the wheat from the chaff when it comes to numbers. In working for different kinds of clients, from Bill Clinton to Bill Gates to Tony Blair, I have learned to pierce through remarkably stubborn conventional wisdom, finding counterintuitive trends in society that can help solve substantial challenges. Imagine for a moment that you are a powerful leader. Eloquent advocates tug at you every day, and the press gives you its opinions. Your advisers chime in. It becomes hard to make the right choice unless you also have the missing ingredient: the numbers. My job was to wade through all the opinions and offer a solid, quantitative view of reality based on the numbers, so that leaders had a true picture when they made their decisions. In my view, words without numbers are as meaningless as numbers without words—you need the right balance, so that eloquent arguments are backed up by reality as depicted by numbers. Later in the book, we talk about rising crime in America—a very difficult subject that has been the focus of countless treatises and theories on everything from unemployment to permissive parenting. But when you understand that the number of felons being released from jail has lately escalated to 650,000 people a year, you instantly have a model of a new threat on the streets and are pointed to a new set of solutions.

In my role as pollster and strategist, I have helped generate winning counterintuitive strategies that follow the numbers. Going after the Soccer Moms in 1996. Helping soon-to-be Senator Hillary Clinton in 2000 look for votes in upstate New York, where Democrats had not traditionally found many. Breaking the mold on advertising for companies by having them pitch their ads to older people, not young ones. Advising the winners of fifteen foreign presidential elections in languages I could not even pronounce, let alone understand, because I stuck to the numbers and not local biases. Often, people are just too close to the situation to see the real facts—and it takes an objective look to tell them what is really going on. Leaders can be even more isolated, often captive to their staffs, and hearing only what local journalists say is going on. Numbers can cut to the chase in any language.

I remember one day telling the new president of Colombia that his people were ready for an all-out war on drugs by an overwhelming percentage. They did not, as most people thought, want to turn a blind eye but wanted to modernize the country. The president was silent on the matter—but finally his chief of staff said, "Mark, you are right, but we would all be killed." He taught me the limits of the numbers that day, but eventually both that president and the country did decide to make war on the drug lords, and risk their lives in the process.

This book is about the power of numbers and how they drive America and the world. Rarely are things what they seem on the surface, and non-quantitative, conventional wisdom is usually not wisdom at all. Hidden right in front of us are powerful counterintuitive trends that can be used to drive a new business, run a campaign, start a movement, or guide your investment strategy. Even though these trends are staring us in the face, we often don't really see them.

Trend Spotters in Context

I am part of a proud line of trend-spotters. Alvin Toffler, who wrote the *Future Shock* series, and John Naisbitt, who wrote *Megatrends*, were some of the first thinkers in the modern era to look at the huge, changing world of human behavior and try to make some sense of it with facts and data. They got it right that the Information Age would change everything.

But one thing in particular that it changed was the nature of looking at trends themselves. As we'll see throughout this book, you can't understand the world anymore only in terms of "megatrends," or universal experiences. In today's splintered society, if you want to operate successfully, you have to understand the intense identity groups that are growing and moving, fast and furious in crisscrossing directions. That is microtrends.

It is very different, however, from what most people do when they "spot trends"—which is itself a growing trend. Lately there is something of a cottage industry of marketers and sociologists who will tell you the Ten or Fifteen Things You Must Know to get through the next two or five or ten years. They define and refine the world around them with ever cuter and cleverer names for the consumer, cultural, and personal changes going on in society. Yes, I aim for some sticky labels in this book, too. But in this book, a trend is not merely a "development," like the declining use of cash. It is not simply a "shift" in how people do things, like more women taking their husband's name. It is not just an evolving "preference" for a product or activity, like the growing use of GPS systems. *A microtrend is an intense identity group, that is growing, which has needs and wants unmet by the current crop of companies, marketers, policymakers, and others who would influence society's behavior.*

Diving In

In *Microtrends*, we will look at seventy-five groups who, by virtue of their daily decisions, are forging the shape of America and the world both today and tomorrow. While some groups are larger than others, what they have in common is that they are relatively unseen—either because their actual numbers are small or because conventional wisdom hides their potential in the shadows, sometimes even emphasizing the exact opposite.

In some of the groups, you will see yourself or your friends, your clients or your constituents. Some groups will seem wildly remote. Some funny. Others tragic. Occasionally, I have documented diametrically opposing trends. Taken together, they are a kind of impressionist painting of America and the world.

At the end, we'll take a step back and look at the portrait. No longer the sum of a few master strokes, America and the world are now a collection of fine dots, to be examined one by one. We'll see what image emerges at the end, and what it means for our future.

PART I

Love, Sex, and Relationships

Sex-Ratio Singles

▲

There is perhaps no feeling more acute than being left out. Everyone remembers what it felt like not to be picked for a sports team, or to be excluded from a friends' night out, or to be the only one not invited to a wedding. What compounds the angst, of course, is the injustice—*why me?* I am a better ballplayer, a more loyal friend, a more gregarious guest—and yet I'm the one left out.

In today's world, more and more women are finding themselves left out of the institution of marriage. Some opt out deliberately, but others fill up the dating Web sites, only to be disappointed. Many blame themselves, wondering what went wrong.

The truth is, there is *nothing* wrong with single women that a few more heterosexual men wouldn't fix. In the Wild West 150 years ago, there were too few women, so they had to import brides. Today, we have the opposite problem. There are too few straight men for all the straight women, and so women are unexpectedly caught in a game of musical chairs—in which at least 3 percent of them are going to be left standing.

In 1994, a National Opinion Research Center study on "The Social Organization of Sexuality" found that 9 percent of men and 4 percent of women said they had engaged in at least some homosexual behavior since puberty. Another study by a team at the Harvard School of Public Health reported that 6.2 percent of men and 3.6 percent of women reported a same-sex partner in the previous three years. A third study reported that 9 percent of men and 5 percent of women who had had at least one homosexual experience said those experiences could be described as "frequent" or "ongoing."

What these studies suggest is that whatever the actual number of gay people may be, gay men outnumber lesbians in America by approximately 2 to 1.

Numerically speaking, when the music stops in heterosexual America, there are a lot of women left standing.

Which means that for the first time in America, there are more single women than ever who are likely to stay that way.

Single Women in America, 1970–2005

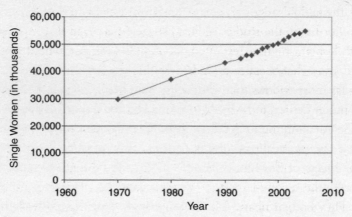

Source: U.S. Census, 2006

Here's how the numbers play out.

At birth, girls have it pretty good. There are 90,000 more boys born every year than girls, setting up a favorable dating ratio. But by the time those kids turn 18, the sex ratio has shifted a full point the other way to 51 to 49, because more boys die in puberty than girls. (Researchers call it a "testosterone storm," which causes more deaths among boys from car accidents, homicides, suicides, and drownings.)

As though that wasn't bad enough—socially speaking, for heterosexual women—the Gay Factor then kicks in. Assuming that about 5 percent of U.S. adults are gay (as experts claim, and polls bear out), there are something like 7.5 million gay men and 3.5 million lesbians in America. If you subtract them from the already lopsided numbers of overall men and women, you get something like 109 million straight women to 98 million straight men—for a straight sex ratio of 53 to 47.

It is even worse for black women. Setting aside the gay factor (which doesn't actually move the black adult sex ratio, since the number of black adults is relatively small), the gender ratio in the black adult community already starts out at 56 to 44, due to the high rates of death among black teenage boys. Then the relatively high incarceration rate of black men—4,700 for every 100,000 black men, compared to only 347 for every 100,000 black women—moves that ratio another point, to 57 to 43. Factor in gender gaps in college education *on top of that*, and it's no surprise that many black women, especially the more successful they are, are single.

It is always possible that there are more secret lesbians than gay men— certainly, the tabloids regularly accuse female public figures of being lesbian. On the other hand, the studies seem to suggest that even if women experiment with lesbianism, they less often choose it as their permanent lifestyle.

We all know that because men die about four years earlier than women, there are far more widows than widowers. But clearly the gender imbalance happens much earlier, too—in the dating years—yet because there has not been sufficient attention to that fact, women too often blame themselves for events that are statistically beyond their control.

Some effects of Sex-Ratio Singles are already evident. In 2005, single women were the second-largest group of home-buyers, just behind married couples. They bought nearly 1.5 million homes that year, more than *twice* as many as single men. Though it would have been unheard of fifty years ago, American women are now regularly buying homes and building equity before they are buying bridesmaids gifts and building families.

A related trend, given the rise of single women, is the number of women bearing or adopting children without a partner—known as Single Mothers by Choice. When the TV character Murphy Brown decided to have a child without a husband in the early 1990s, it was still radical enough to have Vice President Dan Quayle dress her down in what may have been his most famous speech ever (and perhaps the only one by a vice president to engage a fictional character in debate). But at that time, there were only about 50,000 such Moms in America. Now there are an estimated three times that many.

It is possible that the unfavorable straight sex ratio, discouraging as it is for women in some respects, has encouraged women to excel elsewhere. As we'll see in the trend on Wordy Women, young women outnumber young men in fields like law, public relations, and journalism. Women outvoted men 54 to 46 percent in the 2004 presidential election. Women outnumber men in college by about 57 to 43 percent.

Of course, the greatest beneficiaries of the women who are Sex-Ratio Singles are straight men, who—frankly—have never had it so good. Women who wouldn't give them the time of day in college start noticing, eight or ten years later, that there are measurably fewer men in play than there used to be. Suddenly, the balding guy with the solid job, and the reasonably good fatherhood potential, starts looking kind of hot.

And there are more commercial and political implications as well. Home maintenance, home repair, and home security companies have an enormous new market to attend to in single women. How long until Merrill Lynch appreciates the power of single women investing and retiring alone—and changes its trademark logo, the testosterone-charged bull—into something more graceful?

If women actually *want* husbands as much as they want houses, will we someday have mail-order husbands—importing them to Trenton and Tuscaloosa the way we once sent brides to the Wild West?

If women *don't* want the husbands that badly—but they do still want the children—there is a nearly limitless market for sperm donation, and all the financial and ethical regulations that will come with it.

Historians have well documented that a society with too many unattached men leads to war. Will a society with too many unattached women lead to peace?

Cougars

Women Who Date Younger Men

▲

Every era in pop culture reinvents the titillating affair between the older woman and the younger man. *The Graduate* in 1967, in which the worldly Anne Bancroft (Mrs. Robinson of Simon and Garfunkel fame) seduces the naive Dustin Hoffman. *How Stella Got Her Groove Back* in 1996, Terry McMillan's best-selling novel about a successful stockbroker mother who finds unexpected romance with a young Jamaican islander. *Something's Gotta Give* in 2003, in which 50-something Diane Keaton dates 30-something Keanu Reeves (before settling on Jack Nicholson).

But what started out as scandalous, and then became intriguing, has now become downright ordinary.

Older men seeking younger trophy wives is an age-old phenomenon. "Dirty old man" is a universal cliché. But now in America, women's growing financial and sexual independence have made them, too, increasingly interested in younger dates. According to a 2003 study by the AARP, one in three women between 40 and 69 is dating a younger man, and about one-quarter of those men are ten or more years younger.

Although the U.S. Census Bureau tracked these pairings differently between 1997 and 2003, the increase is clear: In 1997, fewer than half a million couples in America were a woman and a man at least ten years younger. In 2003, nearly 3 million couples were a woman and a man at least six years younger.

And between 2002 and 2005, says the online dating service Match.com, the percentage of women in their database who were willing to date men ten or more years younger nearly doubled.

Maybe it's because older women with younger men has been all the rage in real-life Hollywood, too. The woman who played the nation's first female president on *Commander in Chief*, 51-year-old Geena Davis, is married to

Couples Where Woman Is Significantly
Older than Man, 1997–2003

Source: *Pittsburgh Post-Gazette*, 2005, citing U.S. Census data

35-year-old Reza Jarrahy. Sixty–year-old Susan Sarandon has children with 48-year-old Tim Robbins. Nearly 50-year-old Madonna's husband, Guy Ritchie, is 39.

Proof positive of a trend, there's now a *name* for women who date significantly younger men: Cougars. According to Valerie Gibson, sex columnist for the *Toronto Sun* and author of *Cougar: A Guide for Older Women Dating Younger Men*, the term started in Vancouver, British Columbia, as a put-down for older women who would go to bars and go home at the end of the night with whoever was left. But in recent years, it's become more positive — signifying an older, single woman who knows what she wants, has the money and confidence to acquire it, and isn't constrained by desires for babies and a white picket fence.

And so now there are at least a half-dozen Web sites devoted to Cougar dating, complete with mugs and T-shirts. Oprah explored "Older Women in

Love with Younger Men" in 2003. On the wildly popular *Sex and the City*, 40-something Samantha Jones dated "boy toy" Smith Jerrod longer than anyone else in the show's six seasons. In 2005, Fran Drescher, star of the 1990s TV hit *The Nanny*, launched a new comedy called *Living with Fran*, a show about a mother of two who falls in love with a man half her age—apparently based on her real-life experience. VH1 presented *Kept*, a reality show in which a group of 20-something men compete to escort Mick Jagger's ex-wife, the 50-year-old Jerry Hall, for the following year. All of these innovations in entertainment reflect a trend in real life.

A couple of factors have triggered the growth of the Cougars. High divorce rates combined with longer life spans means a greater likelihood of women's reentering the dating market. In fact, according to a 2004 survey conducted by AARP, 66 percent of "late-life divorces"—those that occur in a couple's 40s, 50s, or 60s—are initiated by the women, not the men. Women's success in the workforce means that some women want a man with a less developed career—so that he can move if she needs to, and perhaps be their kids' primary caretaker. (Of course, men have pursued that arrangement for years.)

But according to Valerie Gibson, it's all about sex. A woman's sexual peak is more aligned with that of the younger man. And having either rejected marriage or been through an unsuccessful one, the older woman is looking for something lighter and more frivolous. In her 40s and 50s, says Gibson, sex for women is recreational, not procreational.

Unless, of course, she *wants* children. Over 100,000 women aged 40–44 gave birth in 2004, a 63 percent increase from ten years before. Over 5,000 women aged 45–49 did, too—a ten-year increase of 129 percent. So Cougars come in every stripe.

What's in it for the men?

They, apparently, like the confidence and sexual experience of the older women, and that the women are generally not looking for commitment. And as distinct from decades ago, older women are looking younger every day— thanks to on-demand cosmetic surgery and 24/7 gyms.

As a result, the men, too, at Match.com are interested in older women. Between 2002 and 2005, men interested in dating women five or more years older increased 44 percent. Those interested in a ten-or-more-year difference doubled.

Where do America's Cougars take us? In one sense, Cougars mean that younger men are finally getting even with older men, who since the dawn of time have been poaching their available dating pool. Maybe in that regard, the dating algorithms are all just evening out.

On the other hand, single women—having a hard enough time as it is due to the increasing number of openly gay men—now have a new segment of competition from their older sisters and, indeed, their Moms. (The mother-daughter tension over the same man was the underlying text of *The Graduate* and *Something's Gotta Give*.)

But today's Cougars are the result of the natural instinct for people with success to trade that success for sexual attractiveness. And what was once achievable only by older men with money is now within the reach of women with power and accomplishment (or a good inheritance). Just as billionaire men have to be on the watch for women on the make, biding their time until the money becomes theirs—so now Cougars need to beware of younger men seeking shelter from the storm. They, too, can use detective services to see what their younger boyfriends and spouses are up to; and they, too, need to worry about whether the younger mate will stick around if the older one gets ill, or simply isn't as much fun in later years.

And Cougars need a community. They need guidance as to what kinds of men to seek and to avoid. They need new dating rules regarding finances, sex, and commitment. And they need sisterly advice on how to handle the reactions of parents, siblings, ex-husbands, friends, and especially children. They need the right vacation spots. They even need just the right birthday cards. You may not have a Cougar in your family, but ask around or watch people on a busy street corner for a few minutes, and you will spot them soon enough. They are committed to their lifestyle, and it is an essential element of who they are and what they think about. And they are approaching that magical 1 percent that will make them a microtrend marketplace of interest to politicians, filmmakers, pastors, and marketers.

Mrs. Robinson would be so proud.

Office Romancers

▲

If there was one thing your mother might have warned you against—or your mentor, or your best friend who blew up his love life and his career at the same time—it was Don't Date at Work. You'll compound the heartbreak; you'll compromise your professionalism; you'll expose yourself to sex harassment suits. You'll distract yourself from your job and misplace your affections. The polite aphorism was something like, "Don't mix business with pleasure."

But according to a 2006 employee survey by Vault ("the most trusted name in career information"), *nearly 60 percent* of employees in America have been involved in an office romance, up from just 47 percent in 2003. And of the 42 percent who hadn't had an office romance, 9 percent said they'd like to.

Though many Office Romancers try to hide their affairs, almost everyone knows it's going on: Forty-three percent of employees say there is an office romance currently happening at their workplace, and another 38 percent say there might be. (For many, the discovery is not so subtle: In another survey, by Hotjobs, a remarkable 44 percent of respondents said they've actually caught co-workers "getting amorous" on the job.) But the bottom line is: No one really minds. Fully 75 percent of workers think that romantic and sexual relationships between co-workers—at least if they are peers—are totally okay.

Why the surge? In the long term, it's of course because of the growing equality of men and women in the workforce. The gap has been steadily closing for decades.

In the shorter term, it has to do with the rise of working singles. There are more of them than ever in the workforce (up 22 percent since 1995), and singles aged 25–34 are working more hours per week than they used to—up about 8 percent since 1970. (So really, where else *could* they find romance?)

But of course, some married people are in on the action, too. The Vault

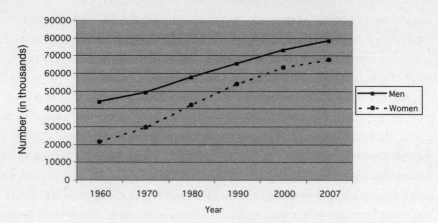

A Shrinking Gap: Number of Employed Men and Women in the United States, 1960–2007

Source: U.S. Bureau of Labor Statistics, 2007

survey found that 50 percent of workers have known a married co-worker to have an affair with someone else at the office.

Not surprisingly, men are more flirtatious at work than women (66 versus 52 percent, according to one survey); and substantially more men (45 percent) say they have had an interoffice romance than women (35 percent). That latter discrepancy either means that women are *serial* Office Romancers; that men are more boastful about this; that women more often leave the workplace after having an affair; or that some of those men's affairs are homosexual. I think the bottom line is this: The office has become the twenty-first-century singles bar. Water is the new gin and tonic, and Muzak the new club beat.

Evidently, some work settings are more conducive to the interoffice affair than others. The Vault surveys found that the number one industries for interoffice hookups are media and entertainment, followed by advertising/marketing and consulting. (Finance and technology, much more dominated by men, are the least likely fields to spawn a fling.) I'm the CEO of a public relations firm and the president of a consulting firm. I am proud to say we have had several interoffice marriages that started as office romances, so a lot of good can come from this—now that men and women are in the workforce with greater equality, and can find people at work with similar skills and interests.

We're not alone in having nurtured office romances into long-term love.

In a 2006 study by the Society for Human Resource Management, over 60 percent of the HR professionals interviewed said that romances in their offices had resulted in marriage. I can attest from personal experience that having married couples on staff can be a big win—they share a passion for our work; they back each other up if there's a crisis at home; and they are productive for the firm even in downtime, since (so they tell me) they wrestle with work challenges even as they give their kids a bath.

The fusing of work and love is nothing new. Moms and Pops have worked side by side since the dawn of agriculture, and again since the dawn of commerce. In fact, married couples make up the majority of business owners in America, with more than 1.2 million husband-and-wife teams running companies. And Americans have always had a special place in their heart for couples who work together (from George Burns and Gracie Allen to Sonny and Cher) and workers who couple together (from Spencer Tracy and Katharine Hepburn to Brad Pitt and Angelina Jolie). Where would music be without famous crooning couples—from Johnny Cash and June Carter, to Beyonce Knowles and Jay-Z? (Where would crime be without Bonnie and Clyde?)

And of course, at-work affairs are not new. "The boss and his secretary" is about as old a horseplay cliché as existed in the twentieth century.

But what's different now is that Workers Who Couple, and Couples Who Work Together, are happening not just in larger-than-life Hollywood or in your basic mom-and-pop shops—although those businesses, too, are growing at record rates—but in big and medium-sized companies, which, as a result, need some new rules. According to the Vault survey, only about 1 in 5 companies has policies regarding interoffice romance. Given concerns about intruding on employees' privacy, most companies have shied away from too much regulation, perhaps just venturing to ban supervisors' relationships with subordinates, or stepping up their reminders about sexual harassment. (Wal-Mart's policies are pretty aggressive, as you probably read about in 2007. After internal investigators found evidence that two high-level marketing executives, one senior and one junior, were having an affair, it fired them both—touching off a public relations storm that ended up with the couple's intimate e-mails splashed across the front pages.)

But are even those policies sufficient? Should even co-equal colleagues who are romantically involved be allowed to share a supervisor? A project? Office space? If all goes well, maybe it's delightful all around—but if the romance sours, one of them could get vindictive.

What about romance with clients, or vendors? How about with employees of competitors—especially if your employee is junior, and the competitor's is senior? Is that some kind of nefarious competitive advantage?

Moreover, as more and more office relationships take off, and more flings turn into rings, it is surely time to revisit the workforce rules, customs, and support systems regarding family employment. Right now in America, there are no uniform U.S. laws that prohibit the hiring of relatives, but it is estimated that up to 40 percent of companies still have rules on their books outlawing "nepotism"—a set of rules from the 1950s designed to stop white, male employees from hiring their underqualified relatives. (The word "nepotism" actually comes from the word "nephew.") Sure, it's still a good idea to stop unqualified nephews from sopping up company resources. But did we also intend to put at risk the jobs of colleagues who get married—and might suddenly violate company policy regarding spousal employment? Did we mean to discourage marriage between otherwise well-suited colleagues? When Congress tried to pass a ban on lawmakers' spouses lobbying on Capitol Hill as part of its ethics cleanup in 2006, some people complained about that very problem, and confusion set in—was our sense of ethics now in conflict with our sense of family? Maybe there's been new meaning given to the old expression that politics spawns strange bedfellows.

Clearly, there is a whole host of HR needs going unaddressed at every level. Co-working spouses want to be reviewed and compensated without regard to the other—but, on the other hand, they would *also* appreciate it if one is laid off, the firm goes out of its way to retain the other. From the employers' side, bosses need some kind of assurance that if co-working couples split up, they'll keep the company out of it, and especially not take up colleagues' time asking them to take sides. And speaking of colleagues, they, too, need some kind of guarantee that when it comes to deciding promotions, awards, or other compensation, the co-workers who happen to be married to the decision-makers won't get preferential treatment. Maybe the new workplace policies, focused less on nephews and more on husbands and wives, should be called "nuptialism."

Beyond formal workplace policies, Office Romancers and Married Colleagues need a community, some fellow travelers with whom to work through shared experiences. What's the best way to handle disclosure of the relationship, and the breakups? Workplace disagreements, or competitions that spill over to home? How about health insurance options, and parental leave? The double humiliation of a spouse's in-office affair?

On all fronts, we might look to universities. As the number of female Ph.D.'s skyrocketed—from about 8,000 in 1966 to over 20,000 in 2002—there was a huge boom in the number of academic couples. As a result, universities have been working for decades on ways not only to permit, but to encourage, positions for double-entry candidates. As this could be a wave of the workplace future, other employers may want to take note.

Finally, couples themselves need to assess what it means to put all their proverbial eggs in one basket. With people working later and later into their lives, a co-working marriage could literally mean 24/7 togetherness for fifty or sixty years. Blissful, I know, for some. For others, maybe a little too close.

It's a new workplace out there, and in what was once a male-dominated office environment, where sexual harassment was the number one problem, the power structure is changing and so is the social structure. Sexual harassment remains a serious issue. But we can now look forward to a time where social collegiality, between truly co-equal men and women in executive positions, is a driving force in our work life and our social life.

In the meantime, as the workforce works through these transitions, you are more likely than ever to stumble upon colleagues smooching (or more) on their lunch break. Could be hot gossip for the water cooler. Or, it could be just Mom and Pop, sneaking a little together time before the afternoon presentation.

Commuter Couples

▲

I n May 2006, the *New York Times* splashed a front-page color portrait of Bill and Hillary Clinton under the headline, "For Clintons, Delicate Dance of Married and Public Lives." Here it comes, readers thought. New, lurid details about the most dissected marriage in America.

The story was compelling—although not from the point of view of either gossip or politics. It was compelling because the way that former President Bill Clinton and Senator Hillary Rodham Clinton live—two careers, two houses, seeing each other fourteen days a month, traveling to be together two out of every three weekends—is increasingly a way of life for married Americans. It's called the Commuter Marriage, and the Clintons are far from alone—more than 3.5 million people are doing it.

In 1990, an estimated 1.7 million married people in the United States were living apart for reasons other than separation. Fifteen years later, that number has more than doubled.

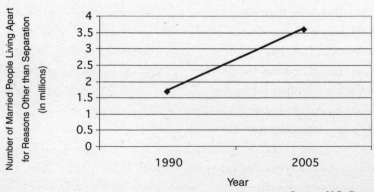

Commuter Marriages in America, 1990–2005

Source: U.S. Census, 2006

Did everyone start taking "A Room of One's Own" just a little too seriously?

The truth is, commuter marriages have always been big in our culture. Ben Franklin had one as our first ambassador to France—though he rarely got back home. Some of America's most important jobs basically *require* them. Active-duty soldiers leave spouses and children for extended periods during deployment. Members of the U.S. House or Senate, like Hillary Clinton—and state legislators in places large enough to have a faraway capital—routinely bed down in apartments near work and then travel home on weekends. (Handfuls of U.S. congressmen live like college freshmen in shared quarters on Capitol Hill.)

But increasingly, regular people—not just soldiers and public servants—are living apart from their spouses, too. Mostly they are dual-career couples who can't, or don't want to, uproot both of their professional lives just because one has to, or can, take a job or get a degree somewhere else. Forty years ago, such a decision would have been unthinkable. Women earned so little, there was such serious stigma attached to women living alone, and travel was so expensive that if a husband had to relocate, the wife pretty much always went along. But now that women make more, nearly 30 percent of American households are people living alone, and air travel is relatively cheap—commuter marriage is just one of the many ways that dual-earning couples are working out their life's work. And, by the way, it's not just for the young and starting-out. According to experts at AARP, the number of married people over 50 who live separately tripled between 2001 and 2005.

While many people in America telecommute so they can spend more time with their families, Commuter Couples are doing the opposite. They are physically where their work is, but using technology to connect them to family. And so while much has been written and advertised about the new Mobile Worker, little has yet been said about the new Mobile Spouse—away, and yet constantly connected through technology. And soon spouses will be able to track each other through the GPS chips in their cell phones, so they will always be able to locate their loved one.

Is commuting dangerous for the marriage? According to the Center for the Study of Long Distance Relationships (LDRs), commuters are not any more likely than geographically close couples to break up. Nor, says Dr. Gregory Guldner, director of the center, are commuting couples likely to be less satisfied in their relationships, or to cheat more. Says Dr. Guldner, so long as couples find a way to share in each other's day-to-day events, find ways to talk about the big issues, and yes, "learn the art of long-distance sex," commuting couples have as solid a shot as anyone.

What do Commuter Couples mean for America? At a political level, you suddenly have a greater number of people "belonging" to two states, which could complicate the rules about voting, taxation, and school enrollment, all of which are based on place of residence. There are also significant marketing opportunities, including financial planning, communications, travel, and special event planning. When being apart is the norm, being together can take on special meaning. Perhaps one reason why these marriages seem to be working is that people really have to appreciate each other to tolerate a commuter marriage—and yet the special feeling of being together, something easily lost in one-house marriages, is constantly renewed. In addition, they afford a degree of space and privacy that conventional marriages don't have—and that space may just be the pressure valve that gives these marriages an equal or better chance of success, in a world where divorce is the norm.

Commuter Couples also affect the workforce. You might think commuters are the least loyal employees, the first to leave on a Friday afternoon to rejoin their distant lovers for the weekend. Or the grumpiest around the office, because they're so lonely without their spouses and kids.

But the truth is, while they're in the city of their employer, commuter spouses probably have far fewer distractions than their counterparts with families or busy single lives. They may actually be more capable of giving their employers a full 24/5 workweek, and a full 24/7 one when it's an "off" weekend. So in an era of high job turnover *anyway*, it may be that the *most* attractive employees are the ones who look like drifters—unattached and unrooted—except a couple weekends per month, and on holidays.

Eventually, one partner or the other generally moves, so most Commuter Couples don't stay that way forever. Since people now change jobs every two to four years, chances are that is how long most Commuter Couples will stay in that state before they reunite. But with so many job changes and two-career couples, the chances that people—at least for some part of their lives—will have a Commuter Relationship for at least a couple of years is skyrocketing. So get ready for the next new condition of modern life.

THE INTERNATIONAL PICTURE

The 3.5 million Americans who are in commuter marriages are hardly alone.

Around the industrialized world, foreign job placements—and dual-career couples—are on the rise. But as a result, more and more couples of every nationality are spending at least some portion of their married lives in separate cities. In every language, it seems, the principle "whither thou goest, I will go" is now less compelling than it used to be.

Whereas many Commuter Marriages are by choice, especially within the U.S., some are by necessity—especially if the first spouse's relocation is to a foreign country. According to a 1999 Global Relocation Trends Survey, of the nearly 50 percent of spouses who had jobs before their significant others were relocated, only 11 percent were able to find employment in the host country. And employers weren't very sympathetic: Just 19 percent aided the partner's job search, while one-third offered no support at all. (The others offered token counseling or job-finding fees.) To make matters worse, only a handful of countries even provide working permits to spouses. So even couples who wanted to live together may end up being commuters.

And indeed, it is probably fair to say that most Commuter Marriages in the world are not among upscale, dual-career couples—but rather among downscale people forced apart by economics. In the U.S. itself, there are millions of guest workers (and illegal immigrants), many of whose spouses are back home. In the Middle East, this phenomenon is often the *majority* situation:

▲ In Kuwait, 63 percent of the population is foreign-born—mainly service workers and laborers from Egypt, the Philippines, Pakistan, India, and Sri Lanka. (An estimated 4 percent of Egyptians go abroad for work, 70 percent of them to Arab Gulf countries.)

▲ In Dubai, just 17 percent of the population is native-born.

▲ In Saudi Arabia, two-thirds of all jobs are held by foreigners. In 2006, these workers sent $14 *billion* back to their families.

Fortunately for many such couples, international travel is faster and cheaper than ever before. So are international telephone calls and e-mail connections. So one can only hope that spousal reunions happen often enough to keep the marriage together—and that, in between, husbands and wives can make do with virtual, and remembered, good night kisses.

Internet Marrieds

▲

It used to be embarrassing to need the Internet to date. It smacked of geeky antisocialness—people who couldn't make it in the "real" dating world. People with something to hide. People so desperate for a date they would seek out strangers at odd hours, from their lonely, maybe even creepy dens. At a minimum, online dating brought to mind older, unsuccessful singles whose dating years were waning and whose biological clocks were ticking. Going online was your Hail Mary effort to find a mate before you got too old. (And the men all figured that the women online were easy—weren't they practically advertising for men?)

But in the last few years, online dating has switched, becoming something of a destination not of last but of first resort. No longer a refuge for people who can't hack "normal" dating, Internet dating is increasingly viewed as a fun way to meet *more* potential dates, while also efficiently weeding out the Totally Undesirable. According to a 2006 study on online dating by the Pew Internet and American Life Project, 61 percent of online Americans do not consider online dating "desperate." Nearly half of online Americans think Internet dating is a good way to meet people.

As a result, nearly 1 in 4 single Americans who are looking for a romantic partner—or about 16 million people—use the 1,000 or more dating Web sites out there. That includes almost 1 in 5 Americans in their 20s, and 1 in 10 Americans in their 30s or 40s. And as of 2004, those Web sites were netting roughly $470 million a year, up from a mere $40 million in 2001. Social networking wasn't invented for politics—it was invented for socializing.

The previous venues for finding mates—religious institutions, mixers, matchmakers—are being replaced by where the new generation is to be found—at the office, and on the Internet.

Sure, Internet dating still has its risks. On www.onlinedatingmagazine.

com—a site devoted to "in-depth coverage of the online dating services industry and dating tips for those who date online"—three of the six most popular articles are "Dangers of Online Dating," "Online Dating Safety Tips," and "Staying Clear of Married Men." But amid the millions who are trying online dating nonetheless, there are a select few for whom e-meeting turns into engagement. According to the Pew study, 17 percent of online daters—or nearly 3 million American adults—have turned online dates into a long-term relationship or marriage. That's exactly the same number of couples in America who say they met in church.

And while there are no firm data on the growth in Internet Marrieds, the trend line is clearly rising. Online dating pioneer Match.com didn't even exist until 1995. eHarmony, which boasts the greatest number of client marriages, wasn't launched until 2000. The hundreds and hundreds of other dating sites—including subspecialty niches, like DateAGolfer, Animal Attraction (for pet lovers), or Positive Singles (for singles with sexually transmitted diseases)—have only just cropped up. And now that it's getting easier to upload pictures and even videos for online prospects, the possibility of bull's-eye matching is only getting more and more real.

In 2007, something like 4.4 million Americans will get married. Almost 100,000 of them will have met online.

In the spring of 2007, we did a short poll of people who met and married on the Internet. While there are Internet Marrieds of every type, it seems that the most typical ones are upscale, urban Democrats who put some serious work into online dating, and are now very, very happy about it.

▲ *Upscale.* Seventy-six percent of Internet Marrieds are employed outside the home, with another 12 percent at home full-time with kids. Seventy percent of the full-time employees are in professional or managerial positions. Sixty-nine percent of Internet Marrieds own their own homes. Sixty-one percent have finished college, including 20 percent who have finished graduate school. A whopping 51 percent have household annual incomes of $75,000 or more.

▲ *Urban.* Almost half of Internet Marrieds live in cities. Presumably people in rural areas already know the locals, but urban environments mean that there are hundreds of thousands of potential matches in your neighborhood that you don't know.

▲ *Democrats*. Seventy-two percent of Internet Marrieds say they are liberal or moderate, with 43 percent identifying as Democrats. (In an average national sample, Democrats would be only about a third of the population.) Interestingly, though, this group is a little more religious than your typical Democrats. Fifty-one percent say they attend religious services at least a few times a month, compared to only 31 percent who attend "never or nearly never." (In a typical Democrat sample, regular services-goers would more likely be under one-third.)

Internet Marrieds had to put some work into the process. Nearly 6 in 10 said they used online dating sites for a year or more before they found their spouse, and about the same number had to date at least six different online matches before they found The One. (Almost a quarter had to date more than ten.) And while the Internet Marrieds did not go into this feeling desperate, they hardly felt joy or confidence, either.

"When you first considered online dating, what were your attitudes toward it?"	
	(multiple responses permitted)
	Percent
Nervous	65
Skeptical	55
Embarrassed	27
Neutral	22
Delighted	20
Confident	10
It was a last resort	10

Source: PSB, 2007

But life has worked out for them. A remarkable 92 percent say their marriages are happy, including 80 percent who say "very happy." Fifty-seven percent think their marriages are stronger because they met online, compared to only 6 percent who think they are weaker. Seventy-three percent think they and their spouse have particular advantages because of the way they met, compared to only 24 percent who think they have disadvantages.

And Internet Marrieds are pleased to spread the word. Eighty-four percent have advised other single friends or family members to date online.

Eighty-eight percent say they would support their children (one day) dating online. And fully 92 percent say they would support their children marrying someone they met online.

Finally, age-wise, Internet Marriage can happen for anyone. Fifty-five percent of respondents are under 35 (about one-third are in their early 30s), but 46 percent are over 35, including almost a third who are over 45. It works for second-timers, too: Thirty-one percent of Internet Marrieds are on their second marriage.

Internet Marriage could be the wave of the future. With marriage rates at an all-time low to begin with, people who want to find a spouse need an effective, efficient way to cut through the hooking-up scene and get right to the real deal. In our poll, when respondents were asked what was the best thing about online dating, their top two answers were "I could narrow my search to people of a certain type" and "I could look over a lot of people in a short amount of time." Marriage isn't something to be taken for granted anymore. If you want to meet The One, you've got to put yourself virtually out there.

In fact, in a world that increasingly emphasizes self-determination, leaving your soul mate search up to singles bars, office romances, and friends of friends seems not only rather passive, but downright negligent. There are 6 billion people in the world, and only a relative handful in your daily orbit. If you really want love, step it up. Do some targeted research, and make that Cupid's Arrow a surgical strike.

As Internet Marrieds grow in number, there are a couple of things we can expect. First, more Commuter Couples. The number of Americans choosing that lifestyle has already climbed to about 3.5 million, but since Internet Marrieds are already more likely to start out in different cities—and are already more comfortable with communication, and intimacy, online—the Commuter Married trend is only likely to grow.

Second, expect more diverse pairings, across race, ethnicity, and nationality. Marital diversity, too, is on the rise—but once the dating marketplace is blown wide open, unconstrained by traditional community or local ties, soul mates of whatever background will have far greater freedom to find each other. (Of course, ethnic or religious minorities who want to find like people will have an easier time of that, too. Just go to www.EligibleGreeks.com, www .EthiopianPersonals.com, www.Muslima.com, or any of the dozens of other ethnically niched dating sites you can find in about two clicks of a mouse.)

Third, look for e-therapists. While Internet Marrieds had the advantage of narrowcasting their love searches, they also likely sacrificed what used to be a cornerstone of the dating world: a personal voucher by the cousin, the roommate, or the colleague who actually knew your intended before you did. Now, with more and more relationships being high-speed but not home-spun, there can be some surprises that call for newfangled counseling. In our poll, the Internet Marrieds (most of whom had spent at least a year on these sites, remember) said that, by far, the worst part about Internet dating was that the people you met could misrepresent themselves. And among the Internet Marrieds who said meeting online had been a *disadvantage*, the number one disadvantage they gave was that they hadn't sufficiently gotten to know their spouse's backgrounds and/or families.

Fourth, look for a lowered online guard when it comes to Internet Marrieds' families. Children of these couples will grow up hearing all about how Mommy and Daddy fell in love over e-mails and chat rooms. How effectively will those parents be able to tell their kids to turn off the computer? And more ominously, will those children have their guard unduly down when it comes to chatting up strangers online?

Like Office Romancers, Internet Marrieds need a community of their own, to work through shared experiences, lessons, challenges, and in-jokes. Throughout this book, I speculate about the need for such communities among many of the microtrend groups. But in this case, I have real proof: While only 37 percent of Internet Marrieds say they know at least several couples who met online, 82 percent say they would like to.

Skeptics may wonder how deep and true Internet-based relationships are, suspecting that people found online will go back online. But what we learned in polling them was the opposite—they choose their mates after going through a wide array of choices, and they are starting out on a very strong footing.

We are a ways off from the offspring of Internet Marrieds hitting the dating scene in major numbers, and it will be interesting to see if it really grows into the mainstream way to date and settle down. But start looking—next to the bronzed baby shoes, have Internet Marrieds framed or bronzed the ads that brought them together? If they have, then the 1990s stigma regarding online dating will be dead, replaced by a pride in searching the earth and the Internet for The One.

PART II
Work Life

Working Retired

▲

There are only a few magic numbers in American civic life. You can vote (and get drafted) at age 18. You can drink at 21. You can become president at 35. You can retire at 65.

But on that last one—do Americans really want to? Now that so many Americans are living healthfully until 85, fewer and fewer actually retire at 65. Today there are 5 million people 65 or older in the U.S. labor force, almost twice what they were in the early 1980s. And that number is about to explode.

U.S. Workforce Participation of Men and Women 65+, 1985–2005

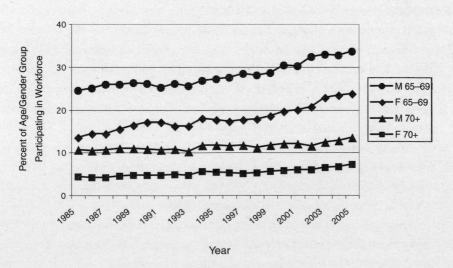

Source: Current Population Survey (CPS), Bureau of Labor Statistics, 2006

Some people are working past 65 because they have to: Health care costs are rising, and Social Security payments—at an average of about $1,000 a month—don't cover what they used to. But the bigger trend in Senior Work is the fact that Americans *love* work—and now that we're living longer, we want to work longer, too. We just can't get enough. My friend and mentor Harold Burson, the co-founder of the global PR firm Burson Marsteller, where I am CEO, just turned 86, and comes to work every day, bursting with ideas.

On average, Americans work over 1,800 hours per year, substantially more than most workers around the world. Although we get fewer vacation days per year than other Western countries (thirteen days, compared to twenty-eight in Great Britain, and thirty-seven in France), we let more than twice as many go unused. And really, what's a vacation to us these days without our BlackBerry? In 2006, almost a quarter of us (23 percent) checked our work e-mail and voice mail while away—up from just 16 percent in 2005. A lot of us *love* to work.

In fact, the impulse to work is so basic that the Fourth Commandment (Third for Catholics) is to take *off* one day a week. Not working for a day is right up there with not murdering, not committing adultery, and not stealing. We tend to assume that most people want off—waiting all week for the Friday afternoon whistle so they can stream out of work. To be sure, many jobs are terrible—even life-threatening—and people reasonably can't wait to get home. But as work overall has become more managerial, consulting, and software-oriented—and as manufacturing jobs have been on the decline—a lot of people have changed their attitude toward work, and the number of workaholics has skyrocketed. How many times have you heard the old saying that no one ever lay on his deathbed wishing he had spent more time at the office? And yet, a lot of people are doing just that. The sandwich generation is going to be in for a shock when they call their 70-year-old parents at the office and find they are just too busy to babysit the grandkids.

Add to America's general obsession with work the fact that it is now the baby boomer generation who is nearing 65, and it becomes clear that the traditional idea of "retirement"—with its gold watch, rocking chair, and golf course—is just about ready for retirement itself.

Boomers reinvented youth in the 1960s and economic success in the 1980s; they are not about to do their senior years by someone else's formula. According to a 2005 survey by Merrill Lynch, more than 3 in 4 boomers say they have no intention of seeking a traditional retirement. Rather, they look ahead to their twenty more years (when Social Security was created in 1935, a 65-year-old could expect just thirteen more years)—and they say Bring It On. Some want to keep their health insurance, or have enough funds for the extra years—but more of the boomers surveyed said they wanted to keep working in order to stay mentally and physically active and to stay connected to people.

And modern changes to the workplace environment have made these desires possible. When more jobs required physical labor, older people who had injuries or pain might have been at a disadvantage. But in the Information Age—well, old folks have more information than anyone. Anyway, drugs like Celebrex have enabled millions of Americans to keep on working *despite* their pain. And if older workers do end up with physical impairments, the Americans with Disabilities Act has helped make their workplaces far friendlier.

The Working Retired mean huge things for America. As a purely numerical matter, they mean a much bigger workforce than anyone had projected. Every year, a little over 2 million Americans turn 65. If just half of them decided to keep working, that would be more than 1 million unexpected participants in the labor force—or almost an additional 1 percent of current workers.

That has enormous implications. First, it puts the squeeze on younger employees, who have been waiting their turn to take the reins. If suddenly people become managers and vice presidents at 40, instead of 35, will they really stick around and wait? If they do, will that breed a more passive kind of leader—because the more aggressive ones will have broken free to start their own ventures?

It has even bigger implications for certain industries. Lower-income older workers tend to work retail, often part-time; higher-income older workers tend to become consultants and independent contractors, either in the field they once mastered or in a hobby they love. And they are far more likely to run their own show: Older workers make up 7 percent of independent contractors, versus only 2.5 percent of workers in traditional arrangements. But either way, expect an easier time for the HR departments of Home Depot and CVS, as well as many technical fields.

In all industries, though, employers need to adjust. The Merrill Lynch study found that very few companies are focused on Aging Workers, preoccupied as they are with hiring younger and healthier workers in order to cut benefit costs. But when it comes to benefit packages, current employee priorities like maternity leave and child care may have to compete with "winter-off" options and prescription drug coverage. Just as the women's movement forced new options for part-time and home-based work, expect new work-place options for cyclical and other kinds of nontraditional work.

I don't envy the manufacturers of golf clubs or the builders of golf courses—the projections of retirees circling the courses all day are likely going to fall short and create a glut. At the same time, the business center may become the busiest place in "retirement communities." And look for growing markets for computers, cell phones, and mobile devices tailored for seniors, as well as a surge in use of reading glasses.

The Working Retired will also affect the political landscape. Older citizens vote, and working men and women retain some of their interest in the economy when they take home a paycheck. Older voters have been becoming Values Voters—especially the grumpy old men. Keeping them in the workforce may keep them voting more on the basis of what's good for jobs and the economy and less on cultural issues.

And look for new legislation and litigation, especially new age discrimination laws. Since 1978, it's been illegal to force workers out before age 70, and since 1986 there's been no compulsory retirement of any form. But currently you get no additional advantage for deferring your Social Security payouts beyond age 70. Why not 73?

And what about subtler age discrimination? Will older workers be forgiven for the little extra time they may need to get the same tasks done? Will it become a "hostile work environment" when the office competitions involve YouTube contests, instead of basketball pools?

The commercial implications of the Working Retired have scarcely been imagined. "Senior" product merchants are still largely focused on golf clubs and walkers. How about "octogenomic" office chairs to accommodate arthritis, back pain, and knee replacements? More nap facilities, for the older people who came to work at 7:00, but need a little shut-eye from 2:00 to 2:30? Defibrillators in every workplace hallway? Sodium-free foods in the office cafeteria?

The Working Retired will also have a big impact on family life. It's unclear how wives will react when suddenly men choose to keep on working instead of spending their Golden Years with them. (Is that insulting? Or is it a huge relief?) And what about grown children? They can no longer count on their parents to pick up the babysitting slack, since their parents are working just as hard as they are—which suggests that the paid child care industry will grow even larger.

And there are public health implications. More than 1 million extra workers per year means significantly more commuter congestion on the roads. And accidents—drivers 65 and older are involved in 7 percent of all traffic accidents, and 10 percent of all fatal accidents.

But the really, really big significance of the Working Retired is that, basically, everything we have been predicting for the last decade or so, regarding the collapse of Social Security, was wrong. There won't, in fact, be ten retirees for every worker, because the retirees will be working, too. The enormous Social Security burdens we've been haranguing about can be addressed, to some degree, by just a few more years of work—and this is largely on the part of people who *want* to do it. According to Eugene Steuerle, an economist with the Urban Institute, if everyone worked just one year beyond expected retirement, we'd completely offset the anticipated shortfall between benefits and taxes in the old age insurance portion of Social Security. If everyone worked five more years, the overall additional taxes to the government alone would be greater than the shortfall.

Could there be a much larger implication than that?

Well—maybe; perhaps the Working Retired will actually extend life itself. Plenty of studies have shown that an active body and mind are key to extending the healthy years. Are we only at the tip of the iceberg for greater life expectancy? Might more and more of us get to 100—not from radical new diets and exercise plans, but from punching the clock well past 65?

And, maybe, the Working Retired could *save* the family—hard as the trend may seem to swallow at first for spurned spouses and indignant grown children. If a person can really work until 90, might that mean a whole new pressure release valve on the work-family dilemma? Could Moms (or Dads) now mainly raise kids from age 23 to 43—and then spend 50 years at work? Surveys of college freshmen today tell us that their highest priorities in life are to make a lot of money *and* raise a family. Can they—at long last—actually do both if suddenly "the working years" are twenty years longer than they used to be?

What used to be the Golden Years are now, in the minds of aging Americans, Golden Opportunities. Yes, this development could cause more traffic accidents, and send the younger generation scurrying to independent ventures—but it could conceivably also avert America's looming Social Security crisis, extend life, and rescue the American family.

Extreme Commuters

▲

There is perhaps no more common experience in America than the daily ritual of going back and forth to work. About 150 million of us work, and only 3 percent of us work from home. So pretty much everyone else— something like 145 million people—leave home every morning, travel to a workplace, and make our way back again at night.

Years ago, there were studies that said people wouldn't tolerate a commute longer than forty-five minutes. Well, we're inching there: Our current average is now 25 minutes, up almost 20 percent since 1980. According to a 2005 *Business Week* report, in 1990 only 24 percent of all workers left their home counties to get to the office. Now, 50 percent of new workers do.

The greater distance between jobs and workers is all about jobs leaving cities for suburbs, and workers leaving suburbs for "exurbs." It's like a big chase to the outer rings, with more and more people paying the price in commuting. But as a result, in 2000, almost 10 million Americans traveled more than an hour to get to work—up from fewer than 7 million ten years before.

And at the extreme of this trend are—aptly named by the Census Bureau—"Extreme Commuters," people who travel *at least 90 minutes each way* to get to work. In 2000, there were 3.4 million such commuters in America, almost double the number from ten years before.

Extreme Commuting is enough of a phenomenon that in the spring of 2006, Midas Muffler held a contest to reward America's Longest Commuter. Attracting thousands of entries, Midas gave the prize to David Givens of Mariposa, California, who drives 372 miles round-trip every day to his job at Cisco Systems in San Jose. (He leaves his house every morning at 4:30 a.m., makes one stop for coffee, and is in his cubicle at Cisco by 7:45. At 5:00 p.m., he reverses the trip, getting home around 8:30.)

Extreme Commuters in America, 1990–2000

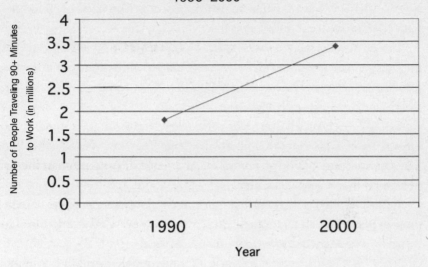

Source: U.S. Census, Journey to Work, 2000

Who are these 3.4 million Extreme Commuters, and why are they working so far from home?

For the most part, people who live far from work can't afford to live near it. New-home prices have nearly tripled since the mid-1980s, and now average almost $300,000. Folks just can't buy houses in the major metropolitan areas where they work. According to Census data, the state that saw the largest increase in commute times between 2002 and 2003 was West Virginia—where housing is still affordable, but more lucrative work in Washington, D.C., Pennsylvania, and Ohio draws workers out of the state from 9 to 5 (or, if you count the commute, from 4:30 a.m. to 8:30 p.m.).

Other Extreme Commuters do it for the quality of life. As land prices decline the farther the land is from cities, people are deciding to endure the long commute in exchange for a bigger house, bigger lawn, less gridlock, and less crime. Not to mention nature. Something like 25,000 people from the Pocono Mountains in Pennsylvania commute for hours into New York City every weekday—but on the weekends, they have hiking, skiing, and cool mountain air.

And some dual-earner couples are becoming Extreme Commuters not so much for economic *or* lifestyle reasons, but rather for logistical ones. As the number of two-worker households increases, so do the chances that one or both will need to trek to work. Princeton, New Jersey, famous for the university, has also become a popular suburb for couples who need to commute to *both* New York City and Philadelphia.

Indeed, the worst commutes in the nation are in the New York and Washington, D.C., metropolitan areas—at an average of thirty-four and thirty-three minutes, respectively. It's serious enough that these commutes, plus high gas prices, are pushing people back to mass transit.

But still, over 3 million people—the magic 1 percent for a microtrend—are waking up with the stars and crossing state lines and even weather zones to get to work, and public policymakers, public health officials, and the business world may want to take note.

First of all, this is a group that cares intensely about gas prices. A whopping 76 percent of all commuters drive alone to work, and that figure is presumably even higher among Extreme Commuters. (It's really hard to rally a carpool at 4:30 a.m., or for your same 125-mile route.) Gas prices can make or break this group's careers. Mr. Givens, the winner of Midas Muffler's Longest Commute award, said that when he won, he was spending about $800 per month on gas. An Extreme Commuter in North Carolina bristled when President George W. Bush said in his 2006 State of the Union address that Americans were "addicted to oil." Are we, she demanded, or are we just trying to get to work? People in the cities may not mind a gasoline tax, but these 3 million people won't be voting for a gas tax candidate anytime soon.

Extreme Commuters are also at greater risk for dangerous behavior like road rage, as well as health problems. Dr. John H. Casada, a specialist in road stress, has said that the longer people's commutes are, the more likely they are to suffer road rage—which can lead not only to violence, but also heart attacks, strokes, and ulcers.

Longer commutes are also linked to obesity. Researchers at Georgia Tech have found that every thirty minutes spent driving increases your risk of becoming obese by 3 percent. In a 2005 ABC/*Washington Post* poll on traffic, 4 in 10 drivers said that while in traffic jams, they eat.

Robert Putnam's 2000 book *Bowling Alone* notably found that for every extra ten minutes you commute, you have 10 percent less time for family and community (unless, I guess, you take your kids with you to day care at your workplace). But since many Extreme Commuters signed on to the bargain in pursuit of small-town life, that seems particularly unfortunate, or particularly self-sacrificing. Many Extreme Commuters do this for their families—to give them a better life with better schools. Others wait for the weekends to enjoy the reason they drive all this way during the week.

The Extreme Commuter group also has important commercial implications. According to a *Newsweek* report in 2006, fast food restaurants are coming out with whole meals that fit in cup holders, and some cars are now outfitted with more cup holders than seats. Gas stations are putting touchscreen menus at the pump, so people can order sandwiches while they're filling the tank and have them ready for pickup when it's time to drive away. Satellite navigation systems now come with real-time traffic options, to help drivers avoid gridlock. The next battleground, say observers, is luxury seats. People who spend more than three hours per day behind the wheel are likely to be very interested in extra-comfort features like back massages. (So far, no one has developed a sanitary, socially acceptable, and portable car toilet.)

Finally, Extreme Commuters are a group with serious time on their hands. Some audio companies claim you need just sixteen hours of their language tapes to go from zero Spanish to a full foundation. At that rate, Extreme Commuters listening in their cars can *habla español* in a week without giving up any other activities. And after a couple months, they could be U.N. translators, if their current jobs don't work out.

Or books on tape. Extreme Commuters are the transportation equivalent of speed readers. They could get through *War and Peace* in twelve days, or *The Da Vinci Code* in five.

Lyndon Johnson said he was declaring war on poverty and beginning massive urban renewal because, he predicted, 95 percent of Americans were going to live in cities. But in fact, people have spread out across the country to suburbs and exurbs faster than anyone could have predicted. (This just proves how hard it is to make assumptions about what America will look like fifty years from now—while you're focused on a few big trends, other microtrends seep in and upset your expectations.) Employers who moved to the suburbs did get closer to *some* of their workforce. But for a whole group of other workers, all their employers' relocation did was encourage them to move farther out—suggesting that for a lot of people, the most important thing is a house, a yard, and a quieter life, no matter what the cost in money or time.

The bottom line is that more and more Americans are on the road—but not so much like Jack Kerouac, looking to find themselves. More likely, they are looking for a cup of coffee and a to-go danish, hoping the gridlock will be bearable today, and knowing that they'll take the exact same route tomorrow.

THE INTERNATIONAL PICTURE

When the European Economic Community (EEC) was founded in 1957, its mission was to tear down trade barriers and ensure that all Europeans could travel freely among the member countries. Little did founder Jean Monnet know that such "free travel" would give rise to today's European Extreme Commuter—and even its jet-setting Mega-Commuter.

Within Europe, the British win the prize for the longest average commute, at forty-five minutes—a good twenty minutes longer than the average commute in the U.S. The overall average commute in the European Union (the EEC's successor) is thirty-eight minutes, with Italy clocking in at twenty-three and Germany at forty-four.

But the interesting story lies not only in the tedious commute time, but in the sheer number of miles that many commuters voluntarily cover. Fully half of passengers in the Chunnel's high-speed train, the Eurostar, which travels over 200 miles between France and England, are commuters—mainly people who live in France and work in London. (In 2007, for the first time ever, a French presidential candidate held an election rally outside France—trying to appeal to the nearly half-million French citizens who live and/or work in London.)

Even more dramatic are the Mega-Commuters who don't just drive or take the train, but fly to work. One European travel firm has predicted that by the year 2016, the number of people who work in the U.K. but live elsewhere—and not just northern France, but also Barcelona, Palma, Dubrovnik, and Verona—will reach 1.5 million. Low-cost airlines make this possible. In 1994, there were *zero* low-cost airlines; in 2005, there were sixty. Airlines like Ryanair, easyJet, and SkyEurope carried some 200 million passengers in 2003 alone.

While Mega-Commuting is growing fast in Europe, the phenomenon is in its earlier stages in Asia. Some emerging discount airlines like Jetstar, Oasis, and AirAsiaX offer low fares, but they still have to compete with the dominant state-controlled airlines. But you can expect that Asians, too, will seize on this trend as soon as they're able. The Chinese already spend *an hour or more* driving to work on average—compared to that, how big a deal are twice-daily flights?

Stay-at-Home Workers

▲

While 3.4 million Americans drive ninety minutes or more to work each day, 4.2 million put on their slippers and head into the home office.

Which might be a fancy paneled den that's off-limits to the kids and has a separate entrance. Or it might be the bed where this worker just woke up, and where—once the pillows are propped up, the cereal bowl is on the night-stand, and the laptop is plopped down in the spot it was named for—he or she can begin productive participation in the U.S. labor force.

Whatever working from home looks like, those 4.2 million Americans doing it represent a 23 percent increase in their kind from 1990, and a nearly 100 percent increase from 1980.

Number of U.S. Workers Working from Home, 1980–2000

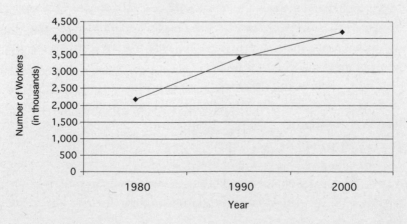

Source: U.S. Census, 2000

Such home-workers don't even include the approximately 20 million Americans who work from home "sometimes." No, these are the people whose regular workday takes place just a couple seconds' walk from their toothbrush.

Why do people work from home? Horror at the Extreme Commutes described in the last chapter is often reason enough—it can be fabulously liberating to skip rush hour, bypass gas expenses, and pay less in car maintenance. The pleasure is only compounded by the ability to stay in one's pajamas—showering optional.

Increased pressure to balance work and family also favors the Stay-at-Home Worker. While it's not likely that one can fully concentrate on work while also being chiefly responsible for (awake) children, many Stay-at-Homers find they can be just as or more productive working at home in the hours that the kids are at child care or in school.

But the biggest reason, of course, that Stay-at-Home Working is on the rise is because it can be: laptops, high-speed Internet access, Black-Berrys, cell phones, and even videophones have made home offices nearly indistinguishable from office offices, and have lately become available with capacities and at prices totally unimaginable in 1980. So whether you're working for yourself or someone else, there is almost no practical difference for your colleagues or clients whether you're in a cubicle or the family den.

Who are America's Stay-at-Home Workers? As of 2000, 53 percent are women—compared to only 46 percent of on-site workers who are women. Eighty-eight percent are white. Sixty-eight percent have at least some college, compared to only 59 percent of the on-site workforce. The large plurality works in management and professional jobs. About 2 in 3 work full-time. Many of them make serious money.

This is a successful, self-driven class of people.

Indeed, a sizable majority of Stay-at-Home Workers (58 percent) run their own businesses, whether formally incorporated or not. Thirty-five percent telecommute, working for private companies or nonprofits located elsewhere. A paltry 4 percent of Stay-at-Home Workers work for the government—which is probably a good thing, considering how many government laptops with citizens' private information on them seem to have been stolen lately.

Stay-at-Home men are an even more successful group. They own the majority of home-based incorporated businesses, and are not only better educated, but also older and wealthier on average than the population in general. These men account for the overrepresentation of Stay-at-Home Workers at the top of the pay scale.

But don't think that only men are transforming the den into a personal office. The "Momtrepreneur" movement—women who take themselves out of the traditional workforce to be with their kids, but also start up part-time businesses for income, satisfaction, or both—is also picking up steam. According to the 2000 Census, more than half of all home-based businesses—which make up half of U.S. businesses overall—are owned by women. Such businesses run the gamut from Avon Ladies—5 million worldwide—to women-owned consulting firms, which are generally started by high-achieving women who build a clientele based on their former expertise. Between 2002 and 2006 alone, the average annual revenue for women-owned consulting firms (home-based and other) grew 45 percent, to over $150,000.

And at every level, people really like being Stay-at-Home Workers. Apart from the control and flexibility that the entrepreneurs have, the 35 percent of home-based workers who don't run their own business, but are employed by other companies or organizations, also report a lot of joy. According to a study by the American Business Collaboration, 76 percent of full-time telecommuters report high job satisfaction, compared with only 56 percent of on-site workers. And it's not because they're taking it easy. People who work from home full-time put in an average of 44.6 hours per week, compared with just 42.2 hours contributed by full-time on-site workers.

Employers are happy not just about all that extra work, but also about the tax credits they get for reducing employees' smog emissions, and increased savings in office space. In my own polling firm, we've eliminated our East Coast phone banks that used to house our callers, in favor of Stay-at-Home Workers. It's not only easier for them, but I can get more people willing to call consumers in Japan—at 3 a.m. New York time—if they can do it from their apartments instead of from my call center. Eventually, all polling interviews will be done this way.

So while Stay-at-Home Workers haven't transformed all of industry—as was once predicted—this seriously growing group of people who work in their slippers has important implications for business and policy.

First, Stay-at-Homers need a way to build community. It is ironic that while we are not actually Bowling Alone, we are increasingly Working Alone. Many Stay-at-Home Workers are tired of eating lunch all by themselves, in the same place they ate breakfast and dinner. We need a virtual water cooler that keeps people connected to their colleagues—not just in an insta-message kind of way, but in a collaborative, shared-space, easy-collegiality kind of way. And there is clearly a market for teaching people how to run and participate in tele-enabled meetings.

Second, as more workplace functions move home, there arise issues of home office safety, comfort, and design. Apparently, the growing incidence rate of fire, injury, and other loss resulting from improperly plugged-in copy machines, computer equipment perched on discarded kids' furniture, and printer wires chewed through by the family dog prompted the secretary of labor in 2000 to call for a "national dialogue" on home office safety. Can you get workers comp if you slip in your home office on your daughter's spilled milk? If your work laptop explodes and burns a hole in your living room couch, should the boss have to pay?

With the growing number of self-employed, Stay-at-Homers—especially successful and assertive ones—maybe we will finally come up with a better system for health insurance and retirement savings than the current employer-based one.

And maybe we will see an increase in "lunch clubs," which used to be the province of martini-drinking men and, in separate rooms, tea-sipping ladies. Professional, white-collar men and women need a place to meet clients and build networks when the family den just won't do. Just as rising divorce rates created a market for longer-term hotel stays like at Residence Inn, the rise in Stay-at-Home Workers triggers a market for shorter-term business locales—one meeting or presentation at a time.

At a minimum, we need to be sure that if videoconferencing becomes standard in people's home "offices," they are fully prepared to get showered, dressed, and otherwise prepared before meetings. It's one thing to have the family pictures proudly displayed on your office credenza. It's another thing to have Junior and the family dog squealing in the background when you're trying to do a strategy call.

Wordy Women

▲

Former president of Harvard University Larry Summers got in a lot of trouble in 2005 for suggesting that women were innately inferior to men in the sciences. But what he didn't say—and what might have gone over better with some of the female faculty who ultimately helped oust him—was that women are on the verge of taking over word-based professions, like journalism, law, marketing, and communications.

Lest I get into the same kind of trouble as Summers, let me be clear that I don't know why men more often go into the sciences and women more often go into the "words." I haven't the slightest idea what role biology, culture, or socialization plays in those choices. But I can tell you that those choices are dramatically changing the face of certain professions, and that could mean big differences for America.

Take journalism. According to the Bureau of Labor Statistics, as of 2005, 57 percent of news analysts, reporters, and correspondents were women. Even 57 percent of TV news anchors—that authoritative role once reserved for the likes of Walter Cronkite—are women. Sure, Katie Couric made big news by landing one of the coveted national evening news spots in 2006. But at the local level, the Mary Richardses of the world had long ago replaced the Ted Baxters.

In public relations—the art of helping people express themselves in just the right way—women make up something like 70 percent of the field, up from 30 percent in the 1970s. (The firm where I serve as CEO, Burson Marsteller, is 70 percent women.) USA Today recently observed that PR may well be the first traditionally male white-collar profession to be redefined by women.

Or look at law, that great province of written and spoken argument. Since 1970, the number of women lawyers in America has grown 2,900 *percent*.

Women are just over half of law school graduates, and nearly half of law firm associates. They are two-thirds of law school vice deans.

Compare all these majority and supermajority numbers to women in the sciences and in business. Women are just 14 percent of architects and engineers. They are about 15 percent of professors in the major technical universities like Caltech and Georgia Tech. They hold only 16 percent of the top officer jobs in Fortune 500 companies. They are a mere 3 percent of technology companies' highest-paid executives.

To be sure, that women flood the wordy professions doesn't mean they always dominate decision-making. In journalism and in law, particularly, women drop off somewhere between the professional schools (where they are the majority) and the corridors of power. Women are only 17 percent of law partners. They are only one-third of full-time journalists working for the mainstream media. But this trend is new, so it may take a long time for it to percolate through to the top.

In the decades that women have joined television news, the number of stories about abortion, child care, and sex discrimination in the workplace has soared. According to a *Washington Post* analysis, during the brief tenure of Elizabeth Vargas as lead anchor of ABC's *World News Tonight*, ABC devoted more time to "sex and family" stories—contraception, abortion, autism, prenatal development, childbirth, postpartum depression, and child pornography—than CBS's and NBC's nightly newscasts combined.

In law schools, Family Law was kind of an arcane elective until the 1970s. Now there are dozens of Family Law journals and it's one of the most popular classes in law school.

The same is true in PR and advertising. Television commercials for tampons, vaginal creams, and "relief from period pain" used to be few and far between. Now you can't watch even a half hour of prime time without seeing them.

The other effect of women moving into word-based professions is that men may very well leave them. In 1971, over one-third of teachers in America's public schools were men. As women surged into the profession, the number of men plummeted to under one-quarter. Already in both public relations and TV journalism, executives are starting to worry about the large-scale evacuation of men. Some claim that the "best" professionals have simply won, but others make the reverse Larry Summers objection: With half the human race underrepresented, can we really reach our full potential?

The truth is, women are in many ways following the traditional routes that new immigrants have found to success. Women entered the workforce with less capital than men, and it is a proven route to upward mobility to flock to these kinds of professions. Wordy professions require human capital, and they are the result of study and hard work, not strength or force. While women dominated first in teaching and nursing, their upward mobility has led to a new tier of professional success beyond those careers.

Wordy professions were a logical choice—a place where women could be successful on their own merits and where they could bring new insights that had been missing from the scene. And so women increasingly became comfortable that these professions were ones where they could excel. They left the physical combat mostly for men, and took on the verbal combat that determines so much in a peaceful democracy.

And you can expect this trend to go global. As women everywhere have entered the workforce and gotten more education, a whole new set of professional jobs is opening up to them.

Of course, one of the biggest-selling writers of all time, J. K. Rowling of *Harry Potter* fame, is a British woman.

Politics is perhaps the next frontier for women. Having long worked with Hillary Clinton, I see how what was once prejudice against women in public life is slowly turning to acceptance and even preference. A whole generation of young women is now watching to see if America, too, will get its first woman chief executive as has already happened in the U.K., Germany, Israel, and Chile. If millions of young women are gaining ground in journalism, public relations, and law, politics is a logical jump—as they require many of the same skills you need for politics. Already many of the most respected policy directors in Washington are women, shaping what the White House and Congress produce that drives our country. We are up to sixteen women senators in 2007—a far cry from fifty, but a huge jump from only one, just twenty-five years ago.

Larry Summers was focused on the wrong side of the issue. Rather than wondering why women were not equally represented in math and science, he might have noticed how well women are doing in the wordy professions and how their success there may lead ultimately to a whole new politics. Their verbal campaign sure had an impact on him.

Ardent Amazons

▲

Wordy Women wouldn't be a perfect microtrend if there weren't *also* an equally intense identity group hurtling in the opposite direction. So now we turn to the women in America who are increasingly choosing work that demands serious physical strength.

They range from athletes to first responders to construction workers to soldiers. First, the athletes. Although the first Female Bodybuilding Competition was essentially a beauty contest in bikinis, there is now such a following of female bodybuilders and weightlifters that, in 2000, women's weightlifting became an official Olympic sport. Female freestyle wrestling joined in 2004. In April 2007, Ria Cortesio became the first woman to umpire a Major League Baseball exhibition game in decades.

Football still brings to mind husky men huddling around a pigskin, but as of 2007, there were actually *three* professional women's football leagues in America, comprising eighty teams—up from fewer than ten such teams in 2000. Women playing rugby—virtually unheard of a couple decades ago—are said to number about 10,000 in college and another 3,000 in high school.

True, they're playing each other—this isn't Billie Jean King walloping Bobby Riggs in a made-for-TV 1970s spectacle—but ask your grandmother if she could have anticipated that, in 2007, there would be *almost 100* professional women's football teams in America.

On the first responder front, America's professional firefighters are about 5 percent female, or over 6,000 women (another 35,000 are volunteers). Among law enforcement personnel, 1 in 4 is a woman, up dramatically from a few decades ago. Of sworn police officers, it's just over 1 in 10.

In 1953, the National Association of Women in Construction started with sixteen members. Today it has almost 6,000 members, and 180 chapters nationwide.

The military has seen dramatic growth as well. In 1960, there were only 31,700 women in the armed forces, or just over 1 percent. As of 2005, there are over 200,000 women serving, or nearly 15 percent of our armed services. (Jessica Lynch, heroically rescued in Iraq in 2003, was only one of over 150,000 American women who have served in Iraq and Afghanistan, as of late 2006.) Altogether, there are 1.7 million female veterans in the U.S.— almost the same number as female elementary and middle school teachers. While few military jobs ever involve combat, the work clearly attracts and rewards the brawnier side of the fairer sex.

In the spring of 2007, we did a quick poll to learn more about these women who choose careers in athletics, police, firefighting, the armed services, or building and construction. In general, they are big, conservative, happy, heterosexual women—ready for a fight and on the way up the economic ladder.

First, they are physically big. Almost 1 in 4 is over 5'7," or in the 90th percentile of white women generally. (Ninety percent of the overall sample was white.) They are also heavier, with 58 percent clocking in above the 150-pound mean, and almost 1 in 3 registering over 170 pounds. Perhaps not surprisingly, 8 in 10 were athletic as girls, and many more had brothers than sisters. (Almost half had at least two brothers.)

Ardent Amazons also skew to the right—with 76 percent calling themselves conservative or moderate, and only 1 in 4 identifying as Democrats. They are more rural, and less urban, than a typical national sample.

Ardent Amazons adore their work. Forty-four percent *love* it most of the time, and another 52 percent like it most of the time. And nearly all would recommend their jobs to girls or young women considering going into this work—more than half, with vigor.

Would you recommend your job to girls or young women considering your line of work?

	%
Yes, enthusiastically	56
Yes, with some hesitation	30
No, probably not	8
No, definitely not	2
Don't know	4

Their enthusiasm for their work is high *despite* the fact that it hasn't been easy. Six in 10 say they've been discriminated against at work because they are women, and almost 4 in 10 say that in their line of work, women's perspectives get ignored. But the groundbreaking quality of it seems to be part of the thrill. Sixty-four percent said that the fact that the work was traditionally male made them more interested in going into it, compared to only 10 percent who said that that fact had made them less interested. And the male tradition of it is a point of pride in social conversation:

When you tell people what line of work you are in, are you:	
	%
Proud, because it's a traditionally male line of work	76
Hesitant, because it's a traditionally male line of work	4
Don't know	20

Finally, Ardent Amazons have found the ticket up. While fewer than 1 in 4 have finished college, they are making good money—42 percent have annual household incomes over $75,000, including 14 percent who make over $100,000. Money and benefits nearly topped the list of what the women like best about their jobs, second only to the mental challenges.

In terms of marital status, 76 percent of Ardent Amazons are now married, and another 18 percent have been. And while most respondents said they knew someone who was gay or lesbian, only 13 percent—the smallest group of respondents—said such people were their co-workers.

But it appears that working in male-dominated professions either carries the risk of sexual assault or was motivated by such assault. Nearly 4 in 10 respondents said they had been the victim of a sexual assault at some point in their lives, which is quite high relative to the reported experience of women overall. Perhaps the experience of being assaulted moved some of these women toward professions where physical strength is prized, and vulnerability is not.

Physical women on the rise have real implications for society. First, these women love their work, and they're not about to go away. While some women's groups have complained that the number of women in traditionally male roles has not risen nearly fast *enough*, men who would hoard these jobs to themselves frankly shouldn't expect to prevail. They have chosen themselves some of the toughest, most dedicated opponents on earth.

Second, to some degree, women will change these professions. At entry, the positioning is that they can and will perform exactly like men—but once they reach a critical mass (as has happened in law and journalism, and arguably medicine), their perspective will shift the enterprises themselves. In 2002, the National Center for Women and Policing found, based on a study of seven major U.S. police agencies, that women police officers are substantially less likely than their male counterparts to use, or to be accused of using, excessive force. As a result, the average male police officer costs his jurisdiction somewhere between two and a half and five and a half times more than the average female officer in excessive force liability lawsuit payouts. Do female police officers focus more on diffusing tension than battling it down? And while that wouldn't be a winning strategy in every case, wouldn't it, in the grand scheme, be a useful balance to excessive force?

Half of all violent crime calls to police concern domestic violence. Does a woman police officer have a better sense of how to react?

Of course, I wouldn't generalize women's strengths any more than I would their weaknesses. Sure, it was under America's first female attorney general, Janet Reno, that the nation's police forces became focused on "community policing" and preventing crime before it started. On the other hand, the first female national security adviser (and later secretary of state), Condoleezza Rice, helped pave our path to war in Iraq. And first female prime minister Margaret Thatcher deployed the British military more aggressively than any predecessor had in years. There haven't been *enough* women in power to make sweeping generalizations about whether or how they might lead differently from men, but based on what we've seen in law and journalism, I would expect changes in the Amazon professions, too.

The other fascinating thing about Ardent Amazons is that as more and more women take up careers that require physical force, women's average strength is likely to increase. Since the late 1960s, men have improved their record marathon times by three minutes—but women have improved theirs by *thirty-one minutes*. Deprived for so long, in significant numbers, of access to intense physical training, women (and men) have taken it as God-given fact that women are smaller, weaker, and slower than men. But who knows? As a purely evolutionary matter, women are still reaching their prime. For some time, men have been able to sort themselves out on the basis of physical strength. Women are only now getting that opportunity, and millions of women who would never have run a real race or tested their physical abilities are starting to get that chance. This is going to significantly narrow, if not eliminate, the physical differences between the sexes.

Just as many women have discovered the power of words, other women are discovering their own physical power and their ability to compete toe-to-toe with men in the most physically demanding professions. The women who choose these new paths love them and are becoming their own distinctive group—strong, proud, intense, and leading the way for others to follow. Twenty-five years ago, we had a national debate on the Equal Rights Amendment, and one of the big arguments against it was that women might have to serve in the armed forces or be police officers. Today's Ardent Amazons are proving what a silly debate that was.

PART III

Race and Religion

Stained Glass Ceiling Breakers

▲

A final trend about women at work. Women may be poised to dominate America's word-based professions, like journalism, public relations, and law, but women's preeminence gets more complicated when it comes to professions regarding The Word.

In the last two decades, the number of female clergy in America has more than tripled. Women students in divinity school just passed 51 percent. In the last ten years, the number of women majoring in religion or theology more than doubled, while among men it grew by barely half. We are seeing the dramatic growth of a new clergy, with a new set of personal priorities driving them to join the ministry. And while they are being turned out in the divinity schools, they are still searching for their permanent place in religious life in America.

Women who wear the cloth seem motivated by a deep sense that the world needs repair. Women clergy, often more so than their male colleagues, are very active in political and civic issues. According to surveys of women clergy, their top issue, by far, is social welfare, including the widening gap between rich and poor. Next is tolerance and rights, including racism; followed by public order and civility; and then gay rights. Toward the bottom of their list is defense and foreign policy; and in particular contrast to many male clergy in America, women pastors' last priorities are "family values" or the "spiritual and moral concern that the nation is turning away from God."

Perhaps not surprisingly, given that list, women clergy are also liberal, sometimes overwhelmingly so, and generally support Democratic candidates for office. A generation ago, many of these women would have been teachers, social workers, and civic volunteers, but now they are combining their commitment to social justice with their personal faith, and ascending instead to pulpits and ministries.

The rise of women clergy promises some changes in American religion. Both male and female clergy tell survey-takers that clergywomen are more caring about the individual lives of congregants, more nurturing, and more likely to draw on personal experiences when preaching, teaching, and counseling. Women are also reported to be far less interested in congregational politics, power over others, and job prestige. And they are said to be more welcoming to newcomers who had been alienated from the fold.

But for all these contributions, and the rise in their numbers, women clergy face some pretty serious challenges. It starts with personal stress, reportedly far greater than what male clergy feel. In a study conducted of 190 United Methodist clergywomen around the country, 60 percent said their sleep was restless, 56 percent said they felt tearful, and more than one-third (35 percent) said they "could not shake off the blues even with help from family or friends." The biggest challenge by far, the clergywomen reported, was balancing work and family. Round-the-clock pastoral duty *and* primary child care duty at home can be very taxing. And whereas most male clergymen have wives who perform leadership roles in the congregation, women clergy find themselves doing both the wifely duties and the clergy's. Finally, for single clergywomen, dating is a very big challenge. Unmarried clergywomen report that most men are intimidated by them, and those who aren't—like fellow clergymen—are too busy to be ideal partners. (Imagine trying to sell your fraternity brother on a blind date with a minister.)

More generally, even those religions that admit women clergy seem to resist their playing too large a role. There is a widely observed phenomenon among women clergy—known as the Stained Glass Ceiling—that while they finish their training in numbers equal to or greater than men, they rise in congregational work far more slowly. To this day, a very large congregation—in any religion—led solely by a woman is almost unknown.

Some say it's just a matter of time until women clergy break through the Stained Glass Ceiling. They have made solid progress in other professions— especially word-oriented ones—and this field might just be taking longer, in part because the First Amendment bars recourse to anti-discrimination laws. (Which is why, with impunity, male pastors can ban women from their profession by just saying: "When Adam followed the leadership of his wife and ate the forbidden fruit, look where it led.")

But a deeper look at the struggles of women clergy suggests that what's ahead may not be Good News.

In the past fifty years, nearly every major religious group in America that has permitted women clergy has seen a profound drop in membership. And every major religious group that has excluded women clergy has seen a dramatic rise. As the chart below shows, most mainline Prostestant groups that permit women clergy have dropped in membership. Most other denomations that exclude them have grown.

Growth/Decline in Major U.S. Religions, 1960–2002

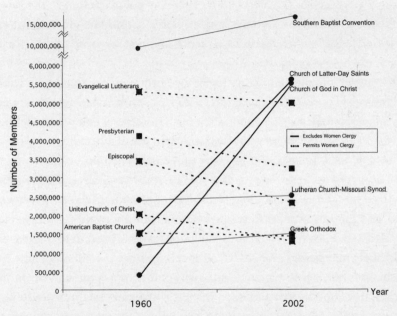

Source: Demographica, Christian Church Membership in the United States: 1960–2002

Catholics in America, whose numbers are too large to even fit on this chart, exclude women clergy and in the past fifty years have grown from 42 million to 67 million. American Muslims, as yet too few to fit on the chart, also exclude women clergy, and grew from 527,000 in 1990 to 1.1 million in 2001, according to the American Religions Identification Survey. (Their numbers may be much larger by now.) Immigration is, of course, also at play, but the pattern holds.

Some will find it tempting to say that women's presence in certain denominations *caused* the flocks to stray. Who needs St. Paul's "I permit no woman to teach or have authority over men"—if you can use empirical trends alone to prove that if you want to grow your religion, bar women clergy.

But more likely, the link is that the admission of women clergy is part of a larger liberalizing trend that is itself becoming unpopular among religious people. Women clergy, rising as they did with the feminist movement, represent the integration of progressive civil society into religion. But more and more, progressivism is not what people are looking for on a Sunday morning. Fully 77 percent of people who regularly attend church say they go for the way it involves their hearts; only 23 percent say they go for the way it involves their heads. For political advocacy, fellowship, and shared ethics, people are figuring they can go to the Sierra Club. If they're going to church, they want inspiration, fear, and conviction. And so women ministers are working on finding a style that gives religion more heart, and that is something quite new for these old congregants.

Of course, congregational membership is not to be confused with truth. All of the world's great religions started small. So while a denomination's fall in membership may say a lot about what the people want, many would argue it doesn't say anything about what God wants, or about what congregants will want over time. The cold statistics now show that this new class of women clergy is having a tough time, as the stricter religions are growing and the liberalized religions are shrinking. But this pendulum has swung many times before, and the role of religion today in so many of the world's conflicts may cause a reaction against religious polarization, and then Stained Glass Ceiling Breakers may be the pioneers of a new movement poised to become the mainstream of modern religion. Consensus and compassion may be on the outs right now, but they are bound to make a comeback. Just as America may be poised for the first woman in the White House, we are also ready for the first female Billy Graham—the first woman minister to catch the imagination of the country through the power of TV and perhaps even the Internet.

Pro-Semites

▲

In one of the funniest scenes in Woody Allen's 1977 hit movie *Annie Hall*, Alvy Singer goes to his non-Jewish girlfriend's house in Chippewa Falls, Wisconsin, to meet her parents. Although Annie and her family are hospitable enough, never mentioning their religious differences, Allen shows us how Alvy imagines Annie's grandmother sees him: an old-world, bearded Chasid, complete with a yarmulke and pais (the side curls worn by traditional Jewish men). Jewish audiences roared at Allen's paranoia. But it wasn't so long ago that Alvy's perception—that non-Jews automatically regarded Jews as foreign and undesirable—was the truth.

Today, that movie scene might be played out differently. Today, Alvy might *actually* sport the yarmulke and pais, and Annie's parents might sit there secretly hoping that Alvy's the boy Annie will marry.

Because today in America, Jew-loving is a bit of a craze. Jews are in demand everywhere. Whatever in the past seemed to trigger envy or rejection of Jews now seems to be triggering admiration and attraction. It used to be the Jews who often sought out relationships outside their faith, hiding their religion in the process. But now there is growing evidence that the opposite trend is happening: Non-Jews are seeking out Jews.

Jewish women, long stereotyped as making reservations for dinner, are now highly sought-after, looked up to by a new generation. And if perhaps it is true that a few of them don't cook, it may be because Jewish women are at the forefront of the professional revolution of the last several decades, racking up unparalleled rates of college graduation, graduate degrees, and high-powered jobs. (Sixty-eight percent of Jewish women aged 25–44 have a college degree, by far the highest percentage of any religious group in America.)

In today's service-oriented, education-based economy, lifestyles that were once seen as out of the mainstream are now highly popular. And so Jewish spouses (of both sexes) are right in the sights of people looking for successful, well-educated mates.

It wasn't always this way. America has had its share of anti-Semitism; in 1939, a Roper poll found that only 39 percent of Americans felt that Jews should be treated like other people. Fifty-three percent believed that "Jews are different and should be restricted." Ten percent actually believed that Jews should be deported. In the 1940s, several national surveys found that Jews were considered a greater threat to the welfare of the United States than any other national, religious, or racial group.

Compare that to a Gallup poll taken in August 2006. When Americans were asked how they feel about people of different religious or spiritual groups in the United States, *Jews rated the highest of any group in America*, with a net positive of 54 percent. No one—not Methodists, not Baptists, not Catholics, not evangelical Christians, fundamentalist Christians, Mormons, Muslims, Atheists, or Scientologists—scored higher in the view of Americans nationwide.

Such "Pro-Semitism" has turned, for some, into a very personal preference. According to J-Date, the most popular online Jewish dating service in the world, as of early 2007, nearly 11 percent of its members were not Jewish. That means that something like 67,000 non-Jews worldwide, and nearly 40,000 non-Jewish Americans, are paying monthly fees for the privilege of proactively seeking out dateable, marriageable Jews. In one of our own polls in September 2006, nearly 4 in 10 non-Jews said they would be "very" or "somewhat" interested in dating or marrying a person who is Jewish.

Those most interested were liberal to moderate, slightly downscale, Catholic men. (A little less Annie Hall, a little more Joey Tribiani from *Friends*.) It is this affinity with Catholics that is driving Pro-Semitism, as both groups typically emphasize big family values and a strong orientation around food—a merger of matzoh balls and meatballs, as it were. Both groups have felt left out or discriminated against at times, and both have lately made significant gains socially. At one point, a Catholic president seemed unthinkable. But with polls like Gallup's—could a Jewish president be in the making?

As of 2006, there were eleven Jewish senators—including one from Oregon, a state that is less than 1 percent Jewish.

Another important part of Pro-Semitism in America is the rise in strong support for Israel from unexpected quarters. Today in America, there are more Christian evangelicals than Jews who support Israel. Senator Bob Bennett, whose Jewish constituency in Utah is 0.2 percent, was recently a lead speaker at a pro-Israel rally. President George W. Bush—whose family was once regarded with great suspicion by the Jewish community—has high popularity ratings in only one country in the world: Israel.

When we polled Pro-Semites, the number one reason they gave for desiring a Jewish spouse was a sense of strong values, with nearly a third also admitting they were drawn to money, looks, or a sense that Jews "treat their spouses better." In 2004, I worked with Senator Joseph I. Lieberman, an Orthodox Jew, on his bid to be president. Although he failed to win his party's nomination, his emphasis on values set a nationwide example that raised the consciousness about Jewish life in America. During his campaign, far more Jews than non-Jews told him a Jew shouldn't run. But his strong sense of principle served him well in 2006, when Republicans and Independents—once unlikely supporters of a Jewish candidate—came to his aid after Connecticut Democrats declined to nominate him for reelection to the U.S. Senate.

Pop culture, too, seems to have discovered Pro-Semitism. When Madonna wrapped herself in Kabbalah, a spiritual movement rooted in Jewish mysticism, a whole new side of America got introduced to Jewish life. Not the *Seinfeld* sort—where Jewish culture hovers faintly in the background—but the uniquely, distinctly, religious kind. Granted, some thought Madonna carried it too far: During her 2004 Reinvention tour, she apparently refused to drink anything but "Kabbalah water," and she wouldn't perform on Friday nights out of respect for the Jewish Sabbath.

Once non-Jews started to make Judaism cool, Jews got into it, too. In 2005, the Jewish reggae artist Matisyahu (whose name is Yiddish for Matthew, or "gift of God"), donned his yarmulke and pais, rapped about the power of God to lift us up, and saw his second CD debut at number two on the *Billboard* charts. What is new here is not that a Jew can make it in rock 'n' roll. Plenty have, like Robert Zimmerman, who changed his name to Bob Dylan, put on jeans and a T-shirt, sang about America, and rocked a generation. What is new is that Matisyahu looks like he comes from a thirteenth-century Polish shtetl, is singing partly in Yiddish and Hebrew, and is drawing in fans from Oklahoma.

As Pro-Semitism spreads, so do distinctive Jewish customs—even when the Jews aren't there. Non-Jews are starting to have bar mitzvahs, the Jewish "coming of age" ceremony when a child turns 13. An entire blog is devoted to the propriety and sensitivity of using a chuppah, a Jewish wedding canopy, in non-Jewish weddings. Matzoh, the "bread of affliction" to which Jews are supposed to limit themselves during Passover to commemorate the haste with which their ancestors fled Egypt, is happily munched down by non-Jews all year.

Perhaps this all started with rye bread and hot dogs, and the deeply held belief that if they were Kosher they were better. My father was in the Kosher poultry business in the 1950s, and he faced a shrinking marketplace as Jews abandoned Kosher food. Today, with the right marketing, he could have welcomed growing demand from Jews and non-Jews alike. If anything, based on this trend, Jewishness is being substantially *under*-marketed today.

According to Jewish tradition, a non-Jew must study, and ask three times, to be able to convert. Maybe in the modern era, they'll shrink that requirement, now that non-Jews are absorbing Jewishness so casually and eagerly. But in the meantime, Jewish singles (like Hebrew National hot dogs) seem to bear an aura of "answering to a higher calling."

Interracial Families

▲

Perhaps no subject in American history has been more important, more fought over, or more all-consuming than race relations. And so it is perhaps remarkable that those couples on the frontier of being truly race- and color-blind have crossed the important 1 percent threshold in America.

Today, over 3 million marriages in America are interracial. And with 83 percent of Americans saying they approve of mixed-race marriages, this trend represents a sea change in American attitudes and tolerance.

My very first poll (when I was 13) was on the subject of race relations in America. I asked the faculty at the Horace Mann School in New York City to take a poll, which CBS had administered nationwide, on black-white attitudes. I discovered that when it came to race, my teachers were far more informed and more liberal than the general public (which was probably a seed of my fascination with the way different groups have opposite passions about the same things). But even among those teachers, there would not have been the kind of acceptance, and eager interchange, we see today in today's younger generation.

In 1970, there were about 300,000 interracial married couples in America, or 0.3 percent of the married population. By 2000, there were over ten times that many—3,100,000– or 5.4 percent of all marriages.

The trend of interracial marriage and its multiracial offspring is significant enough that in 2000, for the first time, the U.S. Census allowed Americans to check multiple boxes under "race"—creating 63 possible racial combinations that don't even include "other."

Who tends to mix it up, racially speaking?

According to Pew Research Center data from 2006, while the majority of interracial couples include a Hispanic, the most common type of interracial couple (at 14 percent) is a white man married to an Asian woman.

U. S. Interracial Couples, 1970–2000

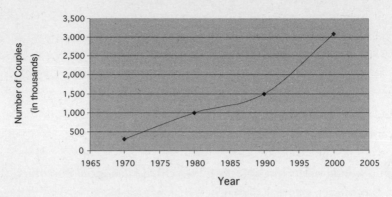

Source: Population Reference Bureau, 2005

Second, at 8 percent, is a black man married to a white woman. (Interestingly, white-Asian pairings are three times as likely to be white men with Asian women as the other way around; and black-white pairings are three times as likely to be black men with white women. Observers have commented on the lagging marriage prospects for black women and Asian men as a result— although those groups do not, as one might expect as a purely mathematical matter, seem to marry each other.)

Moreover, interracial marriage occurs more in the West than it does in the South, Northeast, or Midwest. However, a recent Gallup poll says it is Easterners who say they approve of black-white marriages the most. This is the famous gap between those who just talk the talk and those who walk the walk—in this case actually down the aisle.

Loving across race isn't just limited to romance—it also extends to child-rearing. Between 1998 and 2004, the percentage of foster care children in America adopted transracially (which generally means black children adopted by white parents) leapt from 14 percent to 26 percent. Between 1990 and 2005, the number of children adopted by U.S. parents from other countries, including from China, Guatemala, and South Korea, *tripled*—rising to almost 18 percent of all adoptions, or 20,000 families each year.

Even taken together, the number of interracial families is still just a sliver of American households. But it's steadily growing, and will undoubtedly continue. The main reason is that acceptance of interracial relationships has soared. In 1987, fewer than half of Americans thought it was "all right for blacks and whites to date each other"; in 2003, more than three-quarters thought it was all right.

And today's young people think so even more strongly. Not only were they raised on curricula based on "diversity" and "multiculturalism," today's under-30s are also the most diverse generation in history. Perhaps as a result, over 90 percent of young people accept interracial relationships, compared to just 50 percent of seniors.

And they don't just accept it; they do it. In 2002, 20 percent of 18–19-year-olds said they were dating someone of a different race, up from under 10 percent just a decade before. Of members of Match.com, 70 percent say they are willing to date someone of a different race.

In the future, it seems, race will be less divisive than it was. President Clinton liked to say that humans are bound together by being 99.9 percent genetically alike—and only one-tenth of 1 percent different. It seems that even the dividing power of that .1 percent is diminishing.

With this kind of dramatic growth in interracial couples, families on the frontier of interracial life could use a little support. Nearly half of black-white couples say marrying someone of a different race makes marriage harder. Two-thirds of black-white couples say at least one set of parents objected at the start. Friends and siblings of interracial lovers seem to fly every which way—like the alternately supportive, furious, disgusted, and jealous posses of both Wesley Snipes and Annabella Sciorra in Spike Lee's *Jungle Fever*.

White parents who want to adopt a black child in America are still subjected to "cultural competency" training—a nod to the days (from the 1970s through the early 1990s) when transracial adoptions were denounced as "cultural genocide."

But apart from needing our respect and support, interracial families of all sorts are owed our attention, because very quietly they are eroding the assumptions that have guided America's race-related policies, customs, and habits for decades.

For example, what does affirmative action mean, in an era when people's ancestors were both victims *and* oppressors? Do such people get preferential treatment, or not?

How long will we adhere to the "one drop" rule in identifying people's race? Illinois senator Barack Obama has a white mother, who raised him exclusively, but does anyone (including the senator) tell his story without reflecting on his blackness? Halle Berry has a white Mom, too, who also raised her alone. But the first line of her bio (and the subject of her lengthy Oscar acceptance speech) was her status as the first African-American to win Best Actress. Race scholars contend that race is an experience, not a fact—so if a person is treated as black, he or she *is* black regardless of the number of "drops" involved.

But between stars like these in every field—from Obama in politics, Berry in Hollywood, and Tiger Woods (half-black, half-Asian) in sports—there is no question that the stigma surrounding interracial families is eroding, and that, indeed, its cachet is rising. America has come a long way from the shocked parents of the 1967 film *Guess Who's Coming to Dinner*, when their daughter brought home Sidney Poitier.

And now that Madonna has adopted a child from Malawi, and Angelina Jolie has adopted children from Ethiopia, Cambodia, and Vietnam, it really just couldn't be hipper to build your family as diversely as possible.

Of course, some will argue that in the growing acceptance of interracial relationships, there is also the loss of particularism that each group once brought and has worked to preserve. Native Americans, who have the highest intermarriage rate of any racial group in America, mourn the loss of the customs, language, and identity that used to define them; they have recently opened a museum in Washington to celebrate their culture.

One big theme of this book is that America is no longer a melting pot— that, rather, small groups are now defining themselves in sharper, starker distinction than ever before. To some degree, interracial families are an exception. For hundreds of years, this country had significant racial divisions, and now those divisions appear to be easing in some very significant ways. But at the same time, people can now express and choose their individuality not predetermined by race or creed or date of birth, but rather as an expression of their life experiences and beliefs. And Americans are learning how to be different and accept differences in new ways. Perhaps what makes interracial marriages such a good sign is that it shows how even old divisions can become unifying forces over time. America would not want to repeat the conflicts it went through over race when it comes to religion, politics, art, or culture. As microtrends take America in hundreds of new directions, this central idea can serve to moderate the societal impact of the evolution of society—the ability to bury old differences while not letting new ones rise to the fever pitch of the past.

THE INTERNATIONAL PICTURE

To be sure, interracial marriages are hardly just an American phenomenon. It seems that people all over the world are marrying across ethnicities, borders, and continents—although their reasons may be different from the ones that drive this microtrend here in the United States.

The practice of marrying internationally has hit a new level of popularity in Asia:

▲ In 2005, marriages to foreigners accounted for 14 percent of all marriages in South Korea, up from 4 percent in 2000.

▲ In Japan in 2003, 1 of every 20 new marriages had a non-Japanese spouse. The majority of these marriages were Japanese men searching for foreign wives.

▲ Due to increased opportunities in the workplace for women in Japan, South Korea, Malaysia, and Taiwan—and disproportionately male populations—men in those countries are finding themselves jumping on planes to tie the knot. And women from other Asian countries are happily stepping up. Vietnam is second only to China as Asia's biggest wife-supplier: More than 87,000 Vietnamese women married foreign men in the past eight years. Other countries where women are jumping at the chance include Thailand and Indonesia.

Russia became known during the 1990s as the source for the mail-order bride for Americans; but this, over time, has changed as well. Turkey has now replaced America as Russian women's favorite source of husbands. In 2006, the majority of international marriages in Moscow included Turkish spouses, followed by those from Germany, America, Britain, and the region encompassed by the former Yugoslavia.

There is a dark side to all these transnational marriages, however. While some may be based in love and romance, most happen out of necessity. Some men who look abroad for wives do so out of economic disadvantage; most of them can't compete economically for a wife of their own nationality. Other marriages are arranged for the sole purpose of conferring citizenship, and are promptly followed by divorce. Many also end in isolation and abuse.

But interracial, interethnic, and international pairings are on the rise, as are their offspring. Benetton may have been on to something.

Protestant Hispanics

▲

Guess which country sends the largest number of Catholic immigrants to the United States? Right, Mexico.

Now guess which country sends the largest number of *Protestant* immigrants to the United States? Yep, it's Mexico again.

Protestant Mexicans? Protestant Latinos? In significant numbers?

Everyone knows the Latino influence in America is rapidly growing. In 2006, there were over 43 million Latinos in America, up from about 22 million in 1990. If you count Puerto Rican islanders (4 million), and adjust for what is surely some undercounting, the U.S. Latino population reaches something like 50 million people.

In 2003, Latinos surpassed African-Americans as the largest minority group in the United States. They now make up 14 percent of the U.S. population, and about 8 percent of the electorate—up from just 2 percent in 1976.

But in general, Latino immigrants are thought of as Catholic. And to be fair, 70 percent of Latino immigrants *are* Catholic, and with high immigration rates now, U.S. Latino Catholics are at an all-time high, at about 29 million. Catholicism itself has record numbers of American adherents (about 70 million), and it is predicted that, by 2015, over 50 percent of them will be Hispanic.

But a remarkably important subgroup of Latinos in America are Protestant. According to the 2005 book *Latino Religions and Civic Activism in the United States*, nearly *one-quarter* of U.S. Latinos identify themselves as Protestant or other Christian, including Jehovah's Witnesses and Mormons. That's about 10 million people in America—more than the number of Jews, or Muslims, or Episcopalians, or Presbyterians in the U.S. And of those 10 million Protestant Latinos, nearly 90 percent describe themselves not as "mainline" or liberal Protestants, but as Pentecostal, evangelical, or "born again."

To some degree, this is all part of the worldwide explosion of Pentecostals, who grew from fewer than 50 million to over 400 million worldwide in the last several decades. Clearly, some of the Latino immigrants' Protestant identity took hold in their home countries. But a lot of it is happening here. According to a 2003 study on Hispanic Churches in American Public Life, Catholic affiliation drops almost 15 percentage points between first-generation Latino Americans and their grandchildren. Sure, shedding our immigrant ethnic traditions is an old melting pot story—except that now, it's the opposite. New generations aren't so much "blending in" to America as choosing a *different* niche identity.

Observers of Latino converts say the appeal of Pentecostalism happens on several levels. Pentecostal churches offer services in immigrants' native tongues, and focus strongly on the individual. They place a high value on social and financial mobility, which appeals to many immigrants' personal aspirations. Their focus on laying of hands and physical *healing* appeals to low-wage immigrants, many of whom don't have health insurance. According to one expert on Latino culture in America, Pentecostal ministers in Latino communities are like the old precinct captains in Northeastern American cities. They provide jobs, health care, loans, and social supports. For low-income Latinos, the Pentecostal community is like family.

In addition, Catholic Latinos are said to be drawn to the greater leadership opportunities in the Pentecostal movement. While Latinos make up about 40 percent of all U.S. Catholics, fewer than 8 percent of American Catholic priests are Hispanic, and many of the ones that are come from Colombia and Spain. So for Latino Americans, the Pentecostal movement provides greater, faster opportunities for leadership.

And perhaps most importantly, the Pentecostals are doing aggressive outreach. In some places, they are equipped with full-blown corporate tactics, from direct mail to Latino addresses, to tightly honed messaging, to sanctuary "amenities" that appeal to all comers.

And why is this important? Because Protestant Hispanics—whom many politicians don't even know exist—are a potent political force. In the last two presidential elections, the two main groups who made the difference between President George W. Bush's popular vote loss (and Supreme Court–assisted electoral vote win) in 2000, and his decisive win on both counts in 2004, were white women and Hispanics. In 2000, Hispanics voted for Bush at a rate of only 35 percent. In 2004, they upped their support to 40 percent, with the original exit polls tallying it as high as 44 percent. That was a dramatic shift, and pivotal for the president. But here's what's remarkable. *All* the shift was among Hispanic Protestants. The percentage of Bush voters among Hispanic Catholics in 2000 and 2004 was exactly the same—33 percent. Only Protestant Latinos increased their Bush support, from 44 to 56 percent. Pentecostal Hispanics, unknown to most Americans, were one of the key forces that tipped the 2004 election.

Now following that election, it is fair to say that President Bush and the Republican Party squandered much of that Latino goodwill through a series of immigration proposals that Latinos of every religion found offensive. By the 2006 midterm elections, Latinos had returned, at least at a national level, to the 2 to 1 preference for Democrats that they had historically had. Even the Pentecostal Hispanics felt more strongly about immigration than the issues where they had more in common with the Republicans. But, according to the Pew Hispanic Center, in a half-dozen Senate and governor races, Republican candidates got serious Latino support. And for a different Republican presidential candidate, or in a year not dominated by emotional immigration debates, Latinos in general, and especially Protestant Latinos, can be expected to tune in to Republicans.

Politicians lump Latino voters together at their peril. True, most Latinos are devoted Catholics, and are doing more than their part to revitalize the U.S. Catholic Church. But a growing group of Latinos are Protestant and Pentecostal, and *except* on the issue of immigration, they agree with their Catholic brethren on very little. For example:

▲ According to a poll done by my firm in 2006, a plurality of Catholic Latinos (42 percent) consider the most important issue in a presidential election to be the economy. By contrast, a plurality of Protestant Latinos (44 percent) are Values Voters. Values, to the Catholic Latinos, are the *least* important consideration in a presidential election, with only 23 percent of Catholic Latinos saying that values rank highest.

▲ Latino Catholics are three times as likely as Latino Protestants to belong to a labor union, or have family who do.

▲ Latino Catholics are slightly more upscale than Latino Protestants. Twenty-three percent of Latino Catholics have incomes of $75,000 or above, compared to only 12 percent of Latino Protestants.

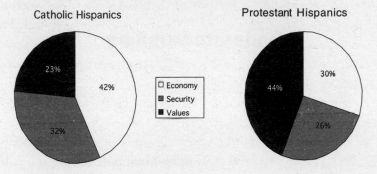

Differences in Priorities Between Catholic and
Protestant Hispanics, 2006

Source: PSB, 2006

▲ More than half of Latino Protestants speak English only, or mostly English with a little bit of Spanish. That is true of only 28 percent of Latino Catholics. Granted, the Latino Protestants generally represent later generations of Americans, but it is consistent with the larger trend that, in the minds of many Latinos, becoming truly "American" means converting to both English and Pentecostalism.

▲ Perhaps most remarkable is the difference between Latino Catholics and Protestants on abortion. Whereas Latino Protestants are strongly pro-life (58 to 26 percent)—again, remember the alliance with President George W. Bush in 2004—Latino Catholics are narrowly pro-choice, at 41 to 37 percent.

But for the immigration debacle of 2006, Republican stalwarts had some serious Latino potential on their hands. Remarkably enough, the fastest-growing religious group within the fastest-growing ethnic group in America looked just like them: nonlabor, pro-life, pro–English language Values Voters. Alas, in 2006, this group swung back to the Democrats.

And the implications aren't just political. More and more Protestant churches need to learn Spanish language and culture, and more and more Catholic ones need to learn what has been so appealing to their "base" about Pentecostalism. Whole new social networks, including for youth, are needed. People pray in surprising ways, and prayers of all traditions are rising from new tongues.

Moderate Muslims

▲

Since 9/11, it hasn't been very easy to be Muslim in America.

Almost half of Americans have a negative view of Islam. When asked to rate their views of all major religions, only Scientology ranks lower.

If one knows a Muslim personally, one's views are moderated—but only a little more than one-third of Americans do know a Muslim personally. Nearly half (46 percent) of Americans believe that Islam encourages violence more than other religions—up from the 35 percent who felt that way six months *after* the 2001 attacks. More than half of Americans say Muslims are not respectful of women. Forty-four percent say Muslims are too extreme in their religious beliefs. Twenty-two percent say they wouldn't want a Muslim living next door.

But if you look at an actual demographic portrait of Muslims in America, there's quite a contrasting picture.

Americans think Muslims are violent? An overwhelming 81 percent of American Muslims support gun control, compared to barely half of Americans who do. Muslims are religiously extreme? Twenty-five percent of Muslims say they attend religious services on a weekly basis—virtually identical to the 26 percent of Americans overall who say they do. Forty percent of Muslims say they're moderate—identical to the American proportion overall.

In fact, if I were to describe for you a cohort of Americans who got married at a rate of 70 percent, registered to vote at a rate of 82 percent, were college-educated at a rate of 59 percent, and were on average making more than $50,000 a year—what group would you guess they were?

Because that's the average Muslim in America. Young, family-oriented, well educated, prosperous, and politically active.

Oh—and growing. Since the 1960s, when immigration quotas that favored Eastern European immigrants were lifted, Muslims have been coming to the United States in steadily greater numbers, mainly to Michigan, Cali-

Attitudes of U.S. Muslims Compared to
Attitudes of U.S. Population Overall

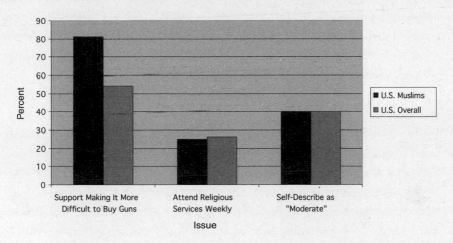

Sources: Project MAPS/Zogby Poll, 2004; Harris Interactive, 2005, 2006; Gallup, 2004

fornia, New York, and New Jersey. There are more than 1,200 mosques in America now, up from about 450 in 1980. Since 1994 alone, the number of mosques grew 25 percent. And while Muslim immigration dropped sharply after the terrorist attacks of 2001, there is no question it is back: In 2005, nearly 100,000 people from Muslim countries became legal permanent U.S. residents—more than in any other year since 1985.

Experts disagree about how many Muslims actually live in America—counting Muslim immigrants, their offspring, and American-born converts to Islam, you'll see estimates ranging from 2 to 7 million. But no one disputes that Muslims are growing not only in number but in political clout. In the 1990s, a group called the American Muslim Alliance set out to place 2,000 Muslims in American elected office by 2000. They got to about 700 before the drop-off in 2001—but in 2006, Keith Ellison of Minnesota became the first Muslim ever elected to Congress.

The real significance in the emerging Muslim community is not so much the change in the number of Muslims, but rather the potential for change within the Muslim community that could go a number of significant ways. As the American Muslim community expands, the internal choices they make will determine how Islam is positioned in America, which could, in some small way, affect how it is positioned in the world.

Already, American Muslims have done a 180 in presidential politics. In 2000, a plurality of them supported Republican George W. Bush against Democrat Al Gore; in the next election, in 2004, *over 75 percent* of them voted for Democrat John Kerry against George W. Bush. Of course, in the intervening years, Bush led post-9/11 invasions of Afghanistan and Iraq that most Muslims construed as attacks not on terror but on Islam—so the turn-around, while dramatic, is possible to understand.

But Americans take note: Muslims are swing voters in their own community, too.

In 2004, the Michigan-based Institute for Social Policy and Understanding surveyed mosque-goers in metropolitan Detroit, one of the most concentrated Muslim communities in the U.S. It found that of the 65,000 or so mosque-goers, 38 percent "prefer a flexible approach" in their religious practice. About the same number—36 percent—were "conservative" (including the 8 percent who identified as Salafi, the most reactionary group, which practices gender discrimination as a matter of divine law, and believes that all non-Muslims will go to hell).

The significance here, though, is that the remaining *quarter* of mosque-going Muslims are open to persuasion—to go either "flexible" or "conservative." M. A. Muqtedar Khan, a political scientist who publicized the study and who is a chief advocate for moderate Islam, calls them "freelancers." As a political pollster, I would call them "swings."

The future of Islam in America likely depends on them. If they decide to go conservative, Muslims in America may start actually matching up more with the stereotype—rigid in their beliefs, segregated by sex, and hostile toward other religions. But if the Swing Muslims go "flexible," there could be the seeds of a genuine Islamic reformation in this country that could work to bridge Muslims and non-Muslims not only in America, but throughout the world.

And they're probably a much bigger group than the survey suggested, since that survey reached only mosque-goers. Presumably the two-thirds who don't regularly go to a mosque are even more open to moderation. So if you add the non-mosque-goers, the flexible mosque-goers, and the swing mosque-goers, and you assume 4 or 5 million Muslims (halfway between the experts' estimates)—you easily get over 3 million Moderate Muslims.

Some institutions are trying to rally them. The American Islamic Congress was formed after 9/11 to denounce Islamic terrorism and promote a greater presence of Muslim moderates in the U.S. A self-styled "Martin Luther for the Muslims" named Kamal Nawash has started the Free Muslims Coalition, intended to denounce religious violence and terrorism more fervently than he felt Muslim organizations were doing post-9/11.

The Pentagon itself has begun a concentrated effort to recruit American Muslims to the U.S. armed forces, hiring imams as chaplains, celebrating Muslim holidays, and ensuring that there are Muslim prayer rooms at West Point and other service academies.

I don't know who will capture the hearts of the Moderate Muslims in America. But whoever does may swing American Islam, potentially shifting American perceptions of the Muslim community and perhaps even creating future international leaders to help bridge East and West. Perhaps Muslims who settle in America have self-selected in ways that make them friendlier to Western culture than is happening in Europe (see below). Or, perhaps, American Muslims remember gratefully how America took strongly anti-Serb, pro-Muslim military positions in Bosnia and Kosovo. Whatever the reason, the difference between the Muslim communities in America and in Europe is striking. But the future course of American Islam is by no means predetermined, and how Moderate Muslims view both domestic integration and American foreign policy could be critical to peace both at home and abroad.

THE INTERNATIONAL PICTURE

While many Muslims in the United States can be characterized as moderate, that is less true in Europe.

Muslims make up about 5 percent of the European Union's population, or 15 to 18 million people—many times the number of Muslims estimated to live in the United States. But that number is growing fast, due to both high immigration rates and the fact that the Muslim birthrate is three times that of non-Muslim Europeans. By 2015, the European Muslim population is projected to nearly double, and Muslims may soon become majorities in several major European cities.

Unfortunately, Muslim population growth may divide Europe, more than enrich it. According to a Pew Global Attitudes Project study on Europe's

Muslims, although European Muslims express far more positive views of the West than do Muslims living in Muslim countries, sizable Muslim groups who make their homes in France, Spain, and Germany describe Westerners as "selfish," "arrogant," "violent," "greedy," "immoral," and "fanatical." And the feeling is mutual: Some 83 percent of Spaniards, and 78 percent of Germans, regard Muslims as "fanatical." (The U.K. and France agree at lower rates, about 50 percent.)

The roots of tension are economic as well as cultural. The Turkish community in Germany is unemployed at a rate of 24 percent—two and a half times the national rate. North Africans in France have a 30 percent unemployment rate—three times France's national rate.

And terrorism looms large. Again according to the Pew study, the Muslim majorities of France, Germany, and Spain are evenly divided on whether or not Arabs were responsible for flying planes into the World Trade Center on 9/11—and 56 percent of Muslims in Britain say they were *not*. Perhaps most disturbingly, more than 1 in 7 Muslims in France, Great Britain, and Spain believe that suicide bombings can be justified in defense of Islam.

It makes sense that U.S. Muslims might be more moderate—those who come all the way here may start with a greater affinity for American values than those who travel the shorter geographic and cultural distance to Western Europe. But it might make Americans all the more interested in affirmatively reaching out to the Muslims who are here, especially the swing, moderate ones.

PART IV

Health and Wellness

Sun-Haters

▲

For millennia, humans have worshipped the sun. We used to do it as an actual god, but now it's more like a cultural obsession, especially on the beaches of Hawaii, New Jersey, Florida, and California. We flock to it for vacation, we turn our faces to it at lunch hour, and if work or school keeps us from getting to it for real, we pretend we've gotten it by lying in tanning beds or spraying ourselves orange. Today in America, there are three times as many professional tanning parlors as there are Starbucks.

And this is *even though* Americans know how dangerous the sun is. According to a 2002 survey, 93 percent of Americans know that too much exposure to the sun is unhealthy, and yet 81 percent still think they look good after having been out in the sun. One in ten vacations in America still involves a beach, with Hawaii our most popular vacation spot. Indoor-tanning is a $5 billion per year industry, with about 30 million Americans having done it—including over 2 million teenagers. According to another study, 1 in 10 children aged 12–18 uses a sunlamp, and only 1 in 3 uses sunscreen.

Unlike smoking, which also grabs us when we're young, we're hard-pressed to say that sun worship involves physical addiction (although remarkably, some are trying). No, it seems that consciously damaging your skin to look better in the short run is just pure vice—the deliberate choice of short-term gratification over long-term pain.

But amid the general brigades of Sun-Worshippers, there is a burgeoning group of dissidents who are on a mission to change all that. They are the Sun-Haters. These are the people who greet summer sunshine with floppy hats that look like Snoopy's World War I bomber gear (complete with earflaps), grudgingly show up at pool parties in full-body wetsuits, and slather on fourteen layers of 50+ sunscreen just to go to work. In an office.

Not that they're wrong. Skin cancer is the most common form of cancer in the United States today, with more than a million new cases diagnosed each year. The mortality rate from skin cancer has increased 50 percent since the 1970s. Between 1980 and 1987, the number of melanomas (the really dangerous skin cancer) increased 83 percent. Skin cancer in teenagers, unheard of a generation ago, is on the rise.

While skin cancer is much more common in light-skinned people, it is more likely to be deadly when it occurs in Hispanics or African-Americans. (One of the most famous people to die from melanoma was Bob Marley.)

And *at least* 25 percent—although it's been widely reported to be higher—of skin damage occurs before a person is 18 years old. Talk about vice—it's virtually child abuse to take your kid to the beach.

So Sun-Haters are out to protect America, and not just with a sun protection factor number stamped on the side of a bottle. Like anti-smokers in the 1970s and organic-food-eaters in the 1980s, they are early adopters of what they hope will soon be a national passion.

So far, they've spawned an industry for sun-safe clothing, which means long-sleeved shirts and pants that are woven more tightly than regular clothes. (A white T-shirt, commonly worn in the summer, provides an ultraviolet protection factor, or UPF, of only 5.) Some of the clothes are fortified with the products in sunscreen, or chemicals like titanium dioxide, which deflect the sun's rays. From a virtually nonexistent industry in 2000, sun-protective clothing now does about $180 million worth of business per year. Not huge potatoes, sure. But ready to grow, especially if the sun-safe manufacturers can figure out a way to make those earflap attachments look less like World War I bomber gear.

The Sun-Haters are also triggering innovations that build sun protection into our daily lives. Just coming onto the market is a product called Sun-Guard, a laundry aid that washes sun protection right into clothes, boosting their UPF level from about 5 to 30. In the cosmetic industry, no one ever heard of sunscreen in makeup until the 1990s. Now the majority of foundations and skin creams contain UPF or SPF of at least 15.

The fastest-growing sun-care product is self-tanners, which work with the skin to alter color. This is apparently the only true way to tan without risk of UV exposure. Sales of these products increased nearly 80 percent between 1997 and 2005. Spray-on tans jumped 67 percent in sales in the early 2000s.

Maybe someone will develop Permanent Sunscreen, much as they developed Permanent Makeup.

How big is the Sun-Hater crowd? If you count all the dermatologists in America (about 14,000), plus their families; the families of people who recently died of skin cancer (about 80,000 deaths between 1997 and 2006); current skin cancer victims (about 500,000), plus their families; and America's Generally Cautious (people who heed dermatologists' warnings the first time, eat only the safest foods, and drive the safest cars)—you get at least 2 million Sun-Hating, fedora-in-August-wearing Americans.

Can they animate public policy?

So far, the U.S. government has not been aggressive about regulating our exposure to the sun. (Given the constant association of suntanning with *worship*, maybe they fear a First Amendment challenge.) But Australia did, once their skin cancer rates hit astronomical levels, and the American Academy of Dermatology has said that if current trends continue, sun-related cancers could outpace lung cancer as the nation's number one cancer-killer.

New York and New Jersey have just passed laws banning children under 14 from tanning in indoor salons. But soon that may seem very timid, indeed. Look for federal agencies and state attorneys general to start going after indoor tanning salons like they once pursued Big Tobacco. If Sun-Haters truly get their way, look for warning signs on beaches, and lawsuits against beach resort owners who don't provide sufficient warnings. And where will it end? Must there be warnings on private swimming pools? Outdoor patio furniture? The entire system of national parks?

Will there be lawsuits claiming "secondhand sun"—to which children are unwillingly exposed at school?

In the shorter term, expect cries for clarity in the definitions and regulations regarding SPF and UPF. At the moment, those SPF numbers on the sunscreen bottles that we take very seriously refer only to the multiple of time it will take to produce a minor sunburn. (If it would normally take you ten minutes to burn, wearing sunscreen with an SPF of 15 will let you take two and a half hours to get it. But you will still get it, if you don't reslather, and the skin damage will be just the same.)

The litigation is already starting. In 2006, Californians filed a class action lawsuit against sunscreen-makers, claiming that the protection assurances were substantially overblown. What is "safe and effective" use of protection against a known cancer-causer, anyway?

The focus on sun danger may coincide with the increasing concern about global warming—which, by the way, some say has exacerbated the skin cancer problem by rethinning the ozone layer. Sadly, in the coming decades, we are likely to get *hotter* without any corresponding comfort that at least we're getting *tanner.*

Moms in America used to say, "Go get some fresh air." Now they say, "Don't forget to put your sunscreen on." Good Day Sunshine just ain't what it used to be.

30-Winkers

▲

Everyone knows you're supposed to get eight hours of sleep. Even as the nutrition experts go back and forth on how many carbs we're supposed to have, and the alcohol experts go back and forth on whether we should drink red wine—the Sleep Experts have been singing the same song for 150 years: People need seven and a half to eight hours of sleep per night.

Well, we're failing. The average American now sleeps less than seven hours a night, which is a drop of about 25 percent since the early 1900s. Thanks to twenty-four-hour-a-day electronics, and expectations, we're awake more than any Americans in recorded history.

Indeed, the number of people who sleep fewer than six hours per night is rising fast—from 12 percent of American adults in 1998 to 16 percent in 2005.

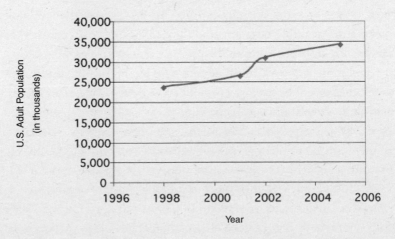

U.S. Adult Population Sleeping Less than Six Hours per Weeknight (1998–2005)

Source: National Sleep Foundation, 2005

That's something like 34 million people who are burning the midnight oil. Or midnight laundry machines. Or midnight Internet solitaire. Or just plain tossing and turning.

It is tempting to think of 30-Winkers as somehow tougher than the rest of us, and some of them definitely cultivate that impression. Margaret Thatcher was said to sleep only five hours a night. Madonna insists she sleeps only four hours a night. Thomas Edison railed against the self-indulgence of sleeping more than five hours a night, and told his staff to do the same. (This is the same staff, though, that said Edison actually slept a lot more than he admitted.) And a good friend of mine in college, money wizard Jim Cramer, never slept more than four hours a night, giving him an edge on some otherwise very competitive folks at Harvard.

Honestly, though, can you think of any activity *besides* sleep deprivation that functions both as a form of torture for enemy prisoners and a badge of honor for super-strivers? You've envied people who say they hardly sleep. If nothing else, in the race for more of everything, they have attained more time. An extra ninety minutes per day adds up—that's 10 percent more awake time per day—or an extra 8.2 years for someone who could expect to live to, say, 82. Through less sleep you could have the life experience of someone aged 91. Now that's tempting.

But the truth is, most 30-Winkers are neither quite so proud nor so hardy. While some are budding young surgeons, or Wall Street climbers making themselves available all day both in the U.S. *and* Asia, most people who under-sleep for work are night-shifters or emergency service workers, like paramedics or utility linemen, and they are at high risk of injury, accidents, and health problems without the promise of lucrative earnings.

And more generally, most people who are up in the middle of the night are up because they *can't* sleep, not because they don't want to. Short sleep is actually statistically correlated with poor health, worry, stress, and low income. Men sleep less than women—although women, especially younger women, are more likely to say they didn't sleep enough. (Fully 76 percent of women aged 18–34 say they experience daytime sleepiness at least once a week.) In the only big sleep study to include substantial numbers of African-Americans, black men were found to sleep a full hour less than average, and with significantly poorer sleep quality than either black women or whites.

30-Winkers on the rise will have tragic, if predictable, outcomes. In the

2005 Sleep in America poll, 60 percent of participants said they have driven drowsy in the last year, and 37 percent say they've nodded off or fallen asleep behind the wheel. The National Highway Traffic Safety Administration says drowsy driving is responsible for over 50,000 traffic accidents a year, including over 1,500 fatalities. Famous disasters like the *Exxon Valdez* grounding and the recent Staten Island Ferry crash were apparently caused by drivers asleep at the wheel.

Less sleep also means less productivity. Two in 10 American adults say sleepiness caused them to make recent errors at work. Productivity costs have been estimated at $50 billion.

And bad sleep threatens domestic harmony. Thirty-nine percent of sexually active American adults—including 64 percent of women aged 35–44—say they pass up sex for sleep. One in 4 adults says their spouse's or partner's sleep problems keep *them* awake, too. And what with men awake more than women, one can only expect greater trouble in terms of online porn, online gambling, and general disharmony when the husband wants company and the wife wants rest.

But perhaps the most surprising implication is the vicious-cycle link between sleeplessness and obesity. Being overweight can cause sleep problems, including clogged airways that constrain breathing. But because a lack of sleep actually triggers the hormones that boost hunger and appetite, sleeping too little can also raise your chances of getting fat. According to the National Center on Sleep Disorders Research at the National Institutes of Health, sleeping just six hours per night raises your risk of developing obesity 23 percent. Sleeping just four hours per night raises it 73 percent.

Too bad Americans don't treat their insomnia with a five-mile run. That would seem to solve both problems.

Some lawmakers are starting to make insomnia their business. New Jersey criminalized "drowsy-driving" in 2003—calling it akin to drunk-driving—although other states have been slow to follow.

The private sector is leaping on the chance both to help people sleep at night *and* help them stay awake during the day. The sleeping pill industry is having a field day: The new, nonaddictive Ambien did a record $2 billion worth of business worldwide in 2004, with the number of people aged 20–44 who use sleeping pills *doubling* between 2000 and 2004. From the stay-awake side, caffeine-packed energy drinks are the fastest-growing sector of the nearly $100 billion domestic beverage industry; between 2005 and 2008, those drinks are expected to bring in more profits than all regular soft drinks and sports drinks combined. And of course, Starbucks, whose house blend has about twice as much caffeine as the leading grocery store brand Folgers, has so deeply permeated American culture that you can barely walk a block without stumbling onto one.

If you can't sleep at night *or* stay up during the day, a company called Metronaps is offering sleep pods in airports, office buildings, and other public spaces. Sure, it's weird to visit Z-land amid strangers in bright daylight—after all, sleep is supposed to be a very private habit. Well, yes—but lack of sleep is a very public problem.

And so while it is hard to imagine a public health campaign to Get More Sleep—the late-night jokes would be too easy, the perky spokespeople too hard to find—perhaps it is time for an American Siesta. Sure, it seems to go against Americans' hardy work ethic, but that ethic was conceived before there was 24/7 e-mail and online shopping. Now, if positioned as a public safety and productivity issue, the case for a midday break could be quite strong. And there have been famous nappers. Winston Churchill worked late into the night but took a serious, pajama-cloaked nap in the afternoon. Both Ronald Reagan and Bill Clinton were said to be big fans of the nap. Is America ready to give over "Early to Bed, Early to Rise," in favor of "If You're Tired, Just Close Your Eyes"?

America has a big choice ahead—either enjoy the extra time awake, and figure out new and more productive activities for it; or say we can't afford *not* to sleep eight hours, and figure out how to get it. Either way, it's no small matter. Our health and life could depend on it.

THE INTERNATIONAL PICTURE

As tired as Americans may be, the rest of the world is hardly doing any better.

According to a sleep survey conducted by ACNielsen in 2005, 7 out of the 10 night-owl nations are Asian. Note that America doesn't even make the top ten.

▲ Sizable numbers of the populations in Taiwan (69 percent), Korea (68

percent), Hong Kong (66 percent), Japan (60 percent), Singapore (54
percent), Malaysia (54 percent), and Thailand (43 percent) regularly go to
sleep after midnight.

▲ Populations in Portugal (75 percent), Spain (65 percent), and Italy (39
percent) also reported regularly turning in after midnight. All three
nations are known to integrate the siesta into their daily routine, perhaps
accounting for these late-night hours. Ironically, the siesta culture
has become such a challenge to productivity in Spain that, in 2006,
the government launched a national campaign requiring all federal
employees to take no more than forty-five minutes for lunch.

In addition to being night owls, Asian nations make up half the early-bird
nations as well—those who wake up before 7 am. Again, America is not known
for its early birds.

▲ Majorities of Indonesians (91 percent), Vietnamese (88 percent), Filipinos
(69 percent), Indians (64 percent), and Japanese (64 percent) rise before
7:00.

▲ The other populations rounding out the top ten are Denmark (66 percent),
Germany (64 percent), Austria (64 percent), Finland (63 percent), and
Norway (62 percent).

What accounts for all this sleep deprivation? Although people all over the
world say "Habit" and "Work Schedule" drive their sleep behavior, one-third
of Americans also cited "Family/Children"—compared to just 17 percent of
Europeans, and 16 percent of Asians. Over half of Europeans said work was
the culprit, while most Asians cited habit.

When it comes down to total sleep hours, Americans are more and more
tired—but they cannot claim to be the *most* fatigued. That distinction goes to
the Japanese—fully 4 out of 10 sleep less than six hours a night. And who gets
the most sleep? New Zealanders and Australians, where 28 and 31 percent,
respectively, get more than nine hours of sleep a night.

Southpaws Unbound

The Rise of Left-Handers in America

▲

A merica is moving to the left.
Left-handed, that is.

While our right-and-left politics have stayed pretty much frozen, there has been a surge in left-handedness. And unless the gene pool is undergoing a hidden transformation, the likelihood is that this lefty rise is related to the societal changes that are at the core of today's microtrends.

Two hundred thousand years ago, when Homo sapiens were creating mankind's first spears and bone needles, some of them were using their left hands. The fossilized teeth of Neanderthals—complete with marks showing which side of the mouth their owners favored—suggest that a bunch of them were left-handed. And among early cave painters, about 50,000 years ago, nearly 1 in 4 was left-handed—about the same proportion of left-handed painters today.

But despite the couple hundred thousand years we've had to look into it, we haven't really nailed the causes or effects of handedness.

Some scientists claim left-handedness is genetic, pointing to evidence that it runs in families. (Queen Elizabeth II, Prince Charles, and Prince William are all left-handed, as was the Queen Mother.) Others say left-handedness is caused by trauma and stress in the womb, pointing to the fact that twins—as well as people with high prenatal exposure to sex hormones like testosterone—have higher southpaw rates.

Then there are conflicting studies on the *effects* of left-handedness. Some studies say it shortens life; some say it doesn't. Some studies say left-handedness increases the risk of breast cancer and/or decreases the risk of Alzheimer's; others say it doesn't. At least one study has found that left-handed people earn more than righties, especially among college graduates; another study found that lefty and righty earnings are equal.

Scientists can't even agree on whether "lateralization of the brain" is uniquely human. The latest findings suggest that chimps favor their right hands, and that there are "minority-sided" fish, who swim the opposite way from the rest of their schools when a predator fish shows up.

But amid the confusion about the impact of left versus right, there's one thing that is almost certainly true: The number of left-handed people in the world is on the rise, and it is likely to keep growing. It's currently estimated at 1 in 10. Look for an increase to possibly twice that rate—and I think it's because of a new approach to parenting.

For centuries, left-handedness has been out of favor. Through the Victorian age and the early twentieth century, lefties were almost impossible to find, because suppressing emotion, difference, and individuality was the order of the day. Indeed, in most cultures in the world, the *left* side of things has generally been associated with evil, sin, and inferiority. Just look at how we talk about it. The English word "sinister" comes from the Latin word for "left." The French word for "left," *gauche*, means "awkward," even in English. In Chinese, the adjective "left" means "improper," and in Norwegian, the expression *venstrehandsarbeid* (left-hand work) means "something that is done in a sloppy or unsatisfactory way." (The opposite is also true. "Right" means "just" in English. *Droit* is "law" in French. *Recht* is "authority" in German and Dutch. *Diestro* is "skillful" in Spanish.)

The anti-left bias comes from, or is reflected in, the fact that in the New Testament, the devil sits at God's left hand, whereas the blessed sit to His right. In Islam, too, left-handedness is a curse—just before the Islamist revolution in Iran in 1979, the Ayatollah Khomeini "proved" that the Shah was cursed by pointing out that his firstborn son was a lefty.

And so left-handedness has been routinely discouraged, or even beaten out of people. China and the Netherlands were particularly aggressive in "hand reorientation" until the twentieth century, and until the 1960s in the U.S., elementary school teachers—most famously in Catholic schools—slapped left-handed children for trying to write with their left hands. Ronald Reagan, Babe Ruth, and Lou Gehrig were young lefties said to be forced by teachers to switch for writing.

But in recent generations, this has all changed. Forcible switching has come to be seen as painful and unnecessary, and now what used to be abhorred in kids is suddenly respected. Just look at the shift in America among people alive today. According to a UCLA study done in 1993, the percentage of Southpaws born in the 1960s was over twice what it was for people aged 60 or above.

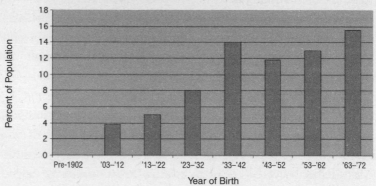

Percentage of the U.S. Population
That Is Left-Handed, by Year of Birth

Source: Hugdahl, K., Satz, P., Mitrushina, M., Miller, E. N. (1993) "Left-Handedness and
Old Age: Do Left-Handers Die Earlier?" *Neuropsychologia*, Vol. 4, pp. 325–33

This means that the "natural" state of left-handedness is some 16 percent
or higher—not 10 percent as is generally thought.

I think the Southpaw rise represents a shift in how we are raising our children, and how we let their individuality come out to help them reach their true
potential. At some point, these days, a parent realizes his or her child is tending
left. The parent panics. Will the child be made fun of? Struggle with writing?
Be left out? In the past, the parent would have done everything possible to
exorcise the tendency. But today? Today, more and more parents shrug their
shoulders, saying it's okay, maybe even something special. Or their attempts to
discourage it are milder, and therefore fail. This is not an isolated reaction. It's
part of the larger trend toward celebrating, rather than suppressing, individuality in kids. From giving children extra time to develop into kindergarteners to
accommodating their vegetarian appetites, parents today are taking their cues
from children, rather than the other way around. It's even related to the greater
freedom young people have today to express their sexual and/or gender identity. Left-handedness is just the tip of the iceberg—in today's world, parenting
is about letting your child develop into his or her own person, not about trying
to stamp him or her into a mold of conformity.

All this is in addition to the fact that we're likely to see more lefties
being born to begin with. Lefties are disproportionately represented among
twins—whose numbers grew by more than half between 1980 and 1997.

They are also more likely to be born to older Moms—according to one researcher, children born to Moms over 40 are *128 percent* more likely to be left-handed than kids born to Moms in their 20s. As everyone knows, Moms over 40 are way up—their childbearing nearly quintupling between 1980 and 2004.

I suspect the lefty boom will bring a surge in the promotion of sheer creative energy, driven by an idea that is at the heart of this book—that small groups of people, sharing common experiences, can increasingly be drawn together to rally for their interests. Lefties in particular represent innovation and self-expression. Einstein was a lefty. So were Ben Franklin and Isaac Newton.

More lefties may also mean more gays. Perhaps unsurprisingly, people who are allowed to follow their urges to the left are also more likely to follow other instincts: In one study, gay participants were 39 percent more likely to be left-handed than heterosexual participants.

More lefties could mean more military innovation: Famous military leaders, from Charlemagne to Alexander the Great to Julius Caesar to Napoleon—as well as Colin Powell and Norman Schwarzkopf—were left-handed.

So were famous criminals Billy the Kid, Jack the Ripper, and the Boston Strangler.

It could also mean more art and music greats—Leonardo da Vinci, Michelangelo, Pablo Picasso, Ludwig van Beethoven, and, yes, Jimi Hendrix and Paul McCartney were all lefties.

It will almost certainly mean better tennis and baseball players. Tennis greats from Rod Laver to Jimmy Connors to John McEnroe to Martina Navratilova have used down-the-line forehands to overwhelm opponents' weaker backhands.

And baseball—where "southpaw" comes from (baseball fields are built so batters can face east, to avoid the afternoon sun, which means that pitchers' left arms face *south*)—will certainly benefit. Left-handed players can't play four of the nine positions on a baseball team—as catcher, second base, shortstop, or third base, they'd have to take too many steps to field the ball and throw to first—but for the same reason, they have a distinct advantage in the other five positions. And from Babe Ruth to Ted Williams to Barry Bonds, left-handed hitters have the upper hand: Not only do right-handed pitchers' breaking balls play to their strength, but their positioning, plus the momentum of lefty batters' swings, gets them closer to first base.

More lefties could also mean more humor: Jay Leno, Jerry Seinfeld, Jon Stewart, Bernie Mac, Ben Stiller, and Matt Groening (and his creation, Bart Simpson) are all left-handed.

And it could mean more executive greatness. Corporate titans Steve Forbes, Ross Perot, and Lou Gerstner are left-handed. So was every U.S. president since Gerald Ford, except Jimmy Carter and George W. Bush. (In 1992, America had its first and only all-lefty presidential campaign: George H. W. Bush vs. Bill Clinton vs. Ross Perot.)

From a lefty's perspective, consumer relief is long overdue. If you are a lefty or live with one, you know how miserable it is for lefties to try to use scissors, can openers, three-ring binders, grapefruit knives, corkscrews, or other basic items designed for right-handed people. The left-handed co–chief executive of Research in Motion, maker of the BlackBerry, has admitted that with its right-side tracking wheel and scroll button, the BlackBerry was designed with only the righty in mind. But so far, it hasn't been cost-effective to design one for lefties.

But now lefties are on the march, growing in numbers—and it won't be long before marketers stop shunning them and instead grab the edge in the lefty marketplace, with more swappable handles on their products and more alternative southpaw versions.

The bottom line is that the rise of Southpaws means not just that we'll have more lefties in school and in the workplace—but also that society is becoming more open, more tolerant, and ultimately more able to *build* on self-expression instead of suppressing it. The percentage of left-handed people may seem like an insignificant detail, but in fact, a society that tolerates people working with different hands, and encourages parents to let their children develop as feels natural to them, is also likely to tolerate a lot of other freedoms. The percentage of lefties in a society may actually be one of the best indicators we have of whether a society is open and flexible or rigid and overbearing. I, for one, wouldn't want to live in a society that didn't encourage handedness of all types.

DIY Doctors

▲

In the past twenty years, the number of practicing doctors in America has nearly doubled. So you would think, with all those new doctors running around, that Americans would be consulting their medical professionals at every opportunity.

They're not. In fact, the biggest trend in American health care is DIYDs— Do-It-Yourself Doctors. These are people who research their own symptoms, diagnose their own illnesses, and administer their own cures. If they have to call on doctors at all, they either treat them like ATM machines for prescriptions they already "know" they need, or they show up in their offices with full-color descriptions of their conditions, self-diagnosed on WebMD.

If they can afford it, they buy their own ultrasound machines so they can check in on their fetuses every night. They sit in corporate boardrooms and compare sizes and shapes of skin moles, trading acquired wisdom about the chances of cancer and best practices on removal. In the old days, homemade medical care meant chicken soup and rest. Now, patients are taking their lives into their own hands, and the old doctor-patient relationship is becoming more like vendor-client—at least for a growing niche of patients who think they know what they need to know.

One proof of the DIYD trend is in the surge of over-the-counter drug sales. In the past forty years, retail OTC sales have grown nearly 10-fold—from under $2 billion to over $15 billion per year. And we're not talking just the occasional plop-plop-fizz-fizz. It's $15 billion worth of analgesics, antihistamines, antacids, laxatives, and lotions. These days, even treatments like Xenical, a fat-absorbing diet pill, are going OTC. In the past, a treatment like that would never have been made available OTC, no matter how safe it was. It would have been left to the doctors. But now, patients want it all for themselves.

Another indication of do-it-yourself medicine is that Americans are flock-

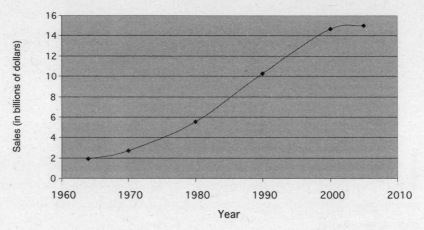

Over-the-Counter Medication Sales, 1964–2005

Source: ACNielsen, 2005

ing to CAM, or non-doctor-provided Complementary and Alternative Medicine, like chiropractic, acupuncture, and massage. In 1997, Americans spent more in out-of-pocket fees for CAM providers than for all of our hospitalizations. As of 2002, more than 1 in 3 American adults (36 percent) said they have used such alternative medicines.

Of course, it is the Internet that is making it *possible* for so many Americans to play a little doctor. While in 2005, 117 million people used the Internet to seek out health-related information, this number jumped to 136 million in 2006—a 16 percent increase in a single year. Health information is now one of the top things people seek out online. And why not? Whereas having a personal medical question used to mean a long, expensive, and potentially embarrassing trip to the doctor, now you can just type into your favorite search engine anything from "bipolar disorder" to "yeast infection," and in a couple of minutes you feel like you went to medical school.

Doctors may not like the trend, but they are part of the reason people are turning to self-care. Between 2000 and 2004, deductibles and co-pays involved in doctors' visits more than doubled. Fully 3 in 5 Americans say they worry about medication errors in the hospital. (As they should—according to the Institute of Medicine, hospital errors kill more people every year than either car accidents or breast cancer. And each year, hospital infections kill five times as many Americans as AIDS.) The truth is, public confidence in people running medical institutions has fallen faster and further than just about any other leading societal institution.

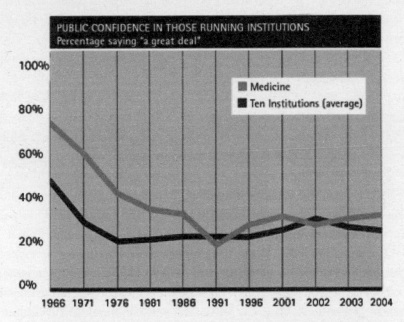

Since 1966, public confidence in leaders of health care institutions has fallen from a greater height than it has for other major institutions. Above, the darker line represents the average of ratings for ten institutions, including the military, the U.S. Supreme Court, colleges and universities, organized religion (except for 1991), major companies, the executive branch of the federal government, the press, Congress, and organized labor (except for 1991 or 1996).

Source: Courtesy of Robert Blendon, from Harris 1966–2004, *Harvard Public Health Review*

So with medicines and medical information directly available—and doctors less well regarded—why not try it yourself?

At the forefront of the DIYD charge is women, which is perhaps not surprising since women make the health care decisions in *over 70 percent* of American households. Women also have a history of medical independence—before the rise of professional doctors, it was mostly "old wives" and "home remedy" makers who delivered America's health care.

DIYers are young, too. That's not only because young people are zippier on the Internet, but also because today's 20- and 30-somethings—having grown up with easy OTCs, and having been treated with more psychiatric medications for depression, anxiety, and attention deficit disorder than any generation in history—think of diagnoses and medicines as a routine part of life. A disturbing number of them even trade prescription meds without their doctors' help. To them, taking charge of their own health management is as natural as arranging their favorite music on their iPods.

DIYDs are having a big impact. Drug companies have seen the power of direct-to-consumer (DTC) ads, like the ones that swamp TV nightly for Viagra, Cialis, and "Ask Your Doctor if the Purple Pill Is Right for You." While they still spend the bulk of their marketing dollars on doctors, the growth in DTC ads has been dramatic: in 1997, drug companies spent about $1 billion on DTC ads; by 2004, it was over $4 billion.

DIYDs also signal an irreversible shift in the role of American doctors. In 1970, *Marcus Welby, M.D.* was watched by a staggering 1 in 4 households in America. He was adored for his nurturing, paternalistic style with his (mostly female) patients. But that era is gone forever. Now reared on the Internet, and increasingly distrustful of doctors and hospitals, more and more Americans—*especially* the women—see themselves as their doctors' partners at best, and their supervisors at worst. Especially when it comes to children. My mother took our pediatrician's word as gospel. My wife, on the other hand, consults three or four doctors (and two dozen friends) on whether or not our four-year-old should get a flu shot. Doctors used to field questions only when things went wrong and the lawyers arrived. Now they play 20 Questions just trying to administer a routine vaccine.

In the future, expect more egalitarian relationships between doctors and patients, including greater e-mail correspondence. In 2005, only 8 percent of adults said they use e-mail with their doctors—but 81 percent said they would like to. Doctors will have to figure out a way to charge for e-mail consults first—they would no doubt like to help patients this way, especially existing patients, but perhaps not at the expense of all their office visits. Once the payment system catches up, though, look for more e-consults.

We can also anticipate even more pressure on the Federal Drug Administration to move more medicines from prescription-only to OTC. Already, we can get about 700 more medicines OTC today than we could thirty years ago, but that may not be sufficient for hard-core DIY Docs.

Is DIYD a good trend? Since people can't sue themselves for malpractice, we may never know. Of course, we may see more lawsuits against drug companies for insufficient disclosure of information, which is even more critical in self-treatment. (Although, really, how much longer or more detailed could those drug warning labels be?)

DIYDs certainly free up a lot of doctor time, if people treat themselves instead of coming in. And since for every person out there studiously investigating his or her own medical condition, there are probably at least a few others failing to just follow the doctor's orders—docs might be able to spend more time being proactive with those who need it.

But a rise in self-medication will no doubt mean a rise in misdiagnoses and drug errors, as well as delays in going to a doctor who might have picked up critical early-warning signs. While it is ultimately up to patients to weigh those risks against the chances of doctor error, and against their increasing suspicion that they know as much as their doctors, it is the doctors who may have to contend with lawsuits that blame them for mishaps *anyway*. It's one thing to happily move the DIYDs off the docket when it comes to weight loss, baldness, and erectile dysfunction—and the drug companies are just as happy to have those people as direct customers. But when patients are second-guessing doctors on cancer treatments, DIYDs are a whole new challenge.

Nevertheless, DIYDs are here to stay. And while Web sites are getting better at providing medical information, it's still not really a well-oiled system. Patients don't *really* know when they can take charge and when they should get to a doctor's office ASAP. They don't really know when they are right and the establishment is wrong. And like all do-it-yourselfers, they don't really know what they don't know. Years ago, basic first-aid was a mandatory course in schools and camps—perhaps it is time for a course in Web medicine, so that young people can acquire guidelines for self-treatment, and learn how to navigate the health care maze. Maybe DIYDs—like nurse practitioners but on a smaller scale—can even become certified to practice DIY medicine. It wouldn't let their Moms brag that Junior is a doctor—but it might make them feel better about the fact that Junior never goes to one.

Hard-of-Hearers

▲

A 2006 survey found that Presidents Ronald Reagan and Bill Clinton have the highest favorability ratings of any U.S. presidents in the past forty years. Here's what else they have in common: They are the only two sitting presidents to have admitted they were hard of hearing.

When they announced it, people sat up and listened, because it was happening to them, too. In 2000, the number of Americans with hearing loss reached almost 30 million, more than double what it had been in the 1970s. That's 1 in every 10 Americans, straining to hear, or missing out on sounds entirely.

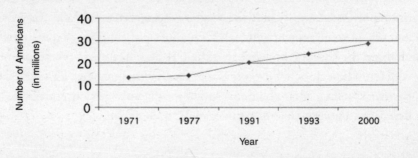

Rise in Hearing Loss Amount Americans, Aged 3 and Older, 1971–2000

Source: American Speech-Hearing-Language Association, 2007

A generation ago, the most common sensory problem in America was poor eyesight. First, contact lenses made glasses practically obsolete, and now Lasik is making contacts practically obsolete. Maybe you heard about how the Navy can't staff submarines anymore, because the sub jobs used to go to sailors whose bad eyesight disqualified them for pilot jobs. But now that eye surgery is not only routine, but free, at the U.S. Naval Academy, everyone wants to be a pilot.

What myopia was for all those prior generations, hearing loss now is. Hearing devices may be small enough these days that schoolkids who need them won't be taunted with cries of "Four Ears"—but deafness is definitely the hot new sensory malfunction in America.

Most hearing loss in the U.S. is sensorineural, which means it's caused by damage to the inner ear or to the pathways between the inner ear and the brain. Since a lot of that happens with aging, our hearing loss incidence is of course increasing. We have more people over 65 in America than ever (about 35 million); and something like one-third of people in that age range are hard-of-hearing. About half of all people aged 75 and older are, too.

But according to the Deafness Research Foundation, about 1 in 3 cases of hearing loss in the U.S. is not about aging, but is purely about noise. And we are bringing it on ourselves. In the old days, when we used to lose our hearing to noise, it was from manufacturing equipment or artillery fire. Advances in technology, and the mainstreaming of protective gear, pushed those causes way down. But now, the hard-of-hearing numbers are actually *higher*, and it's all about leisure and entertainment.

Have you been to a teen movie lately? I can't even sit through the previews without earplugs. It's like when a country with runaway inflation decides to revamp its currency, and suddenly 10,000 rupees becomes 1 rupee. Sitting in the movie theater, with the teens happily munching the popcorn and not even seeming to notice the volume, I feel like someone has suddenly changed the baseline on what amount of noise is "normal."

Here's how aurally toxic our daily life is. Noise reaches the potential for permanent damage at about 85 decibels. Now look at our daily lives. Hair dryers, which some people use every day for many minutes at a time—oblivious to ringing telephones, crying children, and eloquent spouses—come in at 90. A snowmobile comes in at 100. The noise on a subway platform is 105. In an airplane cabin, it's 110. A rock concert is 120. Apparently, *nine seconds* into a rock concert, you experience hearing loss.

And the verdict on iPods is still out. With 100 million of these portable music players around the world tucked into people's ears, lawsuits, and lawmaker inquiries about their effects on hearing loss, have already begun. The French government recently outlawed the sale of MP3s that can play over 100 decibels. Apple, iPod's manufacturer, has upgraded its software to allow consumers (or their parents) to put a volume cap on individual machines.

But whether it's music, movies, hair dryers, or travel, our daily lives are fraying our auditory nerves. Demographically, it's worse for men than for women, with almost 12 percent of men aged 65–74 experiencing tinnitus, or ringing in the ears. Blacks have better hearing than whites or Hispanics. There are geographic differences, too. Southerners have tinnitus at almost twice the rate of Northeasterners. Could it have something to do with being outdoors more?

Entrepreneurs are working hard to capture the growing hard-of-hearing market. When President Clinton went public with his hearing loss, he was already sporting a sleek little digital hearing aid planted deep in the ear canal. It was a far cry from the "Mickey Mouse Ears" that used to hang off a person like a telephone, literally funneling sound deeper into their ears. But even in the past decade, hearing aids have gotten much smaller and more effective. There have also been big advances in surgery that let people with profound hearing loss hear things they never would have.

But as deafness climbs among the boomers, and among vocal young people, there's bound to be a great deal more. Look for bionic ear processors, single-chip implants that can be placed in a body and run without battery replacements for fifteen years. Look for the development of antioxidant drugs, which reduce the presence of free radical oxygen molecules that kill the delicate hair cells of the inner ear. Look for stem cell researchers to tout the possibility of regenerating damaged inner ear cells.

And look for a public health campaign against noise. Like tobacco addiction and sun damage, if it gets you when you're young, you will probably never recover. It's a ripe issue for public activism—except, of course, for the challenge of being heard in Washington *without* shouting.

Already, the hard-of-hearing and deaf community has moved quite mainstream. The first deaf Miss America, Heather Whitestone, was crowned in 1995. Both the National Football League and Major League Baseball have fielded deaf players—Kenny Walker of the Denver Broncos, and William "Dummy" Hoy of the old Washington Senators. In 2001, Rush Limbaugh announced he had suffered sudden hearing loss, caused by an autoimmune inner ear disease. And deaf actress Marlee Matlin, who at 21 was the youngest person ever to win a Best Actress Oscar (for the deaf-themed

Children of a Lesser God), has since had cameo appearances as everything from the hearing-impaired embryologist on *Law and Order: SVU*, to the hearing-impaired tennis lineswoman on *Seinfeld*, to—my personal favorite—the hearing-impaired pollster on *The West Wing*.

And, of course, sign language is very popular. Barely a preschool teacher *doesn't* use her hands to model the words she's speaking, and the phenomenon of teaching infants to sign before they are able to speak has hit near-craze proportions.

The silverest lining in the rise in deafness is that, perhaps, more great innovations will come of it. Two of the greatest communications inventions of the last 150 years, the telephone and the Internet, were motivated by people affected by the loss of hearing. Alexander Graham Bell, whose mother and wife were deaf, invented the phone in part to help magnify sound for the hearing-disabled. Vinton Cerf, widely considered the father of the Internet, is said to have created electronic communication—which became e-mail—out of frustration that he couldn't adequately talk with other researchers (he is partially deaf) or with his deaf wife.

Anyway, check your hearing. Already, kids today can hear high ring tones that many adults over 40 or 50 cannot (hence the "Mosquitotone" ring tone, which students are using to sneak their cell phones into class). It's a problem, unless you're prepared to turn the technology against them—like the shopowner who tried to chase away loitering youth by sending out annoying noises only they could hear. But if you're in the hearing-loss demographic, it is time for a hearing exam—you are probably losing it.

PART V

Family Life

Old New Dads

▲

What do Strom Thurmond, Mick Jagger, Luciano Pavarotti, Charlie Chaplin, and Rupert Murdoch have in common?

They all fathered children after the age of 55.

Actually, if you exclude Mick Jagger, who fathered a child merely at 55, the others all did it after the age of 65. Thurmond, Chaplin, and Murdoch were actually over 70.

Old New Dads are not just a trend of the rich and famous, however. Today in America, there is a new and growing group of men who take painkillers to go out and toss the ball in the yard, not with their grandchildren, but with their children.

In recent years, everyone has made a big deal about Old New Moms, and how women's careers plus advances in fertility treatments are prompting childbearing up to, and even past, 40.

But what's missing is attention to the Dads, who are increasingly older, and who don't face the same biological hard-stop that kicks in for most women around 40.

In 1980 in America, only 1 in 23 births was to men aged 50 or older. In 2002, that share grew to about 1 in 18. At the same time, the birth rate among fathers aged 40–44 increased 32 percent; and among fathers aged 45–49, it increased 21 percent. It went up almost 10 percent for Dads 50–54. A similar trend can be seen in many Western countries, including Israel, the Netherlands, the U.K., and New Zealand.

Having a Dad who's 62 at his child's college graduation is now commonplace.

While the majority of children are still being born to men aged 20–34, the proportion of Dads over 40 is skyrocketing.

Part of the reason is, of course, Old New Moms. As women back-burner

Number of Children Born in U.S., by Age of Father, 1975–2001

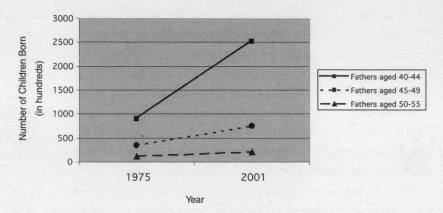

Source: National Center for Health Statistics, 2002

childrearing for the sake of their careers, their mates—who still tend to be a few years older—are likely to be the ones thumbing through *Fortune*, rather than, say, *Maxim*, in the OB/GYN's waiting room.

Another reason is divorce. It's well known that half of marriages end in divorce, but it's also true that men remarry faster, and more frequently, than women do. Somethimes called "Do-Over Dads," more and more older men are trying their hand at fatherhood a second time around, with a younger wife. (Reflecting that trend, vasectomy reversal is up something like 40 percent since 1999. And the urologists say men seeking the procedure are nearly always in their mid-40s or older, with new wives at least eight years younger.)

The third reason is a combination of biology and success. Old New Dads can still physically father children; they have more access to younger women; and they are more likely to have the means to support children later in life.

Are Old New Dads better Dads? They take some flak for being too old for intensive toddler-care, and the very oldest may well not be around when their kids reach key milestones. But many Old Dads say they feel "renewed," and that they are more relaxed and more interested in family life than they were (or might have been) while scrambling early in their careers. Long workdays are less appealing now. Many also say they feel wiser and more reflective with their kids; and that as they start to be more aware of their own mortality, they focus more appreciatively on their children.

I am an Old New Dad myself, with my youngest coming along when I was 48; my kids span the waterfront from 19 to 4. Being an Old New Dad brings concerns about what could happen if I am not around when my kids need me. But it also means that the joys of family life go on well into the 60s. The phases of retirement and empty-nester-hood are shrunk, or eliminated altogether. Every once in a while at ballet class or at a school meeting, I see the young Dads on one side of the room, who have so much left to learn, and the Old New Dads on the other side, far more relaxed. The difference in age is starkest at public schools—at the private schools, Old New Dads blend right in—but at public school meetings we seriously stick out.

The private/public school difference is just one aspect of the commercial and social implications of this trend. Old New Dads are most likely to be richer dads. So for many more toddlers, it means access to wealth and privilege that children born to young struggling parents may never have.

At the same time, these children are also part of an uncharted social experiment. For so long, we have studied the problems of teen pregnancy that we have neglected the opposite end of the spectrum—even though in 2001, the number of children born to fathers over 40 was practically equal to the number born to mothers under 19.

And while Old New Moms have lots of support groups, Old New Dads are a forgotten lot, left to fend for themselves with little guidance, books, or organizations serving their needs. AARP, take note—we may join you at 50, but a growing number of us still have kids in elementary school.

All of this has major implications for our society and its support systems. Old New Dads need to work longer, and retire later, in order to pay for college tuition and other expenses of childrearing later in life.

They need a whole new series of less physical, and more mental, activities they can do together with their kids of all ages.

Old New Dads are likely to be bigger consumers of energy drinks, and parent support books, since they will be doing a lot more carpooling, and less golf, than their empty-nesting peers.

The children, who are more likely to be only children or caboose kids, will need other people who can do the kinds of things younger Dads generally do, like sports and vigorous games. On the other hand, the children will have older role models—which may make them less interested in beer and more interested in wine, less interested in driving fast and more interested in driving safe, and less rebellious and more conservative in outlook.

We may also need to rethink our aging-parent support system, since many older parents will now need help before their kids are able to provide it.

Old New Dads also become a new political force. Already in the U.K., divorced Dads have become militant in seeking their parental rights, making worldwide headlines by breaking into Buckingham Palace.

Finally, if it is generally thought that voters in their 20s focus on personal opportunity, voters in their 30s and 40s focus on family issues, voters in their 50s and 60s focus on college tuition and retirement, and voters over 65 focus on Social Security and health care, then Old New Dads completely disrupt that progression. Now they would be all about kids in their 40s and 50s, college tuition in their 60s and 70s, and . . .

Pet Parents

▲

Americans adore pets. No president since Chester A. Arthur has dared to move into the White House without at least a dog or a cat, and a few of the nineteenth-century presidents took goats, cows, and roosters, too. Sure, pets offer warmth and companionship. They are our proverbial best friends. Several studies have even shown them to lower our blood pressure, reduce our stress, prevent heart disease, and ward off depression.

So what is new about cats and dogs? There is a new breed of pets, and they have a new role in our society. They are replacing kids as the number one companion in America. And as literally the new kids on the block, some pets are being elevated to a new life of luxury, with practically a black American Express Card, a Platinum Frequent Flyer card, and permanent maid and a butler. They have achieved what few have achieved before them—the chance to have high-class problems and a high-class life. In America today, the top 1 percent of pets live better than 99 percent of the world's population.

Here's the story. Sixty-three percent of American households have pets, up from 56 percent in 1988. That's 44 million households with at least one dog, and 38 million households with at least one cat (although interestingly, cats in America actually outnumber dogs by a good 17 million, since cat own-ers are so much more likely to have more than one).

Add to those households a smattering of folks with fish, birds, snakes, and other small animals, and you've got a percentage of pet-owning households in America that is *more than double* the percentage of households with chil-dren. In fact, in the past fifteen years, the drop in the percentage of house-holds with children and the rise in the percentage of households with pets have been practically the same.

American Households with Pets or Children, 1990–2005

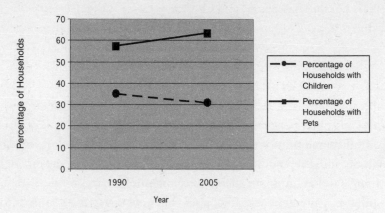

Source: American Pet Products Manufacturers, 1990, 2005–06; U.S. Census Bureau, 2006

And increasingly, women now live alone or as heads of households. These are profound demographic changes that have had some big influences on our country and some small ones.

It is no coincidence that as the number of households without children has risen, the number of pampered pets has risen as well. According to a pet mega-store executive, the average pet product buyer is a woman, aged 24–45, and she doesn't have any children. America's new lifestyles have meant more delayed children, but more accelerated pets. It used to be that children were the drivers of pet ownership—kids saw puppies and pestered their parents until eventually they gave in. And whatever resources went to the pets came at the expense of what went to the children. They shared the resources parents had.

Now the superrich pets are inheriting it all. Not only are there more middle-aged households without kids, there are also more empty-nester households spending more years together post-children. The extension of our life span alone has quintupled the number of empty-nester years as kids go off to college. So whether it's grown-ups who never had kids, or grown-ups who miss the ones they've already raised, there are more and more people in America who, rather than be alone, are adopting more pets and treating them like children.

And clearly, these are some very lucky pets. In 2006, Americans spent almost $40 billion on their pets—up from about $17 billion in the early 1990s—making pet-spending one of the top ten retail segments in the United States. Pet products today are a bigger industry than toys, candy, or hardware. But it is not the mass market that is new—it is the size of the luxury pet market that is new. The top 1 percent of pets probably get 40 percent of all the goodies.

Who needs kids when you can have a pet? Eight out of 10 dog owners, and 2 out of 3 cat owners, buy gifts for their pets on birthdays or holidays. Pet health insurance is on the steep increase. Seventy percent of pet insurance owners and other pet owners interested in it say they would "pay any amount" to save their pet's life. In 2004, Americans bought $14 billion worth of pet food, including record-breaking amounts on "human-grade," gourmet, vegetarian, low-carb, and organic food for our animals.

In 2006, we spent over $9 billion on over-the-counter medical treatments and supplies for our pets—and don't think it was just flea collars and scratching posts. We bought teeth-whiteners, breath-fresheners, fur-glisteners, designer sweaters, doggie jewelry, and yes, animal car seats. We bought kitty chin acne medicine. "Doggles," to protect our dogs' eyes from the glare when they ride in convertibles. Puppy sunscreen. Kitty nail polish. Animal antiaging creams. "Pawfume" (K#9 was, for a while, a Barneys exclusive). And yes, we bought our pets contact lenses.

Some Pet Parents paid thousands, or even tens of thousands, for custommade doghouses. Kennels have been upscaled to luxury hotels that offer hiking, swimming, TV, gourmet meals, and pedicures. The Nashville Loews Hotel (for people) recently introduced "The Hound of Music" package, whereby for $1,600, you can have your dog ride in a limousine to a recording studio and have his barking accompanied and digitally mastered onto a holiday CD. Massage included. For the dog.

And, as every loving parent knows, there are life cycle services. Pet play groups, to encourage socialization. Feline finishing school. Doggie dating services, and, um, weddings. Animal retirement homes, where pets with similar temperaments are grouped together to play between therapy sessions. And, of course, pet funerals, pet memorial stones, and pet grief rituals. Did you know that you can make a diamond from the remains of your beloved pet? Evidently, 20 percent of all created diamonds are so composed.

No wonder *Marley and Me: Life and Love with the World's Worst Dog,*

spent most of 2005 and 2006 on the best-seller list. And the 2006 remake of
Lassie was one of the year's most critically acclaimed films.

What do Pet Parents signify?

Clearly, the market for pet products and services will continue to boom.
And it's no longer just a niche for boutique pet shops; now mega–pet stores
are opening "petiques" to meet Pet Parent demands. Even "human companies" want in. Paul Mitchell hair care has a specialty line just for fur. Omaha
Steaks sells "bag steak pet treats" (although, presumably, not for cows). Clothing, toy, and mattress companies are leaping into the pet product fray like
puppies dancing for Kibbles 'n Bits.

This is big news for animal medicine, too. What with all this high-end
food and treatment, pets are living three and four times longer than they did
30 years ago, so whereas veterinarians used to tackle rabies and distemper,
now they manage obesity, kidney failure, and arteriosclerosis. Veterinary centers around the U.S. are boasting new subspecialties in cardiology, neurology,
and dermatology.

Maybe it's not so bad anymore to be "sick as a dog"?

Beyond unique pet products and services, innovators should attend to
the spaces that people and pets share. In 2005, Honda unveiled the Wow, a
concept car for people who regularly transport dogs. The middle of three seat
rows converts to a pen. The floors are wood for easy cleanup. The back door
has compartments for leashes, brushes, and pooper-scoopers. And more and
more people are working for pets rather than the other way around. Dogwalk-
ers can make $200 an hour for taking a pack of dogs around the block. A pet
stylist can make $100 an hour if he is working for the right Fifi.

Then there are the public spaces. National parks still frown on bringing
pets (have dog, attract mountain lion), but more and more, hotels are not
only allowing pets but offering them plush doggie beds and bathrobes. A
growing number of restaurants offer Doggie Bags for on-the-spot consumption. Stores are putting down water bowls for Fido so "Mommy and Daddy"
can shop.

Look for pets at work, too. The number of companies participating in Pet
Sitters International's "Take Your Dog to Work Day" doubled between 2003
and 2005. We haven't yet managed corporate child care, but shouldn't dog
care be easier?

Pet Parents are pushing a trend toward blurring the distinction in the law
between pets and people. In 2004, a jury in California awarded a pet owner a

record-breaking $39,000 in a veterinary malpractice suit, acknowledging that were the dog to be regarded as mere "property," it had a fair market value of only $10. In 2007, the pet food poisoning scandal sent lawyers scurrying to file lawsuits for what was tantamount to pet-icide. This trend may seem like a big win for pet-lovers, but watch out for the animal rights activists on the other flank who think pet ownership is inhumane. If pets *aren't* property, in the eyes of the courts, why should people be allowed to own them at all?

Another new element is that for a long time, scientists maintained that those cute dog poses were all just instinct, and pets had no real feeling or emotions. Now the scientific world has turned that upside down and admitted the obvious—pets think and act and love, just like real kids. Maybe on a much more limited basis, but the emotional bond between a pet and his or her owner, especially in a childless house, is real and not to be underestimated. When it comes to our kids, there is nothing we would not give them, even when they are cats and dogs.

Pampering Parents

▲

There are few topics that arouse as much passion among Americans as how to raise your children. Dr. Benjamin Spock is still literally a household name—fifty years (and 50 million copies) after his *Common Sense Book of Baby and Child Care* came out—and Americans now snap up the writings of his successors by the millions.

In 1975, America's major publishing houses put out fifty-seven books on parenting; in 2003, they published *twelve times* that many. There are literally hundreds of magazines and thousands of Web sites hawking advice on how to handle your infants, toddlers, tweens, and teens. And the baby product business—which to some degree supports all those publications—is now a whopping $7 billion industry.

The field is not just big, it's contentious. Whereas part of Dr. Spock's genius was that he appealed to practically *every* parent in America, today the field is splintered and a-fightin', like adolescent siblings squabbling over Dad's new portable DVD. Once considered the voice of reason in successful parenting, Dr. Spock is now just as likely to be reviled by the likes of James Dobson for having been too permissive ("the parent must call the shots!"), as he is by the likes of Dr. Sears for having been too strict ("children need attachment, not independence!").

You feel this intense divide when you have a child these days. There you are, thinking you are joining the ranks of the blessed—or the hassled, or however you've come to think of parenting—and boom, where you really are is in the crosshairs of the parent experts and their disciples. Not planning to breast-feed? How selfish. Breast-feeding in public? How barbaric. Your child sleeps with you in bed? How co-dependent. You banished your baby to a crib? How unenlightened, how pathetically *American*.

Amid these intense factions, it's hard to find anything these days that

American parents agree on. But I think I've found two things. First, most parents in America believe that they themselves are strict. Second, they are pretty certain that they are the only ones.

In 2006, we did a poll of Americans with kids under 18 living at home, gauging different groups along a scale of permissiveness/strictness. Some things weren't surprising—the strictest parents attend church weekly or more, identify as conservative, live in the South, and are older. The least strict parents are younger, liberal, live in the Northeast, and were themselves raised by permissive parents. Men are a little stricter than women. Protestants are a little stricter than Catholics.

But when you look at the overall group of parents polled, you realize that one unifying principle is that most parents think they're tough. Fifty-five percent of parents say they're strict, compared to only 37 percent who say they are permissive. Fifty-two percent of parents (and 58 percent of older parents) say it's better to guide children with "discipline and structure" than with "warmth and encouragement." And by more than 2 to 1, American parents say it is more important to make their children good citizens than it is to make them happy.

What's funny is that American parents also overwhelmingly report that *other* parents are not pulling their weight. A whopping 91 percent say that "most parents today are too easy on their kids," compared to only 3 percent who say most parents today are too strict.

So we've got a bunch of parents who think that they're strict, but no one else is. The truth is, they're only half-right—and it's about the others. Today in America, nearly *all* parents are more permissive with their kids than in generations past, despite their self-perception as Bad-Ass Moms and Dads. When it comes to permissiveness, today's parents are, like the title of a popular book, in a state of denial.

It starts with those infant nights. In the first half of the twentieth century, parents were told to keep their infants on strict sleep schedules, even if it meant having to let them "cry it out" in the middle of the night. In the 1950s, Dr. Spock was branded "permissive" for suggesting that, *sometimes*, it was all right to go in and comfort the child—although in later versions of his book, he, too, said it was generally best to let babies cry it out. In the 1980s, Dr. Richard Ferber of Harvard advised parents in his best-selling *Solve Your Child's Sleep Problems* to let the kids gently learn over time to cry it out—a practice now generally referred to as "Ferberizing."

But what do American parents think of Ferberizing? As usual, some swear by it, but most think it is like hanging the kid on the gallows. Sixty percent of the parents in our poll declared that "babies should be comforted whenever they cry"—compared to just 35 percent who said babies should be allowed to cry it out so they'll learn to sleep. And among Moms, who presumably make more of these actual decisions, the split was 66 to 30—or more than 2 to 1—in favor of comforting babies whenever they cry. (The Dads talk big, but then somehow they're more able to sleep through the screams.)

Which is closer to your view?			
	All	Dads	Moms
Babies should be comforted whenever they cry	60	48	66
Babies should be allowed to cry it out at night so they learn how to sleep	35	44	30
Don't know	5	8	4

When it comes to kids and sleep, our entire societal center of gravity has moved to the left of *even Dr. Spock,* who was called permissive in his day. Dr. Ferber himself has gone to great pains in the 2006 edition of his book to clarify that he never used the term "cry it out," and what he advocates is "progressive waiting."

Perhaps the most significant flash point on parenting is around spanking. In 1968, there was near-universal approval of corporal punishment, with 94 percent of Americans saying it was okay to spank your kids. By 1994, approval had fallen to 68 percent, and has held steady at about 65 percent ever since. While 65 percent is still majority approval, you would be hard-pressed to come up with another social trend that has fallen out of favor so far and so fast. Even the death penalty, also now at about 65 percent approval, dropped from only 80 percent.

As if attitudes toward sleep training and spanking weren't enough to show America's increasing permissiveness, what really struck me is how parents say they actually deal with their tweens and teens. Our poll asked parents what they would do if their 9-year-old son cursed at them and said he hated them. Overwhelmingly, the top answers, across age and gender of parents, were "sit down and ask him why he feels that way" and "tell him you're sorry he feels that way, but that you love him anyway." (If the child was a daughter, the numbers on those options were even higher.) Only 14 percent of parents said they would smack him, and among parents under 35, smackers were fewer by *half*. Barely 2 in 10 parents said they would take the child's privileges away for at least a week.

Suppose you had a 9-year-old son/daughter who screamed a curse word at you and said he/she hated you. What would be your likely response?					
					multiple response
The 2 sets of numbers are Son/Daughter	All	Dads	Moms	Parent Under 35	Parent Over 35
Sit down and ask him/her why he/she feels that way	58/64	60/59	57/66	53/63	61/64
Tell him/her you're sorry he/she feels that way, but you love him/her anyway	56/57	44/51	63/60	63/67	51/57
Send him/her to his/her room	44/46	37/38	49/50	51/53	40/41
Take away privileges for up to a week	34/33	39/27	31/35	41/39	30/28
Take away privileges for a week or more	21/25	22/24	21/25	15/26	25/24
Smack him/her	14/14	18/2	11/20	8/20	17/10
Do nothing	0/2	0/4	0/1	0/1	0/2
Don't know	3/1	1/3	4/0	7/1	1/1

Okay, you say—but the child was only 9. And he was just flexing some newfound independence. But we also asked parents what their first response would be if they found out that their 15-year-old was using illegal drugs. And this time, fully 3 *in* 4 parents said they would sit down and talk—with almost 1 in 10 saying they would confide in their kids about their own illegal drug use. Only 15 percent of today's parents would take away privileges (fewer than 1 in 10 Moms would take them from a son), and virtually *no one* said they would hit.

Suppose you had a 15-year-old son/daughter and you found out he/she was experimenting with illegal drugs. What would be your likely first response?					
The 2 sets of numbers are Son/Daughter	All	Dads	Moms	Parent Under 35	Parent Over 35
Sit down and ask him/her why he/she was doing it	68/66	55/70	75/63	73/68	65/63
Take away his/her privileges for a month or more	10/6	16/7	6/5	4/4	13/7
Tell him/her about your own experiences with illegal drugs	7/8	11/9	5/7	8/8	6/7
Take away his/her privileges for up to a month	6/8	13/6	3/9	6/9	7/6
Call the police	4/4	3/3	4/4	1/3	5/4
Get counseling/Send him/her to rehab/Send him/her to a scared straight program	1/2	0/0	1/4	1/1	0/3
Talk to him/her about peer pressure/Tell him/her about the dangers/ramifications of drug use	1/1	1/3	2/0	1/0	½
Hit him/her	0/0	0/0	0/0	0/0	0/1
Other	0/3	0/0	0/4	0/1	0/4
Don't know	3/3	1/2	4/4	4/5	2/2

"Spare the Rod and Spoil the Child" has been replaced with "Have a Good Heart-to-Heart Talk." I won't pass judgment on either approach, but I will observe how dramatic this change has been. While more and more kids are getting a free pass, more adults are going to jail than ever—the judges, spurred by changes in the laws, have gone the opposite direction of the parents. Are parents passing on more problems to the system? Could be.

And yes, the poll data are self-reported—so maybe parents *say* they would sit and talk, when actually they'd yell or hit. But this is the same crowd that skewed strict in describing the best way to raise kids. They think *this* is strict.

What does all this newfound permissiveness mean for America?

It's a loaded question, as each parenting camp derives passion not only from love for their kids, but also from a sense that the future of the world depends on their winning. Social conservatives would say that greater permissiveness, as described here, means kids who will grow up to be self-centered, disrespectful of authority, and criminal. They would point to even liberal black leaders across America who have publicly said that the occasional whack from Mom or Grandma is what kept them in line. And within our survey, they would point to the fact that way down on the list of strict parents, along with the liberals, Northeasterners, and people raised by permissive parents—are also, perhaps surprisingly, *rural* parents. During the great crime drop of the 1990s, rural crime fell far more slowly than either urban or suburban.

Liberals, on the other hand, would point to the decades of studies that say that hitting kids produces short-term compliance, but more severe longer-term problems—including, ironically, disobedience. So that greater permissiveness in America will mean, ultimately, a healthier society.

But either way, the bottom line is that it has become socially unacceptable to discipline children. I was on a plane recently where an overwrought Dad threatened to take away a ski trip if his kids did not shape up. And the other passengers seemed so alarmed—by the Dad's reaction—that I thought we were going to have an intervention right then and there to restrain him. Taking away a ski trip—*that* was viewed as way over the top. Again, I don't know who was right or wrong—but just beware that if you discipline your kids in public, most people will side with your children.

Today's permissive parents have real commercial implications. In the 1990s, it was ardently believed that what busy parents most needed was technology—like V-chips and Internet blocking software—so as to screen out bad influences *before* they entered the house and prompted all kinds of family fights. But it turns out—no one uses them. In 2001, more than two years after the V-chip became standard fare on new televisions, fewer than 1 in 10 parents used it. Our poll showed that while a remarkable 85 percent of parents with computer-using kids monitor them, fewer than 1 in 3 do so with filters or software. Today's permissive parents say they want more slick tech tools, but what they really need is guidance on how to have "The Conversation."

In the old days, kids just got the rod, or at least the riot act. Now they get picked up, timed-out, and negotiated with at great length. The jury is out on whether we'll get a more nonviolent society, or more people unwilling to listen to authority.

Pampering Parents may be more than a microtrend—this trend affects millions of parents, and has enormous societal implications. But what is so counterintuitive about it is how parents think they are being strict, when in fact they have at a minimum redefined what strict is, and turned it from a belt on the behind to a swift chat on the chin.

THE INTERNATIONAL PICTURE

So America is getting more "child-centered," what with all the rushing in to comfort crying babies in the middle of the night and the rapidly declining corporal punishment. But a glance at trends around the world show that the United States is perhaps still stricter than the rest of the world when it comes to spanking, but perhaps not strict *enough* when it comes to academic discipline.

While Americans disapprove of corporal punishment at higher rates than ever, our approval rate is still a near-supermajority 65 percent. And twenty-two states still allow corporal punishment in schools. That puts us in the minority.

▲ ·*Europe*. In Iceland, Poland, the Netherlands, Luxembourg, Italy, Belgium, Austria, France, Finland, Russia, Norway, Portugal, Sweden, Denmark, Cyprus, Germany, Switzerland, Ireland, Greece, and the United Kingdom, corporal punishment is formally banned in the schools; and in many of those countries, it is *also* banned at home. Even the U.K., which as recently as 2004 passed a law ensuring a parent's right to hit a child, may be getting ready to reverse course. A survey conducted by the Children Are Unbeatable Alliance found that 71 percent of British adults now favor giving children the same protection from assault as adults.

▲ ·*Africa*. In Africa, corporal punishment in schools is banned in Namibia, South Africa, Zimbabwe, Zambia, and Kenya.

▲ ·*Asia*. The governments of Japan, China, Thailand, and Taiwan have all told teachers to spare the rod and resort to some other punishment instead. (Of course, in 1994, Singapore was willing to publicly beat an American 18-year-old for vandalizing a couple of cars.)

So America is real tough, globally speaking, when it comes to smacking our kids around, but when it comes to cracking down on the schoolwork, we are relatively and perhaps harmfully lax. According to a survey conducted by Pew in 2006, 56 percent of Americans think that parents place too little pressure on their children to excel in school. But in China, India, and Japan—countries known for their competitive educational environments—solid majorities of parents say parents put too much pressure on their kids.

And of course, Asian students do score higher on certain international exams than Americans. The United States placed 24th out of 29 OECD countries on a global mathematics literacy test in 2003, far below Japan and China. Could this be linked to the fact that, as the RAND Corporation and the Brookings Institution have found, the typical American student spends less than an hour a day on homework?

Maybe we should spare the rod and spoil the teachers—and just make kids sit down and do their homework.

Late-Breaking Gays

▲

In August 2004, Governor James McGreevey of New Jersey stood before local reporters, the national press corps, and 300 million television viewers to announce that he would be resigning because he had had an affair with a man that had left him vulnerable to "false allegations and threats of disclosure."

There were lots of swirling sub-stories. Had public funds been misappropriated to hire the lover as a "security expert" when in fact the guy had no training? Was the relationship an abuse of power, since he had worked for the state? Could a rising politician who lied about sex be trusted on any other matter?

But less discussed was another sub-story: Dina Matos McGreevey. She was the governor's wife, standing loyally by during her husband's announcement. "My truth is that I am a gay American," McGreevey said, as his wife of four years, and the mother of their 2-year-old daughter, watched with a plastic smile.

McGreevey and Matos had met in 1996, after McGreevey had separated from his first wife. They had walked together to her car, and kissed the same night. After a four-year courtship, they got married in a small ceremony in Woodbridge, Virginia, followed by a reception in the elegant Hay Adams Hotel overlooking the White House (where, perhaps, soon-to-be Governor McGreevey aspired one day to live). Two years later, they celebrated the birth of little Jacqueline. And now, nearly four years into their marriage, on national television, Jim McGreevey, age 47, was telling the world he was gay.

Such Late-Breaking Gays are a growing force in America. While exact numbers are hard to come by, experts estimate that there are at least 2 million gays and lesbians who were once married to people of the opposite sex or still are. According to a 2002 survey by the U.S. Department of Health and

Human Services' National Survey of Family Growth, 3.4 percent of *currently* married men aged 15–44—or nearly 900,000—say they've had sex with other men (although such reporting, it should be noted, is broader than reporting that one is gay). When you add in men who were once married, you get over 1.2 million men in America who are or were married and who report having had sex with other men.

Most Late-Breaking Gays, it seems, don't enter their marriages with intentional deceit. Some come to the realization quite late; at least one study has found that 1 in 5 married gay men were past 40 when they had their first homosexual experience. Other Late-Breakers suspected it, but came out only after years of wrestling with their inner truths. Still other Late-Breakers get outed against their will, often by the wife who discovers gay porn or sexually explicitly e-mails on their computer. Or, as in Governor McGreevey's case, by the lover himself. Remember Colorado pastor Ted Haggard, whose paid male lover of several years finally decided he'd had enough of Haggard's public rantings against homosexuality? When the prostitute, Mike Jones, outed Haggard in 2006, Haggard was 50, had been married for 28 years, and had five children.

I suppose Late-Breakers "officially" became a national phenomenon in 2004 when Oprah Winfrey ran a show entitled "My Husband's Gay."

Whence the Late-Breaking Gays? The rise seems directly attributable to the increasing acceptance of homosexuality. Back when most of these men were in high school, well under 30 percent of Americans considered homosexuality an "acceptable alternative lifestyle." Now, in 2006, the trend has reversed, and a solid majority of Americans say they're fine with it. Fully 88 percent of Americans say gays should have equal rights in the workplace, up from just 56 percent in 1977. And gay and lesbian support groups have proliferated to virtually every corner of America.

So what seemed unthinkable a few years ago—when people might chalk up their homosexual urges to onetime experiments, or private fantasies, and walk down the aisle with a woman or man they truly cared for—has now become thinkable. And doable. And so increasing numbers are doing it.

More men, it seems, than women. That is because there *are* more gay men than lesbians, and because, according to experts, wives are often slower to move from lesbian self-awareness to actual divorce. Sure, Ross's wife on *Friends* left him for a hot woman at the gym, and the Mom in Augusten Burroughs's best-selling 2002 memoir *Running with Scissors* (played by Annette Bening in the 2006 movie) had some midlife lesbian affairs. But in real life, the more common situation is like Dennis Quaid in 2002's *Far from Heaven.* Married man in suburbs. Two kids. Upstanding civic life. Burbling homosexual attraction that won't be ignored. Exit closet, age 40.

Late-Breaking Gays in America have needs, especially within the gay community. While it may be easier than ever for teens and 20-somethings to come out of the closet, "middle-aged" debutants often still have lingering discomfort—not to mention a distinct lack of cool in the gay scene. The author of www.comingoutat48.blogspot.com recounts that when he started his new life as a gay man, he had no idea what to wear to bars, and he showed up way too early. *Will & Grace* centered at least a few episodes on Will or Jack "shepherding" a Late-Breaking Gay into their community.

But Late-Breakers' own needs aside, it cannot be overstated how Late-Breaking Gays transform the worlds of their spouses and children. According to a 1990 study on the Social Organization of Sexuality (and substantiated by the Family Growth data cited earlier), there are about 3 million women who were or are married to men who now sleep with other men. In addition, there are about 3.5 million children whose parents came out later in life. Talk about the awkward sex conversation with Mom and Dad.

Straight Spouses Left Behind have a resource in the International Straight Spouse Network, which coordinates nearly eighty support groups in the U.S. and abroad. Their Web site, www.straightspouse.org, reportedly gets 300 visitors a day. And support is needed. According to the experts, spouses of Late-Breaking Gays go through all the stages that one experiences upon a loved one's death—anger, sadness, denial, rage. Sometimes, there is relief, in the form of "it *wasn't* me, it was him." Sometimes there is fear, especially regarding sexually transmitted diseases and AIDS. But almost always, for a Straight Spouse Left Behind, there is rejection, humiliation, and betrayal, and sometimes the forcing of a radical reexamination of one's own judgment, and grasp of truth.

All this, while at a practical level, they are also working through issues of separation, the chance of trying to stay together anyway (which about a third of couples do), and/or the mixed emotions of seeking out new relationships. Many Straight Spouses find themselves in their own sort of closet until it all goes public—at which time they have to endure reams of difficult questions from friends, parents, colleagues, and children. Sure, they now rank alongside the once distraught wives of Oscar Wilde, Rock Hudson, and Elton John—but that doesn't cure the pain.

Two million Late-Breaking Gays rock at least 4 million adult worlds—but they also fundamentally alter the altar prospect for everyone else. Marriage in America is having a hard enough time these days, what with only 7.5 per 1,000 people getting married, down from 10.6 in 1980. But now even the people who aspire to marry, meet a compatible match, and actually walk down that aisle have a new problem to contend with. In fifteen years, will my spouse be Late-Breaking—or worse, secretly *Brokebacking*? Can he say he loves me—and in fact never desire another woman—and yet still leave me for a greater passion when we're 45? How do I turn on the Gaydar *now*, and here, while we're still dating?

Perhaps the dating Web sites, and prenuptial counseling services, will want to add a couple of questions designed to get at latent homosexuality. Hopeful couples today take all kinds of personality tests to learn who matches them, how to anticipate (and diffuse) relationship conflict, and how to maximize the chances of marital bliss. Might it not be a bad idea to make sure people are even on the right dance floor, before they start lining up a partner?

Arguably, if the tolerance for homosexuality in America keeps on rising, the number of Late-Breaking Gays will subside, on the theory that gay people will be just gay from the get-go, and cut out the diversionary detours of heterosexual marriage. Particularly if gay marriage and childrearing gain mainstream approval, gays will lose nothing by choosing same-sex partners, and Straight Spouses will be spared the agony. (As comedian Jason Stuart has said, "I wish you straight people would let us gay people get married. If you did, we'd stop marrying you!")

But that day in America is not coming soon. Fifty-one percent of Americans still consider homosexuality "morally wrong," and nearly 60 percent oppose gay marriage. Many Americans (36 percent) think gays should be less accepted, not accepted the same or more. And so as long as homosexuals are second-class in America, a good number of people with gay feelings will shelve those feelings in favor of a heterosexual wedding, a white picket fence, and biological kids. But if, years later, the feelings recur, or arise in whole new ways, there will be Late-Breaking News about their sexual orientation—and a reorientation for everybody else.

Dutiful Sons

Male Caregivers in America

▲

By now, we know well that Americans are living much longer—a person born today can expect to live well past 70, compared to the life expectancy of 47 if you were born in 1900. And living into your 80s and 90s is increasingly common.

We also know that when people die, they do it more slowly—suffering from chronic conditions like heart disease and Alzheimer's, rather than from some of the quicker-killing diseases of the past.

As a result, most seniors end up needing some kind of end-of-life care, and yet, contrary to popular belief, very few of them get it in nursing homes or assisted care centers. In fact, only *4 percent* of people 65 and older actually live in such places. The vast majority of seniors who need care either get help at home from unpaid relatives, or move in with family members altogether. And that's for an average of four to five years. That's a serious obligation for the caregiver.

Clearly, the bulk of the caregiving burden in America falls to women. There is even a term for professional women who put their demanding careers on hold to care for their aging parents: the Daughter Track— reflective of the Mommy Track that many of these women chose twenty years before, when they put their demanding careers on hold to care for their children.

But while women handle more of the care, and *much* more of the really serious care, there is a quietly growing—and potentially powerful—group of unpaid caregivers in America who are men. According to a 2004 study by the National Alliance for Caregiving and the AARP, nearly 40 percent of the 44 million people in America who provide unpaid care to infirm adults are men. That's about 17 million sons, sons-in-law, nephews, brothers, and husbands caring for loved ones in their "spare" time. Throughout the 1990s, the fastest-growing group of relations providing care to chronically disabled adults was sons.

And it's not just your occasional weekend stop-by to help Dad move the old sofa he can no longer lift by himself. America's caregiving men spend an average of *nineteen hours* a week tending to infirm loved ones. And for some, it's many more hours than that: Almost one-third of caregivers to the neediest relatives are men.

There are some traits of Dutiful Sons that distinguish them from their Dutiful Sisters, and that could in the end have political significance. Male caregivers tend *not* to suspend or cut back on work, and they are much more likely (60 to 41 percent) to be working full-time, with all the additional resources and influence that implies. Male caregivers more often help *other men*—35 percent compared to only 28 percent of caregiving women who do. Third, more so than women, male caregivers choose their situation: Almost two-thirds say they had a choice in the matter, compared to fewer than 3 in 5 women.

Another interesting twist is that Dutiful Sons are disproportionately of Asian descent. While only a handful of male caregivers are Asian-American, 54 percent of Asian-American caregivers are men—compared to only 41 percent of Hispanics, 38 percent of whites, and 33 percent of African-Americans. Indeed, Asian-Americans are the only subgroup in which the *majority* of adult caretakers are male. That no doubt stems from the core Asian value of filial piety, which dates back to Confucius, and in traditional Asian culture is at the heart of a person's moral development. The result is that in Asian families, the firstborn son is generally expected to care for his parents.

Finally, many male caregivers are gay. There was a touching piece in the *New York Times* in December 2006 by Peter Napolitano, a 48-year-old, single, gay man who moved home to care for his 81-year-old mother—mainly because his heterosexual brother and wife couldn't integrate Mom into their already bustling household.

So perhaps guys have been taking a bad rap—many of them are truly thoughtful when it comes to their Moms, Dads, spouses, and partners. Clearly the Asian-American men have a lot to teach the rest of us, but this growth in Dutiful Sons portends some potentially larger shifts in outlook. While it is one of the Ten Commandments to honor thy father and mother, America is not really oriented toward filial piety as a primary value. America is fundamentally child-oriented; we are always talking about the next generation, not the previous one. It is a strength that we're focused on the future—but that is perhaps sometimes at the expense of our parents.

As we see with Old New Dads, the Working Retired, and other groups in this book, this older generation is going to do a lot more than just play golf—they are going to be living longer, getting more involved in their kids' lives, and over time developing much deeper bonds with them. So statistically, the issue of taking care of our parents is going to be a far larger one in our lives and in theirs. This means that while Dutiful Sons are on the rise, what we really need to avoid intergenerational calamity is for the next generations to see their responsibilities more broadly than just "paying it forward." Paying it back is still a very real concept that, increasingly, we have to ingrain in our society and in our values.

Dutiful Sons need more help than they are getting. Like female caregivers, they need more geriatric case managers to help guide them through the mazes of Medicaid and Medicare; backup care if work requires them to go out of town; and the kind of quasi-medical training necessary to care for a loved one who has just been released from a hospital or short-term-care nursing home. A negligible number of workplaces provide any real benefits for elder care, and even though elder care is technically covered under the Family and Medical Leave Act, "parent care" leave has hardly penetrated mainstream culture like maternity leave has. Nor does the maternity leave model really fit senior care. You can chart the developmental needs of kids aged 0–3 and plan for a transition to day care or school. Also, they live with you. Aging parents can be far away, erratic in their health needs, and entirely unpredictable in the length or intensity of care they will need.

But Dutiful Sons could also use some support tailored just for them. Since they are less likely to have been the primary caretakers of children, they may find tending to vulnerable, frustrated, and sometimes unappreciative human beings—even those they love—more exasperating than even women do. Having fewer brothers-in-arms at work, they probably find even less sympathy there when their obligations to care for Mom and Dad make them come late, leave early, or miss work entirely.

Maybe their parents, especially their Dads, are rougher on the sons as they decline than they would be on the daughters. Gay men, in particular, may have a host of complicated issues caring for parents who, perhaps to some degree, never completely accepted them.

Some help is on the way. In late 2006, Congress passed the Lifespan

Respite Care Act, authorizing some $300 million in competitive grants for states and local agencies to help provide relief to people giving long-term, emotionally draining care to family members.

But of course, there is much more to do. Three hundred million dollars is a good start, but the care that family-givers provide is estimated at closer to $300 *billion*. We are just beginning to recognize a problem that is mushrooming, and we are just starting to assess where we will get the home health care workers we need to do this right.

Specifically, as America gets older, and as geriatric specialists decline, we need a greater recognition that more and more of America's 50-somethings are caring for America's 70- and 80-somethings—and they need appropriate accommodation in the workplace. Dutiful Sons have the power and ability to transform this from what has been perceived as just a "women's issue" to a broad societal issue that can finally generate the political head of steam it will take to put this on the table alongside Medicare and Social Security.

And attention is required. In 1997, companies lost between $11 and $29 billion because of departing workers, absent workers, and workday interruptions from employees taking care of infirm relatives. Public policymakers must see the value in that "free" $300 billion contribution caregivers are making. If adult sons and daughters don't do this work, who's going to pick up the slack for America's elderly? The Social Security system that is already buckling under the weight of the boomers?

Democratic presidential candidate Joe Lieberman was said to call his mother every day of his adult life, until she died in 2005 at the age of 90. Teddy Roosevelt was at his mother's bedside when she died. As more and more Dutiful Sons embrace the call to honor their fathers and mothers, they will add yet another moral dimension to life in America—one that has perhaps been on the wane.

PART VI

Politics

Impressionable Elites

▲

Every day in this 2008 election season, I hear two kinds of comments. First, I hear, "If only X or Y candidate were warmer, and friendlier, I would vote for him/her."

Second, I hear, "I like the candidates who address the issues. This is a serious election, and we need a president who truly gets our problems and will help solve them."

Which of those attitudes, do you think, comes from America's Ph.D.'s? The one focused on personality, or the one focused on issues?

The Ph.D.'s, believe it or not, are all about personality. Because a funny thing has happened to the American electorate; it's flipped upside down. America's elite—the wealthiest and best educated of our society—have become *less* interested in America's economic and strategic challenges than they are in candidates' personalities. Go to any upscale cocktail party, and listen in on what they think is most important in the presidential election. I guarantee it—they will start off dissecting the personal traits of every candidate. And there is a good reason for this—today's elites are so far removed from the mainstream concerns like health care, college affordability, job loss, and child care that most Americans face. Perhaps it has always been true that the elites have concerns different from the masses, but in the American meritocracy of the twentieth century, elites were a special breed who had worked their way up the ladder and had a very real appreciation for those now struggling to come up as well. They were, in short, a serious lot who had been through World War II and had a real respect for the seriousness of life and politics. Today's elites have been spoiled longer, and are more removed from the struggles of their parents and grandparents.

While today's elites are reading Tom Friedman's *The World Is Flat*, the rest of America is living it. The elites are seeing unprecedented economic success, while those struggling lower down are getting nowhere. Income data released in March 2007 show that those in the top 10 percent have been getting a raise every year, with the biggest raises (about 14 percent) going to the top 1 percent. The bottom 90 percent of Americans have been taking pay cuts. A rising tide is not, in fact, lifting all boats.

This is what makes it particularly ironic that when you ask elites *why* they are focused on personality, they will tell you that "The Voters"—i.e., lower-income and less-well-educated Americans—don't understand the issues and so *they* vote on the basis of personal traits. But nothing could be further from the truth. The so-called herd in America is better educated and more issue-focused than ever. Come to a political town hall, with America's regular voters, and you'll see that personality never comes up. Voters zero in on health care, education, and friends who are serving in Iraq. They have levels of knowledge about Medicare, Medicaid, our school system, and the global economy that would put many Ph.D.'s to shame. When Hillary Clinton held an online town hall in early 2007, she received 11,000 questions. Ten were about her favorite foods and movies. The other 10,990 questions were about people's real challenges and how she could help address them. Elites today often look down on the general public, but I have noticed that it is the elites who are easily captivated without many real facts, while the larger groups are much more grounded in facts, values, and experiences. Just as college students have always had views that change when they get out and have life experiences, so today's elites are like perpetual college students, far removed from the experiences and struggles shaping everyday American life. And so it is a lot easier to spin America's elites than it is to spin the voters.

The other day, I was on the phone with a reporter from an elite newspaper who kept talking about the importance of presidential personality. He said, "I have an e-mail right here on this from a professor." I said, "A *professor*—is that your idea of the typical American?" America's professors are acting out their vision of non-college-educated voters, and non-college-educated voters are acting like what you'd expect from professors. And when I challenged the reporter on some of his other observations, he said that he'd checked, and "other reporters" felt the same way. Elites look to other elites to reinforce their views, and they convince themselves that the way they see life is how the other 90 percent of America is also experiencing it.

This isn't just my gut. Let's look at the data.

A standard poll question I ask in campaigns is what people consider most important in voting for a candidate: (1) issues, (2) character, or (3) experience. I ask it because I know that all three are important in a leader, and that it can be tough to rank them.

According to a recent poll we did, a large plurality of voters—48 percent—believe that a candidate's stand on the issues is most important, with character a distant second at 32 percent. That preference for issues holds steady whether or not voters have been to college, whether or not they are religious, and across race. Where it does *not* stay constant, however, is across income. Once voters reach the magic line of $100,000 per year, their priority shifts to *character*, by a significant margin. As the table below shows, people earning under $100,000 prioritize issues over character by a serious 51 to 30 percent. But once they reach $100,000, they switch, to character over issues, 45 to 37 percent.

Which of the following is most important to you in voting for president?									
		Education				*Income*			
	All	No College	College Degree	<50k	50k+	<75k	75k+	<100k	100k+
Stands on Issues	48	48	48	50	50	51	46	51	37
Character	32	22	35	28	34	31	33	30	45
Experience	19	29	15	22	15	18	19	18	18
Don't know	1	1	2	1	1	0	1	1	0

That is a *29-point* swing. A shift barely ever gets clearer in polling.

Now while "character" can sometimes mean something core about a person, like dependability or decency, it just as often means something ephemeral or superficial like who you'd like to have a beer with. Sure, likability and buddy potential are important in choosing a president. But are they *more* important than solving health care and creating jobs? Most Americans say no. Frankly, the only people who say yes are the very well-to-do. And the chattering classes, in the media. Publications like the *New York Times*, believing they have been too serious and missed out on the trend toward the personal, now have Maureen Dowd writing psycho-profiles on the op-ed pages, and news reporters like Mark Leibovich filling front pages with personal impressions about candidates' personalities. And the *Times* was just catching up to the *Washington Post*, which had reporters like Lois Romano looking at the personal side for years. In March 2007, even the *Wall Street Journal* blared a piece about Barack Obama's suits, John Edwards's boyish looks, and Rudy

Giuliani's power ties. Suddenly we have gossip in the *Times*, the *Post*, and the *Journal*, and more in-depth issue analysis in the *Cleveland Plain Dealer* and the *Kansas City Star*. Woodrow Wilson would be too stiff for today's elites; he'd be just right for a populist peace movement.

In many ways, the eggheads have become jugheads and the jugheads have become eggheads. And you can see the effect of this rippling through the media. How many talk show guests make less than $100,000 a year? How many reporters talk to many people making less than $100,000 a year? The elite information circle is dominated by people who live in the world of the top 10 percent, and while in the past that helped drive discussion to more substantive levels, today it does just the opposite. Today, the elites are more fascinated with gossip, and they are driving the debate away from the substantive and toward the superficial.

Now all of this would be just a quirky observation about "Tabloid Papers of Record" and "Real-News Rags"—if it weren't for the fact that the different ways the elite and the masses view leadership has an increasing potential to distort presidential elections. Due to changes in campaign finance laws that were meant to *separate* money from politics, a new class of Increasingly Important Donors has sprung up that has more influence over candidate selection and campaigns than ever. Instead of a few donors giving large sums, we now have a lot of donors giving in the $10,000 range. And they all make over $100,000 a year (who else could give away $2,300, once in the primary and once in the general, after taxes, for a politician?). This suggests that they are nearly all, as described above, out of the voters' mainstream.

Here's how the new political donors got to be so important. After Watergate, in 1974, a clean-up-the-mess Congress passed a series of campaign finance reform laws to limit campaign donations and require more disclosure. What they didn't regulate, though, was "soft money"—contributions to political parties that could be used for general "party-building activities," like getting out the vote. So over a few decades, the soft money provisions got abused. In 2002, Congress passed a set of reforms abolishing soft money—but it doubled the amount of "hard money" individuals could give to candidates. (As of 2007, the limits are $2,300 per person per candidate, in the primary and in the general; and $28,500 per person per party, with an overall federal two-year limit per person of $108,200.) But what *this* Congress left unregulated was donations to nonprofit advocacy groups, known as 527s for the section of the tax law that created them. Now 527s (like the Swift Boat Veterans for Truth and Progress

for America on the right, and MoveOn.org and the Service Employees International Union on the left) raise unlimited funds from wealthy party loyalists,
and use these funds to do what the party used to do—like advocate for issues,
run issue-focused TV commercials, and get out the vote.

To my mind, the 2002 reforms have triggered two small groups of intense
and increasing importance. First are the Mega-Donors—the very wealthy
and committed givers who, instead of giving money to party *professionals* to
spend, now underwrite 527 advocacy organizations and call the shots themselves. In the 2006 midterm elections, the 527s raised about $380 million,
at least one-third more than what they'd raised in 2002. In 2004, it was reported that five people, including two who were married to each other, gave
$78 million to Democrat-leaning 527s, which was about one-quarter of the
Democrats' overall receipts.

The second group is the Elite Donors—the couples making $300,000 or
more a year who can give $10,000 or so to candidates without feeling it. They
are well-educated professionals, and they are by and large removed from
what the electorate as a whole is facing. They *have* health care, schools, and
houses. They are almost all drawn from the top 5 percent of America—most
from the top 1 percent. Political candidates in America probably spend half
their time at dinners with these people, and half their time with the other 95
percent.

So between the 527-underwriting Mega-Donors and the increasingly
powerful Elite Donors, we have a new class of givers playing an increasingly
important role in politics—and statistical proof that their heads are nowhere
near the voters'. And not only not near them, but driving the debate in a *more*
superficial direction. Elites may have set up PBS, but that's not what today's
chattering classes are watching.

We are not yet at the critical stage of Nero fiddling while Rome burns—
the classic depiction of ultimate disconnection of the leadership classes. And
the flip side of all this is that the mass of voters have never been truer to the
principle that voters are not fools. They are more alert, more informed, more
educated, and more substantive than ever. So if you can get over all the din
created by the chattering elites and the out-of- touch journalists, you can talk
to some pretty smart people out there.

Swing Is Still King

The Myth of the Polarized Electorate

▲

We hear it every day: America is divided into two camps—red and blue—and the key to elections is just energizing the base. Books have been written about it, careers have been made on it, and movements have been founded on it. But it is simply not true.

The reality is that at the polls, Swing is still King—meaning it is not the ideologues, but rather the pragmatic voters who have little allegiance to any movements, who determine who occupies the White House and runs Congress (and in Britain, who sits in 10 Downing Street). These voters are independent, not party-driven. And more and more, elections are turning on the preferences of middle-aged voters, not senior citizens or the young.

Just look at the math regarding generating turnout for the base versus courting the swing voters. Voting is based on history—the most likely voters are those who voted last time. Based on that, the case for winning with just the base is daunting. Suppose you have ten voters who voted last time, splitting their preferences 50/50. Now if one swing voter changes his or her mind, the vote becomes 60/40. If one new voter gets added to the pool, thanks to your efforts to turn out the base, the vote is still 55 to 45 against you (you have 6 out of 11). If a second voter who didn't vote last time is chauffeured to the polls, you are now back to 50/50, as you have 6 out of 12. In other words, it takes *two new voters* to overcome *one voter who has changed his mind,* and three new voters to overcome his defection. In almost all cases, therefore, it is more strategic to get one voter on the edge to switch opinions than it is to bring two or three new voters to the polls. It's theoretically possible for additional base turnout to be a factor, but in 95 percent of the elections, it is the swing voter who is decisive.

In the 2006 Senate reelection campaign of Hillary Clinton, I predicted that we would not bring a single new voter to the polls, because it was a midterm, low interest election, and so instead we had to work intensively to win over suburban swing voters with a long history of voting. By identifying their psychographics, we "micro-targeted" them into six distinct groups, and reminded them of Clinton's record on issues that matter to their daily lives, like property taxes, video game violence, and local issues. She went from a net loss of nearly 150,000 votes in those key suburban counties to a nearly 150,000 vote advantage—an 18-point increase in her vote from some of her toughest regions.

The myth that America is hopelessly "polarized" gets perpetuated because in Washington, D.C.—where most of the pundits are writing from—everyone has to choose sides to survive. But that's not the way it is in most of America, or Britain or France or Thailand. In fact, because of the increased flow of information, voters are *less* rigid than ever, and increasingly open and flexible. Take a look at the trends.

In the past fifty years, the number of Americans who call themselves Independents, rather than Democrats or Republicans, has grown from under one-quarter to over one-third of the voting public. In California alone, the proportion of Independent voters *more than doubled* between 1991 and 2005. The fastest-growing political party in America is no party.

According to American National Election Studies at the University of Michigan, the percentage of split-ticket voters—meaning people who vote for a Democrat for president and a Republican for Congress, or vice versa—has gone up 42 percent since 1952. That is a radically new willingness on the part of Americans to look at individual candidates, not party slates. It's the sign of a thinking electorate, not a partisan one.

When asked, Americans sometimes display a little swagger and say they definitely will or won't vote for certain candidates or parties. But this turns out to be fairly unreliable bravado. In 1995, 65 percent of voters said they would never vote for Bill Clinton. One year later, they reelected him in a landslide.

Look at what happened at the U.S. midterm elections of 2006—the Democrats won thirty new congressional seats in areas the Republicans had declared too polarized to switch. The Republicans had gerimandered the districts to avoid change, but they were still defeated for the simple reason that if you get just a small flip of independent pragmatists, you get a huge flip in the political landscape.

Or look at what pollsters call the generic congressional ballot—"if the elections for Congress were held today, which party's candidate would you vote for?" Between late 2004 and early 2006, voters swung from a 5-point Republican advantage to a 15-point Democratic advantage. And when the election was held, a Democratic tide undid twelve years of Republican rule. Youth turnout was down to 12 percent from 17 percent of the electorate in the 2004 presidential election, so the Democrats did better with far fewer Democratic leaning voters. The answer is that *contrary to conventional wisdom*, there is a massive swing electorate out there, receiving more information from more sources than ever before, and acting on it.

According to CNN exit polls, in the presidential elections of 1996, 2000, and 2004, between one-fifth and one-third of the electorate made up their minds in the last month before the vote. That's borne out by the fact that in the summer of 2004, voters swung from an 8-point lead for Kerry to a 13-point lead for Bush, and in the end gave President Bush a victory of only 3 points.

Indeed, in the 2004 election, while it is true that overall turnout was higher, it was higher on both sides, canceling out the impact of the appeals to the two bases. It was swing voters—middle-aged women and Hispanics—who made the difference for George W. Bush. The impact of women can't be overstated. In 2004, women were 54 percent of the American electorate, the highest percentage in history. Their interest in and impact on politics has been steadily increasing.

You may recall that in 1996, Soccer Moms were the critical swing voters. Today, those Moms remain at the center of the swing vote, but they are about a decade older, and their kids are going off to college. Now they get their information from the Internet as well as TV and radio, making them the most informed swing voters in history. And while they had little time when their kids were 6 and 8, many of those boomers are now getting some extra time to think about what's going on in America and the world.

The power of the swing voters versus the base is not limited to the United States. In the U.K., there is the same kind of shift making the difference between Labour and Conservative governments. Once again, voters free of the party reins switch back and forth, most often based on who they believe will make the best leader, not which party they believe has the right platform. And in working on twenty-four successful elections around the world, I have increasingly come to see voters won over with TV, media, and message—everywhere from Colombia, where the president I mentioned earlier was not ready to take on the drug lords, to Thailand and Greece. In every one of these cultures, the methods I suggested were similar, even though the cultures were vastly different. Karl Rove, who was hailed as a great strategist in 2000 and 2004, has recently been chastened by his failure to shift strategies after the midterm elections. Just a switch of 2 percent of the voters from one side to the other made a big difference.

Often, the microtrends identified seem to be tearing our society apart, taking it into two more extreme directions at the same time. But this trend—the need for all parties to recognize that their future lies in winning the center—is different. This trend puts the brakes on how far most democracies can go toward one extreme or another.

The impact is profound. The movement to watch is really the global Third Way movement—the triumph of pragmatic, independent thinking over left- or right-wing ideology. It is the growth of mass media and communications that has fueled it, and that gives voters more ability to judge the competence of their leaders and their policies. Though the Internet has seemed to spawn more fragmented movements, the vital center remains the decisive sliver of voters. Over time, this is what will keep many countries out of war and away from radical income redistribution, and into creating more alliances, freer markets, and values that overcome the tensions of the day.

Militant Illegals

▲

If there is one group of people in America that has generally kept a low profile, it is the 12 million illegal immigrants in this country—and generally with good reason. As Edward R. Murrow said in his famous 1960 documentary, *Harvest of Shame*, "migrants . . . have the strength to harvest your fruit and vegetables, [but] they do not have the strength to influence legislation." They have been quiet and in the shadows. As a result, they have been the truly forgotten in America.

Now fast-forward to the spring of 2006. A bill introduced by Republican James Sensenbrenner of Wisconsin, and passed by the U.S. House of Representatives, pushed many illegal immigrants and their families too far. The bill would have made it a felony to be in this country illegally, or to give assistance—like food or medical care—to anyone who was. Deeply wounded, American's illegal immigrants took to the streets.

In broad daylight. In matching white T-shirts, in 140 cities, and in at least thirty-nine states. From Phoenix to Philadelphia, from Boise to Birmingham, hundreds of thousands of illegal immigrants marched in organized parades, in front of TV cameras, to protest the House-passed bill and to call instead for liberalized immigration reform that would not narrow but widen the path to citizenship. In Atlanta, the birthplace of America's civil rights movement, the marchers held placards reading, "We Have a Dream, Too." In Mississippi, they sang "We Shall Overcome" in Spanish. In Los Angeles, the rally in March 2006 was said to be the largest in the history of the city, and perhaps in all of the Western United States. (Referring to the border-long security fence that many lawmakers supported constructing, comedian Carlos Mencia asked, "If you deport us, who will build the wall?")

At this moment, the illegal aliens were *Americans* in the truest sense of the word—using the democratic political system to accomplish their ends.

They may not have been able to vote, and they could have been deported at any moment—but there they were, speaking up for their rights and getting lawmakers to listen.

It is a profound sign of the times that in today's America, hundreds of thousands of America's 12 million illegal immigrants not only felt secure enough to march, but found that they wielded actual political power. For the first time in American history, noncitizens' needs and passions might actually be the critical element that tips a presidential election.

It's not that immigration itself has become America's top concern. While large majorities of Americans followed the news about the marches, and immigration climbed somewhat on the list of issues Americans consider most important, it still lags well behind Iraq, the economy, and terrorism. And as of this writing, Congress still hasn't resolved its differences to produce a new immigration law.

But what did happen is that the passion of illegal immigrants touched a deep chord with *legal* immigrants, who sensed that the animus behind the Sensenbrenner legislation was directed at them, too. And it touched a deep chord with *native-born* Americans who are deeply tied to the illegals— like their children. (When I asked a Latino immigration expert how many American-born Latinos have parents who came here illegally, he said, "Practically everyone.") Suddenly, in 2006, a significant group of Americans was insulted—some say as deeply as when Rosa Parks was asked to move to the back of the bus. And they have turned that indignation into a sense that they can and must influence the course of immigration policy, and beyond.

The number of people feeling that way could be big enough to tip a presidential election. Let's look at the figures.

In the presidential election of 2004, just over 16 million Hispanics were eligible to vote, but only about 8 million did. That leaves at least 8 million prospective American voters who could turn out in 2008, if they felt newly energized.

Could 8 million people swing a presidential election? You bet. In the past fifty years, the average margin of victory in the popular vote for a first-time president has been about 4 million votes. (Even in his *second* term, George W. Bush beat John Kerry by only about 3 million votes.) If even only 2 to 3 million more Hispanic voters turned out in 2008, they could be quite influential, indeed. And Hispanics are the fastest-growing segment of the American electorate. In 1992, they were 4 percent of the vote, and 2004 exit polls said they were 8 percent. That's a doubling of their political power in just three elections.

But it isn't the popular vote that determines who becomes president—it's the electoral vote. Which means that Latino voters need not even tip the entire balance of the electorate—they just have to tip enough of the key swing states where they are already highly concentrated. If Hispanic voters came out in full force in Florida, Nevada, Arizona, New Mexico, and Colorado—which together have 56 electoral votes—their candidate (assuming they had just one) would surely win. Their electoral strength has been increasing not just in numbers, but in their ability to influence the final outcome, because they have been settling in states that are on the verge of tipping from one party to the other.

Key Swing States by Number of Electoral Votes in 2008 with Significant Percentage of Illegal Immigants

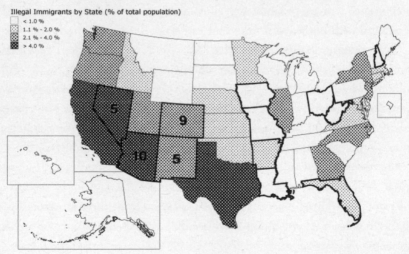

Source: Estimates of the Unauthorized Immigrant Population Residing in the United States, Office of Immigrant Statistics, 2000, 2005

In fact, if you look at the growth of Latino voters in those swing states between the 1992 and the 2004 elections, the rise is remarkable:

Percentage of Latinos in Key Swing State Electorates, 1992 Versus 2004

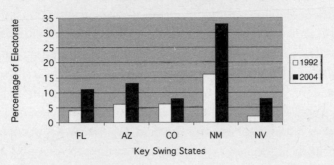

Source: U.S. Census, 1993, 2005

Are Latinos likely to vote? And who will their candidate be?

Offended Latinos seem likely to vote in greater numbers. According to the 2006 National Survey of Latinos, conducted by the Pew Hispanic Center, 75 percent said the immigration debate of 2006 will prompt many more Latinos to vote in upcoming elections. (Indeed, they made up 8 percent of the House race electorate in the 2006 midterm elections—up from just 5 percent in the 2002 midterms.) Sixty-three percent think the pro-immigrant marches of the spring of 2006 signaled the beginning of a new and lasting social movement. And 54 percent think the debate made discrimination against Latinos more of a problem—which itself stirs up participation.

And for whom will they vote? Historically, Hispanics have favored the Democratic candidate for president, with President George W. Bush getting the largest Republican share of Hispanic votes ever in 2004, but that still being only about 40 percent. But the 2006 immigration debate seems to have pushed many Latinos back to the Democrats. In the 2006 midterm elections, they voted about 2 to 1 Democrat, making the 2004 support for George W. Bush perhaps an aberration.

On the other hand, the Democrats' lock on Latinos is not certain. According to the Pew 2006 survey, the percent of Latinos who thought Republicans had the best position on immigration dropped from 25 percent in 2004 to 16 percent, which is pretty darn low. But Democrats didn't actually make up the difference. Indeed, 1 out of 4 Hispanics said that *neither* party had the best position on immigration issues—more than triple the share who felt that way just two years before.

In fact, the increasing independence of Hispanic voters may be the most important consequence of the immigration flare-up of 2006. According to the 2006 Gallup poll on Minority Rights and Relations, 42 percent of Latinos identify as Democrats and 17 percent identify as Republicans—but a remarkable 40 percent identify as Independents. Similarly, a July 2006 poll by the New Democrat Network of registered, Spanish language–dominant voters, found that 54 percent said the immigration debate had increased their interest in voting, but a *41 percent plurality* said it had no impact on which party they were likely to support.

Which means Latino voters will be open in 2008 to strong candidates who speak to their priorities, perhaps from any party. And what are their priorities? Beyond immigration itself, two key issues are health care and education. As of 2005, one-third of immigrants lacked health insurance—nearly two and a half times the rate for American-born citizens. And public schools, public schools, public schools. According to the Center for Immigration Studies, immigrants account for virtually *all* of the increase in public school enrollment in America since the mid-1980s.

As illegal immigrants wield their political influence, Latinos who vote— inspired by the more Militant Illegals—are growing more independent. In this way they will be a growing force in politics not just because their numbers are expanding and because they live in swing states, but *also* because they have shown they will increasingly look at the candidates and not the party alone. For this reason, they may become the most important voting bloc out there. George W. Bush would not have won reelection in 2004 without winning about 40 percent of their vote; and President Clinton, and now Senator Hillary Clinton, draw very strong support from this community. What an enormous mistake Pete Wilson made in the mid-1990s in California, and the congressional Republicans made again in 2006. Voters who want to keep immigrants out are already in the political system, but voters who want America to be true to its heritage of immigration are being awakened, mobilized, and newly activated. So the most powerful political force in the country, and the most important voting bloc in the upcoming elections, may not even be able to vote—but their cousins can. And that may make all the difference.

Christian Zionists

▲

It is often said—and more often assumed—that America's friendship with Israel is driven by America's vocal and well-organized Jewish community.

In fact, support for Israel among Americans in general is extremely strong, with about 65 percent of all Americans having a favorable view of the Jewish state. But here's what's really striking: In terms of sheer numbers, Christians who actively support Israel far outstrip the number of Jews who do.

"Christian Zionists," as they are called—those who believe that their Christian faith itself calls for support for Jewish rule in Israel—are estimated to be 20 million Americans. Even if every Jew in America supported Israel, which they don't, they would barely reach 5 or 6 million.

And so the relative numbers of Christians and Jews for Israel is remarkable. In 2006, a new organization called Christians United for Israel (CUFI) drew 3,500 attendees to its first Washington, D.C., summit and "lobby day." According to CUFI's executive director, David Brog, it took the American Israel Public Affairs Committee (AIPAC) fifty years to draw that many Jews to Washington for its policy conference and lobby day.

AIPAC, with its fifty-year history and reputation for being a strong lobbying force on Capitol Hill, claims 100,000 members. While CUFI does not yet have formal membership, its mailings reach at least *five times* that many Americans.

Sure, Israel is precious to Christians the world over as the land where Jesus lived, preached, and died. But what accounts for American Christians' ongoing, devoted activism to the modern Jewish state? And given so many Christians' passionate support for Israel, why does the myth persist that America's support for Israel is driven mainly by American Jews?

Some part of American Christians' devotion to Israel has to do with politics: Israel is the lone democracy in a fairly totalitarian neighborhood, and is a close strategic and economic ally of the United States. Particularly since September 11, more and more Americans have seen that the U.S. and Israel share not just democratic values and institutions, but also specific enemies.

But what tips Christian *sympathy* for Israel into passionate, pro-Israel *activism* is faith itself. Christians who interpret the Bible literally see God's covenant with Abraham in the Book of Genesis—"I will bless them that bless thee, and curse him that curseth thee"—as a present-day call to care for the Jews and the land of Israel. They read the prophet Isaiah, "For Zion's sake I will not keep quiet," and "Comfort ye my people"—and they hear a direct call to action on behalf of the Jewish state. In addition, many fundamentalist and evangelical Christians believe that before Christ can return to earth, Jews from other lands must return to Israel. In the last decade, something like 600,000 *Christians* sponsored the emigration of 100,000 Jews from Russia and Ethiopia to Israel.

But it must be a pretty small sect of Americans that directly commutes ancient biblical texts to modern-day geopolitics—right? Nope. According to a 2006 poll by the Pew Forum on Religion and Public Life, *more than half of people in the American South believe the state of Israel was given to the Jewish people by God.* (Not the historical land of Israel, but the modern-day state of Israel.) Among white evangelical Protestants, it is 69 percent. Among black Protestants, it is 60 percent. How many American *Jews* think the state of Israel was given to them by God? Probably fewer than 2 in 10.

All this means that while U.S. support for Israel is growing—even as its support is waning among certain intellectual elites—this has at least as much to do with American Christians as American Jews. Indeed, when in July 2006, two Israeli soldiers were captured by the radical militant group Hezbollah and Israel attacked Hezbollah hideouts in Lebanon, CUFI was holding its long-planned conference in Washington, D.C. That week, it was CUFI's 3,500 Christians who descended on lawmakers' offices to advocate giving Israel time to fight its war against America's and Israel's common enemy. AIPAC was there, too, but the new and surprising presence was the Christians.

And that is the new potency of Christian Zionists. While they have been around for ages—evangelical Christians petitioned the U.S. government to create a refuge in the Holy Land for oppressed Jews as early as the nineteenth century—now they are active and skilled in American politics. And they are fired up against the radical Muslim threat to America. As the main organizer of the July 2006 CUFI event, Pastor John Hagee, said, "For the first time in the history of Christianity in America, Christians [are on] the Hill to support Israel as Christians."

The evangelicals' influence on American foreign policy has not gone unnoticed by Christians who take a different view. Jimmy Carter's 2006 book about Israel and the Palestinians—which drew a firestorm from the Jewish community and prompted the former president to apologize for at least a couple of sentences—was actually written less for a Jewish or even mainstream audience, as it was for the Christian Zionists who are at the heart of this trend. According to experts on U.S.-Israel relations, Carter, a liberal Christian, wrote to challenge his increasingly powerful conservative counterparts on the correct *Christian* position on Israel.

Alas, a muddle of religion and politics—with Christians battling out what most people think of as a crisis between Jews and Muslims. And while they battle, American Jews and American evangelicals are finding themselves strange bedfellows. Historically, the two groups have been on opposite sides of most domestic social issues, from abortion to gay marriage—prompting both to wonder how close their alliance over this issue can truly be. Moreover, many Jews, understanding that the Christian vision of Christ's Second Coming involves not just redemption for Christians but also conversion of the Jews, are wary that their political partners may have a hidden agenda in mind.

Other Jews say that's unfounded. Brog, the director of CUFI, calls Christian Zionists "nothing less than the theological heirs of the righteous Gentiles who sought to save Jews from the Holocaust." Compared to the differences that Christians and Jews have with fundamentalist Islam, he says, what separates Christians and Jews from each other is "very small, indeed."

Surging Christian Zionism will surely mean greater pro-Israel activism on the part of Christians as America's evangelical base—at least 40 million strong—increases its political activity. Will that convert American support for Israel to a Republican issue—challenging the bipartisan support it has enjoyed in the past? Will Jews themselves move Republican, despite their long-standing affiliation with the Democratic Party?

Or could Israel actually become *more* important to evangelical Christians than it is to the Jews? Surveys of Jewish college students today show that Israel does not grab them either emotionally or politically the way it did their parents and grandparents. If, in a generation or two, Christians in America who support Israel outpace Jews not only in number but in intensity, to what extent will America's support for Israel look less like an ecumenical, geopolitical alliance, and more like the centuries-old rivalry between Christianity and Islam for the heart of Jerusalem?

At first, one might think Christians for Israel were basically the same people as Pro-Semites—the non-Jews who affirmatively seek out Jews to date and marry. But whereas Pro-Semites are largely Catholic and Northeastern, Christian Zionists are largely evangelical and Southern. Pro-Semites have no particular interest in Israel, but a lot of interest in a Jewish mate. Christian Zionists are just the opposite—they have little interest in a Jewish mate, but a lot of interest in the state of Israel. This phenomenon is perplexing to a lot of people, but perhaps most of all to Jews—who feel their community challenged by the high rates of intermarriage, and yet also stronger with the growing support for the state of Israel.

Newly Released Ex-Cons

▲

D o you remember the 1973 hit single "Tie a Yellow Ribbon Round the Ole Oak Tree"? A man just released from prison is riding the bus home, but he has told his wife that if she doesn't want him back, he'll understand. He says he'll just stay on the bus unless he sees the signal: a yellow ribbon tied around the old oak tree. And, to the delight of the whole cheering bus, the guy sees a *hundred* yellow ribbons tied round that happy tree.

If this were really the scenario for most returning prisoners in America, there would be a boom in the yellow ribbon industry, not to mention oak tree care. Because back in 1973 when Tony Orlando and Dawn were singing that song, there were only about 100,000 people coming out of prison every year. Today, that number has grown by something like 600 percent.

Total Sentenced Prisoners Released from State or Federal Jurisdiction, 1977–2004

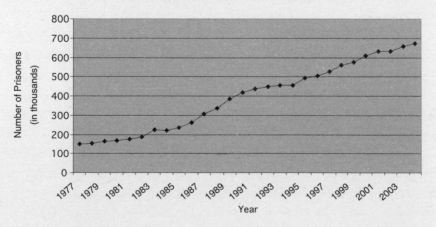

Source: Bureau of Justice Statistics, Department of Justice, Prison and Jail Inmates at Midyear, 1977–2005

These 650,000 or so ex-cons are called "reentrants"—people leaving prison or jail, thanks to either parole or the end of their sentences, to reenter society. They are 90 percent men (with women rising from 8 to 10 percent in the 1990s). Almost half are black; a little more than a third are white; and about 16 percent are Hispanic. Their average age is 34.

The reason there are so many more people coming out of prison now is that, in the last couple decades, we sent so many more in.

Between 1972 and 2004, the combined prison and jail population in the United States went from 330,000 to over 2 million. Add to that 5 million on probation or parole, and you have over 7 million people in America under the jurisdiction of the criminal courts. That's over 3 percent of the adult population, or something like 1 in every 31 adults. It's equivalent to the entire population of Virginia.

In California alone, the prison population grew by more than 500 percent between the early 1980s and now.

This is because in the 1980s and early 1990s, America went on a tough-on-crime spree—imposing longer sentences, more mandatory sentences, and more determinate sentences (meaning less discretion for parole boards to decide how much of, say, a ten–twenty-year sentence a prisoner would actually serve). Forty states passed laws making it easier to try juveniles as adults.

As a result, the U.S. prison population more than quintupled. According to the International Centre for Prison Studies, Kings College, London, America now imprisons 700 people for every 100,000 of population—handily topping all other nations measured, including Russia (680), South Africa (410), England (135), and Japan (50).

But for all this locking up, we don't *really* throw away the key. Over 90 percent of prisoners at some point come out. And so, in 2006, a record-breaking 650,000 people in America left confinement to reenter their communities.

That's more than the entire city of Baltimore. It's practically the entire population of San Francisco. It's almost half as many as come out of college every year.

Everyone knows how Australia was founded largely by prisoners who were bursting through the seams of nineteenth-century British jails. But in the entire eighty or so years of prisoner deportations, fewer than 165,000 criminals total were actually sent over to the new continent. Today in the U.S., we release almost four times that many convicts *every year*. If 150,000 lawbreakers could help found a continent, just think what six times that could do.

But alas, the tale here is not so constructive, at least yet. The typical reentrant in America is a low-income male with little education, who went into jail with a drug problem and didn't get any treatment for it. (Something like 1 in 10 inmates gets drug treatment, compared to the 7 in 10 who need it.) About a quarter were in for violent offenses. Twenty-five percent of reentrants not only have no yellow ribbons waiting for them, but are heading for homeless shelters. Many are mentally ill.

So perhaps not surprisingly, many reentrants fail. According to federal statistics, within three years, two-thirds of reentrants will be arrested again, and almost half will be back behind bars.

This is not only a humanitarian crisis. America spends $60 billion a year on this so-called corrections system.

What's to be done? For at least ten years, policymakers have been calling for attention to reentry, and in his 2004 State of the Union address, President Bush announced a small federal initiative (as yet mostly unfunded) to assist reentrants with jobs, housing, and mentoring. But this is a problem that goes beyond just federal solutions. According to a survey in five large cities, 65 percent of employers said they wouldn't knowingly hire an ex-con. Dozens of professional groups, including manicurists and barbers, have barred ex-cons from their ranks. Most public housing bans them, too.

These people could have been a political force. Nearly every state denies felons in prison the right to vote, but about a dozen states revoke felons' voting rights *permanently*, even after their sentences are finished. In the 2004 election, about 5 million people were disenfranchised due to felony convictions. George W. Bush's margin of victory over John Kerry was only 3 million votes.

In 2000, Al Gore *won* the popular vote by half a million—but had the 400,000 former felons in Florida been able to vote, scholars have concluded, he would have won the presidency, too.

The people who are really bearing the brunt of felons' returns are their families, who, by the way, tend to be pretty tightly concentrated. One study in Ohio found that 3 percent of Cleveland neighborhoods were home to 20 percent of the state's ex-prisoners. Who's tending to the oak trees in *those* neighborhoods? Who's supporting the people whose yellow ribbon commitments could actually make the difference between successful reentry, and a return to the slammer?

There are also the children. In the 1990s alone, the number of children with a parent in prison rose by more than 100 percent—from 900,000 to 2 million. Now, given the reentry surge, we'll have an ex-con baby boom—and given the likelihood of reentrants returning to prison, the number of kids with incarcerated Moms and Dads is only likely to grow.

We made the people who did the crime do their time, but they're coming out now with all-around low prospects and bad social habits, and we need a plan that involves both help and supervision.

The original tough-on-crime proponents would say it is not a coincidence that with all these ex-cons returning, crime is—after fifteen years of decline—back on the rise. But the link just points out how seriously we need corrections reform. Some statisticians have attributed the 1990s drop in crime to *Roe v. Wade* many years before, but more likely it was a combination of the 100,000 cops put on the street by President Clinton, new intelligent police methods, and stricter sentences. In any event, we are now moving from being the free country with the most people in jail per 100,000 to being the free country with the most people *released* from jail per 100,000.

Unless we figure out how to make ex-cons employable, and put job training at the top of the list, this will be a very destructive cycle. Unable to get a job, returning convicts will find they have limited options, and slip back to what they know best, even if they weren't very good at it.

Newly Released Ex-Cons is a microtrend that government and business need to get going on right away. Taking more criminals off the streets only works while they are off the streets—but without a souped-up public-private partnership to reach out to returning felons, we will simply go through another cycle of more lockups and higher crime, once they have done their time.

PART VII

Teens

The Mildly Disordered

▲

When only a minority of Americans went to college, people didn't worry so much about students' different "learning styles," or what may have been actual learning disabilities. If nuanced verbal expression wasn't your thing, you could make a living by lots of other means.

But now that most good-paying jobs in America require college—and most colleges require high-level thinking—there is suddenly greater attention to the skill with which all students read, write, spell, reason, recall, and organize information. And as a result, there has been an explosion in the number of young people diagnosed with learning disabilities, neurological disorders, and other previously unattended to conditions.

To be sure, youth with learning disabilities are not to be confused with severely mentally ill kids, who, sadly, are also on the rise. (Childhood autism has increased 9-fold since 1992. The number of children being treated with antipsychotic drugs shot up 138 percent between 1997 and 2000.) No, most kids diagnosed with learning disabilities today suffer from subtler conditions that would likely have gone undetected a generation ago, but now—thanks to advances in child development research and to more intense scrutiny on the part of parents and schools—are being found out.

The difference is clear as early as toddlerhood. A child who, twenty-five years ago, would have been considered "irritable" is now likely to be diagnosed with Sensory Integration Dysfunction, a condition wherein a child's brain over- or under-perceives sensation, causing lights to seem too bright, noises to sound too loud, or clothes to feel too itchy.

A child who, twenty-five years ago, would have been considered "non-athletic," may well be assessed today with "motor-planning" challenges, or an underdeveloped mental capacity to move from conceiving of a physical movement to executing it.

The new classifications of disorders keep expanding. And so by the time toddlers get to be children and teens, the number of them being diagnosed with problems related to reading, writing, speaking, listening, and math simply explodes. In the past thirty years, the number of kids served under the federal Individuals with Disabilities Education Act definition of "specific learning disabilities" has gone up 82 percent.

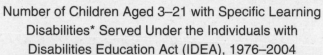

Number of Children Aged 3–21 with Specific Learning Disabilities* Served Under the Individuals with Disabilities Education Act (IDEA), 1976–2004

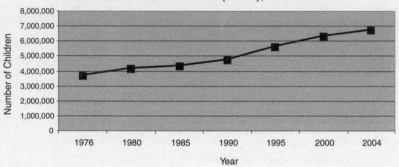

* Specific learning disabilities include problems with oral expression, listening comprehension, written expression, and reading or math skills

Source: U.S. Department of Education, National Center for Education Statistics, 2006

No one is sure whether it's *just* that we're paying more attention that we're finding more nameable problems. There are very likely environmental and other factors contributing to the surge. But there's no doubt that once we examine, label, and classify kids more closely, we see more problems.

And who is encouraging the most scrutiny? The affluent, of course. While learning disabled kids span the spectrum of family incomes, it is practically a fad in the upper middle class. (Who else, after all, would spend serious time and money to find out why their kids are *merely* average?)

Today's most elite, expensive schools offer not just teachers, but also "learning specialists" who attend to each child's developmental milestones. Readin', writin' and 'rithmetic today generally also includes a focus on attention spans, sensory integration, and motor planning. The ironic result is that whereas in low-income communities, "special ed" often signals a doomed academic career, in affluent communities, *not* having an occupational therapist, speech coach, or social-emotional counselor by the time you are 12 is practically a sign of parental neglect.

Just look at the SAT. Between 1990 and 2005 alone, the number of students granted extra time to take the SAT *doubled*, to over 40,000 of the nation's 2 million test-takers. And you can't just get this time with a casual request. You have to have documented proof of your learning disability from a psychologist, plus proof that you have been using all the accommodations recommended by that psychologist on your regular high school tests. Who's getting all that? You can bet it's largely the families with the time and money for specialists, evaluations, and treatments (not to mention the advocacy skills required to seek out and secure the extra time).

And so, as of 2005, more than 40,000 high school juniors are taking extra time on the SAT. That's numerically equivalent to the entire entering freshman classes at the main campuses of Ohio State University, the University of Texas, the University of Pennsylvania, the University of North Carolina, the University of Virginia, Oral Roberts University, Vanderbilt, Texas A&M, and Yale. Combined.

And where affluence is, industry follows. The intense scrutiny of parents has propelled after-school tutoring into a $4-billion-a-year industry, with 15 percent annual growth. Both Sylvan Learning Centers (now with more than 1,000 sites nationwide) and the Kaplan-owned SCORE! Educational Centers have started offering tutoring not just to struggling teens, and ambitious tweens, but to *4-year-olds* whose super-conscientious parents are already worried they are falling behind.

If I were living in a country now that was just beginning its push for universal college, I would invest in its equivalent of Sylvan Learning Centers. A decade from now, after-school tutoring, and toddler catch-up, will be all the rage.

Watch, however, for the "Disorder Divide." While regular folks may still see a stigma in kids' disabilities related in any way to the brain, the affluent wear them like a badge of honor, aggressively explaining why their children undercompete.

And watch for the impact on children in general. With so many more affluent kids regularly sent to specialists and diagnosed with disorders, it may be that society's "best and brightest"—the youth most likely to get good educations and go to college—are subtly internalizing the message that they need a great deal of outside help to be "normal." Already the Millennials, born after 1980, are the most medicated generation in history. Now that they are in college, studies show that of the nearly 1 in 10 college students who seeks mental health counseling, 25 percent are on psychotropic medicines—up from just 9 percent in 1994.

Some will say I've exaggerated the focus on new childhood disorders. But the explosion of new conditions starts at birth. In 2005, the main medical manual on the *mental health of infants*—that is, babies aged 0–3 years—was revised to include two new subsets of depression, five new subsets of anxiety disorders, and six new subsets of feeding behavior disorders. So parents are starting young.

Americans are comforted by the idea that any setback their child faces is not self-inflicted, but rather the result of an outside and previously undiagnosed hardship that must be overcome. The testing system has become something of a game, now that everyone knows that tutoring makes such a difference in scores—so any parents who can get extra time for their children are just playing the game another way. Hey, what's wrong with that kid? Hopefully something—but nothing too serious. That is the answer that opens up extra help, extra time, and a little extra attention. And that is the answer more and more kids are turning to as the explanation for why they are not performing as well as they could or should.

Young Knitters

▲

My 4-year-old daughter is getting ready to apply to kindergarten, and I was recently looking through the Web sites of some of the hottest private schools in Washington, D.C. One of them streamed footage of an extracurricular offering for seventh-graders in knitting. Knitting? In the twenty-first century? In the nation's capital? Were they kidding?

Alas. It is I who was out of touch.

In a nation where you can buy sweaters and scarves at Kmart for under $15, something like 20 million people in America are knitting their own. And the fastest-growing groups of people who knit (that's with two needles) or crochet (that's with one, hooked needle) are teens and 20-somethings.

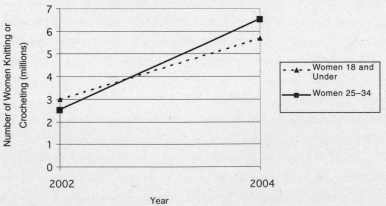

Young Knitters, 2002–2004

Source: Craft Yarn Council of America, 2006

For an activity that is twenty-five centuries old, knitting is very hip.

This trend is, of course, *doubly* counterintuitive. When you think knitting, you think grannies in rocking chairs; and when you think teenagers, you think all-tech all-the-time. And yet there they are, 6 million junior high and high-schoolers in America, clicking and purling away, led by fabulously trendy knitters like Julia Roberts, Cameron Diaz, and Sarah Jessica Parker.

Practically overnight, knitting has gone from frumpy to chic. There are knitting blogs, T-shirt campaigns to "Take Back the Knit," and Knit-Outs (and Knit-Ins) that attract tens of thousands of people in cities all over the country. Scripps Howard's Do-It-Yourself Network features *Knitty Gritty*, a weekly romp through crafting patterns marketed as "fresh, fierce, and fabulous." VogueKnitting has just launched a magazine for knitters under 25. Debbie Stoller's *Stitch 'n Bitch: The Knitter's Handbook*, made the *New York Times* best-seller list in 2004 and has sold something like 100,000 copies. A sequel, *Stitch 'n Bitch Crochet: The Happy Hooker*, sold 25,000 copies in its first couple of months.

Teen knitters aren't some reclusive, anti-technology faction. Thousands of members of MySpace, the wildly popular social networking site, affiliate with knitting subgroups, suggesting that today's teens are comfortable with having their high-tech and low-tech sides—well, meshed together.

Even a few boys are getting into the act. Crafts experts estimate that about 4 percent of needlecrafters nationwide are men, with teen boys in particular increasingly sporting homemade caps for chilly mornings of surfing and snowboarding. (If Cameron Diaz isn't their role model, they can look to football great Rosie Greer, who apparently knitted and needlepointed on the sidelines between plays. According to www.MenKnit.net, women have falsely assumed credit for the history of knitting; it was actually male fishermen who first made heavy sweaters for the high seas, and male soldiers who mass-produced warm socks in World War II.)

But if we are fighting over the heritage of knitting, it's clearly way hipper than we thought. So, who put the vogue back in knitting needles?

In general, the rise in knitting may be part of a larger "nesting" trend that took place after 9/11. Cooking shows shot up in popularity, as did family reunions, and tips for making life simpler. Handicrafts in general got a lot of play (with sewing machines doubling in sales between 1999 and 2005), and, in particular, knitting—with its regular, rhythmic stitching—is said to relieve stress and lower blood pressure. Ex-smokers swear it's helped them quit. People use phrases like "the zone" to describe the experience of knitting, calling it the "new yoga" and the "new meditation."

It's therapy, with a hat to take home afterward.

But for young folks, the appeal of knitting is even greater, combining the best of a few of their worlds. Knitting is social like MySpace, with groups gathering to do it communally—and enjoy the conversation that has apparently flowed from it for twenty-five centuries. It is skill-oriented, like video games—with the chance to take on increasingly harder challenges and get intense satisfaction from accomplishing them. And in today's self-defining, self-actualizing teen world (which comes in handy when positioning oneself for college), handmade clothes and accessories can be a smart, creative way to brand one's unique identity.

On top of all that, who doesn't want a nattily designed cell phone case, bikini top, or guitar strap, handmade by you or a friend?

But there's more. Just like the grown-ups who knit to relieve stress, teens, too, are increasingly looking for a break from 24/7 connectedness and from the college-prep intensity that can begin in pre-K. In some cases, adults are seizing on this need *on behalf of* youth, urging knitting upon them as a way to improve focus and concentration, strengthen creative thinking, and build math and motor skill development. Some sites claim that knitting calms ADD. The independent Waldorf Schools have made knitting part of their grade school curriculum.

So this is another story of how for every action, there is a reaction—for every high-tech movement, there is a low-tech movement embraced by millions of people. And it underscores the basic idea that even though, on the one hand, people find their time is limited, many are looking for calming distractions. And that in a service economy, people want the pleasure of creating something themselves and being able to say, "I made that."

The implications of Youthful Needlers are sizable. In the crafts marketplace itself, there is likely to be a growing demand for richer colors, jazzier patterns, and "fashion yarns," which are fuzzier, furrier, lacier, and more metallic than the ones that composed your old gray crew neck from L.L. Bean. According to the Craft Yarn Council, between 2004 and 2005 alone, fashion yarn purchases rose 56 percent.

Within the world of fashion, we should expect more knits on the runway, and more handmade looks in haute couture. I, for one, didn't know they could make hand-knit bikini tops—but then, until recently, I also didn't know that ten new Knitting "Meet-Ups" were forming *per week* in cities all over America.

However, the real significance of Teen Knitters is that techie clichés notwithstanding, many of today's kids have longer attention spans than we give them credit for; and they are passionate about creating—not *just* cyberprofiles, but also tangible, useful products that mark their presence in the world. They can click and drag with the best of them, but they like the click-click-click of knitting needles, too.

Move over Madame Defarge, whose knitting of shrouds for the victims of the French Revolution made her one of the most famous (and villainous) knitters in literature. Today's knitters are neither old nor "crafty" in the villainous sense; they're stitching and purling because it's peaceful, practical, physical, and people-oriented.

Which also suggests that as teens today turn from one fad to another, there is room for a lot of make-it-yourself products. Nike just launched a Make Your Own Sneaker kit, complete with custom colors and fabrics. Companies are offering new ways for people to design their own makeup, and engagement rings. But how about guys making their own ties? How about jeans-making kits, so kids can put rips in all the right places? As people are customizing their bodies, and ordering customized monogrammed polo shirts, the market is wide open for knitters, and for new ideas that let people both relax *and* have something they can just slip on just after they're done.

Black Teen Idols

▲

There is perhaps no group in America more stereotyped than teenage boys—and in particular, black teenage boys. In 2002, the Casey Journalism Center on Children and Families found that *over 90 percent* of news stories covering youth in America focus on crime, violence, abuse, and neglect, compared to fewer than 5 percent that focus on constructive topics like child care, child health insurance, or youth volunteers. In the media, teenagers are bad news.

Yet, the truth is that there is a new generation out there—and the stereotypes of the 1950s and 1960s have to give way to the reality of the first decade of the twenty-first century. The progress that has been made by a segment of the black community is nothing short of amazing. While several hundred thousand black teenagers get in trouble with the law each year, several hundred thousand are also in college and planning first-rate careers. Black youth are the fastest-growing group of college graduates, and when they get out, there are often lucrative job offers waiting for them. The emergence of this new class of black super-achievers is changing American culture, breaking old stereotypes, and tearing down the race barriers in offices and in the corridors of power. It is less and less about how black youth have gone wrong, and more about how they have gone right. For a growing microtrend of black youth, the system is working.

Perhaps underpinning this good news is the values-oriented nature of these young people. When compared on the three leading indicators of good citizenship—churchgoing, volunteering, and voting—black youth are either outdoing whites or are overrepresented relative to their population.

In the area of churchgoing, black teens have completely flipped with their white peers. In the 1970s, over 4 in 10 white twelfth-graders regularly went to church, compared to only about one-third of black twelfth-graders. In the past thirty years, that trend has completely reversed. Now over 4 in 10 black twelfth-graders regularly go to church, compared to *less* than one-third of white twelfth-graders.

Percentage of Twelveth-Grade Students Who Attended Religious Services at Least Once a Week, by Race, 1976 Versus 2004

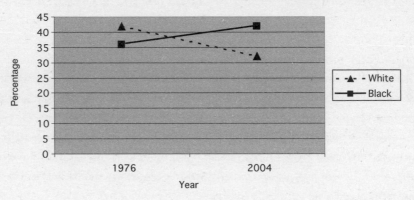

Source: Child Trends, 2004

Moreover, among twelfth-graders in 2004, over half (54 percent) of black students said religion played a very important role in their lives, compared to only about one-quarter (27 percent) of white students. While churchgoing is not the only measure of religiousness, studies show that taking religion seriously is strongly correlated with lower drug and alcohol abuse, later sexual activity, and altruistic attitudes and behavior. It is also correlated with lower delinquency, lower risk-taking, greater amounts of exercise and self-care, and less trouble in school and with the police. Yes, blacks' high school dropout rates are higher than whites, so some of them don't make it into that twelfth-grader study. But the dramatic contrast here suggests that it is time to reassess some teen stereotypes.

On the volunteering front, while youth volunteer rates among blacks have traditionally been lower than among whites, the number of black twelfth-grade volunteers has been steadily rising over the past ten years, and is now equal to (and, in some recent years, higher than) white rates. When you stretch the age group to 15–25, blacks are the most likely among all racial/ethnic groups to say they believe they can personally make a difference in their community. And when you look just at the men, young black males actually have *higher* volunteer rates (63 percent) than either young whites (57 percent) or young Hispanics (48 percent). In the premier community service program City Year, in which 17–24-year-olds do a year of service after high school, blacks make up over 32 percent of the volunteer corps—which is more than twice their representation in the general population.

Finally, when it comes to political activism, voting, and civic studies, young blacks also outdo their peers. According to a 2007 study by CIRCLE, the Center for Information and Research on Civic Learning and Engagement, young African-Americans have the highest rates among 15–25-year-olds of both voter registration and political activity. They are also the only racial/ethnic group of young people to have *increased* their turnout at midterm elections. Young blacks are also the most likely group to view voting as important; and at 72 percent, are by far the biggest supporters of making civics or government classes a requirement for high school graduation.

This kind of civic devotion and constructive democratic participation is just not the rap that young black men generally get. Black teens are an area where old stereotypes die hard, and where, as a result, opportunities for and investment in these youth lag well behind potential value.

While there haven't been comprehensive studies on the backgrounds of Black Teen Idols, they seem to come from families who also value religion, volunteering, and/or civic engagement. (Almost half of all black adults—46 percent—volunteer through a religious organization, which is a substantially higher rate than among whites or Hispanics.) And these youth know what they're after in terms of doing good and giving back. They are drawn to churches that give leadership roles to youth. When they volunteer, they are drawn to activities like mentoring and tutoring (while white volunteers outpace them in activities like "fund-raising" and "supplying transportation"). Politically, they are generally Democrats, but a 2002 study reported that over one-third of blacks aged 18–25 call themselves Independent. The bottom line is: Most young blacks in America are serious, engaged, independent, and ready to make a positive difference in people's lives.

These developments among black youth are part of a larger trend whereby young blacks are doing better than ever in America. High school dropout rates among black youth have fallen from about 30 percent in the late 1960s to 10 percent now. Black college enrollment among recent high school graduates has grown to almost two-thirds, from just 45 percent in 1972. Between 1976 and 2004, the number of black men graduating from college every year almost doubled (and the number of black women almost tripled). Black master's degree conferees grew by more than twice in that time, while white master's-degree-earners grew by only 39 percent.

And as compared to fifty years ago, the number of prosperous black families has grown dramatically. More than 40 percent of black households are now middle-class, up from about 20 percent in 1960. Forty-two percent of blacks own their own homes, and among black married couples that figure rises to at least 75 percent. Black-owned businesses grew 45 percent between 1997 and 2002. A few of them are so well off they just might even become Republicans.

What this means is not only that the black middle class is larger than most of America would think from watching the evening news—but also that there is an emerging group of black youth poised to enrich and lead society in substantial ways. Indeed, *most* black teens in America—including the boys—are in school, relatively pious, committed to American democracy, and doing their part (or more) to make America better. They are not only a serious target market for the technology, apparel, sports, and entertainment industries, they are also ready recruits for college, job, volunteer, and leadership opportunities at every level.

True, too many young blacks in America are struggling, and a nation as prosperous as ours must turn some substantial attention to their challenges. But the media and the marketers need to get some of the clichés right, too, given how much extraordinary citizenship *most* black youth are modeling. The black super-achievers are out there, gaining significantly on their white counterparts. It is only a matter of time before this success-oriented group drives fundamental change in the black community. They are a testament to what is right in America at a time when so much seems so wrong.

High School Moguls

▲

When I was 13, I started my first business—I sold stamps for collectors on approval through the mail. By advertising in the *New York Times*, I developed a clientele for my stamps and it was my first experience with business. I kept double-entry books, bought wholesale at auctions, and sold retail through the mail. I just couldn't wait to check the P.O. box after school on my way home. I did not have many friends back then who were doing the same thing.

Today the Internet and eBay make teen entrepreneurship easier than ever, and the sunglasses you are buying on the Web may just be from a High School Mogul on the other end. Lemonade stands, greeting cards, and baby-sitting are out; the Web is in. In fact, according to *Business Week*, as of 2000, 8 percent of all teens—or about 1.6 million young people in the U.S.—were making money on the Internet.

Sure, some of them were just selling their fathers' old baseball cards on eBay, or unloading the Christmas camera that was a whole three months behind the times. But increasingly, kids are turning their favorite activity—interacting online—into serious business. And part of the reason is that they *can*; when your face to the world is an elegant Web site—and all your transactions go through secure and efficient PayPal—who needs to know that your *actual* face needs extra-strength Clearasil?

Do you know www.ChocolateFarm.com, the Colorado-based company that has about a dozen employees and several thousand hits a day, sells its award-winning Brown Cows, Pigs in Mud, and Pecan Turtles to chocolate-lovers around the country? Founder and CEO Elise MacMillan starts college in 2007. She began the company when she was 10, while her brother Evan, then 13, managed the Web site. Or take AnandTech.com, a pioneer hardware-review site that gives 130,000 viewers per day up-to-the-minute news and analyses of digital cameras, video cameras, and other computer hardware. Anand Shimpi, of Raleigh, North Carolina, started it in 1997 at age 14.

Some of these businesses reap serious rewards. According to *YoungBiz Magazine*, the top 100 entrepreneurs in America aged 8–18 in 2001 earned a total of $7 million in profits.

And kids today love this stuff. According to Junior Achievement, more than 7 in 10 teens say they're interested in becoming entrepreneurs, up from just 64 percent in 2004. Nearly half say it's because they "have a great idea/ want to see it in action"; another quarter say it's because they want to "earn more than they could working for someone else." These are not the teens of yesteryear who delivered papers and babysat to earn cash for movies (now they can download the movies, anyway). Today's kids want to create and run their own show.

Called "'treps" by *YoungBiz Magazine* (short for ent*rep*reneurs)—or "eTreps" if their main storefront is online—High School Moguls are getting some serious national attention in the media, not to mention college scholarships. Camps, summer programs, extracurriculars, and nonprofits are growing up to stimulate more and more Youth Biz. In August 2006, the U.S. Small Business Administration launched "Mind Your Own Business"—an online resource aimed at helping teenagers move a start-up from idea to revenue. They might consider "Don't Sell Weed—Sell Widgets," as a slogan.

Private industry, too, has leapt on the trend. Internet-based companies troll for young, part-time workers with skills and drive. A host of new books advise young people how to make and manage way more money than their parents ever had. *Rich Dad, Poor Dad for Teens: The Secrets About Money— That You Don't Learn in School!* has sold over 50,000 copies in two years.

Of course, youthful business initiative is not brand-new. Jim Casey founded the predecessor to UPS in 1907 at age 19. Paul Orfalea founded Kinko's in the 1970s just out of college. But those guys waited years, if not decades, to see their companies develop. These days, teens build their customer base to millions within months, or they know it's time to move on to the next thing. (Like their English homework.)

What with all this burbling teen capitalism, one might ask if kids these days will even still want to go to college. So far, they do; the overwhelming majority of teens say college is important for starting a business. In fact, the creation of a successful high school business is often one of those great, distinguishing stories to tell on a college application. But what about business school? For their own reasons—having to do with being able to tout graduates' higher average starting salaries—business schools have been making their classes older and older, anyway. To this generation of 17-year-olds, will B-school even be relevant when they're twice that age, with serious business experience under their (hip-hugging) belts?

And High School Moguls may not have the patience to work their way through other people's companies. Already, there are a host of books detailing generation gaps at work—whereby 60-something bosses see 20-something employees e-mailing during meetings, and nearly demote them for insubordination—when in fact the young employees were just skillfully multitasking. But when kids make money so young—not just by being dedicated, like in the old days, but by being ingenious—will they wait around in their 20s to pay their corporate dues?

One of the biggest problems teen entrepreneurs have is that the laws were written to protect them—so as a result, few people will do business with them if they know their age. Almost anything a teenager says is not binding in most states; they can get out of contracts with a wink. And who wants to be responsible for a teenager and the bills they can run up? We may need to have some changes in the laws on teenage responsibility—if they can be tried as an adult for crimes, why shouldn't they be allowed to operate as an adult in business?

Now when we talk about the world being flat, we have to add Global Teenage Entrepreneurs to the mix, and the millions of new businesses that can now bring their products to market on a global basis. Years ago, I was pretty amazed that I could take out a classified advertisement in the *New York Times*. Today, a High School Mogul in Dubuque can bring in orders from Hong Kong. America may not have all the engineers it needs to win the global science contests, but we should seize and celebrate our Teen Moneymakers. They are a sign that the country's creative spirit is alive and well, and that America is nurturing innovation at the earliest possible opportunity in uniquely American ways.

Aspiring Snipers

▲

I have been a pollster for thirty years. With every new poll I read, whether it's for a presidential candidate or a corporate client—here in the U.S. or elsewhere in the world—I learn something new about what people think. Part of the reason I love this work is that every day I find out some new aspiration, hope, or concern people have, and I get to help my clients shape their products and messages based on those findings.

But after thirty years and hundreds of thousands of polls, there's not that much that is out-of-the-box new. Things intrigue me, yes; refine my understanding—most definitely. But it's the rare moment that a poll stops me in my tracks and reorients my understanding of things.

One of those moments happened in December 2006. My friend and colleague Sergio Bendixen, president of Bendixen and Associates in Miami and a preeminent expert in Hispanic public opinion research, conducted a cell phone poll of 600 Californians, aged 16–22, and asked them (innocuously enough), "What do you think you will most likely be doing in ten years?" It was an open-ended question, meaning that the respondents could give any answer they wanted (rather than being guided by a list of possible answers). As expected, almost 70 percent of the young folks said they'd be working, some in a specific career or running their own businesses. Twelve percent said they'd be in college, and 12 percent said they'd be raising a family. One percent said they'd be in the military. And then, like a bolt from the blue, another 1 percent of California's young respondents volunteered that, in ten years, they would most likely be **snipers**.

Now in an open-ended question, for every one respondent who says something spontaneously, several more are thinking it. So this was truly news: A new ambition of the younger generation—not of a lot of them, but enough to be on a scale—is being a sniper.

"What do you think you will most likely be doing in ten years?"	
	(Open-Ended)
Working (specific job or career)	37%
Working (general)	23%
Attending university	12%
Married with family/kids	12%
Working (own business)	8%
Military (general)	1%
Military (sniper/sharpshooter)	1%
Other	6%

New America Poll, Californians Aged 16–22, November 2006

Well, you say, it's just 1 percent. It doesn't mean anything. But as I hope I've been proving throughout this book, 1 percent of folks can and *do* make a big difference, whether in business or politics or the social sector. And here, the fact that we have 1 percent of young people in California telling us that, in 2016, they want to join the military, specifically to be a sniper, is new. In the past, being a fighter pilot was probably the most sought after military career. This is a new idea completely.

When a lot of people think snipers, they think criminals. Especially for those of us who live in the Washington, D.C., area, it's hard to think "sniper" without thinking of the two men who, over twenty-three days in October 2002, randomly killed ten people with long-range firearms from their car. And the major sniper Web sites—yes, there are major sniper Web sites (like www.snipersparadise.com, and www.snipercountry.com)—don't do an enormous amount to disabuse anyone of the stereotypes. One of them posts, in its "Quotes and Poems" section, "God grant me the serenity to accept the things I cannot shoot, the courage to shoot the things I can, and the wisdom to hide the bodies."

But the actual fact is: A sniper is an elite marksman. He is an infantry soldier trained to shoot from a hidden location, generally with a long-range precision rifle, and generally at a human, unsuspecting target. In the world of warfare, the sniper represents the ultimate surgical strike—he inflicts maximum damage, in terms of threat removal and enemy distraction, but with minimal collateral damage, escalation of engagement, or home-team exposure. And he is *efficient*. As an Army sniper instructor once explained to a reporter from United Press International, "In the Vietnam War, the Army shot thousands of rounds per kill. Snipers shoot 1.3 rounds."

Snipers have become increasingly important in modern warfare. In Iraq and Afghanistan, where anti-American forces hide not in foxholes but among urban civilians, the U.S. military is increasingly called on to do battle more surgically. Here at home, with threats of terrorism being lodged against some of our most crowded cities, U.S. defense forces have to be increasingly prepared to face down threats without jeopardizing civilians. The U.S. Army Sniper School (yes, each of the armed services has a sniper-training outfit) is reportedly planning to triple its number of annual trainees. As the fighting in Iraq gets more intractable, it's also considering all-sniper platoons.

Jack Coughlin, co-author of *Shooter: The Autobiography of the Top-Ranked Marine Sniper*, told the *Dallas Morning News* in 2005 that the Aspiring Sniper is "usually the country kid, the kid who grew up in the hills of Tennessee or Texas or something, who grew up with a love for hunting." For sure, hunting would help. But in the California poll conducted by Bendixen, all of the Aspiring Snipers were urban blacks and Latinos. This is a whole new category of Urban Sharpshooters. (Although one thing hasn't changed—all the aspiring snipers were boys.)

And why the sudden interest? Part of it, no doubt, is an increasing respect for the military and law enforcement in America. Following a low point during and after the Vietnam War, Americans have come to regard the armed forces as one of our most trusted and respected institutions. In March 2007, even as barely 4 in 10 Americans thought sending troops to Iraq was the right decision, a whopping 84 percent had a favorable view of the soldiers fighting there (a sea change from the way Americans regarded soldiers in another unpopular war, Vietnam).

Viewed in light of this new patriotism, the aspiration to become a sniper can be quite patriotic. And not just loyal—but also the few, the cool, and the reserved. To become a sniper, an infantry soldier has to be not just courageous, but also patient, self-controlled, and smart enough to master complex mathematical formulas like how distance or wind might affect the path of the bullet. Snipers are the elite of the very well regarded.

But this is quite a change in the role that Americans generally think of themselves playing in war—whether you were John McCain or John F. Kennedy, fighting was about being on the front lines, and exhibiting bravery right in the face of the enemy whom you could see and who could see you. Today, there is more of a questioning about being a front-line soldier, when you can do more damage to the enemy and be safer behind the scenes.

General George S. Patton was so concerned about his men being gung ho on the front lines that he admonished them that no soldier ever won a war by dying for his country; he won it by making the other side's soldiers die for their country. In a sense, the sniper movement represents an acceptance of that philosophy, as we now attempt to fight wars with fewer casualties and fewer risks to soldiers than in the past, when killing was done on a massive scale. And it represents a change in the definition of bravery. People have always felt a little uneasy about snipers—were they fair? Now, they are seen by this generation as not only fair, but smart, efficient, and desirable as a career aspiration.

This is also the generation that was raised on a lot of shooter video games. From *World of Warcraft* to *Sniper Elite* to the U.S. Army's own *America's Army*, kids today are comfortable stalking the enemy and taking him out, at least on screen. These games may be responsible for the renewed interest in joining the military, and the Army is aware of it—these games may serve as a kind of early training ground, and even an SAT of sorts, for future soldiers in a modern army.

Finally, the statistically significant appearance of Aspiring Snipers says something about the post-9/11 culture in America. More so than in decades, young people today are unabashed in wanting to take down Bad Guys. Before 9/11, a lot of people in this country would have called that kind of attitude "primitive," or "simplistic," or at least "insensitive." But since September 11, a growing number of us find the idea of skilled, unflagging marksmen on our side very reassuring. Police, firefighters, and other first responders are now our heroes in ways they haven't been for decades. What's 1.3 shots from an undisclosed location, and a villain on the ground, compared to a now safe subway or building or city full of Americans? Small price to pay.

And if you think about it, the "human hunt" has actually been just below the surface of our culture for some time. Richard Connell's short story "The Most Dangerous Game," in which a big-game hunter goes after human prey, has been widely assigned to American middle schoolers for generations. And dozens of movies and TV shows, from James Bond's *Octopussy* to *Gilligan's Island* to *The Simpsons* to *Xena the Warrior Princess*, have featured literal man-hunting in some way or another.

So whether it strikes you as off-putting or heroic, sniping is a mainstream business. Dozens of gun companies and makers of night vision equipment flock to sponsor annual "Sniper Weeks," multiday conferences at which military and law enforcement personnel from around the world gather for lectures, presentations, trainings, and competitions. And now the U.S. military is actively recruiting and training these fighters for warfare of the future.

So the 1 percent that affirmatively wants to be snipers could change the way we run wars and change the kind of army we have. It is also a symbol of the way people would like to strike in this country—stealth is in, openness is out.

Ask anyone in politics and they will agree—they face "snipers" every day who are trying to find one flinch, one out-of-place word to put on Drudge and YouTube. Deep Throat brought down an administration. There has never been so much political criticism leveled so anonymously as there is today, and for that reason alone, perhaps it is not surprising that so many young people admire snipers—whether on the Internet, in politics, or in the police or military.

PART VIII

Food, Drink, and Diet

Vegan Children

▲

In the old days, the classic American family dinner was meat and potatoes. Mom cooked. Dad praised, and had seconds. Kids cleaned their plates or could have no dessert. Fido got the scraps.

These days, Dad might have cooked, or maybe Mom ordered out. The kids may have barely stopped IMing to come to the table. Maybe Fido's wearing a bib and sitting on a dining room chair. But of all the changes in the American dinner table since the 1950s, the starkest one of all may be that what's on the kids' plates is meatless.

About 1.5 million children in the U.S. between the ages of 8 and 18 are vegetarians, up from virtually zero fifty years ago. That's a million and a half kids who pass over *all* meat, chicken, and fish. Nearly 3 million *more* pass up just meat, and another 3 million pass up just chicken. Then there are also a smattering of pescans (fish only), and vegans, who turn away all foods derived from animals including eggs, milk, cheese, and sometimes honey. Many of them won't even wear leather.

Some of those kids are vegetarian at the encouragement of their vegetarian parents—but more and more, young people are rejecting fleshy food on their own. Especially girls. A sizable 11 percent of girls aged 13–15 say they don't eat meat. While Veggie Kids are fairly evenly distributed around the country, the Midwest slightly edges out the rest of the country at 8 percent—which has got to be disappointing to those meatpacking industry hubs of Chicago, Kansas City, and Fort Worth.

Why the veggie craze? Wasn't it *spinach* that got all the bad press in 2006?

Part of the reason for the rise in Vegetarian Children is the rise of vegetarianism generally, and the growing availability of meatless alternatives, not to mention increasing social acceptance. There are now something like 11 million vegetarians in the U.S.—one-third to one-half of whom are vegans, which is up from fewer than 5 percent in the early 1990s. Even Burger King, of all places, offers a veggie patty. So these days, Veggie Kids can follow their impulses more easily than youth of prior generations.

Another factor in the rise of Vegetarian Children is the rise of parental permissiveness in general—and the premium on individuality, at every age, that permeates practically every trend in this book. A child in the 1950s who told his parents he didn't want to eat meat was probably lectured on nutrition, and conformity, and then threatened with no dinner at all. These days, he will be celebrated for his independence and probably his sensitivity to animals as well. Indeed, the fact that children increasingly go vegetarian of their own accord probably has less to do with practicality, or even parental tolerance, than it does the remarkably steady stream of information that kids today receive regarding the environment. Sure, we've had Earth Day since 1970, and every neighborhood I've ever lived in has periodic Clean Up The Park days. But my 4-year-old comes home from preschool singing "We Recycle, We Recycle" to the tune of "Frère Jacques." She is growing up with a whole new sense of what is politically correct—and kids can have some of the loudest and most uninhibited voices around the household. I am not a smoker, but anyone who is gets an earful from their children. I better darn well not put tin cans or newspapers in the regular trash, or I will get looks. And the meat industry is not faring too well in school, either. Fishing, hunting, and chicken-farming are not some of the most favored activities in school.

In fact, if you think about it, what's really remarkable is not so much that more and more kids are becoming vegan and vegetarian—but that kids today eat as many animals as they do. Have you spent any time lately reading children's books? There is barely a human being in them, until you get to at least Tween Lit. And I'm not just talking about *The Three Bears* and *The Three Little Pigs*, although those are good places to start. From the bears, cats, and worms in Richard Scarry's books to *Curious George* the monkey to the pig family in *Olivia*, there is practically no object of kids' love that *isn't* an animal. And TV and movies are no better. From 2006's *Wonder Pets* on Nick Jr. to that year's hit movie *Happy Feet* (with the singing penguins), how is it, frankly, that children are *ever* persuaded—even by the most nutrition-conscious parents—to let animals pass their lips?

Alas, increasingly, they're not. And nutrition experts increasingly say that a vegetarian diet can be just as good for kids, if not better. So schools, camps, families, and every type of restaurant will be getting ready to provide vegetarian options, and the quality and variety will expand dramatically. Salads have become the fastest-growing fast foods. Don't be surprised if the next fast food events are tofu-based. And maybe some tempura broccoli, or Cajun cauliflower. The industry has done a great deal with different forms of chicken, but they have yet to really run through what can be done with zucchini fries. Aside from the salads, the industry appears stuck in the meat and potatoes syndrome, believing that vegetables are something that kids will eat only under extreme duress. They are missing the trend—a lot of kids now genuinely like vegetable-based foods.

The meat industry is so concerned about what is happening that, in 2003, it launched a counteroffensive. Targeting those teenage girls who have been driving the trend, the Natural Beef Council launched a carefully tailored pro-meat education campaign, with the basic underlying message, "Real Girls Eat Beef." If the Veggie Child trend is sustained through adulthood, the industry's future could be at risk.

It could mean a healthier America, too. Vegetarian men have been shown to have a 37 percent lower risk of heart disease than nonvegetarian men—and vegetarians of both genders are *half* as likely to develop dementia—even when other differences in lifestyle are controlled for.

Of course, vegetables can be dangerous, too, as we saw in the Taco Bell debacle of 2006. Since there is no "kill point" in vegetable preparation—unlike in meat preparation—producers, parents, and the Vegan Children alike have to stay vigilant, even in their healthier lifestyles. So far there has been little appetite for food irradiation, even though it is the sure way to extend shelf life and eliminate the potential for disease from veggies. But faced with billions of new portions of vegetables, the industry might turn to irradiation as the only way to serve spinach and sleep at night.

The battle for the stomachs of our children will be a hard-fought one. The ranchers and the farmers are going to hang in there. And the vegetarian toddlers may well have a counterreaction as teenagers, believing that they have been repressed from enjoying meat, and switch back in record numbers. But more likely, this trend will continue, and more kids, especially girls, will reject the carnivore culture and combine a desire for dieting with new demands for designer veggies. Given, in addition, the move to ethanol and growing demand for corn and cellulose, don't be surprised if soybean futures turn out to be a great investment in the coming years.

Big Momma's Heartache

▲

Everyone knows America is getting fatter. In the early 1960s, the average man weighed 166 pounds, and the average woman weighed 140. Now the average man weighs 191 pounds, and the average woman weighs just about what the average man *used* to weigh—164.

In the last two decades, the number of Americans who are considered "obese"—essentially thirty or more pounds overweight—has doubled. Perhaps more tellingly, the number of people who are considered "morbidly obese"—100 or more pounds overweight—has quadrupled. Today in America, there are estimated to be 9 million morbidly obese people. That's more than twice the number of Americans who suffer from Alzheimer's. It's more than the population of North Carolina or New Jersey. It's a staggering burden to carry.

Of course, we've all heard how our sagging bellies are changing American life. The health care industry has had to make bigger ambulances, larger wheelchairs, wider CAT scan machines, and longer needles. Public transportation has had to adjust, with the Chicago Transit Authority officially widening its bus seats, and airlines having to charge some people for two seats. Commercial innovations abound, like carmakers who are experimenting with swivel seats that make it easier for obese people to get in and out—and caskets that are two-thirds wider.

To be sure, some industries are having a field day. While some stores for petite women are trying to close, Lane Bryant, a leading maker of "fashionable plus-size clothing," is opening hundreds of new ones. The food industry is thriving, as are fast food chains in particular. So, to a lesser degree, is the weight-loss industry. (Although it's not clear that each of these industries has completely done its homework. Alabama, one of the fattest states in the nation, has over 100 KFCs, but only one Jenny Craig. Kentucky—fittingly—

also has over 100 KFCs, but only four Jenny Craigs. Do they know something we don't, or are they not paying attention?)

Even public policy has gotten into obesity—as it should, since our extra weight is costing about $120 billion per year. The Federal Aviation Administration recently added ten pounds to the average weight per passenger in calculating plane cargo loads. Medicare announced it would cover obesity as a disease, which means that more and more weight-loss surgeries may get covered. In 2004, the U.S. Food and Drug Administration launched an "Action Plan to Confront the Nation's Obesity Problem," vowing to step up calorie counts on food labels, nutritional information in restaurants, and better obesity drugs.

But for all this generalized attention, no one seems to be truly focused on the fact that morbid obesity is not evenly distributed, demographically speaking. While we're all *generally* getting fatter, the real burden of morbid obesity is falling disproportionately on one group of Americans: black women. According to a 2002 study in the *Journal of the American Medical Association* (*JAMA*), women in general are about twice as likely as men to be morbidly obese, but a sobering 1 in 6 black women is that overweight—almost more than three times the prevalence rate for any other subgroup of women or men. In fact, despite all the talk about rising obesity, the U.S. population overall is only now experiencing the obesity rates that black women experienced thirty years ago, and black women's rates in that time have nearly doubled.

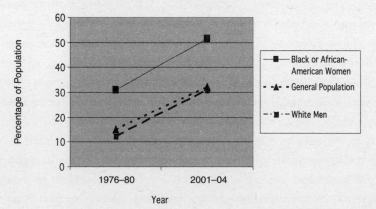

Obesity Rates Among Selected U.S. Populations, Aged 20–74, Late 1970s–Early 2000s

Source: U.S. Department of Health and Human Services, 2006

If you think about it, you've seen this at play in pop culture. Oprah Winfrey, the most popular black woman in America, regularly and publicly discusses her challenges with weight loss. (Does Ellen, or Katie?) One of the hottest dance bands of the 1980s was Two Tons of Fun—two large black women whose number one hit "It's Raining Men" has been remade successfully again and again for two decades. And men, apparently, just can't get enough. Eddie Murphy has practically made a career out of playing big black women—from the *Nutty Professor* films to his 2007 *Norbit*, Murphy has based entire plotlines on little more than the apparent hilarity of the fact that such enormous women (played by himself, a skinny guy) exist. Martin Lawrence did something similar in *Big Momma's House*, and *Big Momma's House 2*. Even Tyler Perry, with his 2005 *Diary of a Mad Black Woman* and 2006 *Madea's Family Reunion*, made more serious films, but still got a lot of mileage out of dressing in drag as plus-sized Aunt Madea.

But in real life, here's what that disproportionate burden means. There are a little over 18 million black women in America. If 1 in 6 is morbidly obese, that's just over 3 million black women carrying an extra 100 pounds or more. According to a 2006 *JAMA* study, morbidly obese people tend to be concentrated in the 50–59 age group, which means the heaviest black women are in their working and grandmothering prime. And here's the worst part. Also according to the *JAMA* study, which tracked its subjects for seven years, middle-aged, morbidly obese women had almost double the chance of dying during the study than women of normal weight. That puts middle-aged black women at perhaps one of the highest mortality risks in the nation.

Can you appreciate the enormity of prematurely losing some 2 million middle-aged black women in America? Although black women make up only about 6 percent of the U.S. workforce, they make up 7 percent of all educational service workers. They make up 23 percent of America's service industry overall.

Black grandmothers are raising or helping to raise 44 *percent* of the black children in America—well above twice the grandmother-raising rate of any other racial group in America.

In 2004, black women turned out to vote at a rate of 60 percent—twice as high as the voting rate of Hispanic women, and just under the white female turnout rate. And black grandmothers are the cornerstone of every black community in America—just ask any preacher, teacher, or person who's ever grown up in one.

One is hard-pressed to say just why black women bear this burden more than black men, or nonblack women. A 2005 study of women's health in New York City found than black women earning less than $25,000 a year were most likely to be substantially overweight. The *New York Times* cited health officials as saying that "lack of access to quality food, the cheapness of unhealthful fast food and processed goods, as well as more subtle societal influences, like differences in acceptable body images among different ethnic groups, all contributed to greater obesity among women with lower incomes and those in certain ethnic groups." And traditional Southern foods that many of the women grew up with were high in fat, sodium, and calories.

While we focus on many of the challenges of the black community such as improving education and creating new opportunities for young people, this clear and statistically significant problem remains essentially unaddressed, effectively swept under the rug, despite high human and social cost. The FDA's "Action Plan to Confront the Nation's Obesity Problem" barely mentions black women. Often in this book we draw out statistical trends that are hidden; this one has been well documented by researchers, but little addressed by policymakers, who will spend billions in additional health care costs as a result. No one—myself included—likes to hear about their weight. And no one wants to be singled out as a group in need of special help in this area. And it is easy to see why politicians would be skittish about addressing this issue for fear of appearing to minister to this politically active constituency. But the facts here are pretty clear: Big Momma's heartache is no laughing matter.

THE INTERNATIONAL PICTURE

Americans are not alone in their widening waistlines. The rise in weight gain has become so universal that the World Health Organization has given a name to this impending epidemic: "Globesity."

For sure, hunger and malnutrition remain serious problems (and perhaps faster killers) in much of the world. But to put the numbers in perspective, there are an estimated 1 billion people worldwide who are overweight, compared to about 800 million who are undernourished.

"Obese" people worldwide now number over 300 million, up from just 200 million in 1995. The World Health Organization predicts that in the next few years, obesity-related killers like heart disease, stroke, diabetes, and hypertension will be the leading worldwide cause of disease and death.

What's most notable about Globesity is that it's not just affecting developed nations. In *developing* countries, says the *New England Journal of Medicine*, as many as 60 percent of households with an underweight family member also have an overweight one. Indeed, except for countries in sub-Saharan Africa, there is hardly a country in the world where the average body-mass index (a more precise measure of fatness than weight) has not been climbing to levels that portend serious chronic disease.

▲ Mexico, for example, is the second-fattest country in the thirty-member Organisation for Economic Cooperation and Development—just behind its neighbor to the north. And in the mostly Hispanic population that lives just on either side of the Mexico-U.S. border, fully 74 percent of men and 70 percent of women are overweight or obese. Diabetes is now the number one cause of mortality in Mexico, up from thirty-fifth place in 1968. That is a higher rate than any other large country in the world.

▲ In China, since the late 1990s, the proportion of overweight men has gone from 4 to 15 percent. The proportion of overweight women has gone from 10 to 20 percent. By 2010, more than half the people in the world with diabetes will be Asians.

And to bring it all back home to the U.S., where African-American women are suffering morbid obesity at dramatically higher rates than anyone else, let's look at Africa. The malnourishment rates there are higher than anywhere in the world. Yet—

▲ More than one-third of African women, and one-quarter of African men, are overweight, and the World Health Organization projects that those numbers will rise to 41 and 30 percent, respectively, in the next ten years.

▲ In South Africa, 56 percent of women are obese or overweight, compared to fewer than 10 percent who are underweight.

▲ In Cameroon, Gambia, and Nigeria, something like 35 percent of the population is obese or overweight.

To be sure, the diabetes rate is still only 2 percent in Africa, compared with nearly 8 percent in Europe and North America—but Africa is quite ill-equipped to diagnose it early or treat it effectively. So while diabetes may seem like a "rich man's," well-fed disease, it can actually take a far worse toll when it afflicts the poor.

Why the crazy, global explosion of fat? Experts say it's all about the worldwide shift in diet from vegetables and grains to highly refined foods and saturated fats. Across the globe, food Is cheaper than it has ever been, but especially calorie-laden food. Our meals and snacks are more drenched in sugar and oil than they have ever been. Mexicans—the second-fattest country in the OECD, you will recall—now drink about as much Coke as milk.

And whereas folks used to walk and ride bicycles, now cars, or at least scooters, are practically universal. Urbanization, TV, and much more sedentary lifestyles have turned everyone into couch potatoes.

Ironically, obesity is a symptom of growing prosperity: Food is cheap, and most of the world can get it. But when it's mostly empty calories—combined with decreasing levels of both manual labor and exercise—it turns into sagging waistlines, and all the health problems that go with them.

Starving for Life

▲

As we just discussed, America is fat. Childhood obesity is up, diabetes is up, and they're having to make our seats wider in buses and airplanes. We know—it's a national crisis.

But maybe because Big People tend to crowd the view, it is possible that we are paying too little attention to a group of Americans who are literally, physically wasting away—not because of want, or illness, or out of political protest, but in a very deliberate quest for longer life.

These Thinning Thousands are not your garden-variety anorexics (although sadly, they, too, are on the rise). They are not chasing a particular body weight, and they're not necessarily repelled by food.

Nor are these people your super-fit Gym Junkies, working out every day and boasting teen-type weights in their Golden Years. (Americans 55+ are said to be the fastest-growing group of gym members.)

No, these apple-for-breakfast, lettuce-for-lunch Century Chasers are a discrete, intense group of people who believe—based on some decent scientific evidence—that cutting their calories to near-starvation levels will lengthen their lives by ten to twenty years.

Crazy? It's been proven over and over in other mammals. In the 1930s, a scientist at Cornell found that cutting rats' calories by 30 percent lengthened their lives by 40 percent, mainly by reducing cancer and other age-related diseases. Similar experiments have shown the same effects in mice, hamsters, spiders, worms, fish, flies, monkeys, and dogs. And when they eat that much less, these animals not only live longer—they are healthier and more vibrant right until the end.

One indication that Calorie Restriction (CR) works the same way in people comes from the Biosphere 2 experiment in the 1990s, when eight bioscientists locked themselves in an airtight terrarium for two years, only to find that the ecosystem, intended to be self-sustaining, barely produced enough food to keep them alive. But rather than abandon the experiment, they were persuaded by their physician, Roy Walford—who fifteen years later founded the Calorie Restriction diet—to live at mere subsistence levels. When the Biospherians came out from their bubble, doctors said they were healthier in every respect than when they'd gone in.

And more recent studies seem to keep proving it. Scientists have found that people on CR diets have lower blood pressure, lower levels of LDL (the bad cholesterol), lower body temperature (which may slow aging), and lower levels of clogged arteries.

Here's what also draws people in. The society with the largest proportion of centenarians in the world—34 out of every 100,000 inhabitants, compared to just 10 in 100,000 in the U.S.—is the Japanese island of Okinawa. Apparently, Okinawans exercise a lot, have low-fat diets, and eat a huge amount of soy. But in addition, they practice a dietary philosophy called *hara hachi bu*, which means "eight parts out of ten full." In other words, they eat to only 80 percent satiation, or about 1,800 calories a day—compared to the average American's 2,500 or more.

You mean that instead of cycling through fad diets—from low-fat to low-carb to brown bread to just-lamb-and-pineapple—I should just eat . . . less? And that would not only make me skinnier, but add years or even decades to my life . . . ?

Calorie-Restrictors think so, and some of them take in as few as 1,200 calories a day. Their (tiny) meals are what you'd expect: fruits, vegetables, nuts, wheat germ. They're as rail-ish as you'd think. And while some experts warn that CR can risk bone brittleness or reproductive problems, even the ones who doubt the claims that CR extends life by 6 or 7 percent admit that it probably does so by 2 percent.

But *it means no food.* Are people really doing it? According to the North Carolina–based Calorie Restriction Society, lifelong CR adherents are a small group, numbering in the low thousands. But something like forty new members join every month. And in the next few years, extensive CR research underway at the National Institutes of Health will raise greater and greater awareness of this approach, especially if the results are good.

CR is unlikely to sweep the nation as the next Atkins, or South Beach. At least those diets traded one vice for another—you had to cut down on potatoes, but you could eat more butter. In CR, the rules are: Eat Practically

Nothing. Given the abundance of food in America, that's like sending a 10-year-old into a candy store and telling her she can only have one jelly belly.

No, at the moment, Calorie-Restrictors are more like an elite secret society at Yale—a small group of people convinced that someday their formula will be the formula for life success. They are smug in the knowledge that the rest of us are eating ourselves into the grave—although at the same time, they struggle daily to reject the pleasures of food beyond subsistence.

Even if the approach never gains more than tens of thousands of hard-core devotees, greater publicity around it could reorient the way Americans think about food. If we suddenly started thinking about food in terms of *life span* rather than *waistband*, it could be a rather serious paradigm shift. And that may have real implications in modern life. Now that more and more people are delaying childbearing until their 40s, might they not seriously ask themselves: Do I want an extra 500 calories a day, or do I want to live to know my grandchildren?

Of course, we won't go instantly from Fast Food Nation to No Food Nation. There won't suddenly spring up "No Eating" sections in restaurants, and Jack Black and Roseanne Barr won't turn overnight into Calista Flockhart and Twiggy. But if enough people shift their orientation toward food, it could trigger changes in our culture. Restaurants and food manufacturers may take more pains to tell us just how many calories we're ingesting. And policy-wise, low-cal eaters are likely to become increasingly impatient with the overindulgent rest of us. If they are going to live significantly longer, they'll want public resources saved for Social Security and other elder needs—not used up on the medical care of people who wouldn't stop scarfing down 2,000 or more calories a day.

And healthy, long-lived CR devotees would be a sweet, sweet prospect for insurance companies—the Met Life–sponsored Calorie Restriction Public Awareness Campaign could be just the beginning, as they offer double indemnity for people who reach 100.

Diet and body image go in cycles, with different cultures at different times favoring either the full-figured or the svelte. But (with the possible exception of Social Security actuaries) the desire for long life goes in just one direction: up. If it can really be proved that in humans, too, fewer cals in the extreme lengthen lives, that finding might give food a run for its money.

Caffeine Crazies

▲

Perhaps the most obvious trend in America is the vast and increasing consumption of bottled water.

In the early 1980s, the idea of paying for bottled water, instead of taking it perfectly free from the tap, was laughable. But these days, you almost never see anyone—from athletes to blue-collar workers to business executives—without their little brand-name H_2Os. As of 2004, Americans drank over twenty-three gallons of bottled water per person per year—almost ten times the amount we drank in 1980. In 2006 alone, sales of Coca-Cola's Dasani and PepsiCo's Aquafina (both of which, by the way, come from local tap water) grew by more than 20 percent, putting them both on the list of top ten refreshment beverages in the United States.

Add some vitamins, minerals, flavors, and/or fizzies to our water, and we leap even higher. According to consumer surveys, people drink bottled water because they think it is cleaner, healthier, and safer than tap water—and if the bottlers add something "useful" to it like vitamins or minerals, we're even happier. According to the Beverage Marketing Association, in 2006, beverages with "functional benefits" grew at two to three times the rate of conventional beverages.

But while some of us are seeking the purity of bottled water, others have gone in the opposite direction, driving the high-caffeine drink to new heights of profit. The totally artificial, stimulus-producing, murky brown stuff that couldn't be more different from water in taste, texture, and packaging. As of 2007, almost 6 in 10 Americans drink a cup of coffee every day, up from under half just three years ago. At-work coffee drinkers are nearly 1 in 4, up from only 1 in 6 in 2003. Starbucks revenues *alone* grew from $1.7 billion in 1999 to a phenomenal $5.3 billion in 2004.

Coffee shops say they're getting espresso customers as young as 10 and 11.

Even church groups lure youth in with coffeehouse-like atmospheres—complete with coffee.

And, of course, carbonated soft drinks are towering over other American beverages—at a staggering 52 gallons per person per year. According to a 2005 study, soft drinks are now the leading source of calories in the average American diet, accounting for almost 1 in every 10 calories consumed. (In the early 1990s, the leading calorie source was white bread.)

Even tea sales have more than tripled since the early 1990s. And innovators are launching new caffeinated breakfast products—like "Buzz Donuts" and "Buzzed Bagels." In case it was too much work to ingest your morning carbs and your morning caffeine in two separate mouthfuls.

Indeed, some people in America will give up the social aspect, and the flavor, of coffees and colas—if they can just have the caffeine straight. By far the fastest-growing beverages in 2006 were energy drinks, like Red Bull and Monster. Your basic 12-ounce can of Coke has 34 milligrams of caffeine. Red Bull has 80. Rockstar Zero Carb has 120. The new "Censored" Energy Drink—known until May 2007 as "Cocaine"—has 280.

In 2006, nearly 200 new such energy drinks hit the shelves, propelling the industry to 50 percent growth and nearly $4 billion in sales. From virtual obscurity just a couple years ago, Red Bull now ranks number seven in U.S. refreshment beverage company revenues, well ahead of Ocean Spray and just a notch or two behind Kraft Foods (which makes Country Time, Crystal Light, Kool-Aid, and Capri Sun). Apparently, Red Bull is the third-largest source of beverage profits in convenience stores across the U.S.

And no one thinks this trend is easing. In 2007, both PepsiCo and Coca-Cola are launching drinks with two to three times the caffeine content of their regular brands.

Yes, even back when I was in college in the 1970s, kids took No-Doz to cram the night before a big exam. But No-Doz has only 100 milligrams of caffeine per tablet, at most. What's a little 100 mg pill compared to Cocaine (the formerly named drink), at almost three times that dose? Indeed, the combination of high pressure to perform, lackluster judgment, and easy availability of caffeine is causing teens and young adults to drive the hyper-consumption of hyper-caffeinated drinks. According to a three-year study of calls to a Chicago Poison Center released in October 2006, the average age of caffeine overdosers—many of whom required hospitalization and, in some cases, intensive care—was 21.

Why the caffeine craziness? What is all the raging buzz for *buzz*?

Part of it, of course, is the 24/7 wakefulness of American life. From round-the-clock shopping and entertainment, to round-the-world colleagues and clients, life in America today is a rest-less frenzy. Americans already sleep an average of 25 percent less per night than we did 100 years ago, and so to some degree we are trying to make up for it with beverages turbo-packed with caffeine. Today's students, especially, feel themselves to be under more pressure to excel than students of prior generations—and with late nights out, 24-hour convenience stores, and little adult supervision, more and more of them are going Caffeine Crazy.

Another reason for the surge in booster drinks is that energy is at an all-time premium in American culture. For a population that is as old as it's ever been, we value vim, vitality, and vigor like never before. Gym memberships are soaring, especially among seniors. Plastic surgery—to make us look younger, at least—is on the rise. Viagra use, between 1998 and 2002, grew over 200 percent among men aged 46–55—and *over 300 percent* among men aged 18–45. Can it be that regular human performance is simply not enough these days? Many of us want to be super-alert, super-charged, and super-men. And if Red Bull, or a venti latte, can get us there—even if we're 12 years old, or if it's our third such drink that day—so be it.

The health effects of the Caffeine Crazy trend are worrisome. It is well documented that caffeine, especially in high doses, can cause insomnia, anxiety, headaches, stomach problems, cardiac arrhythmias, and weight gain—especially if lashed to sugary soft drinks and caramel macchiatos. The quest for super-energy, ironically, can weigh us down.

It's even worse for children, who may be the fastest-growing subgroup of caffeine consumers. Not only are American kids already becoming obese at alarming rates, but a child who drinks one can of caffeinated soda apparently experiences the same effects as an adult who drinks four cups of coffee. While the full effects of energy drinks like Red Bull have yet to be determined, some countries—like France, Norway, and Denmark—have outlawed them entirely because of alleged links to sudden deaths.

Of course, some will rise to defend caffeine's impact on health. It can make athletes more alert, especially if they are not regular users; and many a drowsy driver has probably stayed alive thanks to coffee. Caffeine has been linked to lower Alzheimer's rates, less diabetes, fewer gallstones, lower rates of Parkinson's, and less colon cancer. It is also said to support the delivery of other vitamins or healing agents (which is why there are surprisingly high quantities of caffeine in over-the-counter pain relievers). One study says caffeine grows brain cells, potentially improving memory and the ability to learn. Another study says it cures male baldness (although you need something like sixty cups a day to make it work, so scientists are working on creams that let you just smear it right onto your scalp).

Americans are becoming big drinkers overall. Our poor little kidneys don't know what to make of all the increased hydration and dehydration. (Since 1980, the average American's beverage consumption has grown by an astounding 30 gallons per year—putting pressure on not just our personal plumbing systems, but on the nation's in general.) But Americans are not consuming more alcohol; that consumption has dropped since 1980. They are looking for a very different sort of buzz—drinks that pick them up, not drinks that bring them down. In today's 24/7 world, it should not be a surprise that more and more of them are reaching for caffeine. How else will they be able to stay awake longer hours, or multitask all the time? So hold the martini and pass the Monster; it's time to set up caffeine bars where stimulus-hungry Americans can mix and mingle around their common interest—staying awake.

PART IX

Lifestyle

Long Attention Spanners

▲

It is conventional wisdom that America's attention span is shrinking. A couple of decades ago, we cut our sixty-second TV ads down to thirty, and now apparently the "right" length of an Internet ad is fifteen seconds. We reduce presidential platforms to bumper stickers. We speed-date. When we insta-message our friends, we can't even bother to spell out whole words.

How much more ADD could America be?

But—slow down a minute. (Yes, a whole minute.) For every *Tuesdays with Morrie*, there is a Tom Wolfe novel. For every frenetically animated, two-second pop-up ad on your computer screen, there is a carefully scripted thirty-minute infomercial on your TV—an industry that rakes in over $90 billion per year.

Some people operate on a totally different wavelength. From books to movies to products to news, they want more depth, more information, real answers to more of life's questions. They want substance, not style and flash. So while many marketers and politicians have been perfecting communications aimed at "ADD America"—packing wallops of a message into the nanoseconds they think their audience will give them—they would be wise to pay some attention to America's "LAS," or Long Attention Span folks, too.

How do we know the LAS are out there?

Let's look at sports. Fully half a million Americans run marathons, races of 26 miles or more. Almost 200,000 try triathlons, the toughest of which are ironman triathlons—marathons *plus* a 2.4 mile swim *plus* a 112-mile bike ride. It's not like they could just as easily win a 50-meter sprint. These are people who wrap their heads (and bodies) around something and stick with it for far, far longer than one could reasonably expect. They are in it for the long haul.

Golf, which takes easily four hours per round and is as much a game of the head as it is of the body, has grown in the last twenty years into a $62 billion industry, well outpacing the shorter-term-gratification "amusement, gambling, and recreation" industry. The much faster moving game of tennis has been declining in interest, as more people want to slow down, take their time, and immerse themselves for long periods of time, lost in thought or sport.

Or look at reading. Even as the average Internet page gets about sixty seconds per hit, magazines with 13,000-word, reflective articles like *Atlantic Monthly* have increased their readership to nearly half a million, or almost by half since 1980. Between 2002 and 2005 alone, the circulation of *Foreign Affairs*—truly a publication of all words and no pictures—grew 13 percent.

The real kicker is puzzles. Apparently, 50 million Americans do cross-word puzzles, which can mean anything from ten minutes to three hours of wrestling with arcane synonyms, bad puns, and your own limited spelling. Puzzle-lovers are especially found on the West and East Coasts, where we think of time as being the most hurried.

And of course there's Sudoku, the insanely addictive game where you have to fill in the blank squares of a grid so that each nine-cell row, column, and mini-grid contains all the numbers from 1 to 9. In 2003, practically no one had heard of Sudoku; now Sudoku books fill *several shelves* in most mainstream bookstores, and generate over $250 million in global sales.

Whether it's half a million marathoners or *Atlantic Monthly* readers, or 50 million crossword-puzzlers, LAS Americans are not just the Fringe Attentive. In fact, despite what you learned in marketing school, tuning in for the long haul is really quite mainstream.

The biggest-grossing movie *ever* in America was *Titanic*, which ran for more than three hours.

24, the TV show that took five Emmys in 2006, makes you watch a whole season just to know what happens in one day.

Harry Potter, the most popular book series on earth, proved that not only do we love long stories, we'll wait in lines as long as Lord Voldemort's snake to get the next installment. Long novels, from Thomas Pynchon to James Michener, are huge sellers. Series fiction, from John Updike to Patricia Cornwell, sustains our attention for literally decades at a time.

In fact, in 2005, the best-selling books in America were, on average, more than 100 pages longer than they had been ten years before. And even back in 1995, the average top ten seller was a hefty 385 pages!

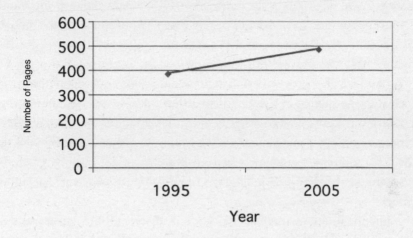

Average Length of Best-Selling Books,
1995–2005

My favorite is political speeches. Every public speaking expert on earth will tell you that short and sweet means powerful. The Gettysburg Address, they recall (with a wistfulness that makes you think *they* think they were there), was under 300 words and took President Lincoln less than three minutes to deliver. But in 1995, President Clinton gave a 9,000-word State of the Union address that took seventy-six minutes to deliver—and it was both the longest and one of the most successful in history. Nearly every year, more than twice as many Americans watch the State of the Union address as watch the final game of the World Series.

So while many politicians try endlessly to cram big thoughts into a few small words known as a sound bite, President Clinton mastered the art of issues-based campaigning. He took the issues and the voters seriously, and rather than give them just "red-meat speeches" (that, say, John Kerry was famous for), he explained issues in a thoughtful and detailed manner. Senator Hillary Clinton is this kind of politician, as was, for all his other troubles, Richard Nixon. No doubt some voters regard their speeches as boring or wonky. But candidates like that do it out of a distinct respect for people, and a belief that, as I mentioned in the Introduction, V. O. Key said fifty years ago, "the voters are not fools."

As I mentioned in the Introduction, Key had a profound influence on how I approach polling and the voters. He systematically studied presidential races in America and determined that each one has been decided on the basis of real, rational, and thoughtful reasons, not on the basis of who wore the better tie. His thinking is the basis for a lot of the work I do—that the rational side of people is far more powerful in many areas of life than the purely gut or emotional side. For every person who decides in a Blink, there is someone who decides only after a serious, intellectual mud-wrestle. And it is the latter type of voter who generally decides elections—the swing voters who go through a process of making real judgments, not snap ones.

The importance of the Long Attention Span in politics should not be underestimated—America itself is a country founded on long intellectual documents embodying powerful ideas that were debated long into the night. And in most other countries, when my colleagues and I bring in American-style political advertising on issues, it handily defeats old-style song-and-rally spots.

Finally, in the commercial world, look at some of the "upset" brand advertising like Dyson vacuums. Here a CEO painstakingly details the physics of the vacuum he invented, and sweeps market share away from the leader.

So be careful before you accept the conventional wisdom that Americans can't concentrate, that we are too distractable for sustained narrative, and that political office always goes to the candidate with the cleverest tag line. In fact, a sizable number of us—often the most interested key decision-makers—will listen for as long as you can talk, read for as long as you can write, and follow for as long as you are willing to explain something. Sometimes people say less not because they are such clever marketers, but because they have less to say.

Neglected Dads

▲

It took fast food marketers a couple of years—and the development of $200 billion in children's direct and indirect purchasing power—to realize that marketing to kids was a really smart way to boost sales. Ronald McDonald, you may recall, with his enormous red shoes and goofy clown face, wasn't meant to attract the people *driving* the family to McDonald's for dinner.

That strategy worked well until the mid-1990s, when Moms started paying more attention to what their children ate. Then, despite the pleas for Happy Meals, Moms started overruling their kids on fast food. (In Britain, they call these Moms the "female handbrake"—Moms who won't let sports-dominated satellite TV into their households.)

The fast food industry stumbled, gauged the trend, and refocused its energy, this time on Moms—adding foods like salad that they could feel comfortable eating along with their kids. If it sounded like a lot that children influence $200 billion a year in spending, women control something like $7 *trillion*.

The Mom focus reached its height at McDonald's in 2004, with a new "McMom" initiative offering everything from an online newsletter with tips on parenting, women's health, and nutrition, to individual McDonald's locations featuring "Mom Corners" and "Mom parking." In 2005, one company executive summed up the industry giant's strategy simply as "It's All About the Moms."

Indeed, the only group still hanging on to anything like that level of attention from fast food marketers is what industry analysts call the "young and hungry men"—males aged 18–34, who eat more than anybody else and are known to eat anything put in front of them. ("Supersizing" was for them, not for the Moms.)

But before getting too comfortable with the two-pronged strategy of

hurried-and-worried Moms and young-and-hungry men, the fast food industry might want to watch the emerging trends again.

In fact, at a recent company retreat to discuss Moms, McDonald's executives asked me what the next trend is that they should be thinking about. And
I looked around at their McMom strategy paraphernalia, and said, "Dads."

Since the 1970s, Dads have been spending more and more time with
their children. According to a 1999 University of Michigan study, in the late
1970s, the average father in a two-parent home spent about one-third as much
time with his kids as the average mother. By the early 1990s, this percentage
had jumped to 43 percent. By 1997, Dads living at home spent 65 percent as
much time with their kids as the mothers did on weekdays, and 87 percent as
much time on weekends.

Two key trends have contributed to the rise in Dad time. First, as more
women have gone out to work, they are tired when they get home and ask
Dad to put the kids to bed. On Saturday, many simply say, "It's your turn."
The second trend is the rise in divorce, which means that, more and more,
kids have regular and exclusive time under Dad's roof.

This is serious father-child interaction time, say the researchers—which
means meals. But where is the McDad initiative? Who's targeting the volunteer coaches, who need a place to take the kids after Saturday's practice?
Who's got the game on *in* the restaurant, so no one has to miss a beat while
spending quality time with the kids *and* relieving Mom, who's exhausted
from her own full-time workweek?

Unlike Mr. Cleaver of *Leave It to Beaver*, who got great respect, today's
Dad gets none. It is almost as though marketers see today's society as an Amazon tribe, where women make all the decisions and men just go along for
the ride.

If you are a Dad actively raising your kids, and perhaps taking them to
their games on the weekend or after school, you are simply ignored by today's
marketers, policymakers, and politicians. In 1996, when I helped identify
Soccer Moms, it was because women with young children were playing a
unique role in politics, serving as the critical swing vote. In the 2006 midterm
elections, it was actually married men who did the swinging. As manufacturing jobs have disappeared, a new breed of "Office Park Dads" has become
the norm—better educated, working in new kinds of jobs, and much more
involved in family life. In fact, 4 million Dads today have substantial child
care duties while their spouses are the chief wage-earners.

The changing role of Dads in families has many untapped marketing implications. Billy Joel's book on being a Dad is a runaway best-seller because it's the one-in-a-hundred children's book that features a Dad. Where are the Daddy-and-me books? Equally ignored are the Dads buying back-to-school clothes, or holiday presents for the kids. (Do an Internet search for "Dads buying gifts for kids," and all you will find is sites that help kids buy gifts for Dads.)

And, dare I say it, what about marketing household cleaners? A 2003 study from the University of California at Riverside showed that school-age children who do chores around the house with their *fathers* are more likely to get along with peers and have friends, and less likely to make trouble at school or become depressed. Not only that, but according to research from the "love labs" of Dr. John Gottman at the University of Washington, when men contribute more to household chores, their wives find them more attractive. (Gottman says wives interpret husbands' domestic contributions as a sign of love and caring, and are therefore more sexually attracted to them.)

But of the hundreds of commercials made annually for household cleaners, has any of them even targeted a man—let alone a Dad? A man's world is a-changin'. A typical man changes more diapers than ever before, and gets less credit than ever before. And in some parts of the world, fathers are staging violent protests to get guaranteed visitation with their kids. Men are spending more time with the kids, but neither Madison Avenue nor the media has picked up on it, and the potential of Daddy-and-me relationships remains untapped.

In the past fifty years, we have had a sea change in the power of women at work and at home, as the majority of women now work and play an increasingly important role in everything from voting to car-buying. At the same time, over the last decade or two, we have finally begun to see men adapting to the new realities of life—becoming more involved in the family, sharing responsibilities, and becoming closer to their kids either from within the nuclear family or through divorce.

And so Dads need some marketing attention, too. I am Papa, hear me roar.

Native Language Speakers

▲

O ne of the great, abiding myths of America is that we are a melting pot—a big, warm stew of all the ethnic and cultural differences that formerly separated us, now blended together into a smooth, supremely palatable *American*.

Language, of course, was the prime example—within a generation or two, immigrants to America were expected to shed their Gaelic, Chinese, Tagalog, or Italian mother tongues for accented—and ultimately flawless—English.

But ironically, in an era when the world's lingua franca is overwhelmingly English, there are a skyrocketing number of people in America who not only have limited proficiency in English, but who live in households where *no one* speaks English very well. The U.S. Census calls these households "linguistically isolated," and the number of people living in them has shot up in recent years—by more than 50 percent, to nearly 12 million people.

Number of U.S. Residents Living in Linguistically
Isolated Households, 1990–2000

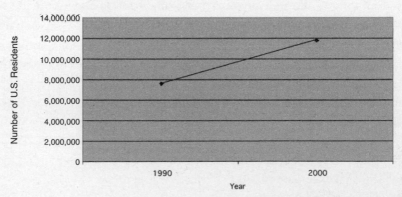

Source: U.S. Census, 2000

That's about 1 in 25 households. It's nearly the population of Guatemala.

The total number of people in America today who speak English either "not at all" or with limited proficiency is nearly 25 million. That's more people than live in Taiwan.

Qué pasa?

Of course, one reason for the surge in Non-English-Speakers in America is the surge in immigration. Since 1970, the number of immigrants living in the United States has more than tripled, from about 9 million to over 28 million. These are the highest immigration levels since the turn of the twentieth century. So it is not surprising that we would be having—as we did then—a burst of linguistic isolation, even if the new immigrants were learning English as fast as possible. (And by many accounts, they are. In 2006, 1.4 million adults were taking government-subsidized English for Speakers of Other Languages classes, and there were waiting lists in at least fourteen states.)

But other factors suggest that the linguistic isolation numbers may not come down so fast. First, because the jobs that draw immigrants to America today, unlike in past decades, are primarily the low-skilled jobs that native-born Americans pass up, today's immigrants come to America with less foreign language training, and less education generally, than used to be the case. Before 1970, fewer than one-third of foreign-born immigrants to America spoke English "less than very well." In the 1990s, that proportion was over 60 percent.

Second, the myth of dramatic improvement generation by generation doesn't seem to be holding up. According to the 2000 U.S. Census, in *over two-thirds* of the households classified as linguistically isolated, the head of the household wasn't even born in a foreign country; *they were born right here in America.*

That remarkable fact may be related to the third reason, which is that for the first time in America, there is the practical possibility of passing English over. In the old days, when American immigrants came in small clumps from many lands, each group had to sink or swim, language-wise. Today, there is a critical enough mass of immigrants from one language—Spanish—that the possibility of staying comfortable in your native-born tongue is higher. Low-wage workers in particular can work, shop, and socialize entirely in Spanish, and there is a good chance their children can get by in school without speaking much English, either. Throw in Univision, Telemundo, CNN en Español, and *People en Español*, and English can seem downright unnecessary.

You can see this attitude emerging if you scrutinize the data on Latinos and English. While it is true that Latinos display near-universal support for teaching English to the children of immigrants, and majorities of Latinos across every income, education, and political group say that "immigrants need to speak English to be part of American society," there is a sizable, and arguably growing, minority that disagrees.

According to a 2006 survey by the Pew Hispanic Center, over 4 in 10 Latino immigrants say that immigrants *do not* need to speak English to be part of American society. Of native-born Latinos, the percentage who feel that way is even higher, at 46 percent.

And even more tellingly, among young Latinos, *less than half* think that immigrants need to speak English to be part of American society. Whereas 69 percent of older Latinos say that immigrants need English to be part of America, *only 48 percent* of Latinos aged 18–29 do. Now it is possible that in answering that question, younger respondents felt defensive about their parents and grandparents who don't speak English but who nonetheless have contributed mightily to American society. They might not have been referring to their own circumstances in saying that English isn't core to being American. But combined with the Census numbers about American-born heads of linguistically isolated households—this could be a trend to watch.

The old cliché was that second-generation Americans served as their parents' navigators, leaping at all the opportunities of the New World, but there may be a small group of second-generation immigrants today who would rather stay tied to the old country.

What are the implications?

Some are gloomy. According to the U.S. Department of Education, people with limited English are less likely to be employed, less likely to be employed continuously, and more likely to work in the least desirable sectors. And their earning potential reflects it. According to Census data, linguistically isolated households are ten times more likely to have incomes under $15,000 than over $100,000.

Non-English-Speakers are also an increasing challenge for hospitals—63 percent of which report seeing patients with limited English proficiency either daily or weekly (and for large hospitals, it's 96 percent). With no systematic way to translate, hospitals end up dispensing worse primary care and overusing expensive diagnostic tests and emergency care.

Others see a silver lining—like in the fact that the Spanish-speaking market is taking off like never before. Spanish-language TV dwarfs English channels in several major American cities. And while Spanish-language radio has topped ratings in Los Angeles, Miami, Chicago, and New York for nearly ten years—as of 2005, it is *also* beating English-language stations in smaller markets like Dallas, Phoenix, and San Diego. And it is growing increasingly popular in places like Des Moines, Tulsa, and Omaha.

So with something like $700 billion in Latino purchasing power in the U.S., many U.S. companies are leaving the assimilation debates to the sociologists and just advertising in Spanish. In the early 2000s, when most companies were cutting their overall advertising budgets, many were maintaining or even increasing their Spanish-language share.

As a matter of policy, if Americans want to close the language gap, we should commit to providing English education to everyone who wants it. At the moment, state support for English lessons is pretty haphazard—Texas, with the third highest immigration rate in the country, spends the minimum required by the federal government, while Connecticut, with its middling immigration rate, spends seven times that. And beyond just numbers of classes, we will likely need to come up with creative, flexible ways to teach English, since many immigrants have low educational backgrounds to start with, are working multiple jobs, working odd hours, and raising children.

And speaking of children, we are squandering a big chance if we don't focus on language support for immigrant youth, since one's foreign language ability apparently falls off precipitously after age 12. (That immigration opponents want to deny public education to the children of illegal immigrants seems particularly ironic in this regard.)

But most importantly, let's get over the melting pot myth. The truth is we're more like a Tower of Babel, doing remarkably *well* at communicating given the fact that U.S. residents today speak over 300 languages. (And who says that's a lot? It's about the same number as was true at America's founding, and we now have sixty times more people.) The bottom line is that so long as we're understanding each other—and no one (not even President Bush, who criticized it) misunderstood "The Star-Spangled Banner" when it was sung in Spanish at the 2006 immigration rallies—then we're doing pretty well.

Vive la différence.

Unisexuals

▲

Since the feminist revolution of the 1970s, we've seen plenty of men doing "women's jobs," and women doing "men's jobs." Male nurses have more than doubled since the early 1980s. So have male au pairs, just since 2001. On the other side, there are sixteen women in the U.S. Senate as of 2007—sixteen times as many as there were in 1981. Since 1972, women in active-duty troops have increased from 2 to 14 percent.

Beyond this kind of "gender-bending" at work, we've also heard a lot lately about "metrosexuals"—heterosexual men who buy their own (fashionable) clothes; use cologne, body wash, and skin care treatments; and even get pedicures, waxing, and cosmetic surgery. And of course, women who play lacrosse, drive race cars, and lift weights competitively.

But today in America, there is a growing number of people who don't just "cross the gender line" when it comes to jobs and hobbies—they reject the very line itself. To them, the binary gender classification system is arbitrary, limiting, and even oppressive. It fails to account for the gray area between male and female that they say more accurately describes them, and arguably everyone else, too.

Some of them want to do away with baggage-laden words like "boy" and "girl," and start again with "boi" and "grrl," and maybe "ze" in place of he and she, or "hir" in place of him and her.

The names for this group are evolving as fast as the movement. Unisexual is one. So is "pomosexual," for "postmodern." "Genderqueer." "Gender-fluid." Within the black community, they are "transsistahs" and "transbro-thas." Within the Native American community, they are "Two Spirits"—a group that was traditionally accorded special respect. Old-fashioned, Latinate types may still be good with "androgynous," or "hermaphrodite."

The most general term is "transgender," which refers to people whose biological sex (the one they were born with) does not match their gender identity (their "inner sense" of being male or female). They are the "T" in what has become the fairly mainstream "LGBT" label, joining them with lesbians, gay men, and bisexuals.

The transgender umbrella includes:

▲ Transsexuals, who have had sex change operations and/or take opposite-sex hormones.
▲ The "intersex"—the 1 out of every 4,500 or so children who are born with ambiguous sex organs. (Jeffrey Eugenides's 2002 Pulitzer Prize–winning novel, *Middlesex*, was about one such person.)
▲ Children as young as 5 who display strong predispositions to dress like the opposite gender—and who are triggering a large, new tolerance movement in schools and communities.
▲ Those who, for a host of personal, political, and/or aesthetic reasons, simply reject the male/female classification.

No one is absolutely sure how many transgender people there are. The World Professional Association for Transgender Health estimates that about 1 in 12,000 males and about 1 in 30,000 females are transgender—which translates into about 17,500 such people in America.

Still, their profile is growing. In 2005, *Desperate Housewives'* star Felicity Huffman played the lead in the Oscar-nominated *Transamerica*, a film featuring a man who was becoming a woman, who learns that s/he has a runaway son. In the same year, the Sundance Channel produced *TransGeneration*, a documentary with the tagline "Four College Students Switching More Than Their Majors." In 2006, *All My Children* became the first American daytime drama to feature a transgender coming-out plotline—with Zarf, a showy rock star played by Jeffrey Carlson, announcing to his friend Bianca that he is actually Zoe, the woman he has felt himself to be all along.

But for such a small group, transgenders' clout is remarkable. Up from zero in 1995, there are now *seventy-four colleges* and universities—including Ivy League schools, public universities, historically black colleges, and community colleges—that ban discrimination not only on the basis of gender and sexual orientation, but also on the basis of gender identity and expression. That's over 1 million college students in America now protected from a form of discrimination that, a decade ago, essentially no one had ever heard of.

Fourteen colleges and universities—including Duke, California State

Polytechnic, Tufts, and Antioch—have changed all their official student forms to allow students to check "male," "female," or "self-identify."

In 2006, the University of Arizona announced that students were allowed to use whichever restrooms on campus corresponded to their gender identity. The Los Angeles Unified School District requires that students be addressed with "a name and pronoun that corresponds to the gender identity."

The newest front in education is "gender-blind" housing, which translates into coed rooming. Ever since higher ed went coed in the 1960s and 1970s, the one thing you could be sure of was having a roommate of your own sex. No more. In 2003, Wesleyan University was the first campus to affirmatively allow coed rooming; since then, Brown, the University of Pennsylvania, and several others have followed suit. Think *Will & Grace*. Now two best friends, a gay man and a straight woman, can be college roommates. (You might think heterosexual couples would be racing to sneak in under these provisions, but so far, they're not. Apparently the year's housing commitment is longer than most college couples are ready to embrace.)

Transgender issues have gone beyond schools and campuses and into the workplace and state legislatures. Over 100 major corporations, including ChevronTexaco, Ernst & Young, and Merrill Lynch, have added gender identity to their nondiscrimination policies. Eight states, plus a host of municipalities that together cover over 30 percent of Americans, ban gender identity discrimination. In December 2006, New York City stopped just short of adopting a policy that would allow people to change the sex noted on their birth certificates, even if they hadn't had a sex change operation.

In 2004, the International Olympics Committee ruled that transsexuals can compete as their new gender, so long as it's been at least two years since their surgery.

While such Unisexuals are few, some say they're the next wave of the civil rights movement. How long before the U.S. Census, too, has a third-sex category beyond male and female—much like in 2000 when it allowed us to check "multiple" races? How long before it's considered impolite, or illegal, to ask a child's gender on an application for school?

Will we stop separating men and women in the military, in public restrooms, in hospital rooms, in prisons, and in the clothing departments at Wal-Mart?

Will there be a Boys and Girls—and Other—Club of America?

Anecdotes aside, Unisexuals are the extreme version of a trend that has become increasingly comfortable for years. Sure, only a few people take opposite-sex hormones, or dress up in their spouse's clothes, but since the 1970s there has been a substantial blurring of the line between "male" and "female" in terms of habits, tastes, and fashions. And the marketers are picking up on it. Designer house Blue Cult has just come out with a brand of jeans that fits both men and women. Mainstream fragrance-makers like Calvin Klein and The Gap sell shared fragrances, or "uniscents." The current rage is "Boyfriend Jeans"—lower rise, tight around the rear, but more relaxed in the legs.

Unisex names—like Cameron, Hayden, Madison, and Quinn—are popular again in ways we haven't seen in centuries.

To my mind, the key reason Unisexuals are interesting is not so much that they blur gender lines—gender-bending has been around, of course, since Hermes and Aphrodite were joined in a word. What's so interesting to me about Unisexuals is that they may be the ideological heirs of the feminist—and revolutionary—principle that *biology need not be destiny*. Today's young women don't actively carry this mantle: Some of them think "feminism" means "un-feminine," and young female professionals long ago rejected the boxy blue suits their mothers wore to work in favor of belly shirts and leopard-print sling-backs. But the transgender population, along with its remarkable number of allies, has reseized this idea, readvancing the principle that identity is less about one's DNA than about one's inner being.

Public policymakers, architects, and fashion leaders beware—it ain't so simple as boys and girls anymore.

PART X

Money and Class

Second-Home Buyers

▲

Second homes" in America bring to mind lavish beach houses, or vast Texas ranches.

Second-home buyers, it would seem, have money to burn, an awful lot of leisure time, and a hankering for opulence in not just one residence but two. Exclusive Resorts has even made a new business of luxury second-home timesharing, requiring a quarter of a million dollars as the price of entry.

But the truth is, middle-income people are the fastest-growing group of second-home buyers. Sales of second homes soared in 2005, accounting for a record-breaking 40 percent of all residential housing sales. And it wasn't because Oprah Winfrey needed another multimillion-dollar townhouse in Aspen or because the Kennedys got another "compound." According to the National Association of Realtors 2005 report, the typical vacation-home buyer earns just $71,000. The median income of investment-home-buyers is $85,700. The median purchase price of second homes is under $200,000.

Second homes are a middle-class craze.

How did this happen? First of all, second-home buying got easier in 1997, when Congress created a tax break for two-home owners who sell their primary residence. Middle-class empty-nesters (the core of the baby boomers) can now cash out their family homes and buy two smaller homes instead.

Second, for many Americans, 9/11 raised the allure of a remote home where people can truly retreat, or hide if necessary.

Third, as the stock market got less reliable, real estate began looking pretty good. Of the 3.34 million second homes purchased in 2005, 2 million of these were investments.

Fourth, people began buying second homes for work—either because their major clients were far away; because they were cultivating clients in multiple places; or because their spouses were already settled in a different city. Whereas couples used to pick up and move if one of them got a job in a new city, it is now estimated that over 1.5 million couples maintain two residences in order to preserve both jobs.

And of course technology has made it *possible* for people to work from multiple sites—with a laptop, a cell phone, and a BlackBerry, one can keep in touch with one's clients (and employees, and bosses) from one's woodsy porch as easily as from one's cube.

But perhaps the biggest reason people are buying second homes is family. Whether it's the Florida couple who buys a condo in Philadelphia so they can easily visit their son at Penn; or the grandparents in Chicago who buy a Savannah home so they can gather their grandkids from Houston, Asheville, and Miami on weekends—family seems to be a driving force behind the surge in middle-class second homes. In a 2005 survey of two-home owners, a plurality said their main goal in life was family happiness/being a successful parent; and an equally large plurality said that the biggest crisis facing America at that time was the dissolution of family. (That was nearly double the number who said the biggest crisis facing America was terrorism, or the war in Iraq.)

Living in second homes has become so widespread that a new term has developed for people who regularly go back and forth: Splitters.

According to www.splitters.com (created by WCI Communities, a home-building company), Splitters are "people who own at least two homes and split their time between them for recreation, work-life balance, or to connect with family and friends." Whereas snowbirds shift residences once or twice a year at most, Splitters go back and forth five times a year on average, and some go as often as several times a month.

There are even Super-Splitters—people who divide their time among three or more homes. But before you think Oprah and the Kennedys again, note that in the National Association of Realtors study, *one-third* of current second-home-buyers said they were very likely to purchase another home, in addition to the ones they currently owned, within the next two years—giving new meaning to the phrase "Bet you can't eat just one."

This is creating not only a rising market for vacation-home builders, and furniture companies, but also great growth potential for the second homes' local economies. Most people savoring family/getaway time will pay local workers to cut their grass, clean their houses, and check on the properties while they're away. According to the WCI Communities' survey, Splitters pay far more into their new communities than they take out—they don't use the schools, but they do buy phone, cable, satellite TV, and local recreational attractions, and they spend close to $2,000 per year on home repairs, upgrades, and remodeling.

As a policy matter, the surge in middle-class second-home buying means that the second-home mortgage deduction may not be the "sop to the rich" that it may at first glance appear. Picture an aspiring politician with a populist impulse. He's looking for new issues to appeal to middle-class voters, and he calls for eliminating the second-home mortgage deduction because he assumes it was planted in the tax code by and for the wealthy. To his surprise, he's ticked off a bunch of very ordinary people, who then send him 5 million pieces of complaint mail. People are passionate about their homes, including their second homes. There is a lot of potential in organizing second-home buyers—they have product needs like bill-paying, revolving credit, and insurance—and they have political needs like low interest rates and high home appreciation.

On a societal level, the second-home buyer trend also represents a rejection of the 1990s philosophy of putting your savings into the stock market instead of your home. Now, it goes into your homes. This shift will make Americans less liquid, Social Security more dependent again on real estate values, and perhaps promote more savings. Unlike the stock market, though, the real estate market depends almost entirely on leverage to succeed.

Moreover, with millions of middle-class Americans having tied up their savings in real estate, there is suddenly a profound new interest in what the Federal Reserve might do. Beyond the business and government elites, did anyone used to care who the Fed chair was, and what his cryptic pronouncements meant? Now there are millions of regular people whose financial stability depends on those quarter-percent increases and decreases. If the Fed gets it wrong, policymakers can expect anger from new quarters. It's a whole new group of people intent on something, ready to lash out if this interest feels threatened. And if the Fed is not careful, it could raise interest rates and push a lot of middle-class people into bankruptcy who bought second homes on credit, but find they can't pay the two mortgages.

The American Dream used to be two cars in every garage. Now it's two garages for every car.

Modern Mary Poppinses

College-Educated Nannies

▲

With more and more Moms working, there has been an explosion in the child care industry. The demand for nannies has gone through the roof, nearly doubling in the past fifteen years. This has bid wages up, increased competition, and also created a new class of nannies: the well-educated nanny.

Often coming from families with lots of children and missing the excitement of that kind of household, this well-educated nanny takes full control of the kids while Mom is at work, perhaps under the supervision of a nannycam.

The role of nannies in the upper class has changed from mother's helper, when Mom was at home; to primary caregiver during the workday (until preschool kicks in) and afternoon caregiver after that. Even in the toniest of families, women are choosing to go back to work, and this is creating demand for a new kind of nanny.

The formal nanny system is really from Europe, but Americans have been entranced with the idea, especially in pop culture, for decades. *Mary Poppins*, the 1964 film about a nanny who literally blows into town and shows children how to find magic all around them, is to this day the biggest Oscar-winning movie in Disney history. In the fall of 2006, it was made into a multimillion-dollar Broadway extravaganza.

The Sound of Music, in which nun-in-training Maria leaves her convent to care for a widowed Austrian's seven unruly children, is one of the most popular American films of all time.

In the 1990s, the hit series *The Nanny*, starring Fran Drescher as the jilted lover/cosmetic saleswoman who ends up caring for the children of a wealthy British Broadway producer, was wildly successful, ultimately playing on four continents.

And the two nanny shows of 2005—Fox's *Nanny 911* and ABC's *Supernanny*—both of which reaffirmed the stereotype that hefty British schoolmarms know more about childrearing than hapless American parents ever will—pulled in millions of viewers each week.

These pop culture nannies are well groomed and respected by their employers, and for the most part considered their emotional and intellectual equals. Indeed, both Maria in *The Sound of Music* and Fran in *The Nanny* end up marrying the men who hired them—raising from subtext to story line the idea that nannies are as worthy and as cherished as Moms.

Of course in real life, nannies aren't always revered the same way. According to Domestic Workers United, a New York City–based advocacy group, most in-home workers are low-income, poorly educated, or both. Many are illegal, and care for other people's children because the informality of home-based hiring helps them fly under the radar of the immigration authorities.

Now there's nothing new about the fact that there might be a gap between popular culture and reality. What is new is that after all these years, fact is actually inching closer to fiction. Increasingly, upscale, college-educated Americans who can compete elsewhere in the workforce are choosing to stay home with other people's kids. The industry is as yet too unregulated to have precise data on this. But two things are happening. First, there is an intense desire on the part of well-heeled parents for nannies with a college degree. Second, there is an increasing interest on the part of college graduates to help raise well-heeled kids. They are having their own children later, so their availability during the post-college years, when they previously would have been taking care of their own kids, has skyrocketed. The irony is that these nannies delay having their own families in order to take care of someone else's.

From the parents' point of view, well, there is little that many upscale parents today *wouldn't* do to help prepare their child for adulthood, from fighting fiercely for private school admission, paying for tutoring for IQ and other tests, and coaching aggressively toward top athletic performance. About 25 million Moms are in the workforce now, compared to just 13 million in 1970. Something like 1 million households now employ nannies, with the greatest proportion of them being high-income. If you're an upscale parent who can get someone to discuss Shakespeare with little Ashley *while* preparing her peanut butter and jelly—well, who wouldn't want that?

That demand has jacked up salaries. In 2005, the average national nanny salary was $590 a week, or $532 for live-ins. Nannies with a college degree are said to earn 20 to 60 percent more. So for a college graduate, that's an average annual salary of about $43,000—well over the $22,000 that the average 18–24-year-old female makes coming out of school with a bachelor's degree. More pay, less stress.

Moreover, from the nanny's point of view, in-home child care can be a perfect way to prepare for a career in teaching, child development, or child research. Or, dare I say it, parenting. Since fewer and fewer American women marry, and those who do delay childrearing until later and later, people who really love kids might find that nannying gives them time with some, for now, that they can really enjoy.

And finally, as demand for and supply of college-educated nannies grows, the systems for linking them are becoming more efficient. What used to be a word-of-mouth, luck-of-the-moment, neighborhood-based undertaking is now a serious national industry. In 1987, there were forty-five nanny agencies in America. By 2004, there were 900. And what with chat rooms, electronic databases, and elaborate matching systems, there is practically no reason to limit oneself. Want to spend two years in San Francisco before deciding if you should go to business school there? Find yourself a nice local family and hunker down with the kids.

It even turns out that there can be career growth, within the same family. Parents who have come to enjoy having a steady, warm adult around the house may not want to give her up just because the kids have outgrown her. Those with college educations who *don't* aspire to business school can readily be promoted to "nanny" the parents, serving as a sort of personal assistant, managing travel arrangements, bills, research, household renovations, and other household employees. Maybe from there she moves to work in Mom's or Dad's company. It's not a bad set of options.

Maybe—like Robin Williams's second wife—one moves from nanny to personal assistant to *wife and Hollywood producer*. Now that's something.

The rise in college-educated nannies means a couple of key things. First, the nannies have needs. Apart from a place to stand at tee-ball practice—go to any sports activity for upscale preschoolers and you'll see the parents and the nannies gracefully self-segregated on the sidelines, with the college-educated nannies hovering awkwardly in the middle. But more broadly, the nannies need a community. A way to share both child care tips and boss-related exasperation. Something like a chat room expanding upon *The Nanny Diaries*, the 2002 best-selling novel (and 2007 forthcoming movie) chronicling an NYU student's romp as the nanny for a spoiled, dysfunctional New York family.

Employers have needs, too. Parents who think they've found a gold mine in a nanny who can help their kids with calculus may think twice in a few years, when (a) their private lives are splashed up on the big screen; or (b) their employee has led the drive to publicize industry-wide mistreatment, underpay, and/or overexpectations on the part of employer parents. How long, really, until there are nanny unions?

Third, think of the other nannies. As much as Modern Mary Poppinses could threaten employers' relatively unregulated freedom, they could pose an even greater threat to the low-income and immigrant women who have come to regard nanny work as theirs. Depending on their own industriousness, this group might either start demanding "household management" and other nanny-improvement courses, to keep them valuable to their employers in an ongoing capacity — or they might retreat to a less popular form of caregiving: the elderly. From an economic and health care perspective, this could actually be a welcome development. According to a report from the 2005 White House Conference on Aging, America needs 1.2 million more paid caregivers, including nursing and home health aides, by 2010. Maybe they'll come from the ranks of displaced nannies.

Here's another thought. If it is true that when it comes to nannies, pop culture leads reality, we might also want to keep our eye out for male nannies, sometimes known as "mannies." At the moment, men probably occupy only about 1 percent of all domestic child care positions. But to look at pop culture, you'd think it was an equal-gender calling. No fewer than nine prime-time shows in recent years have featured male nannies — including the top-rated *Friends, Ally McBeal, Murphy Brown,* and yes, *The Nanny.*

So mannies may be coming. Nanny salaries are growing; stigmas about men doing "women's work" are eroding; more and more single Moms want steady male influences for their children; and the rise in obese children has triggered a demand for more "athletics-focused" caretakers. It's an atmosphere ripe for mannies. According to the British Web site www.celebrity. com, Britney Spears already has one (although the guy's Mom insists he's really more of a bodyguard).

With the decline of manufacturing jobs, the expectation that women will work outside the home, and a majority of Americans at least starting college, college-educated nannies are suddenly available, and they match the new desires on the part of Moms to have nannies who reflect their own personalities and lifestyles. Child care has had an ambivalent but growing role in the American household, and the glut of college dropouts suggests that we will see a lot of previously low-skilled jobs taken by a new class of worker. (Just ask your massage therapist, hairdresser, or flight attendant the name of her sorority, or what her major was.)

And, of course, watch out—and make sure you have a signed nondisclosure agreement—or your family's private conflicts and shortcomings might get exposed to the world, via the cunning pen of your onetime nanny/liberal arts major from Yale.

Shy Millionaires

Americans Who Live Below Their Means

▲

Millionaires loom large in our national imagination. *Who Wants to Be a Millionaire* was the most watched game show ever. We grew up on Richie Rich comic books, Thurston Howell III in *Gilligan's Island*, and J. R. Ewing in *Dallas*. For an astounding eleven years, America watched *Lifestyles of the Rich and Famous*, where week after week, Robin Leach showed us how millionaire celebrities spend lavishly on cars, houses, and other trappings of Lots of Cash.

And while some of today's superrich—like Bill Gates and Warren Buffett—are giving away their money to charity, others—like Paris Hilton—are living tabloid lives that embarrass and fascinate us no end.

But perhaps as a result, we have a bit of a skewed perception about American wealth. According to recent surveys, most Americans think there are far more millionaires in America than there really are—by about 4-fold. A survey done in the late 1990s—when only about 4 percent of households had net assets over $1 million—showed that the public believed that 15 percent of households were that rich. (Today, there are 9 million people in America worth $1 million or more, exclusive of their homes.)

Similarly, most people mis-guess what millionaires look like. With Mr. Howell—or maybe Daddy Warbucks, or Montgomery Burns of *The Simpsons*—in mind, they picture opulent mansions, chauffeured limousines, luxury watches, and maybe some kind of faux British accent. They figure most rich people inherited their wealth, or got it through impossibly privileged circumstances, including private elementary schools and elite universities.

But in fact, according to the authors of the best-selling *The Millionaire Next Door: The Surprising Secrets of America's Wealthy*, the average millionaire in America went to public school, drives an American-made car (and not this year's model), and received zero inheritance.

His accent is likely as plain as his penny loafers.

And he isn't that interested in telling you how much money he has. Most millionaires would not be caught dead in a limo. It is the antithesis of what they believe in. Even the limo companies have had to shift to SUVs.

According to a 2003 survey and analysis by Harris Interactive, there are actually six different kinds of millionaires—and the biggest group is the quietest one. Here are the six:

1. "Deal Masters" (think Gordon Gekko of the movie *Wall Street*)
2. "Altruistic Achievers" (think Bruce Wayne, the public face of Batman)
3. "Secret Succeeders" (like "Citizen" Charles Foster Kane)
4. "Status Chasers" (Scarlett O'Hara)
5. "Satisfied Savers" (Oliver Wendell Douglas of *Green Acres*), and
6. "Disengaged Inheritors" (Dudley Moore's Arthur)

While the cliché of the Really Rich is that they are either ambitious and domineering (like Gekko) or petty and spoiled (like Arthur)—it turns out that those two kinds of millionaires actually represent the smallest groups, together making up less than a quarter of all American rich people.

The largest group, by far, is the Satisfied Savers, who are those millionaires who have worked hard, saved much, and live below their means. When given the choice, they identify with Ford over Mercedes; they aspire not to material gain, but to a long, healthy life; and they splurge on little to nothing. According to the authors of *The Millionaire Next Door*, the majority of American millionaires are not heiresses or movie stars; they are welding contractors, pharmacists, and pest controllers. They wear inexpensive watches and drive used cars. They got rich by investing well and being frugal—and now that they are rich, they still live the same way.

One of the next largest groups of millionaires is the Secret Succeeders— those who didn't expect their wealth, and fear at any moment they will lose it. These are the people who still shop at Target and worry that people may find out they have money. Together, the Satisfied Savers and the Secret Succeeders make up more than 40 percent of America's rich. (But if you have the chance to choose a dinner partner, go with the Satisfied Savers. They'll probably pick the Olive Garden over the Four Seasons, but at least they won't stiff you with the check.)

What is the significance of America's Shy Millionaires—and rich people in general who live well below their means?

America's Millionaires, 2003

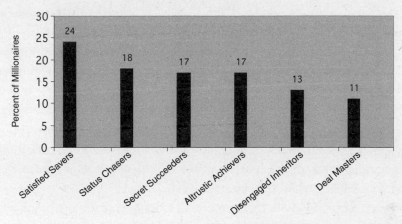

Source: Phoenix/Harris Interactive Wealth Survey, 2003

First, their presence suggests why "class warfare" polemics rarely win in American politics. (See, e.g., Al Gore, circa 2000.) Promising to give the rich their comeuppance on behalf of "the little guy" has its shortcomings when many Americans believe that they, too, can be millionaires. Class warfare language directed at people who have worked hard to get where they are is a very unpredictable way to talk to American voters. It is quite different in Britain, where privilege is presumed to be behind success, but in America, equal opportunity is one of our most cherished values.

Under-the-radar millionaires have particular implications for the estate tax, known to its opponents as the "death tax." As of 2006, any estate worth more than $2 million at the time of its owner's death is subject to a tax as high as 46 percent on the portion that exceeds $2 million. A heated debate regularly takes place in Congress regarding the propriety of this tax, the size of the exemption, and so forth. While only a tiny percentage of Americans are directly affected by the tax, opposition to it has always been more popular than you'd expect, and this group might be one reason why: Shy Millionaires don't want to flaunt their wealth, but they do want to hold on to it.

Finally, while Shy Millionaires are evidently not good targets for opulent jewelry, designer clothing, or luxury cars, there are three places they do put their money.

First, they invest, and many do so with the help of financial services experts. They respect people and strategies that make their money work for them, and financial planners and brokerage houses would do well to look for customers not just in country clubs but in much more pedestrian venues. Charles Schwab sponsors golf tournaments, but these millionaires spend too much time working to be found there. They are more likely at Staples and Costco, looking for a good deal.

Second, Shy Millionaires pay for private school. According to the authors of *The Millionaire Next Door*, only 17 percent of millionaires ever attended a private school, but more than half send their children to one. This is the sea change in families that acquire wealth. Not only does it signal the increasing flight of many successful families from America's public schools, but it also underscores an intense growth in demand for private K–12 education — triggering all kinds of unexpected strategies among private school parents, including holding children back a year to make them more competitive.

Third, Shy Millionaires give to charity. Along with Altruistic Achievers, Satisfied Savers are the most generous of the millionaires, and they see part of their core role as helping to assist others who are less fortunate. So just as marketers need to dig beneath the opulence for potential customers, nonprofits need to dig beneath the big foundations for potential funders. And in that case, if you hit the Shy Millionaire jackpot, you might just find your nonprofit organization bequeathed a huge gift from the estate of that quiet, unassuming fellow with the twenty-year-old suits who used to say he admired your work.

The bottom line is that while Richie Rich might not be living next door, Marty Millionaire is. And very quietly, he's looking for financial services professionals, schools, and nonprofit organizations that share his regard for hard work, discipline, and the value of a dollar.

As America approaches fully 10 million millionaires, it's true that, at one level, a million bucks isn't what it used to be. (Remember Dr. Evil in *Austin Powers: International Man of Mystery*, who schemes to hold the world ransom for "One MILLION dollars" — only to be nudged by Number Two that that won't go very far. "Okay, then," he declares, "we hold the world ransom for one hundred BILLION dollars!") But by any measure, a million bucks is a sweet accomplishment — and those who are bashful about it are doing a lot more for their "class" than the billionaire braggadocios.

Bourgeois and Bankrupt

▲

In France, they used to parade you naked through the street as they seized your estate. In Dickensian England, they locked you in debtors' prison—which was better than putting you to death, which they were also allowed to do. In sixteenth-century Italy (as suggested in Shakespeare's *The Merchant of Venice*)—they could literally take a pound of flesh. In colonial America, they branded your palm with a "T" for thief, so that in the future everyone would know not to do business with you.

Ah, the bad old days of overextending your credit. Today in America, going bankrupt—while still a source of shame—is more like a personal finance management tool. In the past twenty-five years, personal bankruptcy filings in the U.S. have climbed nearly 350 percent, going from 1.2 per 1,000 people in 1980 to nearly 5.4 per 1,000 people in 2004. To put it in historical perspective, that's eighty times greater than the rate in 1920, when 6 people per *100,000* went bankrupt.

In raw numbers, the bankruptcy surge looks like this. In 1985, fewer than 350,000 people in America filed for personal bankruptcy protection. In 2005, filers topped 2 million.

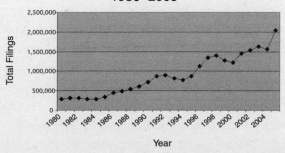

Total U.S. Nonbusiness Bankruptcy Filings, 1980–2005

Source: American Bankruptcy Institute, 2005

As Harvard Law Professor Elizabeth Warren has noted, that was more Americans than were diagnosed with cancer. More people went bankrupt in America in 2005 than graduated from college.

And this is as the economy has been growing.

Now we're not talking here about those innocuous, "reorganizing" corporate bankruptcies, like even Donald Trump does from time to time. Personal bankruptcy is, quite simply, the breaking point at which your credit card bills, mortgage payments, and medical debts so outpace your income that you just can't function anymore without the intervention of a court.

In some parts of the country, bankruptcy is practically a way of life. In Tennessee, Indiana, and Ohio, more than 10 out of every 1,000 people file for bankruptcy. (In Massachusetts, fewer than three do.)

But who are America's bankrupts, really? It's common to assume they're deadbeats—extravagant spenders who buy sixty-inch TVs and sports cars, and then realize they can't pay the mortgage. More than a few policymakers have claimed that the *reason* bankruptcies are rising in America is because there's no longer *enough* shame in overspending.

But according to Professor Warren, the high-on-the-hog bankruptcy-filer is a lot like the Welfare Queen of the 1980s—persuasive politics, but factually untrue.

The typical bankruptcy-filer is a white, middle-class head of household with children and a full-time job. Nearly half of bankruptcy filers are married. They are slightly better educated than the general population. Almost all of them suffered a catastrophic personal event, like job loss, divorce, or a serious medical problem. (Of those who suffered a medical problem, fully three-quarters had health insurance when it started.) The fastest-growing group of bankruptees is seniors, who endure growing medical expenses not covered by insurance; but close on their heels are 20-somethings, whose student debts are at record highs.

Bankruptcy has become a Middle America event.

And why so many? The reason most often given for the recent surge in bankruptcy is the rise of easy credit. In 1970, only 51 percent of families had ever used credit cards; now, over 80 percent have. And you don't even have to have *good* credit to get one—in the 1990s, the rate of subprime lending (to people with troubled credit) grew even faster than the credit industry overall. Lenders complain about deadbeats, but the truth is they make more off interest and late fees from *struggling* customers than they lose from the complete defaulters. And with easier credit comes easier overextension.

Another commonly cited reason is America's abysmal savings rate. In 2005, we saved at a *negative* rate—for the first time since the Great Depression. 'Nuf said.

Finally, many experts say bankruptcy is up because its stigma is down. As new laws make filing easier (which they did until 2005), and more and more people file, more people know someone for whom it all worked out just fine. This justification may be more speculation than fact, however. Economists have calculated that, in fact, the bankruptcy stigma is alive and well; and three-quarters of filers say they were depressed after going through a bankruptcy.

According to Professor Warren, however, what is really going on here is the rising cost of being middle-class. Good public schools have become rare enough that in the neighborhoods they serve, there is an unprecedented bidding war for housing, and mortgages have shot through the roof. Add to that rising health care costs, and college tuition that is far outpacing inflation, and you have a very strapped middle class. And so while household income may be way up, *discretionary* income is down.

Which means that when crisis hits, there's no longer any cushion. In the typical middle-class family, Mom *already* works, so she can't go get a job for emergency income. The family *already* stretched to buy the cheapest house in the lowest passable school district. In today's middle class, finances are so taut that if a family is struck by job loss, divorce, or illness, they snap.

What does this mean for America?

Ironically, some of the bankruptcy rise is rooted in good news. When illness used to just kill us, we didn't have ongoing, astronomical medical bills. When college was only for a select few, most people didn't drown in student loans. When hardly anyone could get credit, hardly anyone defaulted.

In fact, the option of a dignified bankruptcy is considered one of the healthy underpinnings of our economy. While the U.S. frets about personal debt, some in Europe and Japan are pressing for *more* bankruptcy options in order to generate more risk and entrepreneurship. Failure is a product of trying, of taking risk. If we never tried to go to the moon, we would never have had the *Columbia* space shuttle accident. Or, as the CEO of the now bankrupt Eastern Air Lines reportedly said, "Capitalism without bankruptcy is like Christianity without hell."

But even if, at some level, bankruptcy reflects general societal progress, the current rush of Americans in financial ruin is cause for serious attention. At the macro level, it reflects the trouble in our education system, if so few districts are passable that people overspend on housing just to get their kids a reasonable education; and in our health care system, if even the insured can be hurled into ruin with one major medical event.

And at a more immediate level, the fact that there are 2 million people stretched to the breaking point means there is a growing market for credit-counseling, finance-coaching, and money-management training. Why is it that we wouldn't let a 16-year-old on the road without a driver's license, but two years later we'll give her a credit card without so much as a basic financial literacy test? Almost no school in America teaches personal finance instruction, and yet 1 in 3 high school seniors has a credit card.

So if you are one of those companies holding a lot of subprime loans, watch out. Your portfolio is likely to take an unexpected whack if these trends continue, and you will be owning a lot of real estate in the decade to come. We are likely to see fewer infomercials on how to get rich quick with real estate—and instead more on "how to get out from under the crush" of all those houses you bought. Since you can almost always keep your house in Florida when you go bankrupt, that state has been a powerful magnet for the famously bankrupt.

If personal bankruptcies keep rising at current rates, there will be nearly 8 million people going bankrupt a year by 2025. While this is a country that was built on the backs of opportunity for all, America has instead in the last few years seen the squeeze of the middle class and the rise of the bankrupt class. And that is a critical challenge for us all for the future.

Non-Profiteers

▲

No country in the world is more closely associated with free markets, capitalism, and the private sector than the United States. This is the Land of Opportunity. "Rags to Riches" is practically our national mantra. *Show Me the Money!*

Those who can, earn a bundle; those who can't, regulate them. Or, as Ronald Reagan put it (and what, in a partisan moment, I might say has been a self-fulfilling prophecy for the Republican Party): "The best minds are not in government. If any were, business would hire them away."

I personally disagree, of course. Although I've spent my whole career in the private sector, some of my best friends, closest colleagues, and favorite clients do government work with brilliant results. But lately, the public-private sector tension has become less and less relevant. Since the late 1970s, neither business *nor* government has grown at a very impressive rate, in terms of attracting employees. What has grown, however, is the "third" sector—also called the independent sector or the nonprofit sector. Compared to business's and government's lackluster employment growth rates of 1.8 and 1.6 percent, respectively, between 1977 and 2001, nonprofit employment grew at a robust 2.5 percent.

Here's what that means in actual jobs. In 1977, 6 million people worked in the nonprofit sector. By 2001, that number had more than doubled, to 12.5 million.

With 12.5 million employees, the nonprofit sector is still the smallest of the three, but it's by far the fastest-growing. And work within nonprofits is now so varied, and so relatively well supported, that you can make a serious career in America without ever stepping foot into government *or* the hallowed halls of business.

As a result, there has been a quiet rise of the Nonprofit Class. People who spend whole careers never thinking about shareholders, profits, or year-end bonuses; people who aspire to compensation that grows incrementally, not

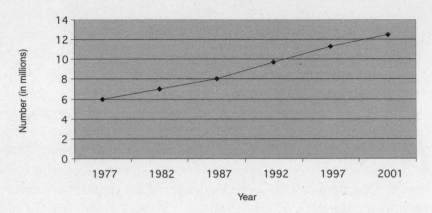

Number of Employees in the Nonprofit Sector,
1977–2001

Source: Independent Sector, *Nonprofit Almanac*, 2001

exponentially; people for whom *Show Me the Money* is just a quirky scene in a 1990s football movie.

Why the Non-Profiteer surge?

First, donors' funds have made it possible. The world's superrich are growing—there were almost 700 billionaires in 2005, compared to 423 in 1996—and the pressure on them to give generously is real. (So are the benefits of the tax deductions.) And so between 1993 and 2003, the number of foundations in America nearly doubled, with assets growing over 150 percent to $476 billion. In turn, the number of registered nonprofit organizations grew to almost 1.5 million.

As a result, nonprofit work can be rich and varied—from hospitals to higher ed, from museums to mosques, from anti-poverty programs to pro-environment efforts. And "nonprofit" doesn't have to mean nonsubsistence. While entry-level salaries in the nonprofit sector tend to be about 10 percent lower than in government and 20 percent lower than in business, a 2005 Pennsylvania study found that the average nonprofit wage in that state was only 5 percent lower than the average private sector wage ($641/week versus $679/week). And at the nonprofit chief executive level, one can do quite well: between 2004 and 2005, the median compensation of the nation's largest nonprofits' chief executives—fully $327,575—rose faster than the bosses' pay at the nation's 500 biggest companies. In 2007, the former head of the Smithsonian had close to a $1 million pay package until Congress got wind of it.

Second, nonprofits may be growing in appeal because the private sector has taken a beating. And I don't mean just the recent Enron and WorldCom debacles, or even Martha Stewart. Since 1981, the percentage of Americans who think corporations need to be reined in has grown from 18 to 34 percent. Between 2001 and 2006 alone, the percentage of Americans saying that corporations ought to have less influence in this country grew from 1 in 2 to nearly 2 in 3. And government isn't any more beloved. Trust in government to handle America's problems has fallen from the low 70 percents in the early 1970s to the low 50s now. So while nonprofits are not without their own public trust problems, they are by and large considered less dangerous, less greedy, and more helpful than either of the other sectors.

A third reason for the surge in Non-Profiteers is that the nonprofit sector itself is maturing, and beginning to tackle social problems that used to belong to the government, with the kind of innovation and discipline that used to belong to business. In the old days, nonprofits meant basically soup kitchens and tutoring centers, and maybe brought to mind rapscallion United Way heads and infighting at the Red Cross. Now a growing number of nonprofits, representing a movement called "social entrepreneurship," are buckling down with disciplined business plans, rigorous metrics, and ambitious plans for scale. Funders support them with an approach called "venture philanthropy," which is hands-on investment, modeled on the private sector's venture capital. As a result, Non-Profiteers around the world are making a big difference, fast—much in the same way that start-up businesses either catch on quickly or collapse. And they're doing it on issues from changing how American colleges look at low-income talent, to franchising public toilets in Africa, to expanding microfinance in India. Given both the idealism and business sense of today's young people—is it any wonder that more and more of them are drawn to this sector? The attitudinal data bear that out: according to a 2006 Harris poll, American adults 65 and older have only lukewarm feelings toward nonprofits—but the feelings of those aged 18–39 are wildly positive.

Nonprofits are hot.

So let's take a closer look at the implications of this growing sector. One is that as the sector grows and attracts more and more talent, it will probably need to get its act together, gender-wise. While women make up nearly 70 percent of the nonprofit workforce—and are a majority of nonprofit executive directors—men still get the lion's share of the money, holding more than half of the number one slots in organizations that have budgets over $5 million. And that disparity arises even when the positions are the same: According to a 2006 study of the nation's largest nonprofits, men are paid over 50 percent more than women even in the same position. Clearly, many women like nonprofit work, perhaps because it is morally rewarding, family-friendly, and/or supplemented by a husband's larger income. But especially in a sector that draws people who want to repair the world, those pay gaps don't seem likely to be tolerated much longer.

Another challenge of the maturing nonprofit sector is turnover. As nonprofits shift and evolve, their annual turnover, at 3.1 percent, is higher than in either the private sector (2.7 percent) or the public sector (1 percent). If nonprofits are to sustain the growth their leaders envision, and their causes require, they will need to invest in top-of-the-line HR systems that grow and retain employees—not to mention ensure that starting salaries are high enough for young employees to pay back their staggering student loans.

Expect greater government scrutiny as well. As the nonprofit sector grows in dollars, people, and impact—particularly given the growth of political nonprofits—expect more resources to be devoted to checking out whether all registered 501(c)(3)s are truly "in the common good" and deserving of their tax-exempt status.

The bottom line is that the sectors are beginning to blur. When enormous foundations take up reforming America's high schools, or addressing Africa's AIDS crisis—or when savvy nonprofits spot under-tapped value and follow aggressive business plans to bring it into line with market forces—the public/private/nonprofit distinction starts to seem important only as a legal matter. The actual work can feel pretty much the same.

Whereas the nonprofit sector used to be regarded as a sort of backwater to the business world, and as a poor cousin to the formidable public sector, it is now increasingly becoming a destination of first resort. Not only is talent flocking there—giving the other sectors a run for their money in terms of employees—but with its emerging blend of businesslike discipline and governmentlike compassion, the nonprofit sector may yet arise to be the one the others look to. Best-selling author Jim Collins, in his *Good to Great* sequel monograph, *Good to Great and the Social Sectors*, claims that the next generation of leaders in America will be the ones who can blend social-problem-solving ability with serious business skills. That combination of skills seems to be just where many modern nonprofits are landing.

And so millions of young people wary of global economic competition in the corporate world, and not so trusting of government service, now have a growing alternative lifestyle—a career as a Non-Profiteer. As a result, more of them are choosing not just to do good for themselves but to do good for others.

PART XI

Looks and Fashion

Uptown Tattooed

▲

What art form has, at different times in its history, signified royalty, loyalty, criminality, circuses, and coming of age in the Ivy League? Yes, tattooing, or the practice of permanently decorating your skin via hot, painful needles. From the Tahitian word *tatau*, meaning "to mark," tattoos have been used throughout human history to identify social status, fulfill religious rites, denote pirates and spies, and declare youthful independence.

And what started in the U.S. as part of the hippie and motorcycle gang movement has gone mainstream—for young people, getting a tattoo is becoming as common as getting your ears pierced. Tattoos have become high fashion.

Hair was once the signature form of rebellion and individuality in the face of parental and societal consternation. Now it seems hair has gone short, with going bald more common among men than going long. Body art has become the way more and more of us like to signal our individuality, in America and around the world. And unlike hair, which everyone can see at a glance, tattoos are usually hidden so they are part our private individuality, revealed only to those who get to see the full inner person, or those who share our locker rooms.

So in case you still associate tattoos with bikers, sailors, criminals, or other lowlifes, you should get over it, and preferably before your 20-something child—the one with the college degree and the excellent job prospects—comes home for Thanksgiving with a red rose, or maybe a Chinese symbol for virtue, stamped on her hip. According to a 2003 Harris poll, more than 1 in 3 Americans aged 25–29 have a tattoo. Nearly a quarter of university students have them. (Something like 13 percent of Americans aged 18–24 have a tattoo *and* a body piercing, not counting women with pierced ears.)

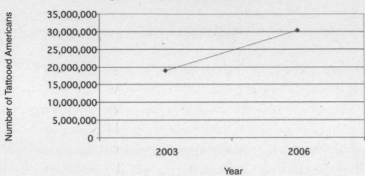

Estimated Number of Tattooed Americans
Aged 18–49, 2003–2006

Sources: *Journal of American Academy of Dermatology*, 2006; U.S. Census, 2003, 2006

Overall, as of 2006, more than 30 million Americans—or nearly 1 in 4 adults—have tattoos, up from fewer than 20 million just three years ago.

This tattoo phenomenon is not only limited to the United States. Folks in Britain, Australia, and Japan are also lining up to paint their bodies. Some 8 percent of Canadian teens have tattoos, according to a survey done in 2000, and 61 percent of these teens are girls.

And so once a signifier of the down-and-dirty, tattooing is now every-person's rite. Boys do it; girls do it; people wearing pearls do it. Indeed, in the Harris poll, the *best-represented* income group among tattooed Americans (22 percent) are people making over $75,000. By contrast, only 8 percent of people making $15,000–$25,000 have gone under the electric paintbrush. In other words, the richer you are these days, the *more likely* you are to have a tattoo.

Part of the appeal is, no doubt, rebellion. A little Japanese pictograph con-notes far greater worldliness than, say, one's provincial parents could ever pull off. A little athletic or cultural symbol locks in one's identity, literally "brand-ing" oneself to peers. Like cigarettes in the 1970s or hot rods in the 1950s, tat-toos are today's edgy-but-not-*too*-dangerous way for middle-class kids to show off their wild side.

But it's not just the liberal, rebel types. To more conservative folks, tat-toos also represent discipline and loyalty. How better to demonstrate the core conservative ideals of permanence and commitment than to burn an idea (or a person) into your very being? According to the Harris poll, 14 percent of Republicans in the U.S. have tattoos. While that's slightly less than the percentage of Democrats, it's still something like 7 *million tattooed Republicans* walking around in America.

Why tattoo? According to the Harris poll, one in three people say it makes them feel sexier, including nearly half of all tattooed women. One in four people with tattoos say it makes them feel more attractive.

And they're in trendy company. Film star Angelina Jolie has at least a dozen tattoos, including a tribal dragon on her left biceps (which used to be nestled under a "Billy Bob" tattoo, until they split up and she had his name lasered off). Rapper 50 Cent's entire back is covered in tattoos. Britney Spears apparently has a fairy, a daisy, a butterfly, the Chinese symbol for "mystery," and three Hebrew letters burned onto her feet, stomach, and neck. Soccer star David Beckham tattooed his arm and back with the names of his wife and sons.

And lest we forget those Republicans, former Secretary of State George Shultz is said to have a Princeton Tiger tattooed on his rear end—a claim he refuses to confirm or deny.

But as the tattoo clientele moves from criminals to coeds, from the dispossessed to debutantes, what are the implications for America?

First, tattoo artists might want to do what every expanding service does—move upscale, set up proper licensing and regulation, increase prices, modernize the designs and graphics, and set up national chains, with a few celebrity spokespersons. (Jolie or Beckham alone could sell millions of tattoos on TV.) There are now estimated to be anywhere from 4,000 to 15,000 tattoo parlors in the U.S., up from 300 just twenty years ago. This is a potential billion-dollar marketplace—in something as elevated as "body art," with mainstream demand—and yet it's still being run by mom-and-pop shops that sell *Dungeons and Dragons* card sets. Where is the McDonald's of tattoos—with standardized brand, safety assurances, and national advertising? (And where is the Le Cirque, with the most elite artists for the most elite clientele?) Such a rolling-up of the business could double the market overnight.

Look for changes in official policies, too. Although the U.S. Coast Guard still rejects recruits with visible tattoos, or ones that cover more than 25 percent of a lower arm or leg, the Army changed its policy in 2006 to allow tattooed hands or necks so long as the tattoos are not "extremist, indecent, sexist, or racist."

Does even that restriction violate the First Amendment? Just as long hair was once ruled protected speech, isn't a tattoo constitutionally protected speech, too? Is the day far off that the Supreme Court will have to get into the tattoo business as well? (Will anyone recuse him- or herself, pleading a personal derma-secret under the black robes?) Imagine the impact of a ruling that tattoos are part of our inalienable rights.

Google and Yahoo! already allow body art on their employees. So do Ford and Wells Fargo. Those organizations with tattoo bans still in place—like Starbucks, McDonald's, Blockbuster, and many police departments around the nation—may soon revisit their policies, since body art bans may exclude lots of fresh young talent.

And the federal government may need a piece of the action, too. To date, the FDA has not put its seal of approval on any tattoo pigments or ink, but what with the numbers of tattoos in America soaring like the butterfly on Drew Barrymore's stomach, the regulatory agency may yet decide it needs to step in.

Of course, what's ironic about the Uptown Tattooed is that in their quest to show a little edge—their bad-boy and bad-girl side—they've actually ended up joining a very mainstream crowd. Oh sure, the Asian tiger on the deltoid. Been there, inked that.

So the question is what's the *next* trend, now that ear-piercing is conservative, tattooing is mainstream, and body-piercing is a yawn. Will flesh-as-advertising-space catch on? If you can be art, why can't you be a billboard? How about $10 an hour for walking around the beach with a "Buy at Sunglass Hut" tattoo?

Perhaps the tattoo industry has not developed to the next level because people believe it is a passing fad—like the hula hoop. But more likely, using our bodies to make political, sexual, romantic, and fraternal statements is here to stay, and the technology will develop to enable disappearing tattoos, 3D tattoos, and glowing tattoos. Moreover, since people who have them like to socialize with other people who have them—as the numbers keep growing, the numbers are likely to keep growing.

Snowed-Under Slobs

▲

A merica has always fancied itself a country that values neatness. It has never been a very formal country—but it is one where "put away your stuff" is heard every day in tens of millions of homes.

Neatness is such a craze it has spawned a $6 billion a year industry in home-organizing products, like plastic bins and file cabinets. We lay out $3 billion on top of that just trying to organize our closets. Every New Year's, we resolve to "reduce clutter" almost as much as we resolve to lose weight.

And when Moms aren't nagging us to be neater, religion is. "Cleanliness is next to godliness" is said to be a second-century Hebrew proverb. The so-called Bible Diet promises "40 Days to Cleanliness." In Islam, it is said that "purity and neatness are half of faith." At least one recent study found that two-thirds of us feel guilt or shame about how messy we are.

But despite the commercial, cultural, and religious pressure to Clean Up Our Act, there is a growing group of Americans who just won't, or don't, or can't. And it's not because they love mess, or think it's liberating or inspiring. They are just swamped with stuff, and given the volume of things in their lives, they have simply decided that all the straightening, sorting, and scrubbing isn't worth it.

While my personal philosophy is to keep everything fairly neat, I have adopted a utilitarian approach to filing and neatness. If you are going to look at something at most once, if ever, don't create a file for it. For example, in 2006, just throw all the bills into a bin—"Bills 2006," and don't bother to create a file for every different type of bill. If you ever need to find something, spend the time filing then. It's my own system to keep myself from drowning in useless filing, even though today most everything is online. But more and more people are adopting an even simpler philosophy—just give up and give in—and let the mess begin.

In the spring of 2007, we did a quick poll to find out just who America's Slobs are, and how messy they are compared to everybody else. We carved out "Slobs" as anyone who identified him or herself as "very messy," anyone who said *others* would call him or her a slob, or anyone who said that messiness has in some way slowed them down or lessened their quality of life. The incidence of such hard-core Slobs in America was about 1 in 10. Of 200 million adults in America, that's 20 million people.

The Slobs are not, as you might have thought, overwhelmingly male. Men do outnumber women, but only by 55 to 45 percent. And neither are the Slobs slothful or unsuccessful. More than 2 in 3 are employed full-time, and of those that have kids, most of them have kids under 5. They are significantly *more* likely than Non-Slobs to have finished college and/or graduate school. They are twice as likely as Non-Slobs to make over $100,000 a year. And Slobs identify as liberal at nearly twice the rate of Non-Slobs (37 versus 19 percent), with a remarkable 47 percent of Slobs saying they are Democrats.

Fewer than 1 in 4 make their beds as part of a daily routine. More than 1 in 3 will leave dirty dishes in the sink more than a day. About 15 percent will even leave dirty dishes in their den, living room, or bedroom longer than a day. When they get undressed at night, almost 4 in 10 drop their clothes on the floor. One in 3 lets kitchen countertop clutter go uncleaned for more than a week, if not indefinitely.

In 2007, business experts Eric Abrahamson and David H. Freedman published *A Perfect Mess*, a book out to make the case for sloppiness. They said messy desks are linked to wisdom, experience, and higher salaries (which is consistent with our poll, at least for earners over $100,000). They said sloppiness allows for the qualities critical to greatness—like improvisation, adaptability, and serendipity. (If Alexander Fleming hadn't been sloppy enough to leave dirty Petri dishes lying around his desk, he would never have discovered penicillin.) They even said that messy people make better parents—focused as they are on warmth and hominess, rather than stacked-up toys and ring-free coffee tables.

They even hinted that clean is killing us. Doctors are now starting to credit the "hygiene hypothesis"—the idea that the sharp rise in childhood asthma and allergies today is attributable to the lack of exposure to certain germs. Chlorine bleach, which erases all mistakes one can make in clothing, is said to poison hundreds of kids a year, and may be linked to breast cancer in women and reproductive problems in men. Pesticides, those cure-alls for green trimmed lawns, have been linked to diminution of short-term memory, hand-eye coordination, and drawing ability in children. Suddenly dirt sounds *sane*, if not entirely *sanitary*. The Anti-Antiseptics may be on to something.

But our poll found that most Slobs are not so much embracing the mess as giving in to it. They are less out to prove that disorder is not a disorder, so much as to manage their own experience of it. More than two-thirds of Slobs said they wished they were neater (and none wished he or she was messier). Two-thirds of Slobs agreed that being neat helps people be in control of their lives. Hardly any Slobs defended messiness, with fewer than 1 in 4 saying it helps them be creative. Indeed, over half of Slobs said that even they *could never live with a slob*—pretty near the number of Non-Slobs who said that. This group is not about proselytizing pandemonium. They are just trying to manage their mess.

Because when people were asked *why* their houses get messy, both Slobs and everyone else led not with pride, or indifference, or even lack of time. They pleaded an overabundance of stuff. Having too much, and too few places to store it, made up more than half of the reason why America's Slobs are struggling.

What is the biggest reason your home gets dirty or messy?	All	Slobs
There's too much stuff	29	33
I don't have time to keep it clean and neat	18	22
There's not enough storage	17	18
My home doesn't really get dirty or messy	22	16
I/we don't care if it's messy	4	8
Mess helps me be creative	1	2
Don't know	7	2

And so this is a trend about overabundance in America—making it less like laziness, and more like obesity. We have a glut of possessions, like we have a glut of food. Hence the surge in Slobs among the wealthy. The more we *can* buy, the more we do buy—and get, and win, and collect, and keep. And while many people go out and spend on *more* stuff to help them organize their stuff, the Snowed-Under Slobs simply live amid it all, letting clutter be their natural environment, instead of fighting it one dish and dirty sock at a time.

The implications are significant. First, if you live with a Slob, stop nagging. Fully 76 percent of Slobs said they hate being nagged about being sloppy—much as the obese don't generally appreciate being harangued by (or eat any less as a result of) spouses' complaints. Slobs are not open to rational persuasion on this front; they're feeling bad enough about themselves as it is.

And if we all loosened up a bit, maybe life would be all that much more enjoyable. We are in an age of more permissive parents, greater individual expression, and greater personal choice. Neatness may not be a thing of the past, but for 1 in 10 Americans, it is just another one of those ideals that is unachievable due to the crush of work and responsibility. Failing to live up to modern standards of neatness is, as our poll shows, a "high-class" problem. The richer, more educated, and busier you are, the greater the likelihood you are one of the growing class of American Snowed-Under Slobs.

Surgery Lovers

▲

A very shy, demure friend of mine recently had Lasik surgery, which she found to be wonderfully effective and painless. For weeks afterward, she stunned everyone by asking, "What else should I have done? Do I need a nose job? Should I buy some silicones?"

Had she done either one, of course, she'd have had plenty of company. Cosmetic procedures, both invasive and noninvasive, have become so popular in America lately that between liposuction, Lasik, nose jobs, and tummy tucks—and the latest favorite, eyelash transplant surgery—it seems like it's the rare American who *hasn't* volunteered to go under the knife.

What used to be the genteel secret of aging, wealthy, white women is now spreading to everyone—including younger, middle-income, and non-Caucasian people. In 2005, 41 percent of surgeons surveyed said they're treating teens. Only 1 in 8 people considering plastic surgery have an income over $90,000; the biggest group (at 41 percent) have incomes between $31,000 and $60,000. And from 1999 to 2001, the number of African-Americans, Asian-Americans, and Hispanics seeking facial cosmetic and reconstructive surgery grew by over 200 percent.

Oh, and men. Of the 12 million cosmetic procedures performed in 2004, more than 1 million were performed on men. (In 2005, there was a 417 percent boost in the number of men who had "ablative skin-resurfacing"—which means peeling off the top layer of skin with a laser and heating the collagen underneath to "regenerate" it.) Ten years ago, a man wouldn't be caught dead on the plastic surgeon's table. Now, men are trying to stay competitive at work by looking more youthful and energetic, and they're trying to keep up with their perpetually youthful wives.

In fact, 1 in 3 surgeons surveyed in 2005 said they see husbands and wives coming in for cosmetic enhancements together. One-fifth of surgeons said mothers and daughters come in together—the numbers say that's probably a face lift for Mom and bigger breasts for Daughter. The family that "lifts" together shifts together.

What used to be a wink-wink secret for ladies (if their eyes could still flutter) is now an open pursuit for everyone. New technologies have made it a breeze. You can zip in and out in a day, or during lunch for Botox, and unlike the old days where one took a "vacation abroad," today there's hardly any recovery time. Many procedures cost less than a nice laptop. What's not to love?

Nothing, apparently. Since 1997, there has been a 444 percent increase in the U.S. in the number of cosmetic procedures, whether it's face lifts, breast enhancements, skin-resurfacings, or fat injections (into the lips). Americans spent almost $12.4 billion on cosmetic procedures in 2005—about the same amount we spent on physical fitness and exercise. Why work to improve your body if you can just buy a better one?

But here's what's really interesting, and kind of disturbing. While the number of cosmetic procedures has skyrocketed, the number of people undergoing them has risen at a slower rate. In other words, a significant number of cosmetic procedures in America are being done on the same people.

These aren't the painfully addicted people, who turn to surgery the way some people succumb to eating disorders. There are people, sometimes called "scalpel slaves," who get dozens of cosmetic surgeries, constantly thinking the next one will fix some gnawing problem in their lives. If the doctors don't turn them away, they can end up looking rather bizarre, even grotesque. (Michael Jackson, anyone?)

But short of truly ill "scalpel slaves," there is a growing group of regular, healthy Americans who try a modest cosmetic enhancement or two, and decide they are so fabulous that they just have to have a couple more.

In 2005, *over half* of facial surgeons' patients got more than one procedure—up from just 28 percent in 2001.

True, some of that dramatic growth reflects greater use of the interventions that call for ongoing treatment, like Botox and chemical peels. But that's *just* people getting facial work. If the rate were even half as high for people getting any cosmetic procedures or, say, over three years instead of one, you'd still have well over 2 million people in America who've gone for repeat elective cosmetic work on their bodies.

Some in the industry certainly want it that way. While the American So-

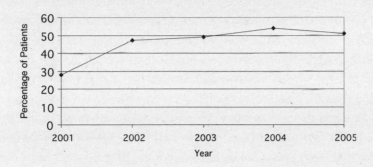

Percent of Plastic Surgery Patients Getting Multiple
Facial Procedures in Same Year, 2001–2005

Source: American Academy of Facial Plastic and Reconstructive Surgery, 2006

ciety for Dermatologic Surgery warns against doing multiple procedures at
once, plenty of Web sites, where the average American is more likely to turn,
hawk the idea. They claim that since overall recovery time is shorter, the in-
terruption to your life is smaller, the cost is lower, and there is no additional
risk to being under anesthesia for longer—then why not get your breasts en-
larged while you're getting them lifted, or get your face lifted while you're
getting your tummy tucked? Two-fers are a good deal, it seems, no matter the
industry.

And pop culture seals the deal. On ABC's 2002 show *Extreme Makeover*,
ordinary Americans can fulfill "lifelong dreams and fairy-tale fantasies," as
teams of plastic surgeons, dentists, dermatologists, Lasik surgeons, and "master body sculptors" come into their lives to fix everything that Nature didn't.

The explosion of plastic surgery in America reflects a virtually out-of-
control obsession with youth. Even as America ages, and the boomers at
60+ are the most populous generation, they still want to look and feel like
30-somethings. And our culture says Go For It. As we have seen elsewhere
in this book, Americans are living in an era of militant self-determination.
People are readier and abler than ever to date whomever they want, vote
however they feel, breed whenever they want, and worship however they
like, without regard to either the biological or cultural limitations that constrained their parents and grandparents. Who cares what I *used* to look like?
Who cares what 50-year-olds "naturally" look like? I will take control of

the information, resources, and experts available to me, and I will remake myself as I desire.

There will be consequences. *New York Times* columnist Maureen Dowd has mused, "What happens genetically when a man who has his nose done, chin augmented, and ears pinned back is attracted to a woman who's had her eyes done and her lips plumped up and her face lifted? And they have a baby and look at each other and moan, 'My God, where did this ugly baby come from?'" Plastic surgery for babies, of course.

And there's a Catch-22 in Hollywood. No one can get the big roles today without a perfectly smooth face, so everyone runs off to get Botox. But with cosmetically engineered faces, no one can really act with any lifelike facial emotion. Are middle-aged film characters done? From now on, every character in a blockbuster film is under 25? Even if they're played by a 40-year-old?

And what about the medical profession generally? At the moment, plastic surgery is a relatively small specialty among board-certified physicians. But increasingly, doctors trained in OB/GYN, general medicine, and even ER work are realizing that the Medical Beauty Business—what with its few emergencies, zero night calls, independence from insurance companies, same-day payments, and low malpractice costs—is a very sweet place to be. At least, for them. Unfortunately, there is already a serious doctor shortage on the horizon, given the expected medical needs of the aging boomers. If more and more doctors are drawn to servicing the healthy rather than healing the sick, that situation is only going to get worse.

Nonetheless, expect a boom in "Aesthetic Medicine," and a bit of a turf war among doctors as to who gets to practice it. (Can gynecologists really do facial peels?) Look also for lawsuits by patients who bought new eyebrows from doctors who, it turns out, were actually trained only in internal medicine.

People may not live forever. But for many, the appearance of living forever is enough, and they are willing to undergo surgery after surgery to make it real. While for most people, the goal is to *avoid* doctors, Surgery Lovers feel just the opposite—they crave the latest and greatest procedure to give them a boost of youth. Perhaps this trend will yield a generation of narcissists. Or it may spawn a generation with the self-confidence to overcome the luck of the draw when it comes to looks.

THE INTERNATIONAL PICTURE

Americans seem to be more alone than not, globally speaking, as they rush to plastic surgeons for a tummy tuck or a nose job. According to a survey conducted by ACNielsen in November 2006, 80 percent of people across forty-one countries said that plastic surgery is "not an option." Asia frowns on the practice even more, registering a disapproval rating of 86 percent.

That said, however, there are people throughout the world who would like to be waiting with the Americans in the plastic surgeon's outer office.

▲ Significant populations in Russia (48 percent), Greece (37 percent), the Baltic republics (35 percent), Ireland (31 percent), and Turkey (29 percent) said that they would "consider cosmetic surgery when I'm older." The Czechs, the Dutch, the Norwegians, and the Hungarians were wildly against it.

▲ While most of the top ten surgery-considering nations were European, Korea did buck the Asian trend by expressing interest at a rate of 28 percent. While many Asians disapprove of plastic surgery (94 percent in Hong Kong, 92 percent in Indonesia), Korea has 1,200 plastic surgeons, the highest per capita in the world. (To put this in perspective, California has only around 900.)

As in the U.S., surgery-loving men are on the rise. Wealthy Iranian men are flocking to get nose jobs, Kurdish men are secretly seeking out age-concealing treatments and hair transplants, and Korean men flock for procedures of all types.

▲ One survey of South Korean men between the ages of 25 and 37 showed that 86 percent believe that if they have a good appearance and fit body, they will be more competitive in the workplace. An estimated 56 percent were dissatisfied with their body.

The other global piece of the Surgery Surge is that more and more people are hopping in planes and engaging in "plastic surgery tourism"—in order to get the best price for their procedures. Favorite destinations include Venezuela, Brazil, the Dominican Republic, Colombia, Ecuador, Mexico, Thailand, and South Africa.

Powerful Petites

▲

There is no shortage of accounts—including in this book—about how America is getting bigger. Men are nearly three inches taller, on average, than we were a century ago. Both men and women are twenty-five pounds heavier, on average, than we were forty years ago. Like Peter Gabriel in his hit song "Big Time," our cars, our houses, our eyes, our mouths, are getting big big big big big. So much larger than life.

But while much of America is supersizing, there is a substantial group of little women who insist that size doesn't matter. Or rather, it does matter (if it's theirs)—and they don't intend for their small physical stature to give them short shrift.

They are America's Powerful Petites.

They came to America's attention in May 2006, when the *New York Times* reported that three of the country's most influential department stores—Neiman Marcus, Saks Fifth Avenue, and Bloomingdale's—had drastically shrunk or eliminated their petite departments.

A hue and cry arose, from five feet off the ground. From Houston to Orlando to Philadelphia to Fresno, the Petite Flap was reported on, opined about, and fretted over. By the end of June, Saks had changed its mind, and some of the clothing designers, who had shut down their petite lines in response to the department stores' decisions, reopened.

Little Women are apparently Big Business.

In retrospect, it seems that the department stores had made a reasonable judgment. Whereas petite sales were a growing industry overall—up 11 percent to $10 billion in 2005, with stores like The Gap and Ann Taylor expanding their lines—petites had fallen off as a percentage of department store sales. The retailers wanted to make room for bags and shoes and jeans, which were selling better.

But the Little Ladies of America would have none of it.

It turns out that most of the really vocal protesters were elite shoppers (this was Saks and Neiman Marcus, after all) and they were decades-long customers, meaning they were older. Indeed, some of the news stories speculated that one of the reasons the stores had tried to do away with their petite departments was that they were trying to lose their association with older, drabber, and pushier ladies—precisely the ones who came out swinging.

But peeved matrons aside, the Great Petite Flap of 2006 tells us something about short women in America.

Because even as the American frame grows longer, there have never been as many petite women in America as there are today.

In the garment industry, "Petite" means clothing for women 5'4" and under. Along with "Juniors" (teens), "Misses" (women starting at 5'5"), and "Plus-Sizes" (sizes 14–28), "Petite" completes the universe of women's clothing. In addition to shorter hemlines, petite clothing generally also means narrower shoulders, higher armholes, smaller buttons, and shorter waist-to-hip lines. If you're 5'1" and try to wear Misses clothes, you will find yourself not only tripping on pant legs and pushing up sleeves, but also contending with droopy inseams and NFL-like shoulder pads. It's embarrassing.

So why the rise, so to speak, in Petite Ladies?

Part of it is that today's women are living longer. An American girl born in 1900 could expect to live to 43; an American girl born in 2000 can expect to live to 80. As the population ages, more of America's women have the genes of an earlier era, when people topped out a little shorter. They've boosted the petite count.

Second, all that aging means a fair amount of shrinking. Beginning at age 50, the discs that cushion our spinal column start compressing, and we lose height. By age 80, we lose an average of one and a half inches. Not to mention the shrinking that comes from osteoporosis and compression fractures, changes in posture, flattening of the arches, and increased curvature of the hips and knees—all common to aging. A few of those symptoms in combination could knock a lifetime Misses shopper smack back to Petites.

But most importantly, the predominant immigrant populations in America are shorter, on average, than the native-born. The Dutch, considered the tallest people on earth, topped out in terms of immigration to America back in the 1880s. Sweden peaked around then, too, and Norway in 1900. For the last half-century, the overwhelming majority of America's immigrants have been Latino and Asian, who skew a good two to three inches shorter than the average American woman. While they haven't been numerous enough to bring down America's average height, they do—at more than 1 million per year—push up the petite count.

You would think that the growing petites would have clothing manufacturers scurrying to outfit them. But for the most part, clothes-makers are chasing the obesity trend, trying to keep up with America's Full-Figured Gals and Big and Tall Men. Lane Bryant opened seventy-five new outlet stores in July of 2006 alone. Who's dressing the tiny ladies?

Here's the other important implication of being undersized and under-the-radar. The Powerful Petites have brought to light the remarkable truth that apparel-makers don't actually know how big *any* of us are. The standard sizes that America's clothing manufacturers use—like the 6-8-10-12 system that most women assume was established back when Eve was fitted for a fig leaf—was actually created in the 1950s, fairly haphazardly, and for a far smaller, more homogeneous population than America has now.

Not until 2004 did the Department of Commerce join with merchandisers to remeasure America—subjecting 10,000 underwear-clad volunteers to a white-light closet that produced hundreds of accurate body measurements in under a minute. But so far, they've publicized almost nothing, and experts say they're unlikely to revolutionize everyday America's clothing anytime soon.

What the researchers did reveal is that whereas the typical American female shape used to be an hourglass, now it is a pear. Hips are now officially wider than shoulders. We are tall, short, and everything in between—just like *Sesame Street* always said. But as a result, there is a seriously under-tapped market out there.

While runway designs may never accommodate anyone but the gauntly statuesque, the rest of us may have learned something from the Powerful Petites. It may be time for us all to storm down New York's Seventh Avenue, with our hips bulging and shoulder seams pinching. *Half* of American women say current styles don't flatter them, and when they do find clothing they like, they can't find their size. Whether people are shrimpishly short or terrifically tall, they'd all like some clothes that fit, please. And whichever clothes-makers come around to accommodating that are sure to have a serious advantage.

PART XII

Technology

Social Geeks

▲

The Geek in America is as entrenched a personality as the Jock, the Cheerleader, the Punk, and the Rebel.

But a funny thing happened on the way to the *Star Trek* convention. Technology crossed over from being a thing for introverts to being a thing for *extroverts*. While the cliché still hangs on that devotees of technology—people who use it constantly, know its lingo, and race to buy the latest gadgets—are social "losers," the truth is that the most enthusiastic users of technology in America are also the most social people in America.

Geeks as we knew them have all but disappeared, possibly even becoming anti-tech—seeking solace in being cut off and disconnected. Once upon a time, working with technology provided an outlet for brilliant but antisocial people who found comfort in machines that responded to them in ways people did not. Now, technology plays the opposite role. And with new music players like Microsoft's Zune now connected to everyone else's, even the solitary act of listening to your own music in headphones is about to become part of a social community. The social uses of technology, with its new emphasis on "connection," have far outstripped the antisocial, individualistic purposes technology used to serve.

The implications for technology marketing are staggering. Whereas tech companies used to target their products to pasty, lonely guys, now they sell having a great PC or cell phone as cool—as much fun and as social as buying a great car. Being tech-savvy was once socially disdained. Now it is at the center of organizing friends, parties, and the social life of the family.

Here's the proof. In a recent poll, we overlaid some Myers-Briggs personality test questions with questions about people's habits, attitudes, and preferences regarding personal computers, cell phones, handheld devices like BlackBerrys, and portable music players. If the old Geek cliché were right, the most devoted techies would be the most introverted, antisocial personalities, right?

In fact, the opposite is true. Although the U.S. adult population as a whole is about 49 percent "extraverted" (defined by Myers-Briggs as folks who draw their energy from the world and people around them), nearly 60 *percent* of the most enthusiastic tech users are extraverted. These are the people who read about advances in consumer electronics and digital devices; are described by friends as into the latest technology and knowledgeable about computer software; and who look forward to new versions of operating systems. But these are *also* the people who are the most busy juggling family, work, and school, and who are living the most active and engaged lifestyles. They go to movies, exercise and play outdoor sports, and listen to recently downloaded music from iTunes far more than those at the other end of the spectrum who were very reluctant to use technology. By more than 2 to 1, the techies opted for "nightlife/hitting the town" as a form of entertainment more so than the "reluctants."

It's the reluctant users—the ones who buy and use technology only when they have to—who turn out to be the introverts, by the significant margin of 57 to 43 percent. These people are not only less interested in technology, they are also less interested in sports, news, magazines, and fashion, and they tend to be more conservative and cautious all around. The people who shy away from social life now *also* shy away from computers—associated as they are with extroversion, ironically enough.

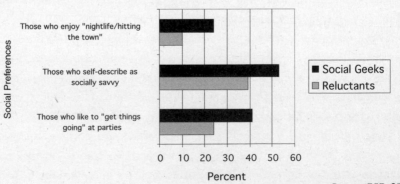

Social Preferences of "Social Geeks" Versus "Reluctant Technology-Users"

Source: PSB, 2005

In fact, the Geek cliché is completely turned on its head when people are asked about their social habits. Fifty-three percent of the "super-engaged" and "enthused" technology-users consider themselves to be socially savvy, compared to only 39 percent of reluctant technology-users. Fifty-eight percent of enthused technology users say they can "talk easily to almost anyone for as long as they have to," compared to only 40 percent of the reluctant tech people.

And when it comes to being the life of the party, the contrast is even more striking. Forty-one percent of very engaged technology-users like to "get things going" at parties, versus only 24 percent of the reluctants.

What used to be a refuge for the socially inept is now a gateway for the socially ambitious.

There may be no greater demonstration of this phenomenon than the extroverted adoption of technology in the form of AOL's instant messenger, or facebook.com, which allows high school and college students to interact, share pictures, and message one another. Facebook.com has grown to more than 8 million postings and, according to comScore, is rated one of the top-trafficked sites in the United States. Even more popular is the online social community MySpace, ranked the number one U.S. Web site in July 2006 by Internet tracking firm Hitwise.

If the old cliché was that techno-geeks had no friends, now it is the case that techno-geeks have a crazy, impossible number of friends. The most popular person on MySpace is one "Tila Tequila," who, as of the spring of 2006, had over a *quarter of a billion* visitors to her MySpace profile. Part singer, part fashion designer, part glamour model, and all-around hot new celebrity, Tila (turned "Tequila") Nguyen was recently interviewed on MSNBC by Tucker Carlson. When he asked her how much time she spends on MySpace, responding to and cultivating online friends, Tila replied, "I spend about twenty-four hours a day on there, pretty much."

So if you are looking to socialize today, get geeky. From dating Web sites to SMS messaging to IM, people today socialize through the typed-in word. Or, more precisely, the typed-in abbreviation. "LOL" for "laughing out loud." "TTFN" for "tata for now."

This new reality opens the way for a spate of publications in the area of "technology life." Technology as social glue is a very different story from the one told in the PC buff books or in serious tech magazines like *Wired*. *Net* is great for product reviews, but it is not *People—Tech Edition* (still waiting to be written)—featuring the top ten tunes celebrities have on their cell phones, how to organize a block party, or what kind of hidden Bluetooth mike Tom Cruise was last seen wearing,

This fundamental change in the role of technology has yet to seep down where it can do the most good—to our schools. While *using* technology has become very social, building technology still has a ways to go. In 2004, the U.S. turned out almost 5,000 psychology doctorates and fewer than 1,000 computer science doctorates. The result is that U.S. technology companies must import more talent from abroad, since there are simply not enough Americans to fill the high-quality tech jobs being created. But as more and more of today's Social Geeks become parents, they may encourage their children to go back to the basics of science fairs and Web site design contests. Some sponsored robot contests are taking off. But it will take there being as much prestige in saying "my son the Internet king" or the "my daughter the computer wizard" as there is now in saying "my child the doctor" or "lawyer." Only then, when this generation of Social Geeks spawns the next one, will studying and using technology reach its full potential.

New Luddites

▲

Have you ever wanted to smash your computer against the wall?

If it was because you were frustrated that it wouldn't do some advanced procedure—like attach your two-megabyte PowerPoint, or upload your digital photographs without reordering them—then you're probably not a New Luddite. Just an ordinary PC user with a shockingly short tolerance for glitches you hadn't even heard of ten years ago.

But if you have taken a conscious stance against gadgets and gizmos, declined to use the Internet for fear of invasion of privacy, or ruled out dating someone because he or she carries a BlackBerry—then you may qualify.

The Luddites, of course, were an early 1800s group of English workers who smashed textile machines to protest the changes—especially the loss of their jobs—that were brought about by the Industrial Revolution. They didn't win, but they've come down in history as mythic members of the Resistance—people who fought for artistry over automation, humanity over productivity.

Today we've shrunk machines to microchips and stored our creativity on servers, but our own Information Revolution has produced dissidents just the same. They aren't smashing other people's cell phones (yet), but in their own small ways, they are Just Saying No.

The New Luddites are to be distinguished from those Americans who lack computers or Internet access because of age, geography, or income. According to a 2003 study by the Pew Center on the Internet and American Life, something like 70 million people (of America's 300 million) are "Tech-Nos"—people who don't use computers at all. But the bulk of those are aging boomers and seniors who find technology too intimidating; rural Americans who don't yet have computers at the same rate as people in and near cities; and low-income Americans who still find them too expensive.

This kind of TechNo will phase out, presumably, as technology continues to get cheaper and more accessible.

But New Luddites are not people who lack technology due to environment or circumstance. They have every technological opportunity, but Still Say No.

In 2000, according to Pew, 13 percent of the people who said they do not use the Internet had had experience with it but quit. By 2002—as most of the country was leaping at the chance to get online—the number of people dropping *offline* had grown to 17 percent. That's about 15 million Americans who've been online and stopped.

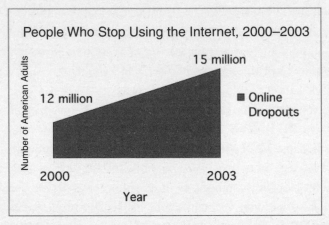

Sources: Pew Internet and American Life Project, *The Ever-Shifting Internet Population*, 2005; U.S. Census, 2006

Eight in 10 such people said they knew of a convenient public place where they could go to use the Internet (like a public library), and that it would be "very" or "somewhat" easy to do so. But they didn't want to.

Who are these New Luddites?

It turns out they are a distinct breed. According to the Pew study, whereas most non-Internet users are older, rural, and lower-income, people who affirmatively reject the Internet are young, urban, and employed. One in 4 said they stopped using the Internet because they didn't like it, it wasn't interesting or useful, or it wasn't a good use of their time.

These people are the flip side of the Social Geeks just described. Unlike those very gregarious people who use technology to advance their outgoing approach to the world, the New Luddites are more pessimistic, more cynical, and lonelier. According to the Pew study, nearly half are dissatisfied with the way things are going in this country today, and over 60 percent say you can't be too careful in dealing with people. Over half believe that most people would take advantage of others given the opportunity. Twice as many Internet dropouts say they have hardly any people they could turn to for support when they need help.

Internet-users tend to believe they have control over their lives. New Luddites don't. In fact, some New Luddites reject technology because they hope it will help them *gain* control. From their point of view, the technology that was supposed to make our lives easier has only made them busier and more stressed. Whatever time we saved with instant communication seems to have been filled up with *more* communication. Do Americans work less, or take more vacation, now that knowledge and communication are at the (increasingly calloused) tips of our fingers? Hardly. We even work more while on vacation.

So the New Luddites are staging their own protest. They're tired of having friends interrupt personal conversations to respond to incoming e-mails from other people. They're tired of having their kids come home from school and go, glazed-eyed, into their computer screens. They're tired of BlackBerrys at the dinner table, drivers on cell phones, and iPods that prevent people from even noticing that other people are trying to talk to them.

They are striking back, with their pens, legal pads, index cards, and scraps of paper in pockets containing all their to-do lists. They may be less outgoing than the Social Geeks, but they are standing firm for the old-fashioned obligation to look people in the eye and say hello—not just IM them, "how r u?" And they may be gaining ground. As of early 2007, the much touted plan to allow passengers to use cell phones on airplanes seems doomed. Apart from lingering concerns that the phones would interfere with plane navigation equipment and on-the-ground calls, it turns out that people didn't want to hear other people yakking in their cell phones in midair. A USA Today survey in 2005 found that almost 7 in 10 Americans favored keeping the airplane cell phone ban in place.

In the last generation, while most people were swept up in TV, some people said no. (Janet Reno's mother reportedly never let her four kids watch; she said it would turn their brains to rot.) In this generation, people are taking a stand against the Internet.

And so there are commercial implications. On the one hand, their strong stance may be reflected in smaller ways among even the bulk of us who like technology. Even the most mainstream cell-phone- and PC-users have got to ask from time to time if we really need *all* those bonus features. At some point, we just want stuff that works.

But for the New Luddites themselves, as well, there are some serious marketing opportunities. They don't want Jetson-like insta-food, they want slow-cooked stews and multicourse meals, both at home and away. They don't want hyper-souped-up cars; they want quiet ones. If they are going to get blisters on their fingers, they want them from knitting and gardening, not from punching tiny missives into their BlackBerrys. The yoga, massage, and spa industries should be on high alert for these people. So should book publishers, crafts-makers, and religious movements. These are America's great un-rushed, and they are looking for low-tech ways to spend their time and money.

Of course the trick is finding them—unlike everyone else, they won't be on the Net.

Tech Fatales

▲

We just debunked the idea that high-tech, gadget-loving computer types are antisocial. In fact, research shows that unlike in earlier times, tech geeks are among the most social people in the world.

But a subgroup of these people—the ignored among the ignored, as it were—are the Tech Fatales: the women and girls who don't just use technology, but drive, shape, and decide the majority of consumer electronics purchases in America.

Would you know, for example, from the clunky design of your eight-pound "laptop" that women outspend men on technology 3 to 2? Yes—all that tech advertising on the show 24 is hitting one target of early adopters, but it is the Claire's shoppers who are scooping up the cell phones and iPods.

Would you know from the fact that today's BlackBerry belt clips are no more dress-friendly than *pager* belt clips were fifteen years ago that women influence almost 57 percent of technology purchases, or in 2006, about $90 billion in consumer electronics sales?

Like women car-buyers, whom we'll discuss next, this is not just an up-and-coming trend. It's not a Brave New World prediction, where in Futuristic Someday, e-commerce and e-lectronics will need to be designed with e-strogen in mind. That day is here. When it comes to buying techno-stuff, women already rule. Women are the majority in law school, the majority in college, and the majority of the voters. Now women are also leading the nation's high-tech binge.

Especially girls. According to the Consumer Electronics Association, girls are more likely than boys to use mobile phones (88 to 83 percent), digital cameras (54 to 50 percent), satellite radios (24 to 18 percent), and DVD recorders (21 to 19 percent). Girls and boys use TVs, VCRs, DVD players, and PCs about the same. The only gadgets on which girls lag are portable MP3

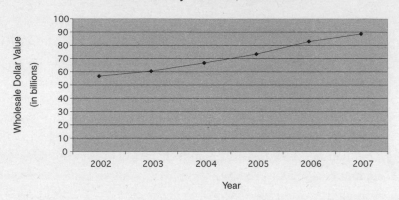

Value (in Wholesale Dollars) of Consumer Electronics Purchases Influenced by Women, 2002–2007

Source: Consumer Electronics Association, 2007

players and videogame consoles—although even there, Nintendo made big strides in 2006 with the Wii, designed with girls (as well as boys) in mind and selling well beyond analysts' expectations.

I well remember that in 1976, the Science Center at Harvard was essentially an all-male fraternity, and there are still fewer girls doing math and science as an academic pursuit. But girls have become heavy users of technology. After all, the principal use of much of the technology today is communications, and it is girls—not boys—who love to communicate all the time.

And yet, if you walk into a Best Buy, do the blue-shirted sales guys, or the super-eager Geek Squad, feel like they're focused on females? Would any woman rank Radio Shack among the stores where she *loves* to shop? These stores are literally tossing away customers. The new Apple stores with their softer colors are generally more inviting, but no one has opened a serious tech store just for girls.

To be fair, these stores know they are missing the boat. Best Buy has just begun a multiyear commitment to soften its lights, lower its music, and offer personalized shopping consultants, for just this reason. It's even retraining its employees so that in addition to counting megapixels, they will ask customers how they want the technology to fit into their lives. Even Radio Shack now aggressively recruits female store managers, and is up to about 1,000, of its 7,000 stores. But, just as with car dealerships, the transition will be slow. Almost 75 percent of women still say they're ignored, patronized, or offended by the salespeople in electronics stores. Forty percent say they're treated better if they're accompanied by a man.

But the truth is, Tech Fatales have far deeper implications for the industry than just sales and marketing. First, women need to be *not ignored*. It's been widely reported that when the first state-of-the-art, voice-calibrated video-conference systems were introduced, they forgot to account for the decibel ranges of women. The camera literally did not hear women's voices.

But that was just a first step. When it comes to product utility and design, in study after study, women express different priorities, different preferences, and different concerns regarding technology. They want their gadgets light, durable, and effective—not fast, sharp, and zillion-faceted.

According to at least one major electronics company, what women want specifically are keyboards that don't snag fingernails, headphones that don't smudge makeup, and cell phones that can be found more easily in dark, crowded purses. After all, if women still can't clip their PDAs to their waist-bands like men—or don't want to, for fear of finding out years from now that cell phone rays damage ovaries—then for goodness' sake, give them a way to find their buzzing phones inside their purses without interrupting meetings; spilling wallets, tampons, and lipstick all over the floor; or missing the calls altogether.

When it comes to home electronics, women want products that accentuate, not take over, the living room, bedroom, and kitchen. Hence the immense popularity among women of flat-screen TVs. Slim, slender, gracious, and less obviously indicative that football will take over on Sunday afternoons. Sharp recently came out with a flat-screen brand softly named AQUOS, which it advertises not just on sports channels and prime time, but also on Lifetime and the Food Network.

But apparently—and here is where the market is deeply underserved—girls and women are deeply open to technology as fashion. Cell phones with diamond "bling kits" apparently fly off the shelves. So do bejeweled ones created by the hottest designers in women's fashion. Yes, there are some laptop bags out there now with woven fabrics and contrasting stitching and special side pockets for makeup—but we haven't come close to exploring the full extent of gadgets and their accessories as personal style. Ask any modern woman whether she'd rather lose her cell phone or her latest pair of shoes. The cell phone *is* the center of a woman's universe of friends and family. She can't go an hour without checking it. And yet, when it comes to integrating this deep part of her personality with style, the best the tech companies can do is black versus blue for the keypad?

The Starbucks economy is coming to technology—and the Ford economy of one-color PCs and laptops is on the way out. Sony is one manufacturer that has started to make multicolored laptops. Apple allowed for engraved iPods. Dell is adapting to the changes in design appeal of technology. The cell phone rack is starting to glitter a little more in its choices.

But the question "What do women want?" may well be the most important question for technology-designers in the coming years. Would Windows for Women look fundamentally different from Windows Vista? Before running into its other problems, the cigarette industry was a model of male/female differentiation—different brands of the same product appealed to different male and female markets. Was the Virginia Slims cigarette really fundamentally different from the Marlboro? The tech industry is changing, but it has been so *Marlboro* for so long that there isn't yet that kind of spot-on differentiation. Like women car-buyers, this is a case of the market having grown up in spite of the industry—and someday soon, someone is going to come along and tap into it in a fundamentally different way, and walk off with not just a niche market, but the largest and fastest-growing piece of the tech puzzle. If you are a Tech Fatale, you are not alone—you are just waiting for someone out there to hear you.

Car-Buying Soccer Moms

▲

The car commercials on the 2005 Super Bowl were testosterone heaven.
Of the nine different ads for cars, seven of them had as their dominant theme speed, craggy mountains, and/or toughness. Honda Ridgeline's ad, called "Rugged," flashed a series of men's belt buckles up close, followed by their wearers engaging in extreme sports. Ford Mustang's "Frozen in Fargo," in which a man freezes to death in his driver's seat rather than wait for warmer weather to drive his convertible, ends with a deep male voice saying, "We Make You Tough."

In fact, of the nine car commercials aired during the Super Bowl, six had no dialogue at all, six had no women, and three had no people at all. In the one that actually had both dialogue and a woman, the Dad chased down his eloping daughter in order to say it was fine for her to run off, so long as she took her mother's car.

Detroit (or rather, Chicago, where the ads are made for Detroit) has got what makes men tick.

Women — not so much.

Which would all be fine if it were only men who watched the Super Bowl (actually, 55 million women do), or if it were only men who bought cars. But that is not the case. Women car-buyers are not just on the rise, they are *the majority* of car-buyers in America today. And with women increasingly living without husbands, that number is only going to increase.

Yet, just as in the technology story in the last chapter, most car ads are targeted at men, whether for the Super Bowl or not — and the feel of car-buying is still so masculine that 70 percent of women say they're intimidated by automobile showrooms. Car-marketers, mistakenly, still think men are the only ones in charge.

Fifty years ago, Dodge launched La Femme, the first American car to expressly target women. The car was pink, and it came with a matching rain bonnet, leather shoulder bag, compact, lighter, lipstick, and cigarette case. Marketed as the car "for Your Majesty, the modern American woman," it flopped. But not because Dodge didn't have the right instinct about attending to women's tastes—it just didn't have the right market research.

As Super Bowl ad-makers well know, men shopping for cars are drawn to power and luxury. But that is not true for women, who over and over have been proved to care more when it comes to cars about affordability, practicality, and safety. According to 2005 Kelley Blue Book data that track new-car registrants by gender, the average horsepower of the top five cars bought by men was 367. The average horsepower of the top five cars bought by women was 172.

Which makes sense, given the way men and women probably use their cars. If women are lugging children, groceries, and sports equipment around all day, they probably care less about going from 0 to 60 in under 5 than about keeping their kids and cargo safe, and having to tend to auto maintenance as little as possible.

Indeed, in the first concept car to be designed and marketed exclusively by women, a 2004 Volvo, low maintenance was a high priority. In the design that emerged, an oil change would be needed only every 31,000 miles. There was no hood—drivers wouldn't be tinkering in there, after all—just an engine access suitable for mechanics. Windshield wiper fluid could be refilled through a little hole behind the gas tank. There was no gas cap, just a roller-ball valve opening for the nozzle. When it was time for inspection, the car was programmed to send a wireless message to a local service center, which would notify the driver. And the engine—a low-emission, gas-electric hybrid—was environmentally friendly.

These, apparently, are the priorities of the twenty-first-century American car-buyer. She is less interested in truck tires that come up to her chest, promising to lug her bouncing and reeling up craggy mountainsides. (Not that trucks are off the table—women are *also* the fastest-growing segment of truck and SUV buyers, purchasing 45 percent of all SUVs and nearly as many full-size pickups as minivans.) But ad campaigns for trucks that just focus on rock-climbing, rather than on utility and family, will likely fall flat for women.

Car-makers, take note. Women car-buyers have not just arrived, they are the dominant force. Pink roadsters with matching rain bonnets were the wrong product, but the right idea. Women want the safer, studier Pontiac

G6 Convertible, the Suzuki Forenza, and the Volkswagen New Beetle; men want the fancier, tougher Porsche 911 coupe, the Mitsubishi Lancer Evolution, and the Ford GT.

Even car brands don't overlap: women's top five brands are Pontiac, Hyundai, Toyota, Volkswagen, and Suzuki. Men's top five brands are Dodge, Lincoln, Jaguar, Porsche, and Infiniti.

That women are the majority force in automobile-buying ought to transform the industry. Cars should be designed more like the Volvo Concept Car, and marketed more like home appliances. But they're *still* not, despite the fact that women's power is not a prediction, but a fact.

When the industry comes around, it will probably find that as women are better tended to, the overall car industry—from vehicle design to service and maintenance—gets stronger. As Jiffy Lube's president has said, "Anything done to attract female consumers is readily accepted by male customers." And as the Volvo president said when they rolled out the all-female-designed and marketed Concept Car in 2004, "We learned that if you meet women's expectations, you exceed those for men."

So perhaps it is time for Ford and GM to stop copying the Japanese, and start copying the Avon Lady or Estée Lauder. Women want safe, easy-to-maintain cars with pleasing design elements. And they want women dealers. Ford is trying to retool its Mercury into its woman brand—but other than adding a "spokesmodel," I am not sure I see changes infused through the system from design to showroom.

The American car industry is having problems—many of them caused by conditions beyond its control, like serious labor shortages and expensive retirement packages. In my work with Bill Ford, we hit upon the idea that to regain their footing, American car manufacturers must again innovate to grow. This is easier said than done, but in the case of the emerging Car-Buying Soccer Mom, it should not be so hard to focus on making the car, and car-buying, more like going to a spa and less like going to the Super Bowl.

In so many areas now, women are the majority, but men and the system are slow to recognize it. Women are the majority of students in college and in law school. Women are the majority of voters. Joining that list, while no one seems to be acknowledging it, is also that women are the majority of car-buyers. That may be the most overlooked marketing statistic in America.

PART XIII

Leisure and Entertainment

Archery Moms?

▲

America is crazy about sports. Over 260 million of us play at least one, up from 235 million just ten years ago. We have something like *two dozen* all-sports cable channels, up from just ESPN in 1979. We put basketball players on our list of Most Admired Men. We elect bodybuilders and professional wrestlers as governors of some of our biggest states. We send football players to Congress.

Ask anyone—sports in America means the Big Four: football, baseball, basketball, and ice hockey. And in our own lives, it means swimming, bowling, fishing, and biking.

So here's what's fascinating. In the past twenty-five years, *except* for football, interest in the Big Four sports has been plummeting. Baseball is actually the favorite sport of only 11 percent of the nation—having not technically been "America's Pastime" since the early 1970s. Basketball had its lowest TV ratings ever in the 2005–06 season. Hockey viewership is so miserable that, in 2005, ESPN stopped airing it altogether.

And in terms of the sports we do, the number of us participating in "regular" ones like swimming, fishing, biking, and basketball is also falling off. So are baseball, tennis, volleyball, skiing, and roller-skating.

So what are all of America's New Athletes doing?

Sports—like music and movies—is niching out. The boardroom hysteria of Major League Baseball notwithstanding, we don't like sports less, we just like *little* sports more.

Since 1995, the National Sporting Goods Association has been tracking the number of American children and adults who participate in various sports. By comparing 1995 to 2005, we can see that while some old standards like baseball, swimming, tennis, and volleyball are declining—by an average of 13 percent—what's on the rise are the more individual, nature-based sports, many of which, twenty years ago, no one had ever heard of.

Changes in Sports Participation, 1995-2005			
			[Selected Sports]
	1995 Participants (in millions)	2005 Participants (in millions)	Percent Growth
Skateboarding	4.5	12.0	166.7
Kayaking/Rafting	3.5	7.6	117.1
Snowboarding	2.8	6.0	114.3
Archery	4.9	6.8	38.8
Mountain-Biking	6.7	9.2	37.3
Backpacking/Wilderness-Camping	10.2	13.3	30.4
Hunting (Bow & Arrow)	5.3	6.6	24.5
Soccer	12	14.1	17.5
Golf	24	24.7	2.9
Basketball	30.1	29.9	-0.7
Fishing	44.2	43.3	-2.0
Swimming	61.5	58	-5.7
Baseball	15.7	14.6	-7.0
Tennis	12.6	11.1	-11.9
Bicycle-Riding	56.3	43.1	-23.4
Volleyball	18	13.2	-26.7
In-line Roller-Skating	23.9	13.1	-45.2

Source: National Sporting Goods Association, 2006

As you can see from the chart above, the fastest-growing sport in America in the past ten years was skateboarding, now done by over 12 million people. That's nearly the same number of Americans who have ever played softball or baseball.

Next was kayaking/rafting, at over 7 million—and then snowboarding. No one ever heard of snowboarding until 1980, and now 6 million people do it. Snowboarders make up almost 1 in 3 users of ski resorts.

Other fast-growing sports in America are mountain-biking, with 9 million participants; archery, with nearly 7 million; backpacking, with 13 million; and—get this—hunting with a bow and arrow, with nearly 7 million.

In the past ten years—since we developed the idea of Soccer Moms—

archery has grown at more than twice the rate of soccer. Hello, Archery Moms?

And in case you think the niching of sports is just a fad among 30- and 40-somethings, it's even more pronounced among teens. Teen NFL viewers under 18 now hold 10 percent of the market, as opposed to 13 percent in the 1990s, and the number of teens who *play* football, basketball, baseball, and ice hockey has fallen off as much as 23 percent in about the same time. But here's what they *are* doing. Since the mid-1990s, the number of varsity high school lacrosse teams grew from 800 to over 2,300. Youth membership in the U.S. Fencing Association more than doubled, to nearly 8,000. Since 1990, the youth members of USA Dance, which includes competitive dancing, grew by almost 7-fold.

And you can bet the national growth in skateboarding and snowboarding didn't come from America's 40-somethings.

What's going on here is that Big Sports have, for some people, gotten just a little too big, and smaller sports give them just a little more space to play, breathe, and engage their hearts.

In the past ten years, watching *and* playing Big Sports have gotten increasingly taxing. More and more, the Big Four are perceived as hypercorporate—what with their (formerly) Enron stadiums, garish wall-to-wall ads, and out-of-control player salaries. Strikes and lockouts have ruined games and whole seasons. The steroid scandals are a big downer. Of course there are still plenty of available fans, but the Big Four are facing some significant leakage to new activities.

And perhaps relatedly, teen participation also got too intense. Kids showing up in sports medicine clinics with "Little League shoulders" and irrecoverably torn ligaments. Hypercompetitive students taking performance-enhancing drugs, and sidelining the regular kids who just wanted a little exercise and team-building. Not to mention the crazy parents on the sidelines, like the Massachusetts Hockey Dad who got in a fight with the father of another 10-year-old in 2000 and pummeled him to death.

Against that backdrop—lacrosse, fencing, and dance start to look interesting. Gentler parents. More chance for more kids to play, and shine. Not to mention, some differentiation for those college applications. Only a few stars are heading for the top-ranked colleges in basketball—but what college wouldn't take a second look at the National Junior Champion in Orienteering?

The niching of sports is a perfect example of how more and more people are splintering off from the crowd to find greater individual satisfaction. Whereas sports used to be the way that the whole school—and later, the whole city—would come together to cheer the community's toughest males in battle against their rivals, now a growing number of people are saying: good luck at the game, but I'm going kayaking.

Notably, not *one* of the fastest-growing sports in America—skateboarding, kayaking, snowboarding, archery, backpacking, mountain-biking, or bow-and-arrow-hunting—depends substantially on teamwork. Sure, like all great sports, they demand persistence, strength, and agility—but today's growing sports are heavy on personal intensity and inner strength, and lighter on playbooks, whistles, uniforms, and manicured fields.

Sports in America are far from declining. They are just shifting from a communal rite to a personal one. What used to be a galvanizing event to bring us all together—like the modern-day version of watching lions tear people apart in the Colosseum—has become the opposite. Now sports help us retreat—often alone, and often to the mountains, the woods, or the water.

Look for niche sports programming, and heroes. Look for it to spill over to not just Archery Moms, but skateboarding politicians.

I would have joked that on the heels of the ragingly successful Fantasy Football, you should look for Fantasy Fishing—but it already exists. Choose your anglers, and bet what they'll catch.

And if the Olympics can get any nichier, it will. When the modern Olympics started in 1896, there were forty-three total events. Now between the Winter and Summer Olympics, there are 386. Is poker next? Don't laugh. The 2005 Poker World Series was a huge draw on ESPN (yes, ESPN—the "E" stands for "entertainment"). But by the 2008 Olympics, watch for ballroom-dancing.

Finally, look for more niche sports in the movies. Since 2003 alone, America's biggest blockbusters have included the Oscar-winning *Million Dollar Baby* (boxing), and the Oscar-nominated *Seabiscuit* (horseracing). But let's be honest. Boxing and horseracing were America's favorite sports fifty years ago, and neither one practically even makes the list anymore for watching *or* playing. In 2005's *The Weather Man*, Nicholas Cage—a Chicago TV personality—was a recreational archer. Weird, right? But onto something.

The growing trend in sports in America skews toward the *individual*, the *quiet*, and the *natural*. No wonder in 2006, Tiger Woods the golfer toppled

Michael Jordan the basketball star as America's Most Popular Male Athlete, after a thirteen-year-reign. The Super Bowl is still the biggest event of professional sports and American TV, but there is a small but growing group that has turned off and tuned out of conventional sports, and turned on to alternative sports instead.

XXX Men

▲

Some of the trends in this book involve a small group creating a big market. This trend involves a huge number of people involved in activities that, despite their frequency, seem to fly under the radar screen.

There is hardly a more taboo topic in America than pornography. Vilified by both religious leaders (generally on the right) and feminists (generally on the left), it is about as widely frowned upon as any pastime in America. But in recent years, the Internet has made pornography so phenomenally easy to access that millions of otherwise upscale, respectable Americans are using it with stunning frequency. Magazine sales may have plummeted, but Internet porn has profited.

About 40 million adults in the U.S. regularly visit Internet pornography sites. That's more than *ten times* the number of people who regularly watch baseball. And which one, again, do we call America's pastime?

In fact, this marketplace is so large that porn is the norm. There is hardly a hotel room in America without easy access to porn. It is just a click away for everyone.

A startling number of people view their porn at work. According to Websense, a vendor of Web security and filtering software, *70 percent* of porn is downloaded between 9 a.m. and 5 p.m. And 20 percent of American men admit accessing porn while at work. Are there five men who work where you do? Try sneaking a glimpse of their computer screens when they're hunched over them, looking like they're working. Chances are, at least one isn't gazing at spreadsheets.

What's remarkable is that these are people who otherwise cleave to really high moral standards. In 2003, *Today's Christian Woman* reported that 53 percent of men at that year's Promise Keepers Convention admitted visiting a porn site the week before. Forty-seven percent of Christians say pornography is a major problem in the home.

Former President Jimmy Carter made it okay to "lust in your heart." The Internet is making it okay to lust at your screen, in private, at low cost.

After all, it was the brilliant viral sex video campaigns that refreshed Pamela Anderson's reputation and made Paris Hilton a celebrity. Both protested that their boyfriends circulated the videos without their permission. But both benefited from the huge publicity and interest they created. Whereas once, such videos would have made these stars untouchable, in today's society, those videos made them stars.

Already a $57 billion industry worldwide, porn generates $12 billion per year in the United States. Apparently in 2001, income from porn was larger than the annual revenue brought in by major league baseball, football, and basketball combined. A 2006 study said that revenue from Internet porn exceeds, by nearly 2 to 1, the combined revenues of ABC, CBS, and NBC.

And porn's share of cyberspace is, as one might expect, vast. There are over 4 million pornographic Web sites, about 12 percent of the total. One in 4 search engine requests on an average day is for pornography. So is 1 in 3 peer-to-peer downloads. Pornographic Web sites are visited three times more often than Google, Yahoo!, and MSN combined.

What is less obvious, though, is that porn has been one of the pivotal industries propelling technology. In the 1980s, when VHS nudged out Betamax to become the videocassette standard, its victory was largely attributed to having the X-rated movie business on its side. Now, according to *Investor's Business Daily*, video disc giants HD DVD and Blu-ray Disc are duking it out to be the standard format for next-generation video discs, and HD DVD's alliance with the "adult industry" is likely to give it the edge.

Today, porn-purveyors are some of the biggest customers of mainstream technology companies. "Sex" is the number one search term people plug into Google and Yahoo! While conservative organizations are quick to boycott firms that advertise in gay magazines, they never boycott the companies selling equipment and services to the porn industry. Why not? While these organizations have few gay members, they have a lot of members who look at porn.

With all of the talk of the effects of porn, one has to wonder if we will see significant changes in actual relationships. Violence was once blamed on TV, but the studies went both ways. Now, as Internet porn has soared, so has Internet dating. Never before have people enjoyed so much access to meeting and dating real people, at the same time they can indulge more of their fantasies in private.

Where this may have the greatest impact is with teens who once bought illicit magazines, and then acquired videos. Now they have access through the Web. Just put something in your Web browser as obvious as "www.sex.com," and see what happens. Pictures young people could never have gotten their hands on without a lot of trouble are instantly available to everyone, with no credit card or ID necessary. The age at which American youth first have sex is declining—down to 16 now—and the easy access to pictures and unlimited information about sex could be one reason why.

But the real "aha" here is for women. The mainstreaming of porn is like a silent hulking presence—a phenomenon completely obvious to men, but almost completely overlooked by women. And when women realize it, will it change the way they view their colleagues, bosses, husbands, and boyfriends? Or do women ignore it on purpose? Do they agree with Jimmy Carter that a little lust is normal, as long as their men stay loyal?

Women are more than a quarter of those who visit porn sites. And more and more women are now living alone. So if there is a trend within a trend, it's that more women are taking the attitude that if you can't beat them, join them.

THE INTERNATIONAL PICTURE

Americans are hardly alone in their passion for porn. TopTenReviews.com claims that the global sex industry is worth some $81 billion per year, with Internet-based porn taking in $3.5 billion. Internet porn pages have grown at a rate of 1,800 percent worldwide over the last five years, and out of the 68 million search engine requests per day around the world, 25 percent are for porn sites. So If you're jumping to cover up the naked people on your screen as the boss walks by, you're probably not alone—someone in the Netherlands is likely doing the same thing.

How popular is porn, really? According to the 2004 Global Sex Survey by Durex (the condom makers), 35 percent of porn-watchers watch it with their partner. Globally speaking, South Africans are the most likely to admit watching porn (60 percent), while Indians (22 percent) and Chinese (24 percent) are the least likely.

Folks around the world get their porn in about the same ways—mainly, through the Internet, telephone, and magazines. But in Europe, the new craze is porn by cell phone. Europeans have spent the equivalent of tens of millions of dollars on cell-phone-compatible porn; in 2004, PhoneErotica. com experienced more than 75 million hits per week. In America, cell phone carriers have been slower to catch on, fearing a public backlash. Nonetheless, researchers say that graphic porn on your cell phone (presumably, right there next to your work e-mail and your digital pictures of the family) will be a $200 million business in the U.S. by 2009.

Naturally, porn is not just for adults. Thailand's *The Nation* reported that in 2002, some 71 percent of its young people (aged 12–25) have visited pornographic Web sites. Forty-five percent are site regulars. One-third of boys aged 13–14 from Alberta, Canada, said they have viewed pornography "too many times to count."

Japan has a particular distinction in the porn field, as a prolific producer of both adult and child pornography. In 1998, the International Criminal Police Organization estimated that up to 80 percent of child porn Internet sites originated in Japan.

Who's got the largest number of registered pornography pages? Germany, at some 10 million. And a tiny country in Africa, São Tomé, lays claim to some 307,000 pages, almost double the size of its population.

It's the biggest, worst-kept secret in the world.

Video Game Grown-ups

▲

Video games in America bring to mind pimply teenage boys, huddled over consoles in dim arcades on sunny days. "Gamers" are antisocial adolescents sitting for hours on end in each other's basements—no fresh air, exercise, or conversation required.

But while old stereotypes die hard, statistics reveal a very different picture. As of 2006, the average video/computer-game-player was 33 years old, up from age 24 just four years before. And not only is he older than you thought, he has apparently been playing for an average of only 12 years—which means that the average gamer didn't even *start* playing until he was old enough to buy alcohol. Video games have become the biggest pastime of adults, not children.

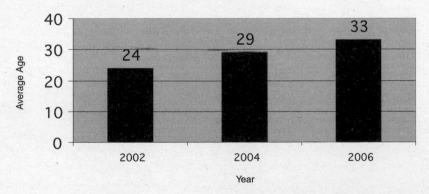

Average Age of Video/Computer-Gamers, 2002–2006

Source: Entertainment Software Association, 2006

According to the Entertainment Software Association, gamers under age 18 actually make up fewer than one-third of all players, and *people over 50 make up 25 percent*. Hard to believe, I know. Along with Bill Cosby and Elton John, one of the star attractions at AARP's 2006 National Convention was Nintendo.

Even adult women—at 30 percent of the video and computer game market—substantially outnumber boys 17 or younger, who make up only 23 percent of the market.

Look out, boys, Mom and Dad are coming down to the basement. But they're not going to take away your video games and make you play outside. They want to join you.

What is going on?

In part, it's the aging of the 30-somethings, who were the first generation to be reared on computers. Whereas "entertainment" to their parents meant buying a ticket to a show, play, movie, or ball game and watching the story unfold, this generation is more comfortable with entertainment that involves clicks, controllers, and interactive narrative.

Second, because they're not threatened by video games, today's parents are actually embracing them as a way to bond with their children. According to the Entertainment Software Association, 35 percent of parents are gamers, and 80 percent of gaming parents play with their kids. Hence the *Dance Dance Revolution* games, in which kids (and their obesity-conscious parents) break a sweat trying to follow along with the video's fancy footwork. And whereas adults and children used to flee from each other at parties, now they can actually have some of the same fun, like having *Guitar Hero* contests *together*. It works across generations.

Third, the entertainment software industry is slowly recognizing its more mature audiences. Along with guns, Goths, and *Grand Theft Auto*, now there are increasingly life-oriented games like *The Sims*, in which players guide fictitious family members through the course of their regular day. In 2005, *The Sims* was the best-selling PC game in North America—and it's wildly popular among women. One of the fastest-growing groups of video-gamers is Moms over 45, whose kids are off to school and who have a fair amount of time, but not a ton of money. They spend more time watching TV than any other group of gamers, and rank second in gaming time. Unlike the reclusive teen geeks of the past, this group wants their games to be easy to play, and *more* social rather than less. It's a whole new world of gamers.

The most popular form of gaming is online cards, enjoyed by 2 out of 3 gaming adults, or probably 35 million people. And for the more-than-casual gamer, there are "MMOGs"—Massively Multiplayer Online Games—in which people interact as fictional characters in a virtual world that constantly evolves, even as the players step away. Nearly 1 in 5 gaming adults, or close to 10 million people, do these. One of the most popular MMOGs, *Second Life*—with over 5 million registrants—allows adults to create virtual characters and have them interact with others in real estate deals, group activities, workplaces, and general social life. Kids aren't even allowed (they have their own version, *Teen Second Life*).

I have to admit that I am an adult PC-gamer. For years, I have played the *Command and Conquer* series of war strategy games in which you control armies with a range of different skills. What I learned is that there is always a way to victory—you just have to keep playing until you find it. Lately I'm shifting to more online Scrabble, but if you notice what people are doing on planes today, it is either watching a DVD or playing a video game. People who use their laptops for work while flying are actually in the minority.

The bottom line is: What used to be a fringe hobby for teen geeks and freaks is now an utterly mainstream activity for American grown-ups. Nearly 100 million adults are considered "active gamers." Video game sales in the U.S. are bigger than movie sales worldwide. Something like 100 U.S. colleges and universities teach courses in how to design and produce video games.

Video Game Grown-ups are a big deal—first for the industry itself. Grown-up Gamers mean a booming industry for "mature" rated games, already the fastest-growing segment, at nearly 15 percent; and a wide-open market for games geared to women. There is also a growing segment of seniors, aka "Gray Gamers." In 2006, Nintendo introduced *Brain Age*, a touch-focused computer game that challenges seniors to a series of on-screen logic puzzles and then tells them how "young" their brain is. Nursing home residents spar to score "Age 50," or "40," while keeping their minds active and maybe staving off Alzheimer's. (Remember how popular Nintendo was at the AARP convention?) This market will only grow as future seniors come to old age with more and more computer literacy.

But even among adults in their 30s and 40s, the market for video games is vastly underserved—just look at the Circuit City displays and the offbeat and grotesque creatures on most of the video game covers. These games could make a serious dent in sales if they had more serious covers, more interesting topics, and new game experiences. There is not a single major game on investing and making money—even though one of the biggest board games of all time was Monopoly. The games all focus on taking over worlds, dating, or killing. But what most 33-year-old men want is to make a killing in the market, or if they want to knock someone off, it's their boss and his corner office. Their female counterparts have just had their first or second baby, and are dealing with child development and sibling rivalry. The untapped marketplaces of human experiences out there are vast, and yet the game-creators still seem lost with the pimply teenagers, and a little oblivious to the lifestyles of their new customers.

Video Game Grown-ups are also a big deal to advertisers. At $10 billion and growing, the video game industry is a serious new marketing venue. While entertainment software is still a small venue compared to TV, Nielsen, whose TV ratings system has for decades helped set the price of commercials on TV, announced in 2006 that it would develop a system of measurements to standardize the market for buying and selling video game ads. As the marketing catches up with reality, look for video game ads not just for cell phones and DVDs, but also home mortgage loans and minivans.

And at a broader level, Grown-up Gamers represent one more blur in the distinction between adults and children. Sure, kids have sex younger than they used to, and call adults by their first names—but increasingly, it is grown-ups who watch cartoons (*The Simpsons*, *King of the Hill*, *South Park*), go to grown-up Chuck E. Cheeses, and now play video games. In all these extra hours that adults are playing video games, they are *not* working, reading, volunteering, or pursuing other community-bettering activities that used to be the hallmark of adult citizenship. Indeed, they are living in imaginary communities. Is that isolation, or mega-connection?

My sense is that, on balance, Video Game Grown-ups will do more good than harm, and the reason is that all this adult comfort with video games is moving beyond entertainment and into education—for them. Gaming is the new frontier of the kind of skill-building and training that adults need to handle some of the world's most serious problems. Dubbed "serious games" by the Woodrow Wilson International Center of Scholars, the next stage of video game technology is game-based learning and simulation, already being developed in areas like disease prevention, terrorism response, and the peaceful removal of dictators. Firefighters are using it to prepare for biochemical disasters. University administrators are using it to reinvent higher education.

Military services are using it to prepare for battle. When the stakes are high and the choices fast-paced and complex, gaming out the options in real time can provide substantial competitive advantage. But it's only as mainstream adults get comfortable with the tools and techniques of gaming—largely in their leisure time—that institutions like schools, universities, and governments will start to mine it for all it's worth.

So what started out as a habit for antisocial teenagers has become the newest way adults are thinking about counterterrorism, education, and war. We "game" not because we're too antisocial to go out, but because we can imagine, plan, and practice for some of life's biggest challenges through software scenarios.

Neo-Classicals

▲

There are a couple groups in America who, every few decades, publicly bewail their demise. Grammarians. Jews. Major League Baseball. Their communal angst is genuine and heartfelt, and they can always point to quantitative data that back it up. But very often—and maybe it's *because* some of that urgency spurs new devotees to action—these groups end up finding new and modern ways to survive.

The latest comer to the I'm-Going-Extinct Party is classical music. Dozens of books, blogs, articles, and, of course, fund-raising drives have been devoted to the tearful lament that Debussy is dwindling and Puccini is perishing. The only reliable lovers of classical music, goes the dirge, are old people—so unless we take drastic measures, classical music, too, will die out within a generation.

They point to some troubling data. Between 2005 and 2006, U.S. sales of classical music CDs dropped 15 percent. In city after city, classical radio stations and professional orchestras are shutting down. Orchestra season subscriptions are falling. School music programs are being slashed in half. And classical music on TV? *Civilized* countries like England still play it, but we don't. We have seemingly 35 MTV channels—but if you want "classic" on TV, you have to mean movies. It's a mournful state of affairs and may well signify our cultural decline.

Alas, the requiem is premature. Classical music is *growing* in popularity, not shrinking. And in the coming years, we should expect it to grow even more.

The reasons are empirical, demographic, and cultural. Empirically, the doomsayers are ignoring some key numbers. In 2000–01, there were over 32 million concert tickets sold, up more than 10 percent from a decade before. Whereas season subscriptions dropped—for example, by 5 percent in Baltimore—single-ticket sales in that city *rose* 46 percent at the same time. That suggests not only that classical music regulars, including retirees, have busier lives than ever, but also that more people than ever are dabbling in classical. Most industries would call that growth.

In 2000, there were more than 36,000 classical music performances in the U.S.—up 10 percent from the prior year and up 45 percent from ten years before. Do *100 concerts a day* in America suggest decline—when in the 1950s (the supposed heyday), orchestra seasons didn't even last eight months?

Orchestra revenues are up; private philanthropy is at record levels; and since 1992, the number of college students majoring in music has risen by more than half. In fact, in 2002, the National Center for Education Statistics had to add to its standard music majors (music, music history, music performance, and music theory) at least three new classical subspecialties: music pedagogy, conducting, and piano and organ.

What did you say was dying out?

Here's my favorite counter-stat. According to Gallup surveys, the portion of U.S. households with a member who plays a musical instrument—54 percent—reached its *highest point ever* in 2003, the last year the study was conducted. And it may be that part of that growth was due to the fact that piano lessons aren't just for fidgety kids anymore. According to the Music Teachers National Association, 25–55-year-olds are the fastest-growing group of new piano pupils.

Even putting aside, for the moment, all the proof points that classical music is thriving and not withering, the big takeaway here is that the doomsayers' key metrics—CD sales and presence on TV and radio—are completely irrelevant. Musically speaking, the Internet is the place to be. And apparently—even though the cliché classical music listener is stodgy and gray—classical music is *more* popular on the Internet than it was in stores. Whereas classical made up only 3 percent of CD sales in retail stores, it accounts for 12 percent of all sales on Apple's iTunes.

Classical music is not only surviving the death of Tower Records, it is actually now spawning a new breed of listener.

The "classic" classical listener was white, elderly, well-educated, and steeped in musical training. While that group still makes up a big portion of classical activity online, a member survey conducted by www.classical archives.com reveals that nearly half of its subscribers are under 50, almost 1 in 5 did not finish college, and 1 in 3 have never played a musical instrument.

When you think about it, it makes so much sense. The Internet is far friendlier to the *casual* classical fan than big-box stores ever were. When you can sample free tracks, or download just one track at a time and listen in the privacy of your iPod, classical music is suddenly not intimidating at all. An unintended consequence of the Internet is that it has opened up classical music to a younger, more diverse, and more adventurous brand of listener.

And if you're a music student—either one of the budding college types or a newbie adult studying piano—it turns out that being able to buy just the track you're studying is a huge boon. Classical music was always so *long*—but now, if you don't want to, you don't have to buy the whole piece!

Now for the demographic reasons that classical music is about to rise. In every generation, the getting-on-in-years wonder why teens, too, don't lap it up. Well, the truth is, they almost never have. Classical music has *always* been an acquired taste, and in *every* generation, middle-aged people come to it for the first time. By that standard, looming U.S. demographics are a classical gold mine. Between 2000 and 2030, the number of Americans aged 55 or older will nearly double—from 60 million to about 110 million. The number of Americans aged 65 or older will more than double—from 35 million to over 71 million. And these seniors will be the healthiest, longest-lived, best educated, and most affluent seniors in history. Even if there were *no* Internet-enabled newbies coming to classical music, the industry should still be celebrating.

And finally, the cultural reasons. Since the 1990s, there has been a group of symphony newcomers who give the lie to the classical-is-*only*-for-old-folks myth: babies. In the 1990s, scientists introduced the "Mozart Effect"—a theory that got popularized as "classical music makes kids smarter." While it turns out not to be quite true, the number of pregnant women, new parents, and schoolteachers racing to buy classical music soared through the roof.

Even better, policymakers bought in. Since 1998 in Florida, all state-funded preschools have had to play some classical music every day. In 1998, Governor Zell Miller of Georgia proposed spending $100,000 a year to give classical CDs or tapes to every child born in the state. Just gave birth? Your maternity ward is likely to pack you off with not just a complimentary diaper and a can of formula, but also *Classical Lullabies for Bedtime*.

And finally, the nail in the coffin of the coffin of classical music may be groups like Bond, an all-female classical quartet who sport a lot of skin on their album cover and spread their legs just a little wider than is absolutely necessary to play the cello. This kind of crossover group is bringing classical a whole new potential audience.

So no swan songs just yet. Classical enthusiasts should be buying up classical CDs now, while they are on sale, because the stores may be *more* crowded soon given the demographic, technological, and cultural changes that are likely to pump up their fan base. Yes, orchestras might have to sell more single tickets than they used to, and they might have to give up up-front recording fees in favor of (large) royalties from digital sales. But the Neo-Classicals are coming. It's the best news classical music's had since Mozart shortened his first name from Johannes Chrysostomus Wolfgangus Theophilus.

PART XIV

Education

Smart Child Left Behind

Kindergarten Hold-Backs in America

▲

O ne of my favorite TV shows in the 1990s was *Doogie Howser, M.D.* It was the intellectual side of the American Dream—if Doogie was smart enough to finish Princeton at 10, then damn the conventions, he could be a Teenage Surgeon. America rallied around young, bursting geniuses who tore through the educational system. Carl Sagan finished high school at 16. Stephen Hawking graduated Oxford at 20. Hell, Mozart toured at 6.

Alas, no more. The biggest trend in education today is the opposite: holding kids back. And the "smarter" they are (or the more likely they are to succeed, statistically speaking) the greater their chances of being delayed.

It's called "red-shirting," after the practice of keeping college athletes out a year while they grow bigger. A U.S. Department of Education report issued in 2005 suggested that nearly 10 percent of American students in kindergarten were actually eligible to have enrolled the year before.

Who's doing this? The typical red-shirted child is a boy, with white, well-educated parents. So well educated that they know how good it feels to be at the top of the class—and they want that for their children, even if their children are currently smaller, less advanced, less developed, or less capable than their peers. So—ever the problem-solvers—they sign them up for peers who are one year younger.

It's particularly popular in private schools and among the well-to-do. An analysis of Connecticut education data showed that wealthy districts red-shirt at rates up to 20 percent, while low-income district rates are 2 to 3 percent.

Once it starts, it's hard to reverse. Soon, even if you're not a hyper-competitive parent, it feels neglectful *not* to hold your child back because if you enroll him in kindergarten at 5, you'll be subjecting him to classmates a full year older. Ironically, of course, the more families do it, the less competitive advantage there is. One observer has called this phenomenon the Kindergarten Arms Race.

Perhaps even more ironically, it doesn't seem to work. Most studies of red-shirted students have concluded that they do no better than their younger classmates in the long term, and that any short-term gains disappear by third grade.

From a trend-spotting perspective, Smart Boys Left Behind would be interesting if only to underscore the widening gap between America's haves and have-nots. As though low-income students didn't already have enough challenges competing against privileged students—what with their college-educated parents and SAT prep that began in the womb—now the lower-income students are also a whole year younger.

But in fact, Older Kindergartners are an even bigger trend than just Elite Boys. Below the layer of kindergartners whose parents hold them back for personal reasons, there is a solidly growing group of students who are being, well, pink-shirted—by the schools—for institutional reasons. If red-shirting means deliberately holding back *eligible* 5-year-olds from kindergarten, what the schools have been quietly doing is changing who is eligible.

In the past twenty-five years—in reaction to bold new standards in the 1980s that aimed to make America's elementary schools more rigorous—nearly every state in the union rolled back its kindergarten cutoff date from December to about September, effectively edging the younger 5-year-olds right into next year's class. In some private schools, kindergartners have to turn 5 as early as April or May of the year they want to start. It's a way to be sure that the schools, too, are more "successful"—at least in the measures people look at.

And so with virtually no central planning, or acknowledgment, America has been rolling back the start of formal education.

The *Chicago Tribune* has called it "the graying of kindergarten."

Whereas virtually nobody used to be 6 in kindergarten, now a serious chunk of children are, including nearly 1 in 5 boys.

Percent of Kindergarten Students Who Are 6 or Older,
1970 and 2001

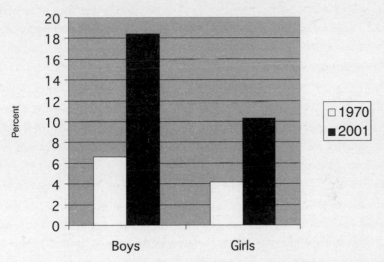

Source: U.S. Department of Commerce, Census Bureau,
Current Population Survey, unpublished tabulations

Does anyone care, besides the parents who have to pay for an extra year of day care, and teachers who might see more roughness at recess? Extrapolated out, it could mean very big things for America. Because you can delay the onset of school, but unless you also unhinge the other life events that are lashed to age, you are going to get some surprising, mismatched results. For example:

▲ *Middle School Sex.* Researchers tell us that the average age at which Americans lose their virginity is 16.9. So if that used to mean tenth grade, now it will mean ninth. Look for a national outcry in the coming years about how *middle-schoolers* are having sex!

▲ *Eleventh Grade Soldiers.* One of the tidy things about having young people graduate high school at 18 was that it set a clear bar for adulthood in terms of legal responsibility, voting, and military service. But now, if boys don't graduate high school until 19, the next time there's a draft, the Draft Board will come looking for America's eleventh-graders. How well will that go over? With those hyper-cautious parents, in particular?

▲ *High School Voters.* We won't need mock national elections in high school—we'll need real ones. Maybe presidential candidates will have to target Get Out the Vote initiatives to high school superintendents.

▲ *Twelfth-Grade Rapists.* If two high school senior sweethearts—he, 19; she, say, 17½—have sex, he could be convicted of statutory rape. And no juvenile hall for him—he's a full-fledged adult.

Of course, one could argue that the aging of schoolchildren, especially boys, is quite good news. Since it's well known that "girls mature faster than boys," maybe a little red-shirting for boys will at long last even the scales. And since girls are far outperforming boys in terms of college enrollment and graduation, maybe red-shirting is as good a way as any to get boys back on track.

And you can certainly understand parents who want an extra year with the children they cherish. What loving parent doesn't look at Junior in the graduation cap and gown, and wonder where all the years could possibly have gone? Especially in this age of fertility treatments, I know that lots of parents feel they worked very, very hard to get their children, and they are not about to give them up one year sooner than they must. And from the children's point of view, too, many of them are being given a great gift, in terms of the extra year to mature, the chance perhaps to shine, the chance perhaps *not* to be bullied. Arguably, that's as important to one's education as algebra.

But, schools of the future, plan on more parking spaces. We may need them in eighth grade.

America's Home-Schooled

▲

Several trends are coming together to produce a growing crop of graduates from "Your Home HS"—as the home-schooling movement is taking root in a significant way. Once regarded as an oddball idea, home-schooling is gaining currency as just about the best way to bring up kids in this crazy online world.

What could parents who home-school their kids be thinking? Maybe they don't think their public schools are any good—a lot of Americans are down on the system. Maybe they are unhappy with the drugs, weapons, and other dangers in school. (America has more school shootings than any other nation.) Or maybe they want more of a religious education than they can get in American public schools, and a little shelter from troublesome theories like evolution. In this world of hovering parents who don't want to let go of their kids, what better way to intensely enjoy them than to never let them get on that school bus?

So home-schooling in America is on the rise. After drawing just a couple of thousand devotees in the early 1970s, when the modern home-schooling movement was born, the number of home-schooled children in America grew almost 30 percent between 1999 (the first year the U.S. Department of Education took a serious look at this) and 2003—from 850,000 students to 1.1 million.

That surge reflected a leap from 1.7 percent of the U.S. student-age population to 2.2 percent. While 2.2 percent may still seem like small potatoes in a student population of over 50 million, home-schooled kids in America actually outnumber charter school and voucher students *combined*.

And yet, who ever talks about the home-schooled?

It may be time. Whereas home-schooling was illegal in most states when President Reagan took office in 1981, now it is legal everywhere. Hundreds

Home-Schooled Students in the U.S., 1999–2003

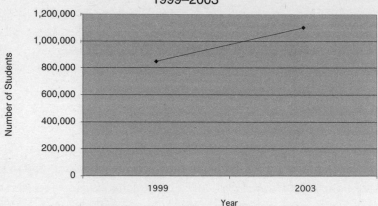

Source: U.S. Department of Education, Institute of Education Statistics, 2003

of organizations, Web sites, and conferences have sprung up dedicated to encouraging and supporting home-schooling. The creation and marketing of textbooks, curricula, videos, and other home-school-centered educational materials is worth an estimated $850 million a year. Major bookstores, movie theaters, and museums now offer special, targeted discounts to home-schooling families.

Even America's colleges, which generally demand strict adherence to requirements regarding uniform transcripts, test results, and applications, have bent the rules to accept parent-described curricula, and student portfolios, in applications from home-schooled youth. In 2000, only 52 percent of colleges had formal policies for evaluating home-schooled students; by 2005, 83 percent did. It didn't hurt that that same year, a study came out showing that home-schooled students score 81 points higher than the national average on the SAT.

The movement has also gained ground thanks to some home-schoolees of national prominence. Although home-schooled youth are barely 2 percent of school-age kids nationwide, they are 12 percent of finalists in the National Spelling Bee. In three of the last seven years, home-schooled students won the National Geography Bee. (The 2002 winner was 10, the youngest in the Bee's history.) In 2001, a home-schooled boy from Montana finished high school at age 15, but didn't feel he was ready for college. So instead he wrote a novel, *Eragon*—which became a best-selling book, and in 2006 was released as a movie starring Jeremy Irons. Even "lonelygirl15"—for a while the top-rated videoblogger in the world—*pretended* to be a home-schooled American teen.

So increasingly, as a nation, we're cool with home-school. In 2001, 41 percent of Americans said it was a good thing, up from just 16 percent in 1985.

Who are they who do science in the backyard, and math at the dining room table or in the supermarket?

More than three-quarters of home-schooled children in the U.S. are white. Sixty-two percent come from homes with at least 3 siblings—which means that parents who home-school their kids really like children to begin with, or that the synergy of a multi-student "class" makes home-schooling all the more attractive. (Imagine the sibling rivalry in those classes.)

While the occasional home-schooling family is superrich—and using home-schooling to accommodate child acting careers, worldwide sailing trips, and what-have-you—54 percent of home-schooling families have incomes of $50,000 or less. Nearly 80 percent earn $75,000 or less.

Over 40 percent of home-schooled students live in the South.

But while the prevailing cliché of home-schooling families is that they are Christian, conservative, and creationist—and it is true that 60 percent of the organizations listed on the Home School Legal Defense Association Web site have Christianity in their mission—the latest U.S. Department of Education study found that only 30 percent of home-schooling parents had as their main reason the intent to teach religion or morality. A comparable 31 percent said their main reason was to get their kids out of negative school environments (be it safety, drugs, or negative peer pressure), and another 16 percent said they were dissatisfied with schools' academics.

So while many home-schooling parents don't want their kids learning evolution—or learning from "government schools" generally—today home-schooling is getting a boost from all kinds of parents who just generally think they can do a better job. And now that the Internet has made it so easy to access thousands of lesson plans—as well as to ease the potential isolation that comes with learning at home—it may be that they can.

The implications are widespread. First, there's a growing industry for home-school retailers—and perhaps especially non-Christian ones. According to the 2003 federal study, fully 77 percent of home-schooling families rely on home-school-specific companies for their curricula, texts, and other educational materials.

Second, look for increasing litigation and legislation regarding home-schooled children. Already there are court cases in which a home-schooling parent is alleged in divorce proceedings to be "neglectful," and veterans benefits are denied to home-schooled 18-year-olds because they are not in approved educational institutions. In 2005, Senator Larry Craig of Idaho introduced the "Homeschool Non-Discrimination Act," intended to put home-schooled youth on equal footing with other students for purposes of scholarships, grants, benefits, and other government aid.

In addition, look for increased calls to regulate home-schooling. As of 2006, only six states "highly" regulate the practice, meaning they require parents to notify authorities, submit achievement test scores, and in some cases have state curriculum approval, parental teacher qualification, or home visits by state officials. On the other hand, ten states require absolutely nothing—not even notification to a school system that home-schooling is happening. One would think that the latter situation might result, at a minimum, in an undercounting of students getting educated, or an overcounting of students "missing" from the system.

As the movement grows, home-schoolers are looking for more recognition and more services. As of 2005, fourteen states had introduced bills that would require public schools to let home-schooled students participate in school extracurriculars like sports, drama, and chess. Since home-schooling parents pay property taxes, they would appear to have a good case that they should be entitled to use local school services.

Home-schooling is a classic counterintuitive microtrend. While schools have grown more complex, education has become more advanced, and most parents are so busy they are spending less time helping their kids with their homework, here you have a group of committed citizens doing exactly the opposite—dropping out of the system and doing it on their own. And they are obviously passionately consumed with home-schooling—you know what they get asked about when they go out for cocktails or dinner.

Home-schoolers have done a great job clearing the way legislatively and administratively for a simple concept. They have cut through reams of rules and red tape to secure a place in the nation, and have already grown beyond anything the movement expected.

But home-schooling may face a backlash from any number of quarters. Fewer students in schools means fewer teachers in the schools. Americans are not always kind to people who do things differently, and home-schooled kids have to get acceptance from public school kids—which could be hard on them socially. Even the losers of the Spelling Bee have complained that home-schooled kids have an unfair advantage, because they could (allegedly) just study spelling all day to the exclusion of math and science.

The bottom line is that as public schools become increasingly worrisome to parents, more and more of them—from every sector—will take it into their own hands to educate their kids. Home-schooling will surely come under attack from defenders of public education, just as vouchers and charters have—although admittedly, home-schooling doesn't require quite the same diversion of public resources. But in the meantime, the burden is increasingly on the American Mom to be not just healer and nurturer, but curriculum designer and science teacher, too.

Will Home College be next? No doubt with the Internet's growing ability to use video, be interactive, and set up social communities, there could well be a second generation of home-schooling that is Internet-based, widely available, and goes right through college. Already companies have put the core college lectures on tape, and could build the curriculum. This could start in the U.S., but have even wider application in more remote, rural countries where getting to school or college is impractical. Home-schooling may eventually be replaced by Internet-based school at home, with traditional public school becoming unnecessary for more and more families.

THE INTERNATIONAL PICTURE

With over 1 million students studying from their living rooms, the United States is the global leader when it comes to home-schooling. But other countries are picking up on this microtrend, too.

Although legal requirements vary by region, Australia, New Zealand, the United Kingdom, and Canada all permit home-schooling. The number of home-schooled children ranges in the tens of thousands in each country, but the groups are growing.

In a number of countries, home-schooling seems to take place a bit under the radar.

▲ **Japan's** Education Ministry does not acknowledge home-schooling as a viable educational option, and can prosecute parents who keep their children at home. Nonetheless, unofficial estimates put the number of Japanese home-schooled students at 2,000 to 3,000.

▲ In **Israel**, the Compulsory Education Law requires all children to attend school. That being said, exemptions are obtainable via a long and complicated bureaucratic process.

▲ **China** legally requires all children to attend school, but existence of the Shanghai Home-School Association is evidence that some families slip through the cracks.

Germany has strictly required compulsory school attendance since 1938, and goes to great lengths to enforce the law. In 2006, the German government put a father in jail for six weeks for home-schooling, and in 2007 put one girl in a mental institution with the diagnosis of "school phobia." The European Human Rights Court has ruled in favor of Germany's compulsory schooling bill.

Why home-school? Many parents cite the same reasons as Americans: fear of schoolyard bullying, concern over the declining quality of education, and the desire to give children a more religious education than public schools can. And by the way, that's not just Christians. A new Web site called the Muslim Homeschool Network and Resource provides information to home-schooling Muslims in the U.S. and Canada.

Although the Internet cannot be credited for sparking the home-school trend, it has certainly catalyzed its adoption across the globe. America's home-school materials suddenly have a growing international market, as well as the surging market here.

College Dropouts

▲

What do Bill Gates, Ellen DeGeneres, Karl Rove, and Yoko Ono have in common?

They all dropped out of college.

They said—college is too slow for me, I should get right out into the real world faster. Well, more and more people are following this track—but most often, they needed the last few years in college to really get ahead.

The good news from the college front is that higher-ed enrollment is higher than ever. According to the National Center for Education Statistics, 69 percent of students who graduated from high school in 2005 were enrolled in college the following October. That was up from 59 percent in 1988, and up from 47 percent in 1973. Indeed, a record-high 54 percent of all Americans have been to some college. For the first time in American history, going to college is a majority expectation for families—most kids will start college—and over two-thirds of high school grads will. This means that while high school used to mark the end of state-sponsored education, today a basic education includes a year or two of college.

But for all the growth in college enrollment, college *graduation* rates have stayed about the same—about 66 percent for students in four-year institutions. And dramatically lower for community colleges and online colleges. Which means that while more Americans than ever are entering college—and graduating—there are also more Americans than ever dropping out, "stopping out" (which is what they call taking a break with an intent to go back), or being "academically dismissed" (which is what they call getting booted). The latter, apparently, is what Woody Allen and Ted Turner have in common.

According to a 2005 article in the *New York Times*, almost 1 in 3 Americans in their mid-20s are now college dropouts, up from 1 in 5 in the late 1960s, when the Census Bureau started keeping that data. So the biggest

Number of High School Graduates Who Enrolled in a Four-Year Institution (and Completed at Least Ten Credits) But Did Not Graduate Within Five Years, 1970–2005

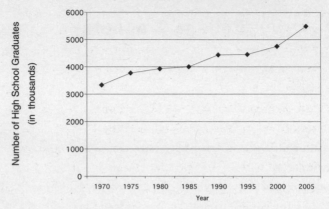

Sources: Institute for Higher Education Policy, National Center for Education Statistics, 2006

national source of educational underperformance has quietly shifted from high school dropouts, and the need to get them to return to high school, to college dropouts, and the need to help them finish their education.

Rampant college dropouts mean fewer people qualified to be teachers, fewer engineers, and fewer FBI agents than we were expecting given how college enrollment has soared. And dropouts are rising. In the decade between 1996 and 2006, America produced something like 28 million college dropouts—a population larger than the entire country of Venezuela.

Who are America's college dropouts?

It is tempting to romanticize them as the Bill Gates/Steve Jobs/Michael Dell–type of dropouts—entrepreneurs with bold ideas who just couldn't sit through four whole years of lectures by minds smaller than theirs. And the truth is, the list of famous college dropouts in America is so large, and so entertaining (Rosie O'Donnell, Nina Totenberg, Rush Limbaugh . . .), that it can start to make you wonder if you, too, could have founded a global computer company or been a talk-radio superstar if only you hadn't slogged through the extra years of business marketing and Psychology 202. (Tucker Carlson, John Malkovich, Barry Goldwater, Gwyneth Paltrow, Edgar Allan Poe . . .)

But the truth is, most people who drop out do so for more pedestrian reasons—usually money. Even if they can eke out the college tuition, they generally need a job to pay for the rest of the expenses of life—or simply because their family needs them and can't wait. And as you might expect, those coming from poorer backgrounds—those who are proudest to go to college in the first place—are the first to answer the practical call to support their families. For those who remember *Spencer's Mountain* (starring Henry Fonda in 1963), college in America, with its rising costs, may still mean parents have to give up their own dreams if they are to get large families to and through college.

But while for many years we have recognized the social costs of high school dropouts, we seem to have ignored the enormous and growing national costs of college dropouts. Nongraduation is very expensive. First, there are costs to the students themselves, like lower earnings. A bachelor's degree holder earns nearly twice what the high school diploma holder earns in a year, and nearly $1 million more over a lifetime.

But then there are the costs to the rest of us. College dropouts are arguably America's greatest untapped resource—the ones who are *prepared* for college, but in the end, don't make that million-dollar difference. And so they pay less in taxes, offer less in ingenuity, and are statistically linked to poorer health, more crime, more divorce, less civic participation, and less volunteerism.

We even pay in the short term. According to a 2005 study by the National Center for Public Policy and Higher Education, half of America's starting freshmen borrow, and 20 percent of the borrowers drop out. That's a lot of defaulted loans. In 2001, there were more than 350,000 ex-students who had begun college six years before, but now had no certificate or degree and little hope of repaying their debt. The *New York Post* declared in 2004 that in the prior five years, college students had wasted more than $300 million in state money by failing to graduate.

Not only are college dropouts a waste of American potential—but it's about to get worse. Between 1995 and 2015, the number of undergraduate students in America is predicted to increase by 19 percent, to 16 million. Eighty percent of the new students will be students of color, and many will be low-income and/or first-generation college-goers. If the dropout and stop-out rate merely stays constant, there will be something like 1 million additional Americans *every year* prepared to do college-level work but not doing it.

And these are the folks who wanted very much to be there. Nearly 6 in 10 college dropouts say they still hope to finish college. Nearly 7 in 10 say they'd have better jobs if they had finished college, and 74 percent say they would be financially better off.

So this is one of those small trends with big national costs. Hovering under the radar for now, it is failing to spawn the industry of government programs, PR alliances ("Got Degree?"), public-private partnerships, or even late-night infomercials that it should.

U.S. News & World Report should be ranking colleges on retention rates, not just admission rates. And not just the retention rates of nonscholarship candidates; every student taking a loan or a grant should know his or her odds of graduating from that college. Educate students up front not just about starting, and adjusting to, college—but about what it is going to take to get through college. And programs like the Teacher Corps can focus on those who are having trouble getting through for financial and family reasons.

A mind is still a terrible thing to waste—and the PR machine that decades ago told people that getting *to* college was everything now has to refocus some of its energies on getting students *through* college. College graduation rates will probably be the most important indicator of whether the U.S. will be able to keep up with emerging Chinese and Indian economies that are turning out millions of competing graduates. And at least one of those techno-geek college dropouts needs to look around and invent the online program for *finishing* the college degree. As noted earlier, America's best professors' lectures are already on tape, and online courses are being developed in almost every subject. If a serious number of American students can't get back to school, then school better find its back way to them—on the Web, when the rest of the family has gone to sleep. Just as we once needed high school equivalency tests, now we need online college equivalency exams. For better or for worse, the market is there, and it is growing.

Numbers Junkies

▲

mericans love numbers—they just don't like arithmetic.
We study less and less math and science in the universities, as more and more students choose fields like psychology. But we are fascinated by the mathematical underpinnings of our daily lives. We may have fewer numbers experts, but we have more Numbers Junkies.

When Larry Summers became president of Harvard in 2001, he told his university community that they lived in a society where few people would admit "to not having read any plays by Shakespeare . . . but where it is all too . . . acceptable not to know a gene from a chromosome or the meaning of exponential growth." And to be sure, at Harvard today, there are only seventy-seven math majors—out of over 6,700 undergraduates. Yale has thirty-eight. That means that this year, these two universities will graduate fewer than fifty people who really understand the ins and outs of higher math.

America has often imported its most brilliant math and science talent. Albert Einstein came from Germany when Hitler took over. Dr. Wernher Von Braun, also from Germany, helped us with our first rockets. While there have been classic American inventors, like Thomas Edison, top math and science people in America have not always been American.

In 2001, a bipartisan commission on American National Security said that the second greatest threat to American national security—behind only terrorist attacks—was the threat of failing to provide sufficient math and science education in America. In 2006 and 2007, Craig Barrett of Intel and Bill Gates of Microsoft testified before Congress that we urgently need more graduates in these fields, and that we will either have to draw from the world's new supply, or face critical infrastructure shortages.

Clearly, degrees in science, technology, engineering, and mathematics (known as STEM) are falling, as a proportion of all postsecondary degrees awarded. In the academic year 2003–04, STEM degrees made up 27 percent of awarded degrees, down from 32 percent just ten years before. And many of those spots are filled not by Americans, but by foreign students using HB-1 visas to complete their education here. By contrast, in China and India, Shakespeare is not as popular as Niels Bohr, but those nations say that they are graduating as many as 950,000 engineers a year. In those countries, the study of math and science is cool—it is seen as the road to a better future. Here, it's not so cool.

But for all the sobering truths about math and science degrees in America, it is also true that the U.S. today is experiencing a growing, and intense, popular fascination with math, science, medicine, and technology. According to a 2007 analysis in *Popular Science*, in this year's television season, there are at least fifteen successful prime-time dramas on the big four networks alone that heavily feature math and science. In the entire decade of the 1990s, there were only ten.

The "it" shows range from the blockbuster *CSI* on CBS, in which forensic scientists in the Las Vegas Police Department solve crimes by reconstructing murder scenes, deducing bullet trajectories, and analyzing blood spatter patterns; to the more niche-y *House* on Fox, in which a genius but ill-tempered Dr. Gregory House spots medical ailments by finding clues about patient behavior that even the patients themselves won't admit. But the appeal goes beyond just medical examiners and practitioners. One of the hottest new shows, with 11 million viewers, is CBS's *Numb3rs*, in which a math genius helps his FBI-agent brother solve crimes using some of the most sophisticated mathematical theorems out there. Indeed, math and numbers have become so ingrained in our modern TV culture that a California reporter called in 2006 for an "Integer Alert"—as something like ten new titles on TV this season are using them, from *The Nine* to *3 Lbs.* to *Six Degrees* to *30 Rock*. (The 2007 movies *300* and *The Number 23* reflect the same integer excitement.)

Sure, science has always been a big part of pop culture, especially in crime-fighting. Sherlock Holmes was the king of science-usefully-applied-to-crime. In the James Bond movies—beyond the women and the fight scenes—one of the highlights of nearly every film is Bond's visit to the labs of Agent Q, who shows off the latest technological inventions that (lo and behold) come in perfectly handy later on. And of course, *Quincy* got all this forensic frenzy started back in the 1970s.

And, to be fair, to whatever degree modern generations of kids have grown up on Barbies and fire trucks, they have also grown up on chemistry sets, Operation, Slinkys, and Rubik's Cube.

But without a doubt, in the past fifteen years, science has gotten a big boost. Educators from Carl Sagan to Bill Nye the Science Guy to even Al Gore have done significant work to bring complex science to America in terms and pictures that everyone can understand. And in movies like 1997's *Good Will Hunting* and 2001's *A Beautiful Mind*, we learned to find math and science geniuses wildly compelling. Then came Dan Brown's *The Da Vinci Code*, and Steven Levitt and Stephen Dubner's *Freakonomics*—and suddenly it seemed like no one in America *wasn't* fascinated with number series, math magic, and data analysis.

But what's happening today is even one step beyond that. *Numb3rs* alone has 11 million people flocking to it on Friday nights not in spite of the math, but *because* of it. When the show was tested with audiences using dials to indicate when their interest was really piqued, the viewers went wild for the math explanations. Why? The explanations made them feel smart, they said.

In many ways, science and technology in America are no longer focused as much on putting men on the moon, or building the world's tallest buildings, so much as they are focused on how to use more Space Ice Cream (the freeze-dried ice cream invented for the astronauts). More and more, we use numbers and technology in our daily experiences, and understanding them and their applications fascinates us. There is more computing power in a Ford car today than fueled the first rocket into space. Our washing machines are becoming computerized. Science and technology are all around us, and we want it demystified.

Look at what has happened to polls. When I started in this business, only the Rockefellers could afford polls—they were hugely expensive, since they were done door-to-door. Now there is a poll done every three days by the major news outfits. We are being saturated with numbers, and the news organizations are pursuing them especially hard because they sell so much better than yet another story on the bombings in Iraq.

At the same time, as more serious news organizations are beefing up their polling, many other organizations are doing "phone-in polls," some of which even earn them a profit from the phone company. This is not real polling, and has no methodological integrity. Moreover, the questions are often slanted to produce a certain result. It is sad that after all that has been developed in the real science of learning what the public thinks, so many TV news and entertainment shows accept techniques that appear scientific, but are not at all. I have seen straight-faced presentations of numbers that may as well have been cooked up in the back.

And most people don't want just the numbers, they want the "aha" from the numbers—they want the analysis and interpretation that give them the satisfaction of turning numbers into ideas. Of course, that is what this book is all about. Behind every trend, there is a reason to be ferreted out, and implications that flow from what people are doing. If Americans keep on working, or teens keep on knitting, there will be changes and consequences from these trends far beyond just the observation. That is why I have tried to be thorough in describing each of these trends, and in thinking through their potential meaning and implications.

Given all the numbers fascination, is America actually at the cusp of reversing the anti-science trend that both security experts and public intellectuals have warned about—or are we just attracted to math and science so long as it's fun and games? TV and movies, yes, but college courses and careers—no thanks? I'm not sure yet that *ER* and *CSI* are sending folks in droves to study chemistry (even though *L.A. Law* once pumped up law school applications). Yes, science summer camps are rising—but schools like MIT seem to be going the opposite direction, and considering revamping their curricula to appeal to *more* mainstream students. Are math and science making a comeback or not?

I recently interviewed one of the heads of the math department at Yale, and he said that the American who made the most money last year—$1.5 billion—was a math major. He was referring to a hedge fund manager who based the success of his fund on his calculations. His point was that there is plenty of money in math. So the popular interest in numbers is encouraging, and I hope books like this will get people thinking about the meaning of numbers.

But it will take a sea change in attitudes, especially among parents and peers, to turn around the number of students going into math and science in America. I hope that as people come to understand the power of numbers more, and as books like this demystify them, more students will take it up. But this is a country founded on the humanities—by a group of writers and thinkers deep into language and history. Ben Franklin was perhaps the exception, and look at all those oddball pictures of him flying a kite. If only he had looked more like Thomas Jefferson.

PART XV

International

Mini-Churched

▲

Do you remember the famous *New Yorker* cover from the 1970s parodying how New Yorkers see the rest of the world? The foreground shows a detailed Ninth Avenue, Tenth Avenue, and Hudson River; then the whole rest of the U.S. gets the space of about three New York blocks, with labels like "Chicago" and "L.A."; and then way off in the vaguely relevant, but not terribly pressing, distance are the flat landmasses of China, Japan, and Russia.

I'm reminded of that cartoon every time I think about how Americans regard religion, not only here in the U.S. but throughout the world. First, we think, there are Protestants and Catholics, with some key subdivisions among the Protestants. Then, there are a smattering of Jews and Muslims in some of America's big cities, and of course lots of Muslims in the Middle East. Mormons live in Utah. And with regard to the world beyond, we're pretty sure that Hinduism and Buddhism are big in places like India; and both Africa and China have traditional religions, although we're not totally sure how Chinese religion and communism go together. Pretty much every other religion is a fringe group, maybe even a "cult."

Moreover, we think, the big religions—Christianity and Islam—are becoming increasingly important to their own followers—witness the rise of the mega-churches in the U.S., and the rise of Islamic fundamentalism in the Middle East. But overall, we think, the world's truly religious must be a minority—or at least on the decline—given the phenomenal spread of science, education, and secularism worldwide. After all, don't we keep hearing about how Americans are a religious *outlier*? And how in places like France and Germany, regular churchgoing has fallen to under 10 percent?

So here are some important truths to orient us. First, despite the predictions of many modern religion scholars in the second half of the twentieth century, the world did not, in fact, get more secular as it got more modern.

In 1968, American sociologist Peter Berger told the *New York Times* that by "the 21st century, religious believers are likely to be found only in small sects, huddled together to resist a worldwide secular culture." Nearly forty years later, in 2006, the same Professor Berger told a global religious conference that his theory had been completely wrong. We don't live in an age of secularity, he said; rather, we live in a world of "explosive, pervasive religiosity."

Yes, and here are the facts. According to the *World Christian Encyclopedia*, which is a survey and analysis of the religious makeup of the entire world, there are nearly 10,000 distinct and separate religions in the world—with *two or three new ones being created every day*. Americans may be witnessing the rise of mega-churches—those sprawling God-o-plexes that offer everything from liturgical enlightenment to teen rafting trips—but worldwide, the opposite is true. What's flourishing is Mini-Churches: small, and seemingly faddish, new groups of intensely devoted followers.

This is, of course, a perfect example of microtrends. While we all want to understand religion through a couple of global megatrends—e.g., "Christianity is moving south," "Islam is moving right"—the truth is that religion around the world today is the sum of tiny, furiously devoted, ever-evolving micro-alliances that push and pull at the landscape of belief.

Of the 9,900 religions identified in the *World Christian Encyclopedia*, some are direct subsets of Islam or Christianity—like the 8 million Ahmadis, a messianic Muslim sect based in Pakistan; or the 300,000 followers of the Toronto Blessing, a Christian Charismatic movement based in Canada. Many are hybrids of traditional religions, like the 20 million Umbandans based in Brazil, who, according to the *Encyclopedia*, blend the traditional African Yoruban religion with native South American beliefs, parts of Catholicism, and nineteenth-century French spiritism.

Who joins New Religious Movements, or NRMs, as they are called? Experts say there is no typical personality type that joins up. Young people who join are generally staking out their independence. Older people who join are looking for comfort their lives haven't been able to provide. Certain ethnic or national groups—like Africans exposed to Christianity—turn to religious hybrids because the hybrids meld the new ideology with more homespun traditions. Almost all NRM adherents are looking for community, connection, affirmation, inspiration, and purpose. The sheer variety and opportunity of NRMs prove that belonging to a group with shared, intense interests—the very premise of *Microtrends*—is a powerful life force in whatever the discipline may be.

The flux, variety, and dynamism of world religions are important for several reasons. First, many of these "micro-religions"—that you can be sure didn't make it on to anyone's *New Yorker*–like map—are quite big. The 20 million Umbandans, for example, outnumber the world's Jews by about one and a half times, and outnumber Unitarians by more than twenty times. It is our perspective that marginalizes these religions, not their number of followers.

Second, as tensions continue to grow between radical Islam and much of the West, the billions of Mini-Churched around the world make it clear that the "clash of civilizations" rhetoric goes only so far. Yes, some segment of radical Islamists is battling some segment of vilified Christians. But when it comes to the impact of religious conflict on the world, the more accurate picture is that billions of people are earnestly advancing thousands of religions, and the resulting tensions—both creative and violent—are propelling world change just as surely as the so-called Muslim-Christian "showdown" that is drawing so much attention.

Third, experts predict that the kind of splintering, evolving, proliferating change that is going on among religions today is only likely to get more intense. Some say it is *because* of the loss of traditional religions' influence (the secularization observed in the 1960s and 1970s) that more, and more varied, religious efforts take root. In that context, militant Islam is less a mere "clashing civilization" than an *example* of one powerful microtrend, and it proves that paying attention to under-the-radar religious groups is important when these groups choose violence as a means of achieving their goals.

Which gets to the final reason that the Mini-Churched are so important. Scholars of these New Religious Movements may be one of the most important law enforcement resources around. While most of the 9,900 religions in the world are seeking peace, comfort, and spiritual fulfillment, there are a *few*, no doubt, that are growing in both intensity *and* violent inclinations. Already the FBI, and its equivalents worldwide, are calling on NRM experts to help them understand which groups are not just growing, but threatening.

And violence aside, other Mini-Churched are growing in their sheer ability to convert. While small groups may seem marginal now, it is worth remembering that all the world's great religions started out as somebody's fringe, heretical revolution. Abraham the idol-smasher was a rebel, as were

Jesus, Muhammad, and Martin Luther. Almost no one used to take Mormons or Quakers seriously, and now they are steady parts of the American religious landscape.

Religion is fractionalizing, and the ability to bring together many people under a single religious banner is dwindling. Clearly Islam, which to much of the West seemed pretty cohesive, has turned out to contain many warring factions. But it's true of all the religions. Organized religion is on the rise, but only through a multiplying of the organizations. Religion, which used to be four-square a part of the Ford economy, is now switching over to the Starbucks economy, tailored to as many individual preferences as we can come up with. These days, you can choose your faith and your prayer community in practically as many varieties as you can choose your morning coffee. It means smaller crowds in the pews, but presumably happier ones.

International Home-Buyers

▲

Ask any real estate broker—actual or caricatured on TV—what the key to home-buying is, and they'll say "location, location, location." You can tear down any house and start again, but you can't create an oceanfront, a mountain view, or a fabulous local school system if it isn't already there. Home-purchasing is all about place.

Which makes it particularly interesting these days that the most sought after places in America are being purchased by people from outside America. We all know that globalization means the economic barriers that separate the continents and the markets are being replaced by a single, unitary system. If you thought an ocean or two would keep you from having to compete with foreigners when it comes to buying a house, guess again. Foreign ownership of U.S. residential real estate could be the hottest trend in the marketplace. Ever wonder why prices in New York apartments keep escalating even though about the same number of people live there? The answer is increased competition for the same space, much of it coming from overseas. The Chinese and Korean governments may be buying our bonds, but the upper classes from around the world are being drawn to American real estate. Amazingly, there are no consistent records of foreign ownership of U.S. homes, so we have to piece together the story from snippets of information out there.

A 2005 survey of Florida Realtors found that 87 percent had closed at least one sale to an international buyer in the past twelve months, and almost 10 percent had a clientele that was *entirely* international. International buyers made up more than 30 percent of home sales in Miami–Fort Lauderdale in 2005, and 15 percent of Florida home sales statewide.

But the trend is not just in Florida. A real estate expert in New York estimated that foreign nationals made up one-third of apartment-buyers in Manhattan in 2004, up from only one-quarter in 2003. A couple of Las Vegas properties are more than 10 percent foreign-owned before they're even built. Houston, Atlanta, Chicago, and Colorado have all seen an uptick in foreign home-buyers. And the U.S. companies that list luxury homes are seeing more international subscribers to their magazines and Web sites, and U.S. realty companies like Century 21 and Christie's Great Estates are opening up more and more offices around the globe.

The makeup and motivations of people buying a place on the continent next-door vary—depending on the buyers.

▲ *Europeans*. In the last few years, the euro rose more than 50 percent against the dollar, and the British pound rose 35 percent. (Even the Canadian and Australian dollars rose 30 to 40 percent against the U.S. dollar.) As a result, American homes seem remarkably cheap compared to real estate in their own countries. And have you ever been to those rocky beaches in England or the grassy ones in Germany? Soft Florida sand and Mickey Mouse are very big draws to our European neighbors.

▲ *Central and South Americans*. Buyers from Venezuela, Colombia, Brazil, and Mexico love the political and economic security of America, and consider U.S. homes both a safe investment and a secure place to live, should instability increase in their home countries. They also appreciate the personal and political freedom that the U.S. affords, not to mention the shopping. Add to that the comparable climate and Spanish-friendly environments of South Florida and Texas, and U.S. homes are highly sought-after.

▲ *Asians*. With the growing economies in Asian countries and the increased flow of business between East and West, having a residential outpost in the U.S. has become increasingly attractive to many Asian families. And U.S. Realtors have been assertively courting them, naming luxury apartments in Chinese and throwing launch parties with Asian cuisine.

In general, the worldwide shrinking of airfare has made it easier to commute to your second home, as well as to visit foreign countries in the first place—which Realtors say is always the first step in buying a foreign home. In addition, new tools like multi-currency mortgages, which let you get a mortgage abroad in your home currency, but then switch if interest rates in the host country get more favorable, are easing the way for foreign home-buyers. And several U.S. banks are adjusting their policies to make it easier for foreign nationals who pay U.S. taxes to get home loans.

In New York, Donald Trump was a major factor in opening up the city to foreigners. Most buildings in New York City had been co-ops, and since co-ops can reject anyone for just about any reason, they looked very carefully at absentee foreign purchasers. But Trump opened condos, and sales of condos are largely unregulated because they offer single apartments, not shares in a corporation. Now that most new buildings are condos, foreign buyers are streaming in.

For the most part, international home-buying is a fairly upscale event; the median price of a Florida home bought by foreigners in 2005 was about $300,000, and nearly 1 in 4 such homes cost over $500,000. But as the middle class grows in Asia and elsewhere around the world, expect the practice to expand.

And foreign home purchases matter, even beyond the buyers and their agents. Surging numbers of international buyers could have some effects on the real estate industry, like more banks shifting their rules on home loans. (Although if foreign buyers stop paying in cash, they could be less attractive to U.S. sellers.) There could be adjustments in the culture of home buys; foreign buyers from some countries like to low-ball their offers, haggle aggressively until the end, and eke out in-kind provisions along with the house — like furniture, or caretakers.

Globalization could affect home design, too. Apparently, some Middle Eastern buyers don't like kitchens right near the entertainment space, as it is not customary for guests to watch women preparing food; and some Latin American buyers don't like having master bedrooms too far from the kids' rooms.

But more significantly, foreign home-buyers have the effect of driving up home prices for the rest of us. When noncitizens buy up one-third of the apartments in Manhattan, that nudges a good portion of middle-level American buyers into slightly lesser Manhattan housing stock, and knocks a good number of lower-end buyers right into Queens. At the luxury level, too, Venezuelans may bid up the prices of high-end Miami homes — but if there's an economic fall-off in Caracas, and they default on their homes, their American neighbors may be left with homes that are plummeting in value. The growing interdependence of our economies now extends to the most local of purchases — real estate.

Some lawmakers believe this trend calls for attention. In early 2007, in response to banks moving to make loans to foreign home-buyers easier, a California legislator introduced a bill to make it illegal for banks to issue mortgages to buyers who don't have Social Security numbers. So far, the bill has largely been dismissed as nativist and unnecessary. But that might not always be true. While America is proud of its role in the global economy, it is actually not so proud that foreigners buy American real estate at much higher rates than Americans buy abroad. Just try buying an apartment in Mexico or a house in Bermuda, and see the hoops they put you through.

And we're protective of our domestic assets. In 2006, when Americans learned that the U.S. was about to hand over ownership of certain New York ports to a company owned by the government of Dubai in the United Arab Emirates, there was a national outcry that lasted weeks and triggered a reversal of the decision. In 2005, when the California-based oil company Unocal was about to be sold to a Chinese company backed by the Chinese government, there was a public backlash that prompted a withdrawal of the offer. As of 2007, Americans are none too pleased that Japan and China own over $1 trillion in U.S. securities.

The purchase of luxury homes one by one, in a couple of communities throughout the U.S., is hardly the same kind of "takeover" of American infrastructure, mega-corporations, or currency. But is it time at least to *measure* trends in foreign purchases of U.S. homes?

Foreign policy experts are quick to point out that a majority of Americans favor international engagement, rejecting the isolationist idea that the U.S. should "mind its own business internationally and let other countries get along the best they can on their own." Yes, but on the other hand, the number of Americans *agreeing* with that isolationist proposition climbed sharply between 2002 and 2005—from 30 to 42 percent, the highest agreement rate since the survey began in 1960. And while, clearly, Americans look more favorably on foreign "investment" (53 percent) than they do on foreign "ownership" (33 percent), it is hard to make the case that home-buying isn't more akin to ownership than investment—especially when over half of the foreign buyers, at least in the 2005 Florida survey, said they bought their homes for vacation and/or part-time work, and barely a third said they bought them as investments.

From the other side of the coin, if you are a foreign purchaser of American real estate, you may want to take a careful look at your investment—did they sell you the bottom floors of an ocean view complex, without an ocean view? Did you pay the full real estate commission, while others typically get a discount? Since many foreign buyers are just looking for some fun and a safe place to put their money in case their local economy tanks, they can be quick to pull the trigger without the same exhaustive shopping of U.S. buyers. On the other hand, while buying U.S. real estate has its pitfalls, it can actually be easier—in terms of U.S. regulations, the need for Social Security numbers, and endless credit checks—than buying stocks and bonds. So purchase away. As Borat says, "Welcome to America."

LAT Couples (U.K.)

▲

Earlier we talked about Cougars—women who date younger men, often without a long-term commitment. We also explored Commuter Couples, people who are wed but live in separate cities, at least during the workweek. Now here's another twist on the unorthodox-ing of family life: long-term, monogamous couples who live in the same city, but in separate residences.

The trend-leaders are in Great Britain, where, as of 2006, fully 1 million couples are committed, exclusive—and living under 2 million roofs.

Marriage is already out of fashion enough. The British marriage rate (the percent of married people per 1,000 of population) dropped from 12.0 in 1991 to 9.2 in 2005, according to the Office for National Statistics. But now, it seems, even *unmarried cohabitation* is too much intimacy. In several Western European countries, the fastest-growing lifestyle is LAT—couples who "live apart together."

In Great Britain, it's 1 million couples—3 in every 20 people aged 16–59. That means there are as many committed, long-term couples who *don't* live together as committed, long-term couples who do.

LAT couples are growing quickly elsewhere, too. In the Netherlands, nearly 1 in 4 people aged 55 or older who consider themselves part of a couple are neither married nor living together, nor have any plans to change their status. Sixty-three percent of the Dutch approve of such "semi-attached couples," of whatever age.

In France, it is estimated that 2 to 3 percent of married couples and 7 to 8 percent of unmarried couples live in separate residences. And here in North America, nearly 10 percent of the Canadian population aged 20 and over are reportedly in LAT relationships. The U.S. doesn't formally track this arrangement, but you can bet it will soon.

LAT Couples are the newest players in the ever-shifting panorama of today's family.

According to demographers and sociologists who are following the LAT trend, the reasons for LAT couples span the spectrum of relationships. Most LATers are young and new homeowners, and don't want to give up their newfound independence. Especially in Great Britain, experts say, where The Home is cherished as one's nest and one's castle, people are loath to give up their houses, or flats, *even* if they're in love.

At the other end of the life cycle, LAT couples are frequently older people who don't want to complicate inheritance matters by introducing even a common law marriage, let alone an actual one, into their plans to leave their property to their children.

Still other LATers are in between, age-wise—and have children from a prior relationship, or aging parents, who are already living in their homes. Introducing a live-in lover or spouse to that family arrangement can unduly complicate matters, and it may be just as easy for both mates to have 24/7 exclusivity without 24/7 togetherness.

Finally, other LATers choose separate hearths because, frankly, one hearth is kind of crowded. Sure, she's your soul mate, but if she moves in she'll make you wash the dishes more than once a week. Hallelujah, he's The One, but if this becomes his house, too, he'll want you to stop burning incense, or he'll expect you to do all the cooking. Many people on their *second* long-term relationship want to avoid the mistakes or the pain of the first one gone bad. LAT is a nice, clear way to say: I love you—from over here, in my own castle—where I am king.

And lots of public "kings" have famously lived apart. Katharine Hepburn and Spencer Tracy kept separate households for their entire, decades-long relationship (although, admittedly, this was in part because Tracy was married to someone else). Woody Allen and Mia Farrow lived in separate apartments in New York. (Although again, arguably not the model marriage, as Allen later declared his love for Farrow's adopted stepdaughter.)

The trend seems kind of shocking to happy, cohabiting couples who can't imagine voluntarily giving up the cozy intimacy of snuggling with their life partner night after night. But the truth is, even among happily married couples who *do* share a roof, it's becoming more and more common to keep separate bedrooms. In the U.S., according to a survey conducted by the National Association of Home Builders, builders and architects have predicted that, by 2015, more than 60 percent of custom houses will have dual master bedrooms. Some of the builders surveyed said that more than a quarter of their new projects already do.

But whatever the reason for living apart, LATers are on the rise, and lots of groups should pay attention. First, those on the prowl. It used to be that a wedding ring would signal "off-limits"; but once unwed cohabitation became so typical, you had to look beyond the ring finger for the ways people talked about their living situations. If they had "roommates," they probably weren't exclusively, romantically tied up. But now all bets are off. Your crush may be ringless and live in a studio apartment, but for all you know she's basically been married for ten years.

Second, parents should take note. You may think your child is carelessly noncommittal, when in fact he's more monogamous than most of your friends. Or you may think you're lucky he's not *too* serious about that girl-friend you don't like, when, in fact, they haven't dated anybody else for years and never plan to.

From a religious or cultural point of view, the rise in LATs could signify a new, and arguably troubling, chapter in expectations about relationships. If "love" and even "monogamy" don't mean the daily engagement in another person's needs, joys, and interests, can commitment really be that deep? Is there *no* sacrifice or adjustment required for love? This is, of course, what the opponents of mere "Living Together" feared back in the 1970s and 1980s. If people just lived together without commitment, how long would it be before they just had sex without even living together? (Oh right, it would be almost immediately.)

Clearly, LATers take relationships more casually than married couples. In a Canadian study done in 2003, only 53 percent of LAT men and 62 percent of LAT women said that "lasting relationships" were important for a happy life, compared to 76 percent of married men and 81 percent of married women who said so.

And one wonders about the effect on children. If there are offspring, will they, too, shuttle back and forth like the children of divorce? Or is LATing part of the larger European trend of having few to no children, anyway?

From a commercial point of view, LATers create new opportunities. Like Commuter Couples, they need shadow home kits—clothes, toiletries, and favorite CDs and DVDs in two places, rather than one. They need double favorite pots and pans. Guest parking in their buildings and on their local streets. Ways to turn off the heat, pick up the papers and the mail, and let the cat out when they don't end up going home for days at a time. These people are worth tending to—after all, if they can afford to keep two flats, they probably have some disposable income lying around.

Perhaps most important, LATers represent a literal *doubling* in the amount of housing stock required. European populations are falling, but the fact that half as many people may need just as much housing could be an important development in the European housing market.

Finally, from a larger sociological point of view, we misjudge singles if we think they're all pining for mates; and we misjudge single homeowners if we think they'll all sell as soon as they fall in love. All the life-cycle-based expectations in the real estate market could be turned on their heads. Nor do we fully understand "households" if we think they are all atomic and independent—there may be more single households than ever in most Western countries, but nonetheless people may be very much living "together."

Maybe LAT couples have discovered something big. Researchers say that while LATers are wary of giving over trust, they are also prudent and independent people, confident enough to be forging a new lifestyle. They may also be far more likely than married people, or even cohabiters, to feel like giddy teenagers before a Saturday night date—absence having made the heart grow fonder, and all that. Maybe the spark lasts longer when the commitment is there, but the incense and dirty laundry aren't.

Mammonis (Italy)

Men Who Don't Leave Home

▲

Free food, free room and board, no curfew, a car when you need one. A lot of young people know a good deal when they see one. And while American kids typically can't wait to leave home, grown-up kids in some less economically thriving countries have been deciding, "What's the rush?" Mom's cooking is pretty good after all.

And so the traditional model of kids growing up, starting a family, and coming back to Mom and Dad's for Sunday dinner is being replaced with a new model: Don't get married, keep the single life of clubs a few nights a week, never give up your room, and stay at home until you are thrown out of—or inherit—the house.

And nowhere is that more true than when Mom's nightly dinner is lasagna, gnocchi, and osso buco. In Italy, a whopping 82 *percent* of men aged 18–30 are still living at home with their parents. No wonder young people are always making out in public in Italy—they have no other place to go.

In Hollywood, Ray Romano hints at the Italian mother's influence in the very popular *Everybody Loves Raymond*, where Italian-American parents Marie and Frank live not with, but next door to, Ray and his family, and Marie's food and opinions loom large in Ray's life. But go to Italy itself, and you'll find not just Ray, but Robert, too, living *with* Marie and Frank. No Debra, no Amy, no kids. Possibly no sports column or police work. Just Mamma, Papa, and the boys, with the boys approaching middle age.

Italian stay-at-homes, or *Mammonis* (Mamma's boys), are the most extreme example, but the trend has been noted and named in other countries as well. They're "kippers" in England, which stands for "Kids in Parents' Pockets Eroding Retirement Savings." They're *nesthockers* in Germany, which translates to "nest squatters." In Japan, they're *parasaito shinguru* (parasite singles), or *freeters*, which is a combination of "free" and the German

Percentage of Males, Aged 18–30, Living with Their Parents (1996)

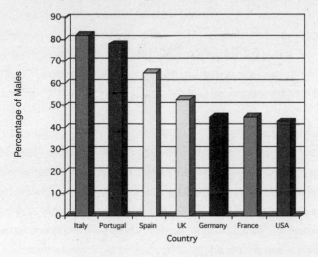

Source: Marco Manacorda and Enrico Moretti, *Why Do Most Italian Young Men
Live with Their Parents? Intergenerational Transfers and Household Structure,*
Centre for Economic Policy Research, 2005

word for "worker," *arbeiter.* In the U.S., they're "boomerangs," "Peter Pans,"
or "kidults." But Italian *Mammonis* take the cake at the astounding stay-at-
home rate of 4 in 5.

What happened?

Most observers say that *Mammonis* have been spawned by Italy's high
youth unemployment, high housing costs, and low and declining fertility.
No jobs, no kids, expensive apartments—why leave home? Other researchers contend that Mamma and Papa actually want the companionship, and
control, and are bribing their kids to stay home. They maintain that late-age
cohabitation with parents causes high youth unemployment, not the other
way around. But perhaps what is most interesting is the idea that economic
distress can cause closer family ties, while economic success can tear apart
the family structure.

Perhaps one of Hillary Clinton's most important insights representing
upstate New York was that "no child should have to leave his or her home-
town to get a good job." The big economic pull of the cities and suburbs in
America is causing better educated kids to leave town to find work—which
has been the traditional pattern since the dawn of the Industrial Revolution.

The result was the breakup of the family, scattering people around the country or even the world.

But in Italy, the opposite is happening. Intense competition from China for its principal products is draining the country of jobs, and the socioeconomic forces are promoting a more carefree life—no kids, no spouse, no responsibilities. But the flip side is that family ties are strengthened—and the nuclear family remains the center of life. Who is to say which system creates greater happiness?

But there are consequences of this change. Today's young Italian adults, according to researchers, have less independence, less initiative, less work and travel experience, and greater trouble forming their own families, than prior generations. They are having children at seriously lower rates (1.2 per woman in 2006 compared to 2.3 in 1950). True, elder care in Italy may pose less of a public burden in the coming years, but child care will be relatively obsolete. And getting a job as a schoolteacher could become impossible, as there will be too many schools for too few kids.

To the extent kidults are a worldwide phenomenon, there are commercial opportunities to mine. Italian parents may like their perpetual housemates, but researchers say that American, British, and German parents don't. The fictitious consultants in the 2006 American comedy hit *Failure to Launch*—who pose as girlfriends to stimulate late-blooming men to move out—may yet become real. Jobs for youth and higher-education programs may want to advertise with AARP and its European counterparts, since the targets (the youth) will be seeing the readers (their parents) every night for dinner.

As for the *Mammonis* themselves—and the kippers, *nesthockers*, and *freeters*—they report being happy enough with their arrangement. Parents and children don't fight cultural battles like they did in the 1960s; now everyone kicks back to watch *Raymond* reruns together. Dinner and laundry are well tended to. The only need they seem to feel is for a bit of privacy for socializing and, of course, sex. Has the European equivalent of Motel 6 seized on the upscale market for rooms by the hour?

Most Americans still regard living at home as an adult as a sign of some degree of failure, particularly in the media. Who does it? George Costanza on *Seinfeld*. Cliff Claven on *Cheers*. For God's sake, Norman Bates in *Psycho*. These are not men who, to use Freudian terms, have healthfully individuated.

On the other hand, Franklin Delano Roosevelt, one of America's most revered presidents, rarely lived in a house that wasn't owned or shared by his mother, Sara.

Perhaps the Italians are pioneering a new postindustrial lifestyle—a homespun counterreaction to the fast-paced and responsibility-laden modern world. Maybe this generation will enter midlife with a sense of relaxation and enjoyment that will be the envy of East and West. Or perhaps this same trend will put Italian society into a deep depression or recession in a few years, as China takes over Italy's manufacturing jobs, and the failure-to-launch generation finds they have to fend for themselves, but without some of the skills they should have gotten from Mamma, including how and when to leave the nest.

Eurostars

▲

Most people have heard about Europeans' lack of interest in having children. While Americans are head over heels for kids, Europeans have largely decided that family is expensive and bothersome, and as a result are seeing a fundamental deterioration of the traditional family structure.

Americans can hardly believe it—Europe's paid maternity leave and subsidized child care policies seem so *generous* compared to ours. But the truth is, fewer and fewer Europeans are using them. Whereas Americans are reproducing at precisely the replacement rate—2.1 children per woman of childbearing age—Europeans are on track to put themselves utterly out of business. The continent's average fertility rate is an un-self-sustaining 1.5 children per woman. In 1990, no country in Europe had a fertility rate lower than 1.3—now fourteen countries do. Another six European countries have a fertility rate below 1.4. Germany alone bore half as many children in 2005 as it had forty years before—suggesting that by the end of this century, the German people might number less than one-third of what they do now.

The reasons for the European birth dearth are biological, cultural, political, and economic. First, as is the case in the U.S., women across Europe are starting families later—if at all—which both increases the risk of infertility and leaves less time for big families. Between 1972 and 2004 in Britain, the number of marriages fell by 36 percent, and the average age of marriage rose from 25 to 31 for men, and from 23 to 29 for women.

From a cultural perspective, the increase in emphasis on self-actualization throughout the Western World has caused more Europeans to forgo having kids altogether, since, clearly, children can be a big disruption to one's work, travel, and leisure. And many left-leaning countries have deep concerns about the environment and overpopulation, causing breeding to be regarded as selfish and destructive. In Germany, it has been reported that a staggering 39 percent of educated women have no kids.

Total Fertility Rate, Selected Countries, 2000–2005

Country	Total Fertility Rate
Nigeria	5.85
Iraq	4.83
Saudi Arabia	4.09
India	3.07
USA	2.04
France	1.87
UK	1.66
Sweden	1.64
Portugal	1.47
Russia	1.33
Germany	1.32
Italy	1.28
Spain	1.27
Greece	1.25
Czech Republic	1.17
Ukraine	1.12

Source: United Nations Population Division and World Health Organization, 2005

Politically speaking, it has been said that the more liberal you are—the less often you attend religious services—the fewer children you will have. No one disputes that, in the past thirty years, Europe has both moved left and secularized. The childbearing-lefty connection may be evident in the United States, too. According to an analysis by USA Today, the fertility rates in the states George W. Bush won in 2004 are 11 percent higher than those in the states John Kerry won. In Utah, where more than two-thirds of the residents are Mormon, the fertility rate is 92 births per year per 1,000 women—the highest in the nation. In Vermont, the first state to embrace gay unions, the rate is 51 births per 1,000 women—the nation's lowest.

But while biology, culture, and politics no doubt play some role in the continental Baby Bust, the main reason Europe is having fewer children seems to be economic. According to a study by the U.K.'s Institute of Public Policy Research, British people aged 21–23 *want* and plan for children at a rate well above replacement. But by age 40, they've had a baby gap of 90,000 fewer children per year than they intended—and the reason seems to be the "fertility penalty" charged to women. Europe's maternity and child care policies may be generous overall, but in Britain, at least, 28 percent of women return to work in lesser paid jobs than they had before they gave birth. Among secretaries, that figure is 36 percent, and among skilled manual workers, it is 50 percent. While some countries have lower fertility penalties than the U.K.'s, it is the case across the continent that expensive child care and soaring mortgages have, crudely put, made the opportunity cost of having children just too high.

The impact of Europe's declining birth rates has been much studied. Demographers and economists predict that Europe's social security problem—the challenge of not having enough replacement workers to support the continent's aging retirees—will be far more drastic than America's. They have warned that in the next fifty years, the ratio of beneficiaries to workers in Europe will be so lopsided that some countries may crumble under the challenge. They have even said that increased rates of Asian or African immigration—which would itself cause social stress—wouldn't compensate for falling European birth rates.

Other challenges of their low birth rate include the likelihood that Europe's market share will shrink; its military power will decrease as it dedicates an even bigger portion of its resources to supporting its elderly; and its proportional influence in the U.S. will decline, especially as America forges greater ties with the homelands of its new immigrants—Latin America, and South and East Asia.

It has even been noted that we're about to have an intercontinental generation gap. Currently, the median age in America is 35.5; in Europe, it's 37.7. But by 2050, the median age in America will be 36.2—and in Europe, it will be 52.7. This means that not only will Europe and America be divided by the Atlantic, but they may have fundamentally different outlooks on the world. Europe will be shaped by events happening now, whereas America will be shaped by a decade that today, has not yet happened.

But for all that legitimate hand-wringing, here's the piece in the whole Baby Bust story that I see being underreported. Yes, birth rates are on the decline, and childless grown-ups are on the rise. But the decline in the overall number of children that European families are having *also* means an increase in the number of single-child families across the continent. Siblings may be fading, but Onlies are on the rise.

In the U.K., 23 percent of women have just one child, up from 10 percent two decades ago. In Luxembourg, between 1970 and 1991, there was a 16 percent increase in the number of families who had just one child. In Finland, the number of Only Children grew 50 percent between 1950 and 1990. In Portugal, it grew 134 percent between 1950 and 1991. And in all of those countries, as birth rates have kept declining, the number of Only Children has kept on rising. Single-child families are the fastest-growing family arrangement in the Western World.

This has serious implications. Since Only Children tend to be pampered, expect a new marketplace for child luxury goods. And who could deny them a pet or two? Look for the mass children's goods retailers to struggle, but for specialized stores to prosper. (Perhaps the mass-merchandisers can make a go of it by catering to the newer, faster-reproducing immigrants.)

As a purely demographic matter, fewer teenagers might also mean less crime, fewer riots, and fewer demonstrations at the universities. There will also be an intense search to fill the schools—which may trigger bringing in more foreign students to fill the higher-level educational system. Teachers, too, will be looking for new jobs as the demand for them shrinks.

But what also lies within this microtrend is the glimmer of hope for a European revival. A generation of Onlies means a rising class of confident, high-achieving, imaginative citizens ready to tackle Europe's problems, big as they may be.

According to birth order researchers, oldest children are highly motivated, responsible, perfectionist, and inclined toward leadership. In the U.S., they are overrepresented at Harvard and Yale, and every astronaut ever to launch has been an oldest child or an oldest boy. Famous eldests are said to include Clint Eastwood, J. K. Rowling, Winston Churchill, and all the actors who have ever played James Bond.

Middle children are compromisers, adaptable, and rebellious—John F. Kennedy was a famous middle, as was Princess Diana. Youngest children are outgoing, manipulative, impatient, irresponsible, and creative; they include Cameron Diaz, Jim Carrey, and Eddie Murphy.

But Only Children, like oldest children, are said to be confident, articulate, ambitious, responsible, and perfectionist. Having had their parents' relatively undivided attention, they are close to their parents, and disfavor radical change. They expect a lot from themselves and from others. They do not take criticism easily; and having been forced less often to share as kids, they can be inflexible. But they are stars: Famous Onlies (in some cases with some faraway half-siblings) have included Tiger Woods, Leonardo da Vinci, and

Franklin Delano Roosevelt. And Frank Sinatra, who, like a true Only Child, did it "his way."

So it is true that Europe faces serious challenges, and has fewer people coming up to address them. But of the ones that are coming, a greater percentage will—thanks to their Only status—be ready to step up in responsible, creative, and successful ways. Devoted to their parents' generation, they will tackle the social security challenge with vigor. Having spent many hours making up their own games while the adults talked among themselves, they may well come up with imaginative solutions no one has yet dreamed of. Their continent's problems loom large, but theirs will be a generation of high-achieving innovators ready to step up. So long as they can master playing well with others, both at home and abroad, Europe may yet experience its Greatest, and Smallest, and Onliest Generation: the Eurostars.

Vietnamese Entrepreneurs

▲

In America, most people still think of Vietnam as the place we became involved in a no-win war, based on a lack of cultural understanding. Fifteen years; 58,000 U.S. soldiers' precious lives; a humiliating escape in April 1975 from the roof of the American embassy in Saigon/Ho Chi Minh City. The failure against which all U.S. military campaigns have been judged ever since. The war itself was based on the domino theory—the idea that if Vietnam became communist, so would country after country in Asia, and the balance of power would fall to communism. Boy, was that theory wrong.

But the belief that Vietnam-style communism would be a repeat of North Korea's was so ingrained that what has actually happened in Vietnam is almost unimaginable to most Americans. While our former enemy the communist government is still in power there, Vietnam has become one of the most entrepreneurial spots on earth. Where America once sent soldiers, and then POW recovery teams, we now send cash. Personal, eagerly shelled out, cold hard cash, for everything from black pepper to coffee to rice to seafood. In 2006, Americans spent *nearly ten times* more on goods from Vietnam than the Vietnamese spent on goods from us.

In the past fifteen years, Vietnam has done more than just about any other country on earth to reduce poverty and build up its middle class. Across the country, the number of abject poor—those who make less than $1 a day— dropped from 51 to 8 percent. Neither China nor India has that good a rate.

In Vietnam's two largest cities, the poor (defined as those making under $250 per month) dropped from 60 percent in 1999 to just 25 percent in 2006. And at the same time, the middle class (making $251–$500 per month) nearly doubled—to more than half of Vietnam's urban population. And "middle class" in Vietnam means what it means elsewhere these days: Almost half of these people have cell phones, almost half have computers, and nearly 20 percent have personal e-mail at home. Vietnamese purchases of beauty and baby products have shot way up. Personal entertainment spending has doubled since 2003 alone. Since 2001, the percentage of Vietnam's city-dwellers who own bank accounts has nearly tripled, to more than a third of the population.

Many of Vietnam's entrepreneurs are in food-related businesses, perhaps because of the large food production industry in that country. From the very successful Dr. Ly Quy Trung—CEO of the Pho 24 restaurant, with fifty locations in Vietnam, Indonesia, and the Philippines—to the low-income mom-and-pops pasting handwritten signs in their front yards advertising homemade *pho* (noodles) or refurbished scooter engines—Vietnamese at every level are leaping into the entrepreneurial fray. Other businessmen and -women are pioneering the high-tech sector, with Vietnam having been called a "second India" of software exports, and rising as a force in telecom.

And all this growth is likely to keep going. Almost three-quarters of Vietnamese children of secondary school age are in school—up from about one-third in 1990—which is a higher rate of growth than either China or India can boast. Infant mortality is down. Life expectancy is up. Foreign money is pouring in. In 2005, the economy grew at a remarkable 8.4 percent, making it one of the fastest-growing economies in the world.

All these happy numbers are reflected in—or driven by—the Vietnamese people's extraordinary optimism. According to world surveys conducted by Gallup International Voice of the People, Vietnam is regularly *the most optimistic country on earth*—with more than 9 out of every 10 citizens saying this year will be better than last. In fact, on that measure, Vietnam beats the second-most optimistic country—Hong Kong—by a good 20 points. (Wondering which country is the most pessimistic? Greece, edging out even Iraq.)

Whence the capitalist fervor, in a land that battled the capitalist superpowers for the right to institute communism, and won? After the Americans left Vietnam, the party tried pure communism, but bad harvests and economic mismanagement nearly caused a famine. Thus was born *doi moi*, or a series of market-based reforms designed to stimulate the Vietnamese economy without sacrificing the party's political power. The U.S. encouraged this direction, with President Clinton in the mid-1990s ending the U.S. trade embargo and normalizing diplomatic relations. By 2002, Vietnam had amended its constitution to guarantee equal treatment for state and private companies, and eliminated several bureaucratic hurdles to the registration of private companies. The rest of the world began warming up to Vietnam, both diplomatically and economically. In 2001, the U.S. and Vietnam signed a bilateral trade agreement, and in December 2006, Vietnam joined the World Trade Organization and the U.S. Congress approved permanent normal trade relations. In perhaps the final chapter of the story of the U.S.-Vietnam military conflict, in 2006, President George W. Bush lifted the U.S. embargo on arms sales to Vietnam.

Of course, it's not all sunshine. Officially, America still regards Vietnam as an "authoritarian" state that abuses human rights. The banks still heavily favor state-owned enterprises, and entrepreneurs have little collateral to offer since the state still owns all the land. Corruption is rampant; intellectual property rights are few; and the court system is still beholden to the Communist Party. Income taxes are high, and power shortages are routine. In rural areas, where the bulk of Vietnam's population still lives, income has not risen nearly as fast as in the cities.

But the rate of economic progress in a place as ravaged as Vietnam underscores a serious entrepreneurial force, which the world would do well to attend to. Look, in the coming years, for substantially increased investment in that nation. The domino theory was wrong because communism in its pure form has been unable to generate a sustaining economic model better than capitalism. Democracy has actually had more trouble getting established than capitalism because enlightened communist states (which do not include North Korea) have been realizing they can hold on to political power if they loosen up on the economic reins. By introducing modest economic freedom, they have been able to enjoy continued political domination—we see that on a huge scale in China and Russia, and now we see it here in Vietnam. These regimes have learned that acknowledging and accommodating economic spirit is the only way to hold on to political power, and that as long as people have economic rights, they may not be so concerned about human rights. America was founded on the opposite principle—that human and political rights must come first—but these states are turning that theory on its head with some surprising success.

Look also for lessons regarding Vietnam's age structure. In most industrialized and developing countries in the world, we are having aging crises—certainly in America, Europe, and Japan, the populations are living longer than ever, and not being replaced at nearly the rates they used to be. In Vietnam, by contrast, over 60 percent of the nation's 84 million people are under age 27. While a youthful age structure is not always a recipe for success—the world nations with the lowest median age are struggling countries in Africa—it could be here, given the country's serious focus on education and the optimism that pervades the country, particularly among young people.

And if you want to start a business, especially selling goods to Americans, hop a plane to Vietnam and see what you can get made there for speedy exportation. The workforce is booming.

Thirty years after the U.S. failed to defeat communism in Vietnam, that country is a model entrepreneurial nation, trading goods, arms, and ideas with some of the biggest capitalist powers on earth. In a sense, this would be the equivalent of Iraq, thirty years from now, having rejected formal democracy but working with the U.S. to teach other nations town hall plebiscites and online presidential chats. It sure doesn't seem likely now. But neither, when you watched Marlon Brando descend into hell in *Apocalypse Now*, did you imagine that one day you'd buy Vietnam's coffee and rice at ten times the rate they're buying ours.

French Teetotalers

▲

There is nothing the French enjoy more than having wine. Except, perhaps, not having wine. French culture has been built around mixing wine with daily life—at brunch, at lunch—whenever a bunch of French people get together, it is usually around wine. And poor cheese—what would it taste like without the addition of a savory wine?

So here's a fact that has French wine merchants gagging. Over the course of the past forty years, no country on earth has *cut* its alcohol consumption more than France (except the United Arab Emirates, where in at least one emirate, people are lashed for possessing alcohol). And it's all about the wine. While consumption of beer and spirits has stayed basically steady in France, the per capita consumption of alcohol from wine fell from 20 liters in 1962 to about 8 in 2001. In glasses of wine, that translates into about 235 per person per year, down from about 425. And it's projected to drop even further and faster by 2010.

Now, to be fair, the French still drink *more* wine than anyone else on earth. Even that dramatic drop still has the average French adult drinking 235 glasses of wine a year—the equivalent of one glass almost every weekday, or one glass every day from New Year's until almost early *septembre*. But it's a dramatic decline nonetheless.

One reason for the dwindling wine consumption is the acceleration of the French meal. In 1978, the average French meal lasted 82 minutes. Plenty of time for a half-carafe, if not a bottle. Today, the average French meal has been slashed down to 38 minutes—and it's more likely than a meal anywhere else in Europe to include McDonald's burgers and fries. Wine is a victim of the disappearance of the leisurely meal. It is not the target of the change, but the decline in wine consumption is a by-product of the emergence of the faster, more modern, on-the-go lifestyle. Having resisted change for centuries, France is becoming modern, and Old World habits are giving way now at a rapid rate. Today's French children are no longer sheltered from the Internet, video games, TV, and fast food. Whereas the countryside had been immune to the changes in the city, now we are even seeing France's boundaries and borders shrink, as high-speed trains break down cultural barriers and connect every corner of France.

A second reason for the wine decline is a recent public safety campaign, mainly focused on road security. As of 2004, there were about 10,000 deaths per year from alcohol-related traffic accidents in the European Union, with France having one of the worst rates per capita. In the U.S., the federal government responded to rising drunk-driving deaths by essentially forcing every state to raise its drinking age to 21, which experts agree has saved tens of thousands of lives. While France hasn't seriously considered raising its drinking age—16—the Ministry of Transportation did crack down on drunk drivers in recent years, and also launched a public education campaign designed to warn people of the effects of driving while intoxicated. Drivers paid attention. So much so that wine manufacturers, whose profits are slumping, sued the government—and launched a counteroffensive to have wine classified as a *food*. That would not only eliminate printed health warnings on wine bottles but radio and TV advertising for wine would be unlimited. Don't laugh. Spain classified wine as a food in 2003.

The third reason the French are drinking less wine is the greater degree of health-consciousness that the French, like many Westerners, feel. Apparently some *French Women Do Get Fat*, and they are attempting to diet and exercise like everybody else. And in 2007, laying to rest yet another quintessentially French habit, the French banned smoking in public places—and some 70 percent of the French population support the ban.

Perhaps also important is that the immigrants coming to France in the last decades have largely been Muslim, and religious Muslims drink no alcohol. The French cannot, therefore, count on the next generation of Muslims to save the wine industry—if anything, the growing Muslim population could exacerbate the problem, and land now used for vineyards could gain more value if used for housing.

Typically, such consumer goods problems have been dealt with by exporting them—if our own French citizens won't drink our wine, we'll ship it out. But, to whom? Upstart winemakers from the U.S. to Australia to China to Brazil have been making their own less expensive, and quite good, wine.

And Americans, for one, are not as interested in French products as they used to be. Fights over "French fries," as well as serious disagreements over foreign policy, have left many Americans with a sense that France is not the role model it once was. Once the standard of all luxury, and a key player in Western history, France is no longer a top-of-mind country for most Americans, especially as compared to China, India, Russia, and the U.K. And U.S. merchants have taken advantage of that fact to grow the share of the California wine market. Two decades ago, wine-tasters held their noses to sample California wines. Today, they celebrate them. And while American wine-drinkers got educated on Merlots and Cabernets, they have lost any sense of what a Bordeaux or a Meursault is. The U.S. industry has been educating its consumers while the French have turned their backs on them, and the results have been dramatic. Meanwhile, Spain, Australia, and other vintners moved in with popular, lower-cost wines, and French wines got isolated as the expensive brand with declining benefits.

Imagine if people in China were to stop drinking tea; or the Japanese were to throw sushi overboard. The dislocations would be cataclysmic. Such are the problems created by the French drinking more Perrier than Pomorol. First, the French vineyards—as rich a part of French cultural identity as Disney World is to the U.S.—are in desperate straits. Having failed to prepare for either the decline in domestic demand or the upstart wine producers in other countries, French winemakers have found themselves with a glut of Côtes du Rhône and grapes rotting on the vine. The crisis has sparked violence with police and triggered heavy government aid packages. French wine merchants used to be elite entrepreneurs, the guardians of French gustatory standards. Now they are the ones rioting in the streets. As of 2006, the European Commission was considering dramatic new ways to reverse the vintners' slide.

Second, while the decrease in wine consumption will likely do good things for rates of French alcoholism, cirrhosis, and other alcohol-related diseases, one might also expect *adverse* health effects, if the claims about the healthfulness of red wine are true. While no one knows for sure if red wine decreases heart disease, the theory has been out there for decades, and France's low rates of coronary disease despite its high-fat diet have certainly fed the mystique. But now, with half as much wine consumption as forty years ago, this will be a real test of the theory—heart attacks should increase, and if they don't, it could reverse one of the great drivers of worldwide growth in red wine consumption.

Of course, some people can benefit. If you are an American entrepreneur, it might not be a bad idea to scoop up some cheap French wine and smack on some labels announcing "REAL FRENCH WINE" for under $10 a bottle. *Some* people in America will still be very impressed.

And if you are a young, growing French family, you are saving money—many euros a day—by drinking less wine, and you are likely putting that cash into modern conveniences and a rising standard of living. You are also probably contributing more to the gross national product, able to do a lot more work because you have more hours per day at peak alertness.

But if you are a French vintner, you are facing the opposite—a lot more time on your hands, and fewer euros in your pocket. Maybe you even take a few extra drinks just to get through the day. All the while lamenting, "Just what has happened to the *ancien régime?*"

Chinese Picassos

▲

There are a couple things everybody knows about China. First, it's a budding economic superpower, with 1.3 billion people—over 500 million of whom are projected to be middle-class by 2010. The sheer size of the market is staggering.

Second, especially here in the U.S., we know that because of China's intense focus on science and engineering, it is turning out hundreds of thousands more undergraduate science majors than we are—and rapidly gaining on us in terms of graduate degrees in science and engineering, too.

It may surprise you to learn, therefore, that China is increasingly an *art* superpower, too. Between 1993 and 2005, China's premier art auction house nearly quadrupled its annual sales volume, from under $2.5 million to $10 million. According to Chinese gallery-owners, domestic demand for Chinese art has grown nearly 10-fold in recent years, and is expected to keep climbing. This is, of course, a reflection of that booming Chinese middle class—who now not only have walls to decorate and fortunes to flaunt, but also want someplace other than the volatile Chinese stock market to put their money.

Yet growing Chinese interest in art—enormous as it is for the Chinese themselves—is not the end of the story. This is a global explosion. Since the 1980s, the price of contemporary Chinese oil paintings on the world market has skyrocketed, in some cases by as much as a 100-fold. Between 2004 and 2006 alone, Sotheby's and Christie's increased their Asian (mostly Chinese) contemporary art sales worldwide from a mere $22 million to a stunning $190 million. Suddenly, Chinese art is one of the hottest things on the international scene.

Not bad for a country that just a few years ago required all "art" to expressly glorify the Communist Party—right? What happened?

First of all, China *used* to lead the world in many kinds of art, like calligraphy and, of course, the porcelain most of us in the West call, simply, "china." But the twentieth century was a low period, what with the communist repression of most forms of artistic expression. After the death of Mao Zedong in 1976, there was a temporary flowering of art, with artists venturing forth in a kind of nervous, avant-garde style of painting—but in 1989, the "China/Avant Garde" show at the National Gallery in Beijing was shut down by the government within weeks of opening. A few months later came the Tiananmen Square massacre, and many artists fled their homeland or abandoned art entirely.

Only slowly, over the 1990s, did Chinese art trek back. In 1992, the communist authorities legalized the private art market and began to ease up on censorship. By 1995, Chinese artists were on display at the Venice Biennale, a major worldwide show of contemporary art; and in 1996, Americans flocked to New York's International Asian Art Fair. In 2004, as part of its obligations as a member of the World Trade Organization, China opened its doors to foreign auction houses; and by 2006, Sotheby's and Christie's had the record-breaking sales of Chinese art mentioned above (although still mostly outside the mainland). Today, the Chinese government affirmatively cultivates international art stars.

Now when you think Chinese art, don't just think pastoral scenes, with those exotic ink brushstrokes. The biggest Chinese painters today present full-scale studies of musicians, prostitutes, families, and acrobats, as well as richly abstract canvases. Some of the edgier ones depict red babies floating through postindustrial landscapes, or yaks cartwheeling across railway lines. And many have become household names around the world, as well known as contemporary Western stars like Damien Hirst and Jeff Koons. Forty-three-year-old Liu Xiaodong of Liaoning Province sold his *A Man with Two Women* to a Chinese entrepreneur for a record-breaking $2.7 million in November 2006. Around the same time, Zhang Xiaogang, 48, of Yunnan Province, known for his photograph-like paintings of the Cultural Revolution, sold his *Tiananmen Square* for $2.3 million at Christie's in London.

And it's not just painting, either. The New York–based Cai Guo-Qiang, born in 1957 in Fujian Province, is best known for casting a rainbow across the East River to celebrate the opening of the temporary Museum of Modern Art in Queens, and for exploding a powder-based dragon across the Thames. Chinese painting, film, video, photography, and performance art have become some of the most innovative in the world.

Maybe we—especially in America—shouldn't be surprised. One of our own Founding Fathers, John Adams, once wrote to his wife, Abigail, that he "must study Politicks and War, that my sons may . . . study . . . Commerce and Agriculture, in order to give their Children a right to study Painting, Poetry, and Porcelain." So maybe it's the natural progression that war gives way to commerce, and commerce gives way to art. Perhaps China's flourishing markets, entrepreneurs, and scientists—rather than being inconsistent with a booming art presence—are art's natural breeding ground.

The implications are big, as is everything in China. The growing class of Chinese artists is in the millions—including the 20-somethings who sell their photographs to eager Western scouts for $10,000 a pop; the 30- and 40-somethings who were born during the Cultural Revolution and now create at the crossroads of, as one observer has said, "an authoritarian regime and rampant consumerism"; and the 50- and 60-somethings who came of age during the Cultural Revolution, and now have the perspective, and some freedom, to criticize it.

There's even a big market for mass-art production, and reproduction. A Chinese town called Dafen, just outside the southern city of Shenzhen, houses hundreds of oil painting shops, wherein thousands of assembly-line workers can re-create for you in minutes whatever masterpiece you want— Chinese or foreign, classical or contemporary. Talk about the entrepreneurial foundation of artistic expression.

Look for a booming industry of Chinese art merchants, marketers, middlemen, and, of course, fakes. State cultural authorities had to pass a law in 2003 requiring all auction houses and personnel to undergo annual examinations to guard against fraud in the enormous but nascent art market.

And viewers are booming, too. Young Chinese apparently love the burgeoning art galleries, making art-browsing one of the fastest-growing pastimes in China. And as a result, both the U.S.'s Guggenheim Museum and France's Pompidou are looking to open branches in China.

Yes, some of the market has yet to mature, both in terms of artists' freedom and buyers' tastes. The government still censors some work, especially if it deals with contemporary politics, and it is disinclined to allow much home-made art to leave the mainland. From the buyers' and critics' side, too, there is some refinement to be had—some galleries still pay painters purely by the *size* of the canvas.

But my sense is that the surge of Chinese artists is good news for everyone. Not just the creative Chinese, who have won back some freedom to express themselves aesthetically; and not just the layers upon layers of Chinese and international art merchants who will build businesses to match the interest. And not even just the people of all nations who may now be able to relate to more Chinese citizens on more levels. No, the art surge is most importantly good news for China—if the incremental liberation of artistic expression signals an expansion of other political and economic freedoms as well.

During the Cold War, Czech poet and playwright Václav Havel used art, before he used politics, to challenge the communist government's grip on his country. In a series of internationally acclaimed plays, Havel cried out for a free and open Czech society. In 1989, Havel became president of the newly democratic Czechoslovakia (and later the Czech Republic)—and without violence. Some day, Chinese artists may herald a new chapter of not just artistic, but also economic and political, reforms in China.

And last, if you want to get in on the ground floor of some budding art communities, go to where business—regular business—is booming. John Adams may have thought he was just musing to his wife about his personal family legacy, but he was also making a keen observation about society. China's size, and its rich history of aesthetic innovation, may make it an exceptionally good place for art to flourish right now. But other countries whose GDPs are also rising steadily include Azerbaijan, Estonia, Trinidad and Tobago, and Ghana. Maybe that Estonian expressionist you've been admiring is actually *also* a great investment. And, of course, Vietnam.

Ask the Medicis—where there's prosperity, there is probably art. And where there is prosperity *and* rapid social change, there may well be important, powerful, even transformative art.

Russian Swings

▲

This trend is about the middle of the Russian electorate. It's about Russians who, in the 1990s, swung toward democracy, and now are swinging back. They not only hold the future of Russia in their hands, but they tell us something important about democracy versus prosperity, which, in the West, we often assume go hand in hand.

The late 1980s were heady days for Eastern Bloc democrats. The Polish Solidarity movement was having real, bilateral talks with its communist government; Hungary was instituting multiparty elections; and the East Germans were marching in the streets for the right to travel. Then the Berlin Wall came down, and the Communist Party ceded power in Czechoslovakia, Romania, Bulgaria, and Albania. In 1990, East and West Germany rejoined, and finally the Soviet Union itself dissolved.

Russians were hopeful. After seventy-five years of communist rule—and centuries of autocratic czars before that—a majority of Russians told the 1991 Pulse of Europe Survey that they thought their country should rely on a democratic government rather than a strong leader to solve the country's problems. Among young Russians, aged 18–34, nearly 6 in 10 said they favored democracy over a strong hand. The promise of both economic and political freedom was powerful, thrilling, and forward-looking.

And by many measures, Russians' hopes have been borne out. After an initial depression in the 1990s, Russia's economy has now grown eight years in a row, surpassing the average growth rates of all other G8 countries. Thanks to rising energy prices and Russia's huge reserves of oil and natural gas, Russian incomes are rising, consumer credit is widely available, the stock market is booming, and consumer demand is growing. The emerging Russian middle class has swelled to between 40 and 50 million people. In this sense, the fall of communism was a great, pro-democratic, even pro-capitalist success.

But today, Russians are telling global pollsters some surprising things. According to the Pew Global Attitudes Project, which inherited the 1991 Pulse of Europe Survey, only 28 percent of Russians now favor democratic government over a strong leader—down from 51 percent in 1991. (In 2002, the percentage favoring democratic government sank as low as 21 percent.) A remarkable 81 percent of Russians—including every demographic subgroup—now say that a strong economy is more important to them than a good democracy.

To put this shift from democracy to strong leader in perspective, Pew compares the Russian shift to trends in the Muslim world, where authoritarian rulers are commonplace. In five out of six predominantly Muslim countries—Morocco, Lebanon, Turkey, Indonesia, and Jordan—majorities of respondents say they would prefer that democratic institutions solve the country's problems than a leader with a strong hand. Which would you have thought would be more committed to democratic rule—those Muslim countries, which most Americans probably couldn't find on a map—or our European ally Russia, to whom the U.S. has furnished almost $2 billion in aid since it did away with communism more than fifteen years ago?

What seems to be emerging is the Russian Swing Voter. The voter who used to march for democracy, but now strongly favors a strong ruler with concentrated power.

Who this voter is is critical to the future of Russia. He is a he, for starters. According to Pew's analysis, Russian men were the biggest democracy boosters in the early 1990s—favoring democracy over a strong leader 58 to 35 percent, compared to women's more lukewarm support of 46 to 42 percent. But now, about two-thirds of all Russians—men and women—prefer the strong leader.

Second, Russia's new Swing Voters are largely the young people who were at the forefront of the pro-democracy movement in the early 1990s. Whereas nearly 6 in 10 Russians aged 18–34 favored democracy then, now those same people, having aged to their 30s and 40s, have switched, favoring a strong leader by an even wider margin (66 to 29 percent).

Also, money has something to do with the swing. The lowest income group in Russia has the least remaining faith in democratic forms of government.

Disillusioned, male, and not quite middle-class. The Swing Voter is he who sees the rising gap between rich and poor, and knows he's on the wrong side. He who is disappointed in Russia's school systems; its miserable public safety (fewer than 3 in 10 Russians feel safe on the streets); and its wide-spread corruption (in 2006 in Moscow alone, 40 percent of poll respondents said they had given a bribe in the last twelve months). This is Russia's swing vote.

Of course, the vote of any sort in Russia is being challenged these days. Probably buoyed by the very surveys that show Russians like strong-man leadership, President Vladimir Putin has replaced regionally elected governors with his own appointments; proposed ending mayoral elections; made it harder for new political parties to form and register; and harassed the umbrella opposition group—known as Other Russia, led by chess great Garry Kasparov—practically to extinction. As a St. Petersburg party leader told the *New York Times* in early 2007, "I would not call the process underway in our country democracy."

Nonetheless, there is deference to popular opinion. Polls and surveys still matter to Putin, who surely watches his own approval ratings, now in the high 70s, with glee. Putin conducts occasional, live Q&A sessions with the Russian people over e-mail and telephone to hear concerns and share plans. While it is widely understood that Putin will handpick his 2008 successor (unless he circumvents the constitution to give himself a third term), observers also say that he began floating candidate trial balloons as early as 2006, to be sure that his choice will be well received.

So Russia is at a crossroads. On the one hand, President Putin seems inclined to make Russia an "autocratic petro-state," as one observer has called it, and to assume the mantle of the global opposition movement to the United States. His February 2007 speech in Munich was described as "the most aggressive speech from a Russian leader since the end of the Cold War."

But on the other hand, Russia's voters—including the swings who once supported democracy—have the power to urge their leaders to remember the growing middle class, attract and not repel more foreign investment, and permit more economic and democratic freedoms. Yes, they were disillusioned by the post-communist depression in the 1990s, and while they appreciate the economic growth under Putin and are impressed by his strength, there is also a growing sense that they're concerned about it, too. Since 2002, those who favor democracy over a strong leader have climbed from 21 percent back up to 28 percent. In fact, in a 2006 survey, nearly half of Russians said they were at least somewhat worried that their president "might try to establish a severe dictatorship, relying on the security forces."

So the Swing Voters can help steer this country through its crossroads. And while American swing voters are aging Soccer Moms, the Swing Voters in Russia are rugby men. They don't mind some fancy footwork with the democracy ball. If anything, these Russian voters reinforce what we are finding all around the world—that people want economic freedom first, and democratic institutions second, once there's a little prosperity. New institutions of democracy have a way of becoming bogged down while developing countries, courageous enough to try liberalizing their economies, need to demonstrate some fast results. And so even in places like Russia, where there is a history of brutal, tyrannical government, the Swing Voters are choosing saving the economy over saving democracy. But if democracy is to gain as well, it will be at the hands of the quintessential democratic tool, the swing voter.

Indian Women Rising

▲

A hundred and fifty years ago, widows in India used to throw themselves on the funeral pyres of their husbands, in a tradition called *sati*. Today, the leader of India's most powerful political party (and one of the most beloved figures in that nation of over 1 billion) is a woman. Her mother-in-law, Indira Gandhi, was India's prime minister for more than fifteen years. Throughout the world, Indian women are rising to the top of business, science, sports, and the arts. For a group that used to have almost no identity beyond the home, Indian women have come a long way.

India itself has come a long way. As of 2007, its economy regularly grows at over 8 percent a year, making it second in growth in the world only to China. Its middle class—at 300 million people—is the size of the entire United States. In the last decade, India has lifted more people out of poverty than the number of residents of Western Europe. In the 1990s, India grew its literacy rate 13 points—now up to nearly two-thirds of the population. By the late 2030s, India is projected to have the third-largest economy in the world, after the U.S. and China.

India's women have enjoyed a good portion of this national boom. In India's urban areas, women's employment has recently grown at over ten times the rate of men's. The increasingly knowledge-based economy has opened more opportunities for educated Indian women, who no longer need to travel to remote factories to rise in the workforce. And at the top of Indian women's professional success are the worldwide superstars discussed below.

Of course, India still has a great deal of work to do, both for national prosperity generally and for women's share of it. India is still home to the largest number of the world's poor, with almost 600 million people living on $2 per day and another 250 million living on half that. Almost 2 million Indian children die every year before their first birthday. Two-thirds of the popula-

Growth in Ratio per Thousand for Employed Men and Women in Urban India, 1999–2005

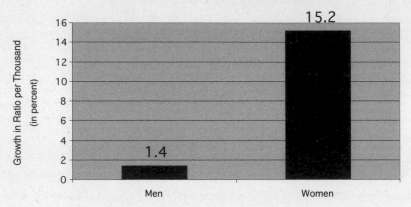

Source: Employment and Unemployment Situation in Cities and Towns in India, 2004–2005; National Sample Survey Organization, Ministry of Statistics and Programme Implementation, Government of India, March 2006.

tion still live without basic services, including 450 million people who have no electricity.

And women's gains have their starts and stops. While urban women are rising in the workforce, the majority of their jobs remain low-paid agricultural and domestic work. Primary education for girls is on the rise, but fewer than half of Indian girls make it to secondary school. *Sati*, mentioned above, and dowry murders—the practice of killing young brides who cannot deliver the price their grooms expected—are formally outlawed, but both still occur. Violence against women throughout India is high; and abortion of girl fetuses seems not only widespread but growing—even among higher-income families. In terms of politics, while there is a mandate at the local level that one-third of legislative seats be filled by women, the bill proposing the same at the parliamentary level has failed over and over to reach consensus.

But as is the case in every democracy on earth right now, the rise of women in India seems certain, and significant. In politics—apart from the stratospheric Gandhi family—the ranks of women legislators are growing, if slowly. In several Indian states, female representation surpasses the required 33 percent, and scholars are now proving what a difference women's leadership makes. According to a 2005 study by researchers at the London School of Economics, raising Indian female political representation by 10 percentage points increases by 6 percentage points the probability that an urban Indian child will get a primary education.

In business, too, women like Naina Lal Kidwai and Kiran Mazumdar Shaw are busting all stereotypes about women and finance. Kidwai, CEO of the European bank HSBC India, was the first Indian woman to graduate from Harvard Business School, and now manages 50 percent of the foreign institutional investment in her country. Within a year of her becoming CEO of HSBC India, reported *India Today*, the bank's pretax profits rose 85 percent.

Shaw, a Bangalorian native who started out as India's first woman brewmaster, and is now chairman and managing director of the biggest biopharmaceutical firm in India, Biocon Ltd., is said to be the nation's richest woman, with a net worth of nearly $500 million U.S.

In the arts as well, film director/writer/producer Mira Nair has made it about as big in both Bollywood and Hollywood as a person could hope. From her wildly successful debut *Salaam Bombay!* to her Best Screenplay–winning *Mississippi Masala* to her Golden Globe–nominated *Monsoon Wedding* to her much acclaimed 2007 *The Namesake*, Nair has decimated any lingering stereotypes about female weakness in male-heavy Bollywood, and through the content of her films arguably has done as much to bridge worldwide cultural understanding as any filmmaker today. Bollywood itself is now such an "it" industry that headliner *Hollywood* actors—like George Clooney—are scrambling to get in.

That kind of international impact is spreading in every field. Indians make up the largest group of international students in the U.S., at nearly 15 percent. Many of them stay—after attending Yale School of Management, Indra Nooyi rose to become chairwoman of PepsiCo, and in 2006 was named the fourth most powerful businesswoman in the world. Kalpana Chawla came to the U.S. to study aerospace engineering at the University of Texas; she was the first Indian-born woman to fly into space, and was one of the seven-member crew lost in the space shuttle *Columbia* disaster.

Swati Dandekar, Democrat of Iowa, is the first Indian-born woman to be elected to a U.S. state legislature. Tennis star Sania Mirza, the first Indian sportswoman to make the cover of *TIME* magazine, drew her own personal fatwa because her tennis outfits didn't comport with the traditional dress codes for Muslim Indian girls.

Evidently, Kidwai, Shaw, and Nair are good friends—Shaw and Nair since childhood—which may say something about the rarefied environment in which prominent Indian women are rising. Yes, in a nation with a half a billion women, there are clearly going to be more women left behind than make up most nations on earth. But there's no question about it, Indian women's ascent is steady and powerful, and with it may yet come huge changes not only for the earth's second-largest country, but for the entire world.

Educated Terrorists

▲

The power of small is biggest when it is destructive.

Small numbers have always been able to pull off assassinations that changed the course of history, but never have so few been able to upset so much as in the modern world. We all know a terrorist cell with a suitcase-nuke could forever change our society.

It took but a single crazy person to turn Virginia Tech into a killing field and put a nation in mourning. It took fewer than two dozen hijackers to bring down the World Trade Center.

But there is a big difference between the two events. The Virginia Tech killings were the product of a single deranged mind whose ideas died with him, while 9/11 was the result of an intellectual and religious movement that has the power to convince even well-educated and seemingly rational people both to give up their own lives and to commit mass murder. If they were willing to ram the World Trade Center, they would have been willing to blow up all of New York if they had had the means.

The power of any such movement should not be in doubt. With over a billion Muslims in the world, al Qaeda could increase its ranks to 10 million if it convinced just 1 percent to join its movement—a force larger than any current army, and a force that could create a global insurgency that would turn the world into a nightmare.

In the twentieth century, mass movements like fascism and communism changed the world and were behind many global conflicts. Today, extreme movements can be small and yet create similar havoc. They need no government, no elections, and no state sponsorship (though they are looking for it), but they can potentially put an end to society as we know it.

Fortunately, al Qaeda still has a long way to go to reach 1 percent.

According to the Terrorism Knowledge Base, a comprehensive databank for global terrorist incidents and organizations, there are a total of 1,255 terrorist groups in the world. Of those, forty-two have been classified by the U.S. State Department as Foreign Terrorist Organizations (FTOs). By far, the largest of the FTOs is al Qaeda, with about 50,000 members, and bases in forty-five countries. In fact, the entire membership of the forty-two organizations is only about 125,000 terrorists, showing how relatively enormous al Qaeda is in this space.

Selected Foreign Terrorist Organizations, as Designated by the U.S. State Department		
Name of Organization	Base of Operations	Estimated Membership
al Qaeda	45 countries	~ 50,000
United Self-Defense Forces of Colombia (AUC)	Colombia	>20,000
New People's Army	Philippines	16,000
Revolutionary Armed Forces of Colombia (FARC)	Colombia	12,000
Liberation Tigers of Tamil Eelam (LTTE)	Sri Lanka	~8000
National Liberation Army (ELN)	Colombia	3000
Aum Shinrikyo/Aleph	7 countries including Japan	>2,000
Hamas	Israel, West Bank/Gaza	>1000
Hezbollah	Lebanon	1000
Kurdistan Workers Party (PKK)	Turkey	>1000
DHKP/C	Turkey	<1000
Palestinian Islamic Jihad (PIJ)	Israel, Lebanon, Syria, West Bank/Gaza	<1000
Popular Front for the Liberation of Palestine (PFLP)	Israel, West Bank/Gaza	800
Shining Path	Peru	500
Egyptian Islamic Jihad (EIJ)	Afghanistan, Egypt	>300
Jemaah Islamiya (JI)	Indonesia, Malaysia, Philippines, Singapore	>300
al Qaeda Organization in the Islamic Maghreb	Algeria, Mali, Mauritania, Niger	300

Name of Organization	Base of Operations	Estimated Membership
Basque Fatherland and Freedom (ETA)	Spain	300
Continuity Irish Republican Army (CIRA)	Ireland, UK	<200
Jaish-e-Mohammad (JeM)	Kashmir, Pakistan	>100
Armed Islamic Group	Algeria	<100

Source: MIPT Terrorism Knowledge Base, 2007

As a percentage of the world's population, 125,000 terrorists is about .002 percent. And if we look just at the radical Islamist groups on the list of forty-two FTOs, about twenty-two of them qualify. Those twenty-two groups—ranging from al Qaeda at 50,000; to Hamas and Hezbollah at about 1,000 each; to Jaish-e-Mohammad in Pakistan and the Armed Islamic Group in Algeria at about 100 each—together make up about 57,500 terrorists worldwide. As a percentage of the world's billion or so Muslims, that's .004 percent. So it is far below a 1 percent microtrend, but it ranks as a critically important and obviously dangerous nanotrend.

It does not need to become a mass movement to be successful. Rather, it needs a growing cadre of smart, sophisticated, tough operatives. Its growth now depends not on attracting hundreds of millions but on successfully creating a leadership class that can mobilize money and resources and carry out operations.

While poverty is often cited as a prime reason for the growth of fundamentalism, the founders of the terrorist movement come from surprising backgrounds. In fact, poverty and despair are remarkably unrelated to either the rich and well-educated founders like bin Laden or to many of the frontline terrorists, including the 9/11 hijackers or the July 7 train bombers in London.

On both sides of the aisle; in the U.S., Europe, and the East; in every religion (including Islam); and in government, business, and academia, leaders have vocally and earnestly linked terrorism to poverty and desperation. When young people's hopes and dreams for material gain are thwarted, they turn to violence, goes the theory. When they have nothing left to live for—and might even earn a little money for their families, or some immortal rewards—by blowing themselves up, they make the ultimate sacrifice. And so scholars to the left have said the U.S. "can no longer afford to allow states to fail." And presidents to the right, like George W. Bush, have said, "We fight against poverty, because hope is an answer to terror."

It sounds so reasonable. But while studies on terrorists are limited, the empirical evidence does not seem to prove that either poverty or economic desperation drives people to strap on explosives and hurl themselves at Western targets. If anything, it's the opposite. When Israel was destroying the houses of its suicide bombers, the interesting point was that they had houses. The impoverished and uneducated may just be too smart to blow themselves up for this cause.

In a 1980 study of radical Islamists being held in Egyptian jails, researcher Saad Eddin Ibrahim found that the typical offender was a male in his early 20s; from a normally cohesive, rural, or small-town family; educated in science or engineering; upwardly mobile and had high achievement and motivation. Not poor and desperate, but educated and rising.

In 2002, professors Alan Krueger and Jitka Maleckova compared 129 Hezbollah fighters who had died in the 1980s and early 1990s to the Lebanese population from which they were drawn. Whereas the Hezbollah militants had a 28 percent poverty rate, the overall population's was a higher 33 percent. And whereas 47 percent of the militants had gone to secondary school, only 38 percent of the general population had.

Similarly, in a 2003 study of suicide bombers in Israel, it was determined that the suicide bombers were less than half as likely to come from impoverished families as was the population as a whole. And more than half of the suicide bombers had been educated beyond high school, compared to less than 15 percent of Palestinians overall in the same age group.

The 9/11 hijackers—and their backers—fit the same description. They came largely from middle-class families and had high-level science and engineering backgrounds. Osama bin Laden himself is a civil engineer, and extremely wealthy.

In a 2004 study of 400 global terrorists, including the 9/11 perpetrators, forensic psychiatrist and former CIA operative Marc Sageman found that three-quarters of the terrorists came from the upper or middle class. Nine out of 10 came from caring, intact families. Almost two-thirds had gone to college (compared to the 5 or 6 percent that is typical in their countries). Three-quarters were professionals or semiprofessionals, mostly in the sciences and engineering. Nearly three-quarters were married, and the vast majority had children. Fewer than 5 of the 400 had a personality disorder. These men knew three to six languages, including a handful of Western ones. As one historian has sarcastically observed, the root cause of terrorism seems to be "money, education, and privilege."

Sageman concluded that what tipped these 400 otherwise intelligent and privileged men to terrorism was their social networks. Because they were so bright, they were sent abroad to study—and once overseas they felt lonely and excluded. They gathered to eat and socialize in and around mosques, and it was there that radical leaders turned them on to violent jihad. Other scholars have said that beyond just social networks, terrorists are motivated by core issues of identity and pride—either at a personal or national level. Suicide bombers have wealth and education, but they feel personally excluded, like nouveau riches disdained by the aristocracy. Or they feel culturally aggrieved, given the fall of Islam from global prominence and achievement. Far from the conventional myths, terrorists are not desperate for material subsistence or, obviously, survival. They are out to change the world by force.

State Department advisor David Kilcullen has mapped out a ladder of potential Islamic terrorists. At the bottom is the vast population of "Mainstream Muslims"—those who could be drawn to terrorism or allied against it, the bulk of whose grievances can be addressed by political reforms. Above them is a smaller group, whom he terms the "Alienated Muslims." These people have given up on reform, and are ripe to join the radicals. To dissuade them, he says, we must deploy ideological conversion, like the way youth in this country are turned away from gangs. But beyond that, at the top of the ladder, are the few who are beyond persuasion or coercion. Those are the ones we have to fear. But when you delve more deeply into who they are, it's quite a surprising picture. It turns out that the soldiers of terrorism are some of the best-educated, most self-sufficient soldiers in the world.

The significance of getting today's terrorists right, of course, is enormous. After all, it is lack of correct intelligence that has been one of America's most dangerous Achilles' heels. And to date, it is unclear whether what America has done to defeat terrorism has been effective or has helped them gain more recruits. What exactly is the right strategy for defeating terrorism depends a lot on who the real terrorists are and how they got that way.

While the typical terrorist may not be Patty Hearst, it turns out that he (or she) could be sitting next to you in the library, in Starbucks, or in your college dorm. Terrorists are dedicated because they believe, and their beliefs are elaborate and sophisticated.

The central terrorist movement of the twenty-first century, unlike communism, will not be defeated with washing machines. On top of the military and social efforts, it will take strong intellectual and religious cohesion—perhaps an interfaith movement dedicated to defining the true path to God that wins back as many converts intellectually as the military is able to find and destroy militarily. The most powerful recruits they are getting—for example, the cell members behind the July 7 train bombing in Britain—are more likely to be found in good schools and on the Internet than in the slums. They are part of a romanticized movement justified by religious doctrine, and we will need to redouble our efforts to shake the intellectual foundations of that movement to stop the flow of these kinds of recruits. The upscale terrorist is not a fluke—the consistent presence of well-educated terrorists shows the power of twisted ideas to twist impressionable young minds, and it shows how seriously we must strengthen our efforts to win the war of ideas.

Conclusion

Microtrending

▲

When Greek philosophers first tried to explain natural change in the world, they were stumped until Democritus, in about 460 BC, proposed the theory that the world was made up of atoms—small but distinct particles whose mix determined the state and character of matter. Many disagreed; even Aristotle was his chief critic. But over time, Democritus was proven right. In fact, even the most solid mass turns out to be made of billions of invisible atoms that determine its character.

As any high school student knows, change the mix of atoms just slightly and you will get profound effects on the strength of steel, the shine of diamonds, or the radioactivity of enriched uranium. This analogy reflects the underlying theory of *Microtrends*—our culture today is increasingly the product of what I have identified as societal atoms—small trends that reflect changing habits and choices. They are often hard to identify, but I have tried to provide a kind of periodic table of trends in the major areas of everyday life. Very slight changes in the mix of the cultural atoms will trigger profound changes in the shape of our globe and the character of our society.

Most people today make judgments much more as Aristotle did—looking holistically at events from their own point of view. But unlike Aristotle, they often claim to see the forest without having truly examined the trees. And especially in today's world of the quick post, they increasingly make judgments based on their own worldview rather than the underlying facts, which they view as hard to determine. The simple truth is that most of the time we can't see the true patterns of people's lives, except through statistics, and yet we claim to understand them based instead on our own limited viewpoints. The tendency then is for conventional wisdom to be both very dogmatic and very wrong.

I have found over the years that there is often a huge disconnect between belief about the economy and the true economic state of affairs. Until the statistics are actually published, people tend to assess the economy primarily through the eyes of the national media. In 1992, when Bill Clinton won the presidency based on worries about the economy, the statistics that came out after the election showed that the period leading up to November had actually been a period of record growth. Attitudes had been most negative at a time the economy was actually turning around.

In 1995, when I was working with President Clinton, Pat Buchanan got on the cover of *TIME* and *Newsweek* trumpeting the ideas that the economy was going down the tubes and no new good jobs were being created. We were becoming a nation of hamburger-flippers, he said, to nodding journalists. I asked the head of the White House Council of Economic Advisers to look into it, and he found that people actually were getting good New Economy jobs, led by the software sector. In his 1996 State of the Union speech, President Clinton said we had the best economy in thirty years—a statement that sent a flurry of reporters to check actual statistics rather than popular political movements and sweeping, politically motivated statements. The more people looked at the facts, the more they agreed, and six months later, there was near-unanimity that the economy was in great shape. Had the economy changed? No, what had changed was knowledge about the true facts of the economy. When people looked at the actual trees, their view of the forest changed.

I learned from this that an average person cannot tell the difference between 4 percent unemployment and 8 percent unemployment. If you have 100 friends, and a few more are employed or unemployed, you can't accurately gauge whether the economy is going up or down. If twenty of them were unemployed, you could; in other words, you can easily see firsthand the complete disasters and depressions. But you can't see the changes in the normal range of most statistics. You can't really see the difference between an economic boom and a recession, which would be the difference between 4 and 8 percent unemployment.

So for most subjects, people rely on a combination of news shows, Web sites, magazines, radio, chatter with friends, and their own gut. And given how unscientific almost all of those sources are, most people end up being wrong much of the time about what is actually going on. They are influenced by what *looks* right, and by what they want to see. They rarely take the time to look at the cold hard facts of what is happening.

I invite you to undertake some trend-spotting of your own at www

.microtrending.com. I have given you a head start with the seventy-five in this book, and no doubt you have spotted several of your own as you read it and it triggered some recollection of trends you have observed. In this book, I have tried to show how by focusing on the facts and the numbers, you can see almost a parallel universe—generally hidden, and yet staring us right in the face. Almost everything in the book has come from publicly available sources; it's all out there for anyone to look at. And a look at the numbers suggests that more people should look at the numbers more often. They are the tea leaves for understanding the changes in society. Maybe Alexis de Tocqueville could understand us from firsthand observation back when America was small and young, but today he would probably not be sending back the right dispatches.

We are undergoing massive change in contradictory ways—a society that is fundamentally older, yet working more; a society that is striving to be healthier, and yet has never had higher obesity or caffeine consumption; a society that is increasingly discussing politicians' style and personality, and yet is more educated than ever before.

And the world itself is undergoing some very counterintuitive changes: As science becomes more important, we have had a rise in religion; as economic freedom and capitalism are winning out, democracy and human rights are lagging; societies that give the greatest encouragement to childbearing are showing some of the greatest population declines.

The new laws of trends are coming into focus. For every trend, there is a countertrend. For every push to modernization, there is a drive to hold on to old values. For every dash to the Internet, there are those who want to knit and seek peace and quiet. For every rush to have instant information, there are people who want it long, detailed, and thoughtful. For every surge in homes without kids, there is a surge in homes with pets.

Microtrends reflects the human drive toward individuality, while conventional wisdom often seeks to drive society toward the lowest common denominator. As I said at the start, we have seen the original Ford economy literally replaced by the Starbucks economy—the multiplication of choice as the driver of personal expression and satisfaction.

Some trends are big and obvious, and affect most of us. But more and more, what is shaping the world is a series of powerful desires and forces that are hidden, operating just under the surface. And in those forces are the seeds of unexpected changes. They explain why the tolerance of war and conflict are on the decline; why economic freedom appears to be irrepressible; and why we are suddenly seeing acceptances of lifestyles and marriages that for thousands of years were bitterly opposed and blocked.

Movements get started by small groups of dedicated, intensely interested people. That is why the al Qaeda model of organization, and the focus on the number of terrorist converts, is critical. Winning movements are not necessarily majority movements, but they have drive and intensity behind them. Ten people with bazookas can overcome 1,000 people with picket signs, but they can't overcome 10,000 people with picket signs. This is the magic of the 1 percent threshold, and the potential of microtrends to be at the center of changing the world.

Many of the trends covered in this book have been fun—but almost all of them have a serious side to them. Pro-Semitism may have its funny side, what with ethnic jokes about finding a spouse who is good at making reservations, but it also represents the tumbling of thousands of years of barriers. Pets becoming the new children may drive up silk dog-bed sales, but it will also fundamentally change people's attitudes toward animals and how we treat them. Sun-Haters may look silly in their long sleeves on the beach, but they could reorient how we regard the outdoors, recreation, and environmental policy. If people are becoming their own doctors, they are going to be a handful when they encounter their real doctors, and lives are going to be lost when these DIY Docs commit "malpractice."

Will young people's interest in activities like knitting signal a return to some of the basics—people getting a chance to make something with their own hands? Or will their interest in becoming snipers lead to more criminal acts of cowardice? Or might it change how we look at warfare altogether?

And clearly, with High School Moguls on the one end and Working Retired on the other, people are looking to work more at both ends of their life—for all the talk of the preciousness of time with kids and family, Americans are flocking more to the rewards of work and less to the rewards of family. Hence, the explosion in the number of single households.

While there is a wave of interest in religion, people around the world are gravitating toward smaller churches and newer religious sects. Some older religions are trying to modernize, reforming their doctrine and adding women to the pulpit. Others are going more traditional. Perhaps nowhere are we seeing more contradictory and swirling microtrends than in religious movements today. But it suggests that what we are seeing now is likely to grow— more and more people will be loosely affiliated with religion, and, at the same time, the intense followers will grow in devotion and influence. We have to be vigilant in watching for the growth of offbeat cults, and also hold the line when religious zealots try to break down the separation between church and state.

And in politics, we are increasingly seeing how both the Democratic and the Republican parties are made up of fragile coalitions whose members are becoming more rigid and intense in their outlook. On the Republican side, the Christian right, the tax-cutting business leaders, the anti-government in-dependents, and the patriotic tough guys are showing their tension as the loose coalition that was their party is fraying at the seams. And on the Demo-cratic side, the historical coalition of union members, minorities, women, and moderates is having to integrate whole new priorities and techniques of the Net Roots and liberal blogoshere.

And so there is talk about third-, fourth-, and fifth-party candidates com-ing in. The current pattern suggests it is only a matter of time before one party or the other breaks apart, and that would be a sea change in American politics. As of the spring of 2007, the Democratic Party is energized and showing greater unity. The Republican Party, on the other hand, is los-ing membership and arguably its identity, and is probably more ripe for breakup.

In critical area after critical area, we are seeing the potential for greater fragmentation, and the impact of microtrends in accelerating that fragmenta-tion. We are watching groups express their individuality in new ways, putting more stress on religion, politics, popular culture, and family structure.

The flip side of this disaggregation of society is that it will continue to increase support for tolerance. If individual choices become more and more important to people, then minority rights become equally important to the expression of those differences. I think we are seeing a new tolerance already for different lifestyles, including an accelerated acceptance of the gay life-style. While gay marriage as a policy failed in many states, the bar for ac-ceptable treatment of gays, blacks, Hispanics, and women has been moving dramatically—and a single insulting comment like the one made by former Senator George Allen of Virginia, former *Seinfeld*-ian Michael Richards, or former shockjock Don Imus can end a career.

If Internet marriage becomes the norm, then by definition the old castes of marriage by religion, neighborhood, ethnicity, and country club will go out the window. This breaking down of barriers, and expanded freedom of choice, are now moving to the heart of all of people's major life decisions.

But the central thesis of this book is that society is changing in ways that few are really appreciating or understanding. By focusing only on the major trends that reach a "tipping point," most observers are missing the fact that you no longer have to reach that point to be a successful trend with a vast potential impact on society.

Over 600,000 felons coming out of jail per year is a tripling of the rate of returning ex-felons, compared to just twenty years ago. Unless we do something completely different to work with these newly released felons, crime will go up, and our society will change as a result.

Immigrants who used to hide in the shadows are flexing their political muscle by deeply touching the millions of legal immigrants who vote and are located in key swing states. Unless their immigration and other key domestic priorities are addressed, they will play a significant—and perhaps decisive—role in politics, perhaps literally determining who our next president is.

If several million more Americans go into the nonprofit sector, declaring that their lives are not about how much money they can make but how much good they can do, that will play an important role in changing the paradigm of success in this country.

And many of the international trends I have highlighted show that no society will be immune from the sweep of the new choices people are making. Entrepreneurs in Vietnam and artists in China are changing the character and image of these countries. Whether it is through renewed economic or artistic expression, swirling microtrends in those countries have a profound impact on everyone in those societies, as more and more people seek greater expression either in those forms or in other innovative ways.

Some have argued that the explosion of choice in both products and identities is confusing, paralyzing—even depressing. As Malcolm Gladwell wrote about in *Blink* and Barry Schwartz described in *The Paradox of Choice*, having twenty-four options of jam will draw shoppers in, but having six options of jam will actually trigger more sales. Having too many choices gives rise to feelings of pressure, overload, and regret. We'd rather not have any jam than look back and fear that we chose the wrong one. We'd rather not build ourselves into independent beings than experience the disappointment of being (inevitably) imperfect.

Maybe. But frankly, that train has left the station. Starbucks isn't going to stop offering us forty-two brands of coffee, five brands of milk, sixteen flavor enhancers, and nine types of sweetener—and the world isn't going to force people back into preset gender, spiritual, or professional roles. So while it is smart to learn to manage choices if they get overwhelming, the bottom line is that, in today's world, the potential for *personal satisfaction* due to individual choice and freedom is at its highest level ever.

Other observers of the rise in choice and specialization have argued that the boom threatens societal cohesion. If everything is up for self-determination—from gender to religion to expectations about marriage—then there can be no *unity*, no *community*—no "One America," no universal peoplehood.

Well, there probably never was as much national unity as mythologizers like to remember. This is a nation that has always spoken hundreds of languages. This is a nation that fought a civil war over the enslavement of one-third of its people. Indeed, the most famous and celebrated of *The Federalist Papers*, the intellectual cornerstone of America's very founding, is James Madison's treatise on "factions," describing the inevitability (and productivity) of America's intensely competitive special interest groups.

No, what is different now is not that the factions of society are so much more numerous, but rather that they are dividing along lines of personal *choice* rather than circumstance, like race—or fortune, like landowning. We are at least as intensely divided as any healthy democracy has ever been, but along new fault lines, related to choice. And yet, if anything, as a result, we now have *more* community. Now 1 million families who want to home-school their children can find like-minded allies and share resources on the Internet—rather than feeling isolated, unprepared, or thwarted in their preference. Now 2 million people who realize in later life that they are gay can live openly with that fact—both they and their families finding support from online communities around the nation and the world.

So while some may consider it pessimistic to say that twenty-first-century societies are equally or increasingly splintered, I think that on balance it's good news.

Sure, in a land of fast-moving and adamantly expressed personal choices, it will be harder for democracies, both emerging ones and old ones like the U.S., to manage all the crisscrossing intensities about both private values and public resources. There will be no simple national solutions, and politicians who try to tell you there can be are fooling you and/or themselves. The world is indeed getting more complex and more differentiated, in terms of the ways people devote their discretionary resources— like money, time, energy, votes, and love.

But the explosion of individual expression will also make it much harder for autocracies, old and new, to flourish. China is giving way to capital markets and artists because, once exposed to the rest of the world's information, its billion people won't stand for anything less. India is giving way to the power of women because, once exposed to the power of their contributions, it won't want to go back. Perhaps extreme fundamentalist Islam will be a paradox, depending on how it develops during the next few years. In some ways, it is a victim of its many splinter groups seeking to lay claim to the religion with self-proclaimed leaders and their fatwas. In other ways, it seems to be trying to reestablish ritual and the subjugation of personal choice as the superior way to live. It is the motherload of counterintuitive trends, and its flourishing is at odds with perhaps all the other trends of modernity. Fundamentalists know this, which is why they have pitted themselves against those trends, even depicted them as evil. The world has repeatedly gone through periods of darkness after some of its greatest advances, from the fall of Rome to the early Dark Ages, because it failed to prepare adequately for the countertrend that grew from a small seed. The weakness of a world driven by personal choice is that mass collective action becomes more difficult to organize and sustain because intense groups who oppose action can become more powerful. On the one hand, this effect should make all wars less likely; on the other hand, it also makes it harder to sustain broad collective action against determined foes.

So the democracies of the future may find it harder to maintain stable coalitions, and will find that issue and lifestyle coalitions (i.e., antiwar activists, or single Moms) will most likely replace the identity politics of the past. More and more actions will be based on 51-percent coalitions rather than a broadly unified public, because personal choice tends to pull people in opposite directions and makes it harder to bring them together. But this also means that it will get harder to unify people on behalf of new dictatorial regimes. The more *either* kind of regime ignores the power of the microtrend, the more it will find itself in trouble with its citizens.

Microtargeting will become the dominant means of advertising and marketing communication, replacing the old one-way TV and radio communications. That is why Internet advertising firms are now selling at such a huge premium—advertising and marketing will increasingly be on a personalized basis. Every communication that can be personalized will be, and this will lead to a huge expansion of the personal communications industry whose job it will be to advertise the right products to the right niches of people. The big online companies are fast becoming the repositories of personal information that can be used to build the marketing campaigns of the future.

Personal choice is also reaching its highest level in social life, as more choices mean more dating and a vastly expanded pool of potential spouses. Never in history has an individual been able to reach so easily out of his or her social circle to find potential mates. The combination of romance at work and online has the chance of shattering any caste system, and creating a new form of marital mobility.

And the broad patterns of choice are clear: more work; more individual fulfillment; new family units; greater social, economic, and physical mobility; wider circles of friends and acquaintances; and greater involvements in society.

The next generation of workers will be better educated and more technologically comfortable, yet they will be more difficult to satisfy unless they are treated in new ways to match their expectations of unlimited choice. Employees will essentially have to be microtargeted from day one—and given matching mentors, motivating messages, and customized loyalty programs.

It is also clear that in many areas, contradictory trends will continue to create good markets at both ends of the spectrum. Healthful food will continue to exist side by side with good-tasting but unhealthful choices. More emphasis on children as the center of life will exist next to more households focused on self-actualization. The tension between religion and secularism will grow with huge segments adopting one or the other viewpoint. While Moms continue to be the center of family life, the new relationship kids have with Dads, including older Dads and divorced Dads, may finally get recognition in the marketplace.

As we step back and look at the culture in America and around the world, the societal atoms that I have called microtrends appear to be driving change in almost every area of everyday life. There may not be a lot of Internet-based marriages yet, but they are changing our social structure. The straight-sex ratio may be only slightly uneven, but it is affecting all of us. The satisfied elites in America, removed from any real economic struggle, are driving much of the media perspective of the world. The number of artists in China may pale in comparison to the number of engineers, but they are beginning to pull the world's biggest country in new directions.

Behind each of these trends, I think, is a level of rationality driving the change. People are sleeping less because they are doing more. Empty-nesters are treating pets as children because they long for the children who have moved on to their own lives. Parents are becoming more permissive because they believe that words are more effective than the back of the hand. Underlying the idea of microtrends is that there is rarely a single right way to do things—and that similar people may make very different choices and start two totally contradictory trends. And yet both of those decisions can be totally rational. Even those choosing the most irrational path of all—terrorism—appear to be making their decisions based on careful study and deeply held beliefs. Long Attention Spanners represent a movement away from split-second decisions and toward deeper, deliberative thinking.

Clearly, the seventy-five microtrends in this book are simply representative of the thousands of new trends out there, and there are new trends occurring each day. The great fear of the future has been that mass societies would become faceless societies, with people forced into conformity—everyone looking alike, dressing alike, and being required to think alike. This was seen as almost a necessary sacrifice in order to feed and clothe growing populations with diminishing resources. But I suggest we are headed in completely the opposite direction—a future in which choice, driven by individual tastes, becomes the dominant factor, and in which these choices are reinforced by the ability to connect and communicate with communities of even the smallest niches.

The future rarely turns out as predicted. The reason is that most predictions are driven by the same conventional wisdom that drives the daily consensus around us, and are usually based on the big, easily spotted observations like the spread of the global economy. But as you dig deeper, you see a world teeming with lesser-known, harder-to-spot developments that really are the small forces that will drive tomorrow's big changes.

Acknowledgments

▲

I had the idea for this book for a number of years and was always going to get around to it "next year." But at the urging of Bob Barnett, this became the year to finally put it all down.

I wish to thank above all Kinney Zalesne, my collaborator, whose brilliant work helped turn the ideas into a reality. I know Kinney from working with her in the 1996 presidential campaign, and she learned polling then and is a great writer as well. I have thoroughly enjoyed our collaboration.

I also want to thank Bob Barnett, who represented the book and whose proddings got it off the ground and whose belief in it led successfully to its publication. He is truly remarkable.

Friends and colleagues who suggested, reviewed, sharpened, and, in some cases, exemplified microtrends include Scott Siff, Don Baer, Sergio Bendixen, Mich Mathews, Jonathan Kessler, Billy Mann, Neera Tanden, David Ginsberg, and J. B. Schramm. And I wish to thank Bill Gates and Bill Clinton for their reviews and help.

I am also very grateful to my editor and publisher, Jonathan Karp, who believed in this project from the first moment and guided it throughout with great skill and enthusiasm. His team, including Nate Gray, Cary Goldstein, Fred Chase, Bob Castillo, and Anne Twomey, are first-rate partners.

I also wish to thank Melissa Wisner, the book's senior research analyst. For a solid year, Melissa threw herself into this project with tremendous energy and devotion, and was the front line in gathering all the numbers that got turned into stories. She did a fabulous job.

Lora Seo, an intern, devoted many months to ferreting out some of the most arcane data in the book. There is no decades-old Census table or obscure corporate data point that Lora cannot wrestle to the ground.

Many people at Penn, Schoen & Berland also gave of their own time and creativity to support the book. In particular, Josh Werman, Nick Danoff, Andrew Claster, Matt Lieppe, and Emily Colligan provided top-quality work over and over. Others who enriched the effort with contributions large and small include Alex Braun, Amy Cohen, Brad Dawgert, Jonathan Gardner, Amanda Keeter, Beth Lester, Amy Leveton, Jonathan Penn, Jay Ragsdale, Merrill Raman, Ian Ritchie, LaDon Roeder, Peter Roehrig, Rachel Schwartz, Payal Shah, Craig Smith, Jessica Trainor, and Grant Zallis.

Finally, I wish to thank all of the trend-spotters out there who are finding new trends every day. Many of you are recognized in the Sources, which I tried to document thoroughly. Some of the trends in the book are brand new; some had been spotted and I developed new implications in the context of *Microtrends*; and some are an amalgam of previous work and new work. I hope this book will both acknowledge your skill and the great value of statistical trend-spotting.

Sources

▲

I. Love, Sex, and Relationships
Sex-Ratio Singles

The Social Organization of Sexuality study was first reported in Edward O. Laumann, John H. Gagnon, Robert T. Michael, and Stuart Michaels, *The Social Organization of Sexuality: Sexual Practices in the United States* (University of Chicago Press, 1994). The third study cited is Samuel S. Janus and Cynthia L. Janus, *The Janus Report on Sexual Behavior* (Wiley, 1994). All three studies are referenced in Paul Varnell, "More Gays than Lesbians," on the Web site the Independent Gay Forum, November 30, 1999, accessed June 2006, at http://www.indegayforum.org/news/show/26996.html.

The data in the graph on the number of unmarried women in America come from U.S. Census, "Marital Status of the Population 15 Years Old and Over, by Sex and Race: 1950 to Present," accessed June 2006, at http://www.census.gov/population/socdemo/hh-fam/msl.csv.

For more on the sex ratio in America, see T. J. Mathews, and B. F. Hamilton, "Trend Analysis of the Sex Ratio at Birth in the United States," *National Vital Statistics Reports*, Vol. 53, No. 20, Hyattsville, MD: National Center for Health Statistics, 2005, accessed at http://www.cdc.gov/nchs/data/nvsr/nvsr53/nvsr53 20.pdf.

The percentage of gay people in America is difficult to measure; see discussion at "Demographics," http://www.glbtq.com/social-sciences/demographics.html. But many studies hover at about 5 percent overall, and polls from Penn, Schoen & Berland Associates (PSB) conducted in recent years regularly yield that percentage.

Data on the gender ratio in the black community come from U.S. Census, "Population by Sex and Age, for Black Alone and White Alone, Not Hispanic: March 2004," U.S. Census Bureau, Current Population Survey, Annual Social and Economic Supplement, 2004, Racial Statistics Branch, Population Division, accessed at http://www.census.gov/population/socdemo/race/black/ppl-186/tabla.pdf and http://www.census.gov/population/socdemo/race/black/ppl-186/tablb.pdf.

Data on the incarceration rates of black males and females come from Paige M. Harrison and Allen J. Beck, Ph.D., "Prison and Jail Inmates at Midyear 2005," *Bureau of Justice Statistics Bulletin*, May 2006, NCJ 213133, accessed at http://www.ojp.usdoj.gov/bjs/pub/pdf/pjim05.pdf.

For information on average life expectancy, see E. Arias, "United States Life Tables, 2003," *National Vital Statistics Reports*, Vol. 54, No. 14, Hyattsville, MD: National Center for Health Statistics, 2006, accessed at http://www.cdc.gov/nchs/data/nvsr/nvsr54/nvsr54 14.pdf.

The National Association of Realtors data on single women purchasing homes was cited in David Calvert, "Dream House, Sans Spouse: More Women Buy Homes," *USA Today*, February 14, 2006.

The data on the rise in Single Mothers by Choice come from Amy Harmon, "More Single Women Become Mothers by Choice," *New York Times*, December 29, 2005.

For information on degrees conferred by sex, see "Bachelor's, Master's, and Doctor's Degrees Conferred by Degree-Granting Institutions, by Sex of Student and Field of Study: 2002–03," National Center for Education Statistics, accessed at http://nces.ed.gov/programs/digest/d04/lt3.asp.

Cougars

The data on dating habits of women aged 40–69 come from a study conducted by Knowledge Networks, Inc., for the AARP magazine: Xenia P. Montenegro, Ph.D., "Lifestyles, Dating and Romance: A Study of Midlife Singles," *AARP The Magazine*, September 2003, accessed August 2006 at http://www.aarp.org/research/family/lifestyles/aresearch-import-522.html.

The census-based comparisons come from L. A. Johnson, "Love for All," *Pittsburgh Post-Gazette*, October 9, 2005. This article also summarized the changes in dating preferences on Match.com.

Valerie Gibson was quoted on the ABC News Web site, "Are More Older Women with Younger Men?" May 5, 2005, <http://abcnews.go.com/Primetime/print?id=731599>, accessed August 2006.

The data on live births to women aged 40–44 and 45–49 come from the National Center for Health Statistics, Vital Statistics of the United States, 1994, Vol. 1, "Natality, Table 1–13," Live Births by Age, Race and Hispanic Origin of Mother: United States and Each State, 1994, accessed March 2007; and the National Vital Statistics Reports, Vol. 55, No. 1, Table 2, "Live Births by Age of Mother, Live-Birth Order, and Race of Mother: United States, 2004," September 29, 2006, accessed March 2007.

Office Romancers

The Vault Survey, cited throughout, is their "Office Romance Survey," conducted January 2006, with 693 responses from employees representing a variety of industries across the U.S., accessed April 2007, at http://www.vault.com/nr/newsmain.jsp?nr page=3&ch id=420&article id=26126479.

The Hotjobs survey was accessed April 2007, at http://hotjobs.yahoo.com/jobseeker/about/press releases/021103.html.

The data on approval of co-worker relationships come from a 2005 CareerBuilder.com survey, "Office Romance," conducted in January 2005 of more than 1,300 workers, accessed April 2007, at http://www.careerbuilder.com/share/aboutus/pressreleasesdetail.aspx?id=pr160&sd=2/7/2005&ed=12/31/2005&cbRecursionCnt=1&cbsid=1da66156dedf4c9e83ee497e5c8abb8d-230303910-J5-5.

Data on singles in the workforce come from Marshall Loeb, "5 Tips to Consider When You Fall in Love on the Job," www.careerjournal.com, September 22, 2005; and Ellen R. McGrattan and Richard Rogerson, "Changes in Hours Worked, 1950–2000," Federal Reserve Bank of Minneapolis, *Quarterly Review*, Vol. 28, No. 1, July 2004.

Data on male versus female behavior come from "Interoffice Romance Survey," a joint survey sponsored by LexisNexis Martindale-Hubbell's Lawyers.com and *Glamour* magazine, August 12, 2004.

The SHRM study is Michael Parks, "2006 Workplace Romance: Poll Findings," a study by the Society for Human Resource Management and Careerjournal.com, January 2006.

Data on female Ph.D.'s come from U.S. Department of Education, National Center for Education Statistics, Higher Education General Information Survey (HEGIS), "Degrees and Other Formal Awards Conferred" surveys, 1976–77 through 1984–85, and Integrated Postsecondary Education Data System (IPEDS), "Completions" surveys, 1986–87 through 1998–99, and Fall 2000 through Fall 2002 surveys, table, prepared August 2003, accessible at http://nces.ed.gov/programs/digest/d03/tables/pdf/table270.pdf.

Commuter Couples

The *Times* story on the Clintons was Patrick Healy, "For Clintons, Delicate Dance of Married and Public Lives," *New York Times*, May 23, 2006.

Data on married couples in 2005 living apart from their spouses for reasons other than separation come from U.S. Census, accessed June 2006, at http://www.census.gov/population/socdemo/hh-fam/cps2005/tabA1-all.csv. The 1990 data come from http://factfinder.census .gov/servlet/DTTable? bm=y&-ds name=DEC 1990 STF3 & CONTEXT=dt&-mt name=DEC 1990 STF3 P027&-mt name=DEC 1990 STF3 P038&-redoLog=false&- caller=geoselect&geo id=01000US&-geo id=NBSP&-format=&-lang=en&-SubjectID=11745086.

The AARP data come from a January 11, 2005, KCET.org radio transcript, accessed June 2006, at http://www.kcet.org/lifeandtimes/archives/200501/20050111.php, quoting Nancy Griffin of *AARP The Magazine*.

For more from the Center for the Study of Long-Distance Relationships, and Dr. Gregory Guldner, see http://www.longdistancerelationships.net/.

In the International Picture, the Global Relocation Survey can be found at http://www.iht. com/articles/2004/03/27/rspouse ed3 1.php#. The Kuwait data come from "Foreign Workers in the Middle East," *Migration News*, Vol. 3, No. 4, December 1996. Data on Egypt and Saudi Arabia come from http://www.migrationdrc.org/research/regions/egypt themiddleeast.html, and the Saudi earnings data come from http://www.enews.ma/foreign-workers i39834 0.html. Data on Dubai come from Eric Weiner, "Thanks for Your Hard Work. Now Get Out!," *Slate*, August 15, 2005, accessed January 2007, at http://www.slate.com/id/2124497/fr/rss/.

Internet Marrieds

The Pew study relied on this chapter is Mary Madden and Amanda Lenhart, "Online Dating," Pew Internet and American Life Project, March 5, 2006.

The online dating magazine Web site was accessed March 2007, at www.onlinedating magazine.com.

Marriage data come from National Vital Statistics Report, Vol. 54, No. 8, "Births, Marriages, Divorces, and Deaths, Provisional Data for June 2006."

The PSB poll of Internet Marrieds was conducted online on March 27–28, 2007.

II. Work Life
Working Retired

The data on seniors in the workforce come from "Labor Force Participation of Persons Ages 62 and Over, 1982–2005," Current Population Survey (CPS), Bureau of Labor Statistics.

The data on vacation days worldwide come from the World Tourism Organization, whose Web site is http://www.world-tourism.org/. For more on unused vacation and working while on vacation, see Stephanie Armour, "U.S. Workers Feel Burn of Long Hours, Less Leisure," *USA*

Today, December 18, 2003; and "Annual Expedia.com Survey Reveals 51.2 Million American Workers Are Vacation Deprived," April 25, 2007, accessed May 2007, at http://press.expedia.com/index.php?s=press releases&item=372.

The Merrill Lynch survey report is "The Merrill Lynch *New Retirement* Survey: A Perspective from the Baby Boomer Generation," February 23, 2005. The survey itself interviewed 3,448 U.S. baby boomers by phone and online in February 2004.

For more on occupations preferred by older workers, see "Old. Smart. Productive: Surprise! The Graying of the Workforce Is Better News than You Think," *BusinessWeek*, June 27, 2005.

The traffic accident data come from National Highway Traffic Safety Administration, Table 63, "Driver Involvement Rates per 100,000 Licensed Drivers, by Age, Sex, and Crash Severity," accessed February 2007, at http://www-nrd.nhtsa.dot.gov/pdf/nrd-30/NCSA/TSFAnn/2004HTML/TSF2004.htm#chap2.

C. Eugene Steuerle, "Working to Fix Our Fiscal Woes," *Washington Post*, April 14, 2006. Thanks also to Dr. Steuerle for personally walking us through some of this analysis by telephone.

Extreme Commuters

Some key Extreme Commuter articles, from which some of the cited data are drawn, include Keith Naughton, "The Long and Grinding Road," *Newsweek*, May 1, 2006; "Extreme Commuting," *BusinessWeek Online*, February 21, 2005; and Debbie Howlett and Paul Overberg, "Think Your Commute Is Tough?," *USA Today*, November 29, 2004.

As of March 2007, the American labor force numbers 146.3 million people. See Bureau of Labor Statistics, "Employment Situation Summary," accessed April 2007, at http://www.bls.gov/news.release/empsit.nr0.htm.

Data on the average American commute come from U.S. Census, American Community Survey, press release of February 25, 2004, accessed June 2006, at http://www.census.gov/Press-Release/www/releases/archives/american community survey acs/001695.html.

Data on national commuting come from Clara Reschovsky, "Journey to Work: 2000," U.S. Census brief, issued March 2004.

The Midas Muffler contest was reported at Gary Richards, "Your Commute Is Bad? Try 186 Miles Each Way," Knight Ridder Newspapers, May 4, 2006.

Data on 2005 average sale prices of new homes come from U.S. Census, "Median and Average Sales Prices of New One-Family Houses Sold," accessed June 2006, at http://www.census.gov/const/C25Ann/soldmedavgprice.pdf.

"Worst Commute" data were reported in D'Vera Cohn and Robert Samuels, "Daily Misery Has a Number: Commute 2nd-Longest in U.S.," *Washington Post*, August 30, 2006.

Dr. Casada's insights and those of the Georgia Tech researchers are courtesy of "The Long and Grinding Road," cited above.

The ABC/*Washington Post* poll data come from Gary Langer, "Poll: Traffic in the United States," February 13, 2005, accessed June 2006, at http://abcnews.go.com/Technology/print?id=485098.

Robert Putnam, *Bowling Alone: The Collapse and Revival of American Community* (Simon & Schuster, 2000).

For articles helpful to the International Picture, see Vernon Silver, "Cheap European Flights Cater to Both Commuting Doctors and Drunken Revelers," *Bloomberg News*, February 23, 2007; "UK Commute 'Longest in Europe,'" *BBC News Magazine*, July 22, 2003; Sean

Coughlan, "The New Commuter Belt," *BBC News Magazine*, July 18, 2006; Matt Welch, "Fly the Frugal Skies," www.reasononline.com, January 2005; "The Rise of the Super-Commuter," www.cnn.com, April 12, 2005; Vernon Silver, "Ryanair Sparks Surgeon Commutes, European Vacation Home Frenzy," www.Bloomberg.com, February 22, 2007; and Keith Naughton, "Tailing the X-Commuter," *Newsweek International*, July 3–10, 2006.

Stay-at-Home Workers

Trend data on Stay-at-Home Workers come from U.S. Census 2000: "Class of Worker for Workers Who Worked at Home for the United States: 1980 to 2000," accessed September 2006, at http://www.census.gov/population/cen2000/phc-t35/tab01-5.xls.

Demographic data on Stay-at-Home Workers come largely from "Selected Characteristics of Workers Who Worked at Home and Workers Who Did Not Work at Home for the United States: 2000," accessed September 2006, at http://www.census.gov/population/cen 2000/phc-t35/tab01-2.pdf.

On the topic of Momtrepreneurs generally, see Mary-Beth McLaughlin, "Moms Spur Growth in Home Businesses," Scripps Howard News Service, November 14, 2006; and Jasmine D. Adkins, "For Women Consultants, Business Is Booming," *Inc.com*, July 19, 2006.

The American Business Collaboration study was cited in Eileen Gunn, "Working from Home Is Losing Its Stigma," *Wall Street Journal Online*, accessed April 2007, at http://www .startupjournal.com/howto/workhome/20041014-gunn.html.

Other articles useful to this chapter included "Getting a Home Office to Work for You," Associated Press, September 3, 2004; Eleena De Lisser and Dan Morse, "More Men than Women Working from Home," *Wall Street Journal Online*, accessed April 2007, at http://www .startupjournal.com/howto/workhome/199906211437-lisser.html; Hugo Martin, "Touting a Telecommunications Trade-Off," *Los Angeles Times*, August 22, 2001; and Jaimee Rose, "The Safety Zone: As Workplace, Home Has Hazards," *Los Angeles Times*, August 14, 2000.

Wordy Women

For more on Larry Summers and the Women in Science flap, see James Traub, "Lawrence Summers, Provocateur," *New York Times*, January 23, 2005; and Cornelia Dean, "Bias is Hurting Women in Science, Panel Reports," *New York Times*, September 19, 2006.

The 2005 data on women in journalism come from the Bureau of Labor Statistics, Table 11, "Employed Persons by Detailed Occupation, Sex, Race, and Hispanic or Latino Ethnicity"; and Paul Farhi, "Men, Signing Off: As More Women Become TV Anchors and Reporters, Males Exit the Newsroom," *Washington Post*, July 23, 2006. Other useful articles on this issue include Suzanne C. Ryan, "The Vanishing Anchorman: The Number of Male Newscasters on TV Has Reached an All-Time Low. What's the Story?" *Boston Globe*, January 15, 2006; and Vicky Lovell, Ph.D., Heidi Hartmann, Ph.D., and Jessica Koski, "Making the Right Call: Jobs and Diversity in the Communications and Media Sector," Institute for Women's Policy Research, 2006, accessed on May 4, 2006, at http://www.iwpr.org/pdf/C364.pdf.

The 70 percent figure on women in public relations comes from Rick Hampson, "Women Dominate PR . . . Is That Good?" *USA Today*, April 25, 2001. As of 2007, it may be closer to 65 percent.

In 1971, there were 9,947 women lawyers. In 2000, there were 288,060. See American Bar Foundation, *Researching Law*, Vol. 16, No. 1, Winter 2005, p. 7. For the rest of the data on women and the law, see "Legal Education Statistics," Fall Enrollment 2004, American

Bar Association Section of Legal Education and Admissions to the Bar, January 25, 2005, accessed May 2007, at http://www.abanet.org/legaled/statistics/fall2004enrollment.pdf; National Association for Law Placement, November 2004, accessed May 2007, at http://www.nalp.org/press/details.php?id=53.

For data on women in the sciences, see the BLS source cited above; and James Dean, "Gender Gap Attracts Scrutiny: Women Remain Outnumbered at Science Schools," *Florida Today*, February 5, 2005. For more on women in business, see Carol Hymowitz, "Women Swell Ranks As Middle Managers," Associated Press Financial Wire, July 24, 2006.

The insights about "women's issues" climbing on the evening news come from the Farhi article cited above.

For more on women in teaching, see Chris Kenning, "Shortage of Male Teachers Worsens in Elementaries; Stereotypes Add to the Imbalance," *Courier-Journal* (Louisville, KY), November 22, 2004.

Ardent Amazons

For more on women's football leagues, see http://www.womensfootballcentral.com/teams .html; http://www.iwflsports.com/teams.php; and http://www.womensprofootball.com/teams .php.

More about women firefighters fighting discrimination can be found at Rick Barrett, "Firefighting Still Seen by Some as 'Last Male Bastion.'" *Milwaukee Journal Sentinel*, September 19, 2006; and at the Web site of Women in the Fire Service, Inc., http://www.wfsi .org/women and firefighting/faq.php.

Data on women police officers come from "Crime in the United States 2004," accessed April 2007, at http://www.fbi.gov/ucr/cius 04/law enforcement personnel/table 74.html.

Information on women in construction comes from the National Association of Women in Construction Web site, accessed February 2007, at http://www.nawic.org/.

Data on women in the military come from Department of Defense Personnel, 1960–2005, accessed February 2007, at http://www.census.gov/prod/2006pubs/07statab/defense.pdf.

The PSB poll was conducted online on April 2–3, 2007.

The study on gender and excessive force is the National Center for Women and Policing, "Men, Women and Police Excessive Force: A Tale of Two Genders," April 2002, accessed February 2007, at http://www.womenandpolicing.org/PDF/2002 Excessive Force.pdf.

The data on men's and women's marathon times come from Laura Pappano, "Gender Games," *Boston Globe*, September 28, 2003, accessed April 2007, at http://www.boston.com/news/globe/magazine/articles/2003/09/28/gender games/.

III. Race and Religion
Stained Glass Ceiling Breakers

Data on growth in women clergy come from the Bureau of Labor Statistics, "Employed Persons by Detailed Occupation and Sex, 1983–2002 Annual Averages." The data on women in divinity school are cited in Neela Banerjee, "Clergywomen Find Hard Path to Bigger Pulpit," *New York Times*, August 26, 2006. Data on religion majors come from the National Center on Education Statistics, accessed September 2006, at http://nces.ed.gov/programs/digest/d05/tables/xls/tabn262.xls and http://nces.ed.gov/programs/digest/d95/dtab242.asp.

The survey of women clergy was conducted by Laura S. Olson, Sue E. S. Crawford, and James L. Guth, "Changing Issue Agendas of Women Clergy," *Journal for the Scientific Study of Religion*, June 2000, and reported in Martin E. Marty, "Women Clergy: The Numbers," accessed March 2007, at http://www.beliefnet.com/story/33/story 3340 1.html; and "Women Clergy: More Liberal, More Political?", *Religion Link*, accessed March 2007, at http://www.religionlink.org/tip 040120b.php.

The survey regarding women clergy being more caring was conducted and reported by Barbara Brown Zikmund, Adair T. Lummis, and Patricia M. Y. Chang, *Christian Century*, May 6, 1998, and accessed March 2007, at http://hirr.hartsem.edu/bookshelf/clergywomen summary.html.

The study of United Methodist clergywomen was conducted by Jesse Shultz et al. and summarized in "UF Study: Female Ministers Face Pettiness, Patriarchy and Pressures," June 9, 1999, accessed March 2007, at http://news.ufl.edu/1999/06/09/clergy/.

The reliance on Adam and Eve to ban women clergy was reported in Marc Schogol, "Black Women's Struggle to Serve from the Pulpit as Well as in the Pews," *Philadelphia Inquirer*, October 26, 1997.

Trend Data on various religions' membership come from http://www.demographia.com/db-religusa2002.htm; U.S. Census, Table 73, "Self-Described Religious Identification of Adult Population: 1990 and 2001," accessed September 2006, at http://www.census.gov/compendia/statab/tables/07s0073.xls; and Cathy Lynn Grossman, "'Code' and the Sacred Feminine," *USA Today*, May 23, 2006, accessed September 2006, at http://www.usatoday.com/news/religion/2006-05-23-code-women x.htm.

The data on hearts and heads come from a poll conducted by PSB in September 2006.

Pro-Semites

The data regarding educational attainment among women of various religions were taken from the study conducted for Brooklyn College, CUNY, by Barry Kosmin and Ariela Keysar, "The Impact of Religious Identification on Differences in Educational Attainment Among American Women 2001," *Religion in a Free Market*, Paramount Market Publishing, 2005.

The Roper survey results cited were obtained from searches of the iPOLL Databank and other resources provided by the Roper Center for Public Opinion Research, University of Connecticut, *Survey by Fortune and Roper Organization, July 1939*, retrieved March 16, 2007, from the iPOLL Databank, the Roper Center for Public Opinion Research, University of Connecticut, <http://www.ropercenter.uconn.edu/ipoll.html>.

The Gallup poll regarding attitudes toward different religions can be found in the Gallup Poll News Service, "August Panel Survey," August 28–31, 2006.

The surprising number of non-Jews on JDate was brought to our attention by Sarah E. Richards, "You Don't Have to Be Jewish to Love JDate," *New York Times*, December 5, 2004.

The PSB poll was conducted in September 2006.

Interracial Families

Data on the number of interracial marriages in America come from Sharon M. Lee and Barry Edmonston, "New Marriages, New Families, U.S. Racial and Hispanic Intermarriage," *Population Bulletin*, a publication of the Population Reference Bureau, Vol. 60, No. 2, June 2005, p. 11. Thanks to Mr. Edmonston himself for helping us navigate the data.

Data on American attitudes toward interracial marriage come from Allison Stein Wellner, "U.S. Attitudes Toward Interracial Dating Are Liberalizing," www.prb.com, June 2005, citing RoperASW, *Roper Reports 03–3* (unpublished study). The Pew study cited is a Pew Research

Center Social Trends Report, "Guess Who's Coming to Dinner," released March 14, 2006. That study also contains views on interracial dating by age. The Gallup study is Gallup Poll News Service, "Acceptance of Interracial Marriage at Record High," June 1, 2004.

Much of the interracial adoption data come from Lynette Clemetson and Ron Nixon, "Breaking Through Adoption's Racial Barriers," New York Times, August 16, 2006. For more on international adoptions, see Sharon Jayson, "New Generation Doesn't Blink at Interracial Relationships," USA Today, February 7, 2006.

Data on youth interracial dating come from Ely Portillo and Frank Greve, "Social Integration in the U.S., Including Cohabiting and Marriage, Is Surging," McClatchy Newspapers, July 20, 2006; data regarding members of match.com come from http://www.miami.com/mld/miamiherald/15084469.htm?template=contentModules/printstory.jsp, accessed October 2006.

The survey of interracial couples was conducted March 29–May 20, 2001, by ICR/International Communications Research for the Washington Post, and reported at "Race, Dating, and Marriage," July 5, 2001, accessed October 2006, at http://www.washingtonpost.com/wp-srv/nation/sidebars/polls/couples.htm.

Another article useful to this chapter includes Steve Sailer, "2000 Census Shows Interracial Marriage Gender Gaps Remain Large," UPI, March 14, 2003.

Data for the International Picture come from Norimitsu Onishi, "Betrothed at First Sight: A Korean-Vietnamese Courtship," New York Times, February 22, 2007; "The Family—International Marriages More Common," Daily Yomiuri (Tokyo), December 3, 2005; "Vietnamese Decree to Tighten Foreign Marriage," Deutxhe Presse-Agentur, July 26, 2006; and "More Russian Women Marry Foreigners," TASS, January 15, 2007.

Protestant Hispanics

Thanks to my friend and colleague Sergio Bendixen for his review of and thoughtful reflections on this chapter.

Data on the Latino population in America come from U.S. Census, "Nation's Population One-Third Minority," accessed April 2007, at http://www.census.gov/Press-Release/www/releases/archives/population/006808.html.

Data on Latinos and Catholicism, including the data on Latino priests, come from Bruce Murray, "Latino Religion in the U.S.: Demographic Shifts and Trends," accessed August 2006, at http://www.facsnet.org/issues/faith/espinosa.php.

The book cited is Gaston Espinosa, Virgilio Elizondo, and Jesse Miranda, editors, Latino Religions and Civic Activism in the United States (Oxford University Press, 2005). The 2003 study on Hispanic churches in American public life is a preliminary study by the same authors.

A useful article on the question of why Hispanics are drawn to Pentecostalism, as well as the Pentecostals' assertive outreach tactics, is Arian Campo-Flores, "The Battle for Latino Souls," Newsweek, March 21, 2005.

The data on Latino voting in 2004 come from Roberto Suro, Richard Fry, and Jeffrey Passel, "Hispanics and the 2004 Election: Population, Electorate, and the Voters," Pew Hispanic Center, June 27, 2005. The data on 2006 Latino voting are also from the Pew Hispanic Center, "Latinos and the 2006 Mid-Term Election," released November 27, 2006, and accessed December 2006, at http://pewhispanic.org/files/factsheets/26.pdf.

The PSB poll of Latinos was conducted by telephone, March 5, 2006.

Moderate Muslims

Data on American attitudes toward Islam come from a CBS News poll, "Sinking Perceptions of Islam," conducted April 6–9, 2006, accessed September 2006, at http://www.cbsnews.com/stories/2006/04/12/national/main1494697.shtml; and Lydia Saad, "Anti-Muslim Sentiments Fairly Commonplace," USA Today/Gallup Poll conducted July 28–30, 2006. Other useful articles on attitudes toward Muslims include Claudia Deane and Darryl Fears, "Negative Perception of Islam Increasing," Washington Post, March 9, 2006.

Most of the data on Muslims' own attitudes and demographics come from "Muslims in the American Public Square," a poll conducted by ProjectMAPS and Zogby International, August 5–September 15, 2004 (hereafter, "MAPS Poll"). Comparison data with Americans in general come from Darren K. Carlson, "Americans Softening on Tougher Gun Laws?," Gallup Polls, November 30, 2004; and Harris Interactive Poll No. 80, October 31, 2006 (on attending religious services), and Harris Interactive Poll No. 19, March 9, 2005 (on political affiliation).

For more on recent Muslim immigration, see Andrea Elliott, "More Muslims Arrive in US, After 9/11 Dip," New York Times, September 10, 2006.

Data on the growth of mosques come from www.usinfo.state.gov, "Demographic Facts," accessed December 2006, at http://usinfo.state.gov/products/pubs/muslimlife/demograp.htm.

For more on the American Muslim Alliance, see its Web site at http://www.amaweb.org/, and Lee Hudson Teslik, "A Muslim for the Hill?," Newsweek, September 13, 2006.

Data on the Muslim electorate's shift in 2004 come from MAPS Poll, cited above.

The Social Policy and Understanding survey was conducted by Ihsan Bagby and reported at "A Portrait of Detroit Mosques: Muslim Views on Policy, Politics, and Religion," Institute for Social Policy and Understanding, 2004, accessed December 2006, at http://www.ispu.us/go/images/F000196/Detroit Mosque Exec Summary.pdf. The report is not without its critics, who claim that the author exaggerates American Muslim moderation. The Khan piece is M. A. Muqtedar Kahn, "The Remarkable Moderation of Detroit Muslims," Detroit News, July 4, 2004, accessed December 2006, at http://www.ijtihad.org/Moderation%20of%20American%20Muslims.htm.

For more on the American Islamic Congress, see its Web site at http://www.aicongress.org/. For more on the Free Muslims Coalition and Kamal Nawash, see http://www.freemuslims.org/ and Don Oldenburg, "Muslims' Unheralded Messenger," Washington Post, May 13, 2005.

Resources useful to the International Section included "An Uncertain Road: Muslims and the Future of Europe," Pew Forum on Religion and Public Life, October 2005, accessed December 2006, at http://pewforum.org/publications/reports/muslims-europe-2005.pdf; and Omar Taspinar, "Europe's Muslim Street," Foreign Policy, March 2003. The Pew Global Attitudes Project was reported at "Muslims in Europe: Economic Worries Top Concerns About Religious and Cultural Identity," Pew Global Attitudes Project, released July 6, 2006, accessed December 2006, at http://pewglobal.org/reports/display.php?ReportID=254.

IV. Health and Wellness

Sun-Haters

The tanning parlor–Starbucks comparison comes from Julie Rawe, "Why Teens Are Obsessed with Tanning," TIME, August 7, 2006, pp. 54–56.

The 2002 survey on attitudes toward suntanning was released by the American Academy of Dermatology on April 24, 2002.

Data on the tanning industry come largely from Helene Blatter, "The Tanning Dilemma Sun-Bathers: Sun-Bathers Know Risks, but Seek Bronzed Skin Anyway," *Riverside Press Enterprise*, July 23, 2006; Jacob E. Osterhout, "Know It All," *New York Daily News*, July 10, 2005; Valerie Nienberg, "Shedding Lights on Sunless Tans," *Jupiter Courier* (Florida), November 17, 2004.

For more on teen tanning habits, see Paul Vitello, "Skin Cancer Up Among Young; Tanning Salons Become Target," *New York Times*, August 14, 2006, <http://www.nytimes.com/2006/08/14/nyregion/14tanning.html?ex=1168491600&en=4e9087ae8e8b00ff&ei=5070>, accessed August 2006; and Alan C. Gellar et al., "Use of Sunscreen, Sunburning Rates and Tanning Bed Use Among More than 10000 U.S. Children and Adolescents," *Pediatrics*, Vol. 109, No. 6, June 2002, <http://pediatrics.aappublications.org/cgi/reprint/109/6/1009>, accessed January 8, 2007.

Unless otherwise noted, skin damage and cancer data come from the American Cancer Society, "Estimated New Cancer Cases and Deaths by Sex for All Sites, United States, 1997 to 2006," Cancer Facts and Figures, <http://www.cancer.org/downloads/STT/CAFF2007PWSecured.pdf>.

Helpful articles on the sun-safe clothing and sun protection product industry include Business Wire, "SunGuard™ Laundry Aid Helps Clothing Block More than 96 Percent of Harmful UV Rays; This Next Generation in Sun Protection Washes-In a UPF of 30," July 27, 2005; Richard A. Marini, "Shun the Sun; Clothing Protects Against Harmful Rays," *San Antonio Express-News*, May 13, 2004; SunGuard™, <http://www.sunguardsunprotection.com>, accessed January 2007.

30-Winkers

Data on Americans' sleep habits come from "2005 Sleep in America Poll," National Sleep Foundation, released March 29, 2005, accessed October 2006, at http://www.sleepfoundation.org/site/c.huIXKjM0IxF/b.2417141/k.C60C/Welcome.htm. Other useful online resources include www.sleep-deprivation.com and www.sleepapneainfo.com.

Articles useful to this chapter include "New Study Shows People Sleep Even Less Than They Think," *Science Daily*, July 3, 2006; accessed October 2006, at http://www.sciencedaily.com/releases//2006/07/060703162945.htm; and Stefan Lovgren, "US Racking Up Huge Sleep Debt," *National Geographic News*, February 24, 2005.

Traffic accident data come from "Drowsy Driving and Automobile Crashes," published at www.nhtsa.dot.gov, accessed October 2006, at http:www.nhtsa.dot.gov/people/injury/drowsy driving1/Drowsy.html.

For more on the sleeping pill industry, see http://www.livescience.com/humanbiology/060323 sleep deprivation.html. For more on the caffeine industry, see Melanie Warner, "A Jolt of Caffeine, by the Can," *New York Times*, November 23, 2005.

The Web site for Metronaps is http://www.metronaps.com.

The international data come largely from a 2005 ACNielson study accessed January 2007, at http://asiapacific.acnielson.com/news/20050228.shtml.

Southpaws Unbound

Caveman southpaw data were reported in Alexandra Witze, "Study Takes Left-Hands-On Approach," *Dallas Morning News*, October 12, 2003.

For more on the causes of handedness, see David E. Rosenbaum, "On Left-Handedness, Its Causes and Costs," *New York Times*, May 16, 2000.

For more on the disputed effects of left-handedness on human health, see Nicole Frehsee, "All Is Not Right in the World of the Lefty," Fort Lauderdale *Sun Sentinel*, October 29, 2005. For more on Southpaw earnings, see Joel Waldfogel, "Sinister and Rich," *Slate*, August 16, 2006.

The discussion of lateralization of the brain among animals comes from Amanda Onion, "The Left-Handed Advantage," *ABC News*, February 17, 2005.

For more on the religious heritage of left-handedness as sin, including the Ayatollah Khomeini reference, see "All Is Not Right in the World of the Lefty," cited above; and Kathleen Laufenberg, "For Centuries, Being Left-Handed Was More than Just Inconvenient," *Tallahassee Democrat*, January 29, 2002.

The UCLA study is K. Hugdahl, et al., "Left-Handedness and Old Age: Do Left-Handers Die Earlier?," *Neuropsychologia*, Vol. 4, 1993, pp. 325–33, cited in Thomas H. Maugh II, "Lefties Don't Die Young After All, Study Reports," *Los Angeles Times*, April 4, 1993.

The higher incidence of left-handedness in twins is noted in "On Left-Handedness, Its Causes and Costs," cited above. The data on the greater likelihood of lefties being born to older Moms come from Stanley Coren, psychologist at the University of British Columbia, and reported at "The Left-Handed Advantage," cited above.

The study on prevalence of left-handedness among gays is cited in "All Is Not Right in the World of the Lefty," cited above.

Famous left-handers are reported in multiple sources, including the "Famous Left-Handers" Web site, http://www.indiana.edu/~primate/left.html.

For more on lefty advantages in sports, see Childs Walker, "Some Lefties Do All Right," *Baltimore Sun*, November 16, 2006; and Alan Blondin, "No Longer Taboo, Golf Is Seeing the Emergence of the . . . Lefties," *Myrtle Beach Sun-News*, September 8, 2006.

The BlackBerry/Research in Motion story comes from Tyler Hamilton, "Business Tries to Right Wrongs for Lefties," *Toronto Star*, August 13, 2004.

DIY Doctors

Over-the-counter drug sale data come from ACNielson research posted on the Consumer Healthcare Products Association Web site, "OTC Retail Sales—1964–2005," <http://www.chpa-info.org/ChpaPortal/PressRoom/Statistics/OTCRetailSales.htm>, accessed March 2007.

The information on complementary and alternative medicine can be found at "CAM Links—Williamson Street Co-op," <http://www.livingnaturally.com/common/adam/CAM_Links.asp?storeID=3ED1FF6A18BD42979FFF73C8E8CD4512>, accessed August 2006.

The figures on Internet use to find medical information come from "Number of 'Cyberchondriacs'—Adults Who Have Ever Gone Online for Health Information—Increases to an Estimated 136 Million Nationwide," Harris Interactive, August 1, 2006, <http://www.harrisinteractive.com/harris_poll/index.asp?PID=686>, accessed August 2006.

Trends regarding health care costs come from "Health Insurance Cost," National Coalition on Health Care, <http://www.nchc.org/facts/cost.shtml>, accessed August 2006.

Trends regarding Americans' trust in doctors are described in "Americans Are Concerned About Hospital Based Medical and Surgical Errors," Harris Interactive, <http://www.harrisinteractive.com/news/allnewsbydate.asp?NewsID=825>, accessed August 2006.

Hospital infections kill between 44,000 and 98,000 Americans per year; see "To Err Is Human: Building a Safer Health System," Institute of Medicine of the National Academies, <http://www.iom.edul/id=12735>, accessed August 2006. Breast cancer is expected to kill about 40,000 Americans in 2007; see American Cancer Society Web site at http://www .cancer.org/docroot/stt/stt 0.asp, accessed April 2007. Car accidents kill approximately 42,000 Americans per year; see data from National Highway Traffic Safety Administration, reported at http://money.cnn.com/2005/08/01/Autos/nhtsa death stats/, accessed April 2007. AIDS kills approximately 17,000 Americans per year; see 2005 data reported at http://www.cdc.gov/hiv/ topics/surveillance/basic.htm#hivest, accessed April 2007.

The graph on public confidence in the medical institution was provided by Robert Blendon at the Harvard Public Health Review, and first published in Cathryn Delude, "Crisis of Confidence," *Harvard Public Health* Review, Fall 2004, <http://www.hsph.harvard.edu/review/ review_fall_04/rvw_trust.html>, accessed August 2006.

Data on women and health care decisions are provided on "Women, OTCs and Health in the United States," Consumer Health Education Center, http://www.checforbetterhealth .org/Chec/Media/Facts_Stats/Women_OTCs_FastFacts.as px>, accessed August 2006.

Data on growth in spending on direct-to-consumer ads come from Milt Freudenheim, "Showdown Looms in Congress over Drug Advertising on TV," *New York Times*, January 22, 2007.

The data on patient interest in e-mailing their doctors come from "New Poll Shows US Adults Strongly Favor and Value New Medical Technologies in Their Doctor's Office," Harris Interactive, <http://www.harrisinteractive.com/news/allnewsbydate.asp?NewsID=980>, accessed August 2006.

Hard-of-Hearers

The survey regarding presidents Clinton and Reagan is from Gallup Poll News Service, "Americans' Retrospective Approval of Clinton Improving," conducted June 1–4, 2006; accessed September 2006, at http://www.galluppoll.com/content/?ci=23362.

Data on Americans' hearing loss come from the Web site of the American Speech-Language-Hearing Association, accessed September 2006, at http://www.asha.org/public/ hearing/disorders/prevalence adults.htm.

The Navy's challenges with eye surgery were reported at David Cloud, "Perfect Vision Is Helping and Hurting Navy," *New York Times*, June 20, 2006.

Data on the elderly and their hearing loss come from http://www.census.gov/cgi-bin/ipc/ idbagg and http://www.asha.org/public/hearing/disorders/prevalence adults.htm.

The Deafness Research Foundation data, including the decibels of household noises, can be found at http://www.drf.org/hearingbalanceresearch.htm.

Demographic data on the hard of hearing come from the National Institute on Deafness and Other Communication Disorders, "Statistics About Hearing Disorders, Ear Infections, and Deafness," accessed September 2006, at http://www.nidcd.nih.gov/health/statistics/hearing.asp; and "Non-Hispanic Blacks May Have Best Hearing in U.S.," June 12, 2006, accessed September 2006, at http://www.insidescience.org/reports/2006/010.html.

Helpful articles on the future of treatments for the hard-of-hearing include Linda Marsa, "Auditory Achilles' Heel," *Los Angeles Times*, January 16, 2006; "Antioxidants May Sound Hope for Hearing Loss," Associated Press, October 12, 2003; "UB, Military Collaborate on Design, Testing of First Drug to Prevent Noise-Induced Hearing Loss," December 2003, accessed April

2007, at http://www.medicalnewstoday.com/medicalnews.php?newsid=4915; and "Stem Cells May Be Key to Deafness Cure," *CBS News*, August 7, 2006.

For more on the mosquitotone, see Paul Vitello, "A Ring Tone Meant to Fall on Deaf Ears," *New York Times*, June 12, 2006.

V. Family Life
Old New Dads

The birth rate data in this chapter come largely from the National Center for Health Statistics, Centers for Disease Control, U.S. Department of Health and Human Services; Mark O'Keefe, "The Joys and Pitfalls of Late-Life Fatherhood," New House News Service, http://www.newhousenews.com/archive/okeefe061504.html, accessed September 2006; and Joyce A. Martin, M.P.H., et al., "Births: Final Data for 2004," *National Vital Statistics Reports*, Vol. 55, No. 1, September 29, 2006. International data come from *United Nations Demographic Yearbook: Focusing on Natality*, "Live-Birth Rates Specific for Age of Father: 1990–1998."

The phrase "Do-Over Dads" was coined, as far as we know, by Carlene Hempel, "Do-Over Dads," *Boston Globe*, November 6, 2005. The vasectomy statistics come from her article as well.

Pet Parents

Pet ownership statistics, as well as data on the size of the pet products industry, come largely from the Web site of the American Pet Products Manufacturers Association, Inc., accessed October 2006, at http://www.appma.org/press industrytrends.asp.

Data on households with children come from U.S. Census, accessed October 2006, at http://www.census.gov/population/socdemo/hh-fam/hh1.xls.

The figure on pet owners paying anything to save their pet's life comes from http://www.emaxhealth.com/116/6885.html, reporting on a 2005 study conducted of Veterinary Pet Insurance policyholders.

Other articles useful to this chapter, from which several data points and anecdotes come, include Janis Fontaine, "Pet Ownership, Related Spending on the Rise," *Palm Beach Post*, May 26, 2005; "Pet Spending at All Time High," *Business Wire*, April 5, 2006; Sandy Robins, "New Products Pamper Pet from Head to Tail," April 27, 2005, accessed October 2006, at http://www.msnbc.msn.com/id/6142671/; Joan Verdon, "Pets Rock! Human Companies Going to the Dogs (and Other Beasts)," *The Record* (Bergen County, NJ), April 7, 2006; and Larisa Brass and Carly Harrington, "For Pet's Sake: More Owners Going All Out for Their Little Charges," *Knoxville News-Sentinel*, December 18, 2005.

For more on Honda's Wow, see Will Iredale, "Dog-Friendly Car Takes a Bow-Wow," *The Sunday Times* (London), October 9, 2005; accessed October 2006, at http://www.timesonline.co.uk/article/0,,2087-1817415,00.html.

Pampering Parents

Benjamin Spock, *Common Sense Book of Baby and Child Care* (Pocket Books, 1946).

The data on the growth in parenting books come from Neil Swidey, "All Talked Out," *Boston Globe*, November 7, 2004.

Data on the size of the baby-product industry come from Matthew Boyle, "The $5 Million Diaper Bag," *Fortune*, April 19, 2006.

The PSB polls were conducted online October 27–29, 2006, and December 13, 2006. Eligible respondents were adults who had children under 18 living at home with them.

For more on "Ferberizing," see the original at Richard Ferber, M.D., *Solve Your Child's Sleep Problems* (Simon & Schuster, 1985); the 2006 version is called *Solve Your Child's Sleep Problems: New, Revised, and Expanded Edition.*

The data on attitudes toward spanking come from Murray A. Strauss and Anita K. Mathur, "Social Change and Trends in Approval of Corporal Punishment by Parents from 1968 to 1994," accessed July 2006, at http://www.dadsnow.org/studies/strauss1.htm; and Julie Crandall, "Support for Spanking: Most Americans Think Corporal Punishment Is OK," ABCNEWS .com, November 8, 2004. The death penalty data come from an October 2006 Gallup poll, accessed December 2006, at http://www.galluppoll.com/content/?ci=1606&pg=1. For more on rural crime dropping more slowly in the 1990s than urban or suburban crime, see "Rural Crime Facts," National Center on Rural Justice and Crime Prevention," accessed February 2007, at http://virtual.clemson.edu/groups/ncrj/rural crime facts.htm.

Data on the use of the V-chip come from a July 24, 2001, press release by the Kaiser Family Foundation, accessed December 2006, at http://www.kff.org/entmedia/3158-V-Chip-release .cfm.

In the International Picture, the data on states and countries that approve corporal punishment come from http://www.stophitting.com/disatschool/statesBanning.php.

For more on the U.K.'s Children are Unbeatable! Alliance, see http://www.children areunbeatable.org.uk/. Their survey data were cited in "Majority 'Support' Smacking Ban," *BBC News*, May 19, 2004, accessed December 2006, at http://news.bbc.co.uk/1/hi/uk/3727295 .stm.

The study on global attitudes toward pressure on kids is Richard Wike and Juliana Menasce Horowitz, "Parental Pressure on Students: Not Enough in America; Too Much in Asia," Pew Global Attitudes Project, August 24, 2006, accessed January 2007, at http://pewresearch.org/ pubs/55/parental-pressure-on-students-not-enough-in-america-too-much-in-asia.

Data on U.S. placement on the global mathematics literacy test come from M. Lemke et al., "International Outcomes of Learning in Mathematics Literacy and Problem Solving," National Center for Education Statistics, 2004, accessed December 2006, at http://nces.ed.gov/ pubs2005/2005003.pdf.

Late-Breaking Gays

Biographical information regarding former governor Jim McGreevey comes from James E. McGreevey with David France, *The Confession* (HarperCollins 2006).

Useful articles for this trend included Melissa Fletcher Stoeltje, "Spouses Feel Pushed Aside When Mate Reveals Homosexuality," *San Antonio Express News*, July 3, 2005; Katy Butler, "Many Couples Must Negotiate Terms of 'Brokeback' Marriages," *New York Times*, July 7, 2006; Jane Gross, "Windows to the Closet," *New York Times*, November 1, 2004.

The National Survey of Family Growth data can be found at William D. Mosher, Ph.D., Anjani Chandra, Ph.D., and Jo Jones, Ph.D., Division of Vital Statistics, "Sexual Behavior and Selected Health Measures: Men and Women 15–44 Years of Age, United States, 2002," Table 7, accessed February 2007, at http://www.cdc.gov/nchs/data/ad/ad362.pdf.

Data on American attitudes toward homosexuality cited in this chapter are summarized by the Gallup Poll, accessed January 2007, at http://www.galluppoll.com/content/Default .aspx?ci=1651&pg=1&VERSION=p.

The blog www.comingoutat48.blogspot.com was quoted in Jane Gross, "When the Beard Is Too Painful to Remove, *New York Times*, August 3, 2006.

Data on spouses and children come largely from Katy Butler's article, cited above.

Marriage statistics come from http://www.cdc.gov/nchs/data/mvsr/supp/mv43 12s.pdf (the 1980 number); National Vital Statistics Report, Vol. 54, No. 8, "Births, Marriages, Divorces, and Deaths; Provisional Data for June 2006."

For the Jason Stuart joke, we are grateful to Joe Kort, "The New Mixed Marriage: When One Partner Is Gay," originally published in the *Psychotherapy Networker*, September 2005, accessed January 2007, at http://www.joekort.com/joekort the new mixed marriage.htm.

Dutiful Sons

The main study relied on in this piece is "Caregiving in the U.S.," National Alliance for Caregiving and AARP, released April 2004.

Life expectancy data come from the Centers for Disease Control: Table 27, "Life Expectancy at Birth, at 65 Years of Age, and at 75 Years of Age, by Race and Sex: United States, Selected Years 1900–2004," accessed April 2007, at http://www.cdc.gov/nchs/data/hus/hus06.pdf#027.

The Napolitano piece is Peter Napolitano, "Modern Love; Close Enough for Momma, Too Close for Me," *New York Times*, December 24, 2006.

Figures on the value lost to companies from absentee workers come from Jane Gross, "As Parents Age, Baby Boomers and Businesses Struggle to Cope," *New York Times*, March 25, 2006.

VI. Politics

Impressionable Elites

The Friedman book is, of course, Thomas L. Friedman, *The World Is Flat: A Brief History of the 21st Century* (Farrar, Straus & Giroux, 2005).

The income data come from David Cay Johnston, "Income Gap Is Widening, Data Shows," *New York Times*, March 29, 2007.

The PSB poll was 806 telephone interviews among likely 2008 presidential voters, including an oversample of 400 very likely Democratic presidential primary voters.

Cited journalists and articles include Mark Leibovich, "Listening and Nodding, Clinton Shapes '08 Image," *New York Times*, March 6, 2007; and Christopher Cooper and Ray A. Smith, "Style on the Stump," *Wall Street Journal*, March 31, 2007.

Useful articles on 527s and their record fund-raising include Chris Suellentrop, "Follow the Money," *Boston Globe*, June 26, 2005; and John Broder, "Campaign 2006: 527 Groups Set to Spend Big on Negative Political TV Ads," *New York Times*, October 11, 2006.

Swing Is Still King

An earlier version of this piece was published in the *Washington Post* by Mark J. Penn, "Swing Is Still King at the Polls," on March 21, 2006.

The data on the growing number of Independents come from Gallup: in January 1966, 23 percent of voters called themselves Independent (see Q98 at http://brain.gallup.com/documents/questionnaire.aspx?STUDY=AIPO0723); in April 2007, 36 percent of voters did (see http://www.galluppoll.com/content/default.aspx?ci=15370).

The California data come from Report of Registration, Historical Registration Statistics, February 10, 2003, and February 10, 2005, accessed February 2006, at http://www.ss.ca.gov/elections/ror/reg stats 02 10 05.pdf and http://www.ss.ca.gov/elections/ror/regstats 02-10-03.pdf.

Split-ticket voter information comes from the American National Election Studies Guide to Public Opinion and Electoral Behavior, "Split-Ticket Voting Presidential/Congressional, 1952–2004," accessed February 2006, at http://www.umich.edu/~nes/nesguide/toptable/tab9b 2.htm.

Congressional ballot data come from Gallup, "Election 2006," accessible at http://brain .gallup.com/content/?ci=4534.

CNN exit poll data for 2004, 2000, and 1996, respectively, were accessed at http://www .cnn.com/ELECTION/2004/pages/results/states/US/P/00/epolls.0.html, http://www.cnn.com/ ELECTION/2000/results/index.epolls.html, http://www.cnn.com/ALLPOLITICS/1996/elections /natl.exit.poll/index1.html.

Militant Illegals

Thanks to my friend and colleague Sergio Bendixen for his review and thoughtful comments on this chapter.

Directed by Fred W. Friendly and starring Edward R. Murrow, *Harvest of Shame* was a documentary aired on *CBS News* on Thanksgiving 1960.

The Sensenbrenner bill was H.R. 4437, the Border Protection, Anti-Terrorism, and Illegal Immigration Control Act of 2005, passed by the 109th Congress on December 16, 2005. It did not pass the Senate.

Data on the Hispanic electorate come from Roberto Suro, Richard Fry, and Jeffrey Passell, "Hispanics and the 2004 Election: Population, Electorate, and Voters," Pew Hispanic Center, June 27, 2005. For 2004 exit poll data, see http://us.cnn.com/ELECTION/2004/ pages/results/states/US/P/00/epolls.0.html.

The state-by-state data on the Hispanic electorate in the graph come from U.S. Census, http://www.census.gov/population/socdemo/voting/cps2004/tab04a.xls (for 2004) and http:// www.census.gov/population/socdemo/voting/p20-466/tab04.pdf (for 1992).

The 2006 Pew Study was Roberto Suro and Gabriel Escobar, "2006 National Survey of Latinos," Pew Hispanic Center, July 13, 2006. Data on actual Latino performance in the 2006 midterm elections come from "Latinos and the 2006 Mid-term Election," Pew Hispanic Center, November 27, 2006.

The 2006 Gallup data on Latino party identification come from Gallup's annual Minority Rights and Relations poll, reported July 6, 2006.

The New Democrat Network poll is "Inside the Mind of Hispanic Voters," conducted June 24–July 1, 2006, by LatinInsights, and released July 19, 2006.

Health insurance and education data among Latino immigrants are drawn from Steven A. Camarota, "Immigrants at Mid-Decade: A Snapshot of America's Foreign-Born Population in 2005," Center for Immigration Studies, December 2005.

Christian Zionists

Data on American support of Israel can be found at Gallup poll, "Perceptions of Foreign Countries," February 1–4, 2007, accessed April 2007, at http://www.galluppoll.com/content/ default.aspx?ci=1624&pg=2.

Articles useful to this chapter included Jane Lampman, "Mixing Prophecy and Politics," *Christian Science Monitor*, July 7, 2004; Bill Broadway, "The Evangelical-Israeli Connection," *Washington Post*, March 27, 2004; David D. Kirkpatrick, "For Evangelicals, Supporting Israel Is 'God's Foreign Policy,'" *New York Times*, November 14, 2006; Richard Allen Greene, "Evangelical Christians Plead for Israel," *BBC News*, July 19, 2006; and Max Blumenthal, "Birth Pangs of a New Christian Zionism," posted August 8, 2006, accessed October 2006, at http://www.thenation.com/doc/20060814/new christian zionism.

The Pew poll regarding views on God's giving the state of Israel to the Jews is the Pew Research Center for the People and the Press and the Pew Forum on Religion and Public Life, "Many Americans Uneasy with Mix of Religion and Politics," p. 20, released August 24, 2006.

Citations from David Brog come from "Righteous Gentiles at the Right Time," Religion News Service, June 5, 2006, among other sources. Thanks also to Jonathan Kessler for informing the discussion of former president Jimmy Carter's book *Palestine: Peace, not Apartheid* (Simon & Schuster, 2006).

Newly Released Ex-Cons

Trend data on reentrants come from Paige M. Harrison and Allen J. Beck, Bureau of Justice Statistics Bulletin, *Prison and Jail Inmates at Midyear 2005* (May 2006), and earlier versions. Demographic data come from the U.S. Department of Justice, Office of Justice Programs, Bureau of Justice Statistics, "Reentry Trends in the U.S., Characteristics of Releases," accessed January 2007, at http://www.ojp.usdoj.gov/bjs/reentry/characteristics.htm. Thanks also to Amy Solomon for helping us navigate the data; and to Jeremy Travis, the true reentry pioneer.

Trend data on the jail and prison population generally come from Table 335, "Adults on Probation, in Jail or Prison, or on Parole: 1980–2004," U.S. Census Bureau, Statistical Abstract of the United States: 2007.

Data from the International Centre for Prison Studies can be found at http://www.prisonstudies.org/.

Data on the transportation of convicts to Australia can be found on the Web site "Convicts to Australia: A Guide to Researching Your Convict Ancestors," accessible at http://members.iinet.com.au/~perthdps/convicts/res-02.html.

Recidivism data come from U.S. Department of Justice, Office of Justice Programs, Bureau of Justice Statistics, "Reentry Trends in the U.S., Recidivism," accessed January 2007, at http://www.ojp.usdoj.gov/bjs/reentry/recidivism.htm.

The figure on children with parents in prison comes from Julie Delcour, "Second Chance," *Tulsa World*, December 10, 2006.

Other articles useful to this chapter include "A Stigma That Never Fades," *The Economist*, August 8, 2002, which cites the survey of employers in large cities and the Cleveland study; Eric Eckholm, "Time Served: The Revolving Door," *New York Times*, August 12, 2006; and Rex W. Huppke, "Rehabilitation or Recycling?," *Chicago Tribune*, March 12, 2006.

VII. Teens
The Mildly Disordered

Autism statistics come from http://www.fightingautism.org/idea/autism.php?s=US&z=s. Data on children being treated with antipsychotic drugs come from Joan Lowry, "US Families Face Learning Disabilities," *Ventura County Star*, December 21, 2003.

Data from the Individuals with Disabilities Education Act come from U.S. Department of Education, National Center for Education Statistics, 2006, "The Condition of Education 2006," NCES 2006-071, Washington, D.C.: U.S. Government Printing Office.

Research on the growing number of students getting extra time on the SAT comes from Mark Franek, "Time to Think," *New York Times*, March 29, 2006.

Data on the after-school tutoring industry come from Diane Heldt, "Tutors Aid More than Rich or Kids with Learning Woes," Associated Press State and Local Wire, October 17, 2005.

The data on college students' mental health is Robert P. Gallagher, "National Survey of Counseling Center Directors, 2005," published by the International Association of Counseling Services, Inc.—Monograph Series No. 80, accessed December 2006, at http://www.education .pitt.edu/survey/nsccd/archive/2005.monograph.pdf.

For more on infant disorders, see Elizabeth Bernstein, "Sending Baby to the Shrink," Associated Press Financial Wire, October 24, 2006.

Young Knitters

Most of the data on knitting and crocheting participation come from the Craft Yarn Council of America study found on their Web site, CYCA News, http://www.craftyarncouncil .com/know.html, accessed October 2006.

For more information on men's knitting groups and their history, see Men's Knitting Site for Men Who Knit, http://www.menknit.net/, accessed October 2006.

Other articles helpful to this chapter included Kate Stone Lombardi, "The Cool World of Knitting (Really)," *New York Times*, February 13, 2005; Nancy Carollo, "Everything Old Is New Again," *New Orleans Times-Picayune*, March 23, 2006; and Denise DiFulco, "Sewing, So Fashionable; Projects Once Humbly 'Homemade' Are Now Touted as 'Handmade,'" *Washington Post*, September 21, 2006.

Black Teen Idols

The Casey study is at "Coverage in Context: How Thoroughly the News Media Report Five Key Children's Issues," February 2002, accessed April 2007, at http://cjc.umd.edu/about/ ContentStudyExecSummary.htm.

The data on twelfth-grade churchgoing come from Child Trends Databank, "Religious Services Attendance," accessed April 2007, at http://www.childrensdatabank.org/pdf/32 PDF .pdf.

The data on volunteering and voting behavior come from Karlo Barrios Marcelo, Mark Hugo Lopez, and Emily Hoban Kirby, "Civic Engagement Among Minority Youth," January 2007, accessed April 2007, at http://www.civicyouth.org/PopUps/FactSheets/FS 07 minority ce.pdf, analyzing data from "Monitoring the Future, High School Senior Survey, 1983–2005" and its earlier version, Mark Hugo Lopez, "Civic Engagement Among Minority Youth," September 2002. Both documents were produced by CIRCLE, the Center for Information and Research on Civic Learning and Engagement, based in the University of Maryland's School of Public Affairs.

The City Year data were provided by Alison Franklin, co-director, Strategic Communications, City Year, via e-mail dated April 18, 2007. For more information on City Year and its application process, see www.cityyear.org.

Data on black adult volunteering come from "Volunteering in America: State Trends and Rankings, 2005 Key Volunteer Statistics," accessed April 2007, at http://nces.ed.gov/programs/digest/d03/tables/dt107.asp.

The information on volunteer preference by race comes from "College Students Helping America," Corporation for National and Community Service, October 2006, accessed April 2007, at http://www.nationalservice.gov/pdf/06 1016 RPD college full.pdf.

The 2002 study on black party identification is David A. Bositis, "2002 National Opinion Poll," Joint Center for Political and Economic Studies, conducted September 17–October 21, 2002.

All data on high school dropouts, college enrollment, college graduation, and master's degrees come from the National Center for Education Statistics. The particular tables are as follows: Table 107, "Percent of High School Dropouts (Status Dropouts) Among Persons 16 to 24 Years Old, by Sex and Race/Ethnicity: Selected Years: April 1960 to October 2001," http://nces.ed.gov/programs/digest/d03/tables/dt107.asp; Table 181, "College Enrollment and Enrollment Rates of Recent High School Completers, by Race/Ethnicity: 1960 Through 2004," http://nces.ed.gov/programs/digest/d05/tables/dt05 181.asp: Table 261, "Bachelor's Degrees Conferred by Degree-Granting Institutions, by Racial/Ethnic Group and Sex of Student: Selected Years, 1976–77 Through 2003–04," http://nces.ed.gov/programs/digest/d05/tables/dt05 261.asp; Table 264, "Master's Degrees Conferred by Degree-Granting Institutions, by Racial/Ethnic Group and Sex of Student: Selected Years, 1976–77 Through 2003–04," http://nces.ed.gov/programs/digest/d05/tables/dt05 264.asp.

Some data on the black middle class come from Robert L. Harris, Jr., "The Rise of the Black Middle Class," *The World and I*, February 1999, Vol. 14, No. 2. The data on black-owned businesses come from Elwin Green, "Black Business Owners on Rise," *Pittsburgh Post-Gazette*, April 18, 2006.

High School Moguls

The very useful *BusinessWeek* article is Rochelle Sharpe et al., "Teen Moguls," *BusinessWeek*, May 29, 2000, accessed January 2007. Other useful articles included Penelope Green, "Barons Before Bedtime," *New York Times*, January 25, 2007.

For more information about the Chocolate Farm and its founders, see www.chocolatefarm.com; http://www.mary-kateandashley.com/mind body soul/article.php?88.

For more information about AnandTech and its founder, see www.anandtech.com: http://www.rediff.com/us/2000/mar/24us3.htm.

The YoungBiz study can be found at Party Mayeux, "Report on America's Top 'Treps," *The 2001 YoungBiz 100*, accessed at http://www.youngbiz.com/aspindex.asp?fileName=yb mag news/2001youngbiz100/main.htm.

The Junior Achievement study on teens' attitudes toward entrepreneurship is "2006 Interprise Poll on Teens and Entrepreneurship," conducted by Junior Achievement Worldwide, August 28, 2006.

Aspiring Snipers

The New America poll of California teenagers was conducted in November 2006 by Bendixen and Associates.

The cited poem comes from www.snipersparadise.com, accessed January 2007.

Useful articles for this chapter included Matthew Cox, "Time to Go SNIPER!," *Army Times*, March 6, 2006; John C. K. Daly, "UPI Terrorism Watch," UPI, July 27, 2005; and Richard Whittle, "Fatal from Afar," *Dallas Morning News*, July 7, 2005.

The 2007 data on American attitudes toward the Iraq War and the troops fighting it come from Jodie T. Allen, Nilanthi Samaranayake, and James Albrittain, Jr., "Iraq and Vietnam: A Crucial Difference in Opinion," Pew Research Center for the People and the Press, March 22, 2007, <http://pewresearch.org/pubs/432/iraq-and-vietnam-a-crucial-difference-in-opinion>, accessed March 2007.

VIII. Food, Drink, and Diet
Vegan Children

The data on Vegetarian Children come largely from a 2005 poll conducted by Harris Interactive on behalf of the Vegetarian Resource Group, April 14–18, 2005, among a nationwide sample of 1,264 U.S. youth aged 8–18; accessed February 2007, at http://www.vrg.org/journal/vj2005issue4/vj2005issue4youth.htm.

The National Beef Council's campaign was reported in Kate Kompas, "1 in 4 Teens Say Vegetarianism Is Cool," *St. Cloud Times*, February 17, 2003.

The studies showing health effects of vegetarianism were conducted on Seventh-Day Adventists, and reported, among other places, in Sharon Bloyd-Peshkin, "Meatless Wonders," *Chicago Tribune*, October 5, 2003.

Also useful to this piece were Jennifer Nelson, "Don't Have a Cow, Mom," *Washington Post*, October 31, 2006; and Virginia Rohan, "Veggie Vanguard," *The Record* (Bergen County, NJ), April 13, 2003.

Big Momma's Heartache

Data on America's weight gain come from Cynthia L. Ogden, Ph.D., et al., "Mean Body Weight, Height, and Body Mass Index, United States, 1960–2002," October 27, 2004, accessed August 2006, at http://www.cdc.gov/nchs/data/ad/ad347.pdf.

Useful articles for this chapter included Christine Gorman, "More than Just a Little Chunky," *TIME*, July 9, 2006; and John Stucke, "Weighty Issues," *Spokesman Review*, March 26, 2006.

The figure on the cost of obesity comes from "Companies Fight Employee Fat, Hoping to Trim the Bottom Line," Associated Press, February 3, 2003.

For more on the Food and Drug Administration's Plan obesity-tackling plan, see http://www.fda.gov/loseweight/obesity plan.htm.

The first *JAMA* study is Katherine M. Flegal, Ph.D., et al., "Prevalence and Trends in Obesity Among US Adults, 1999–2000," *JAMA*, Vol. 288, No. 14, October 9, 2002.

Obesity rates over time come from National Center for Health Statistics, *Health, United States, 2006, with Chartbook on Trends in the Health of Americans*, Hyattsville, MD: 2006, Table 73, "Overweight, Obesity, and Healthy Weight Among Persons 20 Years of Age and Over, by Sex, Age, Race, and Hispanic Origin, and Poverty Level: United States, 1960–1962 Through 2001–2004," accessed August 2006, at http://www.cdc.gov/nchs/data/hus/hus06.pdf#073.

The second *JAMA* study is Kathleen McTigue, MD, MS, MPH, et al., "Mortality and Cardiac and Vascular Outcomes in Extremely Obese Women," *JAMA*, Vol. 296, No 1, July 5, 2006.

Data on black women's participation in the workforce come from Bureau of Labor Statistics, Household Data Annual Averages, Table 10, "Employed Persons by Occupation, Race, Hispanic, or Latino Ethnicity, and Sex," accessed January 2007 at http://www.bls.gov/cps .cpsaat10.pdf.

Data on black women raising children come from U.S. Census, Table 3, "Children Living with Relatives by Type of Relative, Presence of Parents, by Race and Hispanic Origin and Whether Below Poverty Level: 2001," accessed January 2007, at http://www.census .gov/population/socdemo/child/sipp2001/tab03-03.pdf.

The New York City study is "Women at Risk: The Health of Women in New York City," a report from the New York City Department of Health and Mental Hygiene, March 2005, accessed January 2007, at http://www.cmwf.org/usr doc/Final Women At Risk.pdf, and reported in Marc Santora, "Study Finds More Obesity and Less Exercising," New York Times, March 8, 2005.

In the International Picture, the global numbers on obesity and undernourishment, as well as some of the data on specific countries, come from Claire Nullis, "Africa Faces Growing Obesity Problem," Associated Press, November 29, 2006, accessed January 2007, at http://www .breitbart.com/article.php?id=D8LN0P6G1&show article=1.

The worldwide obesity numbers come from http://www.who.int/nutrition/topics/obesity/ en/index.html. A very helpful article here was Jane E. Brody, "As America Gets Bigger, the World Does, Too," New York Times, April 19, 2005.

Mexican data come from "Obesity on the Rise in Mexico," The Economist, December 18, 2004.

Starving for Life

The Cornell and subsequent research on life extension through calorie restriction, as well as the effects of such diets, are summarized in Michael Mason, "One for the Ages: A Prescription That May Extend Life," New York Times, October 31, 2006; and David Schardt, "Eat Less Live Longer?," Nutrition Action Healthletter, Center for Science in the Public Interest, September 1, 2003.

The Biosphere story is told in Julian Dibbell, "Super Skinny Me," The Observer (London), December 3, 2006.

Evidence of health effects of CR is cited in Jack Cox, "Low-Cal Movement," Houston Chronicle, May 2, 2004.

For more on the centenarian Okinawans, see Nicole Piscopo Neal, "Meet the 120-Year-Old Man," Palm Beach Post, January 17, 2004; and Richard Corliss and Michael D. Lemonick, "How to Live to Be 100," TIME, August 30, 2004.

For more on the Calorie Restriction Society itself, and its founder, Roy Walford, see their Web site, www.calorierestriction.org.

Caffeine Crazies

All statistics on bottled water, soft drink, alcohol, and overall beverage consumption come from U.S. Census Bureau, Statistical Abstract of the US: 2007, Table 201, "Per Capita Consumption of Selected Beverages by Type: 1900–2004."

Information on sales of Dasani and Aquafina, drinks with "functional benefits," and energy drinks, comes from March 8, 2007, press release of the Beverage Marketing Corporation, accessed April 2007, at http://www.beveragemarketing.com/news2.htm.

Coffee-drinking statistics are reported in Reuters, "More Adults Prefer Daily Cup of Coffee," citing the 2006 National Coffee Drinking Trends report, March 3, 2007; and Tammy Joyner, "Innovators Come Up with Ways to Get Daily Jolt," Cox News Service, February 16, 2007. The latter article also provided the information about caffeine-laden food.

Starbucks growth statistics were cited in "Gourmet Coffee Popping Up in Unexpected Places," Associated Press, May 2, 2005.

The study on soft drinks being the leading source of American caloric intake was reported in Shari Roan, "Less than Zero," *Los Angeles Times*, November 27, 2006.

Tea sales data come from "Steaming Ahead, America's Tea Boom," *The Economist*, July 8, 2006.

More information about energy drinks can be found in Michael Mason, "The Energy Drink Buzz Is Unmistakable," *New York Times*, December 12, 2006.

The Chicago poison center study was reported by an October 16, 2006, American College of Emergency Physicians press release, "Caffeine Abuse Among Young People Discovered in Examination of Poison Center Calls," accessed April 2007, at http://www.acep.org/webporta/Newsroom/NR/general/2006/101606b.htm.

For more on Americans' sleeping habits, see the 2002 Sleep in America poll, conducted by the National Sleep Foundation, accessed April 2007, at http://www.sleep-deprivation.com/.

The Viagra data come from "Younger Men Lead Surge in Viagra Use, Study Reveals," *Medical News Today*, August 6, 2004.

IX. Lifestyle
Long Attention Spanners

The figure on annual infomercial sales comes from John Larson, "From the Inside Out," NBC News, September 15, 2006, accessed October 2006, at http://www.msnbc.msn.com/id/14856571/.

Data on marathons and triathlons come from the Running USA Web site, at http://www.runningusa.org/cgi/mar repts.pl; and Michael McCarthy, "Ford Joins Forces with Ironman for Tough Sell," *USA Today*, May 19, 2005.

Tennis declined from 12.6 million participants to 11.1 million participants between 1995 and 2005; see National Sporting Goods Association study at http://www.nsga.org/public/pages/index.cfm?pageid=153.

The *Atlantic Monthly* circulation data are self-reported at http://www.theatlantic.com/about/atlfaqf.htm#circulation, as are the *Foreign Affairs* data at http://www.foreignaffairs.org/advertising/circ.

Crossword puzzle data come from Leslie Mann, "Not Your Father's Cr--sw-rd," *Chicago Tribune*, June 25, 2006.

Data on the Sudoku industry come from Martin Fackler, "Inside Japan's Puzzle Palace," *New York Times*, March 20, 2007.

The insights on long novels and series fiction come from "Span of Attention," HypertextNOW, accessed April 2006, at http://www.eastgate.com/HypertextNow/archives/Attention.html.

In recent years, the State of the Union address has been watched by about 42 million people; see http://www.nielsonmedia.com/nc/portal/site/Public/menuitem.55dc65b4a7d5adff3f65936147a062a0/?vgnextoid=a61ff63a16729010VgnVCM100000ac0a260aRCRD. The last game of the World Series rarely gets more than 20 million viewers; see http://www.baseball-almanac.com/ws/wstv.shtml

Neglected Dads

Data on children's and women's purchasing power can be found on the Free Press Web site, "Children's Programming," Free Press, http://www.freepress.net/issues/kidstv, accessed January 2007; and Girlpower Marketing Web site, http://www.girlpowermarketing.com/files/GP WEB Final.pdf, accessed January 2007; among other sources.

The University of Michigan study is W. Jean Yeung et al., "Children's Time with Fathers in Intact Families," *Journal of Marriage and Family*, Vol. 63, February 2001, 136–54.

The University of California Riverside study by sociologists Scott Coltrane and Michele Adams is based on data from the Child Development Supplement, Panel Study of Income Dynamics (PSID), conducted at the Survey Research Center, Institute for Social Research, University of Michigan. It was released in June 2003; the report can be accessed at http://www.eurekalert.org/pub releases/2003-06/uoc--wdc061003.php#.

The University of Washington study by Dr. John Gottman, widely reported in the press, was first published in John Gottman, *Why Marriages Succeed or Fail* (Fireside, 1994).

Native Language Speakers

Thanks again to Sergio Bendixen for reviewing this chapter as well.

The data on linguistically isolated households come from Hyon B. Shin with Rosalind Bruno, "Language Use and English-Speaking Ability: 2000," U.S. Census Bureau, issued October 2003, accessed November 2006, at http://www.census.gov/prod/2003pubs/c2k br-29.pdf.

The figures regarding residents who speak English "not at all" or with limited proficiency, as do the implications for limited English-speaking, come from http://www.us-english.org/inc/official/factsfigs.asp.

Immigration data come generally from the Center for Immigration Studies, whose Web site was accessed November 2006, at http://www.cis.org/articles/2001/back101.html.

Data on classes on English for speakers of other languages come from Eunice Moscoso, "Despite Concerns About Assimilation, Immigrants Learning English," Cox News Service, August 24, 2006.

Trend data on English proficiency of immigrants come from U.S. Census Bureau, Census 2000, "Profile of Selected Demographic and Social Characteristics for the Foreign Born Population Who Entered the United States Before 1970" and "Profile of Selected Demographic and Social Characteristics for the Foreign Born Population Who Entered the United States 1990 to 2000."

The data on heads of linguistically isolated households, including both nativity and income, come from U.S. Census Bureau, Census 2000, "America Speaks: Selected Characteristics of Households by Linguistic Isolation for the United States," accessed November 2006, at http://0-www.census.gov.mill1.sjlibrary.org/population/www/socdemo/hh-fam/AmSpks.html.

Data on Latino Americans' attitudes toward English come from the Pew Hispanic Center, "Hispanic Attitudes Towards Learning English," fact sheet published June 7, 2006.

Hospitals' challenges are described in Olga Pierce, "Hospitals Lack Language Plans," UPI, October 13, 2006.

Spanish success on the radio, as well as data on Latino purchasing power, are described in Hiram Soto, "Spanish-Language Radio Stations Are Rising to the Top," Copley News Service, October 23, 2005.

Information on the supply of English classes comes from Fernanda Santos, "Demand for English Lessons Outstrips Supply," *New York Times*, February 27, 2007.

Unisexuals

Useful articles for this chapter included Paula Dohnal, "Floating Between Two Genders," *Wisconsin State Journal*, October 10, 2005; Elizabeth Weil, "What If It's (Sort of) a Boy and (Sort of) a Girl?," *New York Times*, September 24, 2006; Patricia Leigh Brown, "Supporting Boys or Girls When the Line Isn't Clear," *New York Times*, December 2, 2006; Jenna Russell, "Finding a Gender Blind Dorm," *Boston Globe*, July 27, 2003; Alyson Ward, "Transcending Gender," *Fort Worth Star-Telegram*, August 24, 2005; Kelly Pate Dwyer, "An Employee, Hired as a Man, Becomes a Woman. Now What?," *New York Times*, July 31, 2005; Bonnie Miller Rubin, "Transgender Movement Emerging from the Shadows," *Chicago Tribune*, April 3, 2006; and Chris Rovzar, "Dude Looks Like a Lady," *New York Daily News*, July 23, 2006.

The Pulitzer Prize–winning novel is Jeffrey Eugenides, *Middlesex* (Picador, 2002).

For more on the World Professional Association for Transgender Health, see their Web site at http://www.wpath.org/.

The data on college and university policies come from Gender Public Advocacy Coalition, "2006 Genius Index: Gender Equality National Index for Universities and Schools," 2006.

The data on state policy come from Transgender Law and Policy Institute, whose Web site is http://www.transgenderlaw.org. The situation in New York City was reported at Damien Cave, "City Drops Plan to Change Definition of Gender," *New York Times*, December 6, 2006.

X. Money and Class

Second-Home Buyers

The term "Splitters," as far as we know, was coined by WCI Communities, Inc., a homebuilder with communities in Florida, Connecticut, Maryland, New Jersey, New York, and Virginia.

The data regarding second-home sales and buyers come from Paul C. Bishop, Ph.D., Shonda D. Hightower, and Harika Bickicioglu, "2006 National Association of Realtors® Profile of Second-Home Owners"; and the National Association of Realtors' "Profile of Second-Home Buyers," 2005.

The 2005 survey of two-home owners was conducted online by Analytical One Research Services for WCI, Inc. According to their methodology summary, it included 408 respondents who qualified as Splitters, out of a total of 1,743 respondents.

Modern Mary Poppinses

Useful articles for this trend included Heidi Knapp Rinella, "Minding the Children: Like One of the Family—Demand for Nannies in American Homes Has Sharply Increased," *Las Vegas Review-Journal*, March 15, 2005; Davis Bushnell, "Demand for Nannies on Upswing in Greater Boston," *Boston Globe*, March 13, 2005; and Tracey Middlekauff, "Nannies," *Gotham Gazette*, October 27, 2003.

Data on Moms in the workforce come from "Employment Status of Women by Presence of Child and Age of Youngest Child, March 1975–2005," Annual Social and Economic Supplement, Current Population Survey, Bureau of Labor Statistics.

Comparative salary data come from the Web site of the International Nanny Association, accessible at http://www.nanny.org/images/2006SalarySurvey/index 2.htm; and the Annual Demographic Survey, a joint project between the Bureau of Labor Statistics and the Bureau of the Census, accessed April 2007, at http://pubdb3.census.gov/macro/032006/perinc/new04 019.htm.

For more on career growth in nanny work, see Ralph Gardner, Jr., "Taking Superparents in Hand," *New York Times*, June 16, 2005.

The cited book is Emma McLaughlin and Nicola Kraus, *The Nanny Diaries* (St. Martin's, 2002).

For more on the need for paid caregivers, see 2005 White House Conference on Aging "Annotated Agenda, Final—November 3, 2005," accessed September 2006, at http://www .whcoa.gov/about/policy/meetings.annotated agenda.pdf.

Shy Millionaires

The data on skewed perceptions of millionaires come from a study conducted by Catherine Montalto, sponsored by Consumer Federation of America and Providian Financial; see 2001 press release, at http://www.americasaves.org/downloads/www.americasaves.org/ PressReleases/07.16.01.pdf.

Thomas J. Stanley and William D. Danko, *The Millionaire Next Door: The Surprising Secrets of America's Wealthy* (Longstreet, 1996), was very helpful to this chapter.

The annual Phoenix/Harris Interactive Wealth Survey consisted of 1,496 interviews conducted online by Harris Interactive between March 25 and April 9, 2003, with U.S. adults aged 18 years and over who were financial decision-makers for households with a net worth of $1 million or more, minus any debt and excluding primary residence.

For more on the estate tax, see Stephen Moore and Arthur B. Laffer, "The American Dream Tax," June 14, 2006.

Bourgeois and Bankrupt

Bankruptcy trend data come largely from Thomas A. Garrett, "The Rise in Personal Bankruptcies," Federal Reserve Bank of St. Louis, *Review*, Vol. 89, No. 1, January 2007/February 2007; and the American Bankruptcy Institute, whose Web site was accessed January 2007, at http://www.abiworld.org/AM/AMTemplate.cfm?Section=Home&CONTENTID=35631& TEMP LATE=/CM/ContentDisplay.cfm.

Professor Warren's book is Elizabeth Warren and Amelia Warren Tyagi, *The Two-Income Trap: Why Middle-Class Parents Are Going Broke* (Basic Books, 2003). Much of the data and anecdotes come from this book and Professor Warren's other articles, including David U. Himmelstein, Elizabeth Warren, Deborah Thorne, and Steffie Woolhandler, "MarketWatch: Illness and Injury as Contributors to Bankruptcy," *Health Affairs*, February 2, 2005.

Other articles useful to this chapter included Christine Dugas, "American Seniors Rack Up Debt like Never Before," *USA Today*, April 24, 2002; and Mindy Fetterman and Barbara Hansen, "Young People Struggle to Deal with Kiss of Debt," *USA Today*, November 22, 2006.

For more on the bankruptcy stigma, see Kartik Athreya, "Shame As It Ever Was: Stigma and Personal Bankruptcy," *Federal Reserve Bank of Richmond, Economic Quarterly*, Vol. 90, No. 2, Spring 2004. The information on bankruptees' depression is cited at http://www .bankruptcylawinformation.com/index.cfm?event=dspStats.

The "capitalism without bankruptcy" quotation, attributed to Frank Borman, former CEO of Eastern Air Lines, was cited in Liz Pulliam Weston, "Why Going Broke Is a Fact of Life in America," accessed January 2007, at http://moneycentral.msn.com/content/specials/P87467 .asp?special/bankrupt.

Non-Profiteers

Growth statistics on the nonprofit, for-profit, and government sectors come from the Independent Sector, *Nonprofit Almanac: Facts and Findings*, "Employment in the Nonprofit Sector," 2001, accessed at http://www.independentsector.org/PDFs/npemployment.pdf.

Data on the superrich come from "The Business of Giving," *The Economist*, February 26, 2006.

Data on foundation growth come from the United States Nonprofit Sector, National Council of Nonprofit Associations, 2006, accessed January 2007, at http://www.nonprofitcongress.org/ sites/nonprofitcongress.org/files/theme editor/npcongress/us sector report.pdf. Data on growth of nonprofit organizations come from Thomas H. Pollak and Amy Blackwood, "The Nonprofit Sector in Brief: Facts and Figures from the Nonprofit Almanac 2007," Urban Institute, 2006, accessed January 2007, at http://www.urban.org/publications/311373.html.

Data on nonprofit entry-level salaries come from R. Patrick Halpern, "Workforce Issues in the Nonprofit Sector: Generational Leadership Change and Diversity," American Humanics: Initiative for Nonprofit Sector Careers, May 2006 (hereafter "Humanics Study", accessed January 2007, at http://www.humanics.org/atf/cf/%7BE02C99B2-B9B8-4887-9A15-C9E973FD5616%7D/American%20Humanics%20Workforce%20Literature%20Review% 20and%20Bibliography%204-26-06.pdf. The Pennsylvania study was cited in Bob Fernandez and Patricia Horn, "Nonprofits' Job Engine Transforms PA Economy," *Philadelphia Inquirer*, August 28, 2005.

Data on nonprofit executive salaries come from Noelle Barton, Maria Di Mento, and Alvin P. Sanoff, "Top Nonprofit Executives See Healthy Pay Raises," *Philanthropy.com*, September 28, 2006, accessed January 2007, at http://www.philanthropy.com/free/articles/v18/i24/24003901 .htm.

Survey data on the need to rein in corporations come from David W. Moore, "Little Political Fallout from Business Scandals," Gallup News Service, July 8, 2002, accessed January 2007, at http://www.galluppoll.com/content/?ci=6340&pg=1.

Survey data on Americans' trust in government come from Jeffrey Jones, "Trust in Government Declining, Near Lows for the Past Decade," Gallup News Service, September 26, 2006; accessed January 2007, at http://www.galluppoll.com/content/?ci=24706&pg=1.

Useful articles on social entrepreneurship include Emily Eakin, "How to Save the World? Treat It like a Business," *New York Times*, December 20, 2003; and Nicholas Kristof, "Do-Gooders with Spreadsheets," *New York Times*, January 30, 2007. See also David Bornstein, *How to Change the World: Social Entrepreneurship and the Power of New Ideas* (Oxford University Press, 2004).

Data on generational regard for nonprofits come from Harris Poll No. 33, April 27, 2006, http://www.harrisinteractive.com/harris poll/index.asp?PID=657.

Data on women in nonprofits, as well as on nonprofit employee turnover, come from Humanics Study, cited above.

Jim Collins, *Good to Great and the Social Sectors: A Monograph to Accompany Good to Great* (HarperCollins 2005).

XI. Looks and Fashion

Uptown Tattooed

The 2003 Harris poll is summarized by Joy Sever, Ph.D., at "A Third of Americans with Tattoos Say They Make Them Feel More Sexy," October 8, 2003, accessed October 2006, at http://www.harrisinteractive.com/news/allnewsbydate.asp?NewsID=691. The full poll is accessible at http://www.harrisinteractive.com/harris poll/index.asp?PID=407.

The AAD study was reported by Andrew Bridges, "Survey: 24 Percent Between 18–50 Tattooed," Associated Press, June 10, 2006.

The Canadian study is Health Canada, "Special Report on Youth, Piercing, Tattooing and Hepatitis C Trendscan Findings," March 2001.

For more on celebrity tattoos, see http://www.vanishingtattoo.com/celebrity tattoos.htm or http://www.celebritytattoos.org/.

The George Shultz rumor is reported in a Hoover Institute interview with the former secretary of state at http://www.hoover.org/publications/digest/5956876.html, among other places.

For more on military policy regarding tattoos, see Katie Zezima, "Yes, the Military Needs Bodies, but Hold the Bodywork," New York Times, December 3, 2005; and J. D. Leipold, "Army Changes Tattoo Policy," Army News Service, March 18, 2006.

For more on the body as billboard, see Frank Eltman, "Your Ad Permanently Tattooed Here, There, and Everywhere on New York Man's Body," Associated Press, January 29, 2005; and Melanie Wells, "Hey, Is That an Advertisement on Your Arm?," USA Today, July 23, 1999.

Another useful article was David Brooks, "Nonconformity Is Skin Deep," New York Times, August 27, 2006.

Snowed-Under Slobs

How much Americans spend on getting organized comes from Penelope Green, "Saying Yes to Mess," New York Times, December 21, 2006.

The PSB poll of slobs was conducted online on April 5–6, 2007.

The book is Eric Abrahamson and David H. Freedman, A Perfect Mess: The Hidden Benefits of Disorder—How Crammed Closets, Cluttered Offices, and On-the-Fly Planning Make the World a Better Place (Little, Brown, 2006).

Surgery Lovers

All citations to the survey of plastic surgeons refer to the "American Academy of Facial Plastic and Reconstructive Surgery 2005 Membership Survey: Trends in Plastic Surgery," released February 2006. The survey included 233 completed questionnaires, with data tabulated by ICR in Media, Pennsylvania.

Income data was cited in Paige Herman and Marie Kuechel, "Cosmetic Surgery Has Gone Mainstream," Ventura County Star, January 8, 2006.

Data on men's surgeries and on the plastic surgery industry generally come from "Cosmetic Plastic Surgery Research Statistics and Trends for 2001–2005," Plastic Surgery Research, http://www.cosmeticplasticsurgerystatistics.com/statistics.html, accessed August 2006.

"Scalpel slaves" were identified early in Paddy Calistro, "Looks: Slaves to the Scalpel," Los Angeles Times, July 19, 1987; and Jennet Conant et al., "Scalpel Slaves Just Can't Quit," Newsweek, January 11, 1988.

The Dowd reference comes from Maureen Dowd, *Are Men Necessary?: When Sexes Collide* (G. P. Putnam's Sons, 2005), pp. 247–48, quoting Alex Kuczynski.

More on the medical beauty business can be found in Natasha Singer, "More Doctors Turning to the Business of Beauty," *New York Times*, November 30, 2006.

Most of the data in the International Picture come from "Consumer Attitudes Towards Aging: A Global ACNielsen Report," November 2006, http://www2.acnielsen.com/reports/documents/ global aging attitudes nov06.pdf, accessed Januasry 2007. Other sources include a study by AGB Nielsen Media Research and Men's Health on South Korean men and plastic surgery, cited in Burt Herman, "S. Korea Sees Boom in Male Plastic Surgery," Associated Press, April 16, 2006; Frances Harrison, "Wealthy Iranians Embrace Plastic Surgery," *BBC News*, October 1, 2006; "Bargain Basement Plastic Surgery in Kurdistan," *Iraq Slogger*, March 6, 2007; and Sergio DeLeon, "Tourists Heading to Colombia for Plastic Surgery," *USA Today*, March 14, 2006.

Powerful Petites

The Peter Gabriel song is "Big Time," from the *So* album by Geffen Records, 1986.

The *New York Times* article that started the petite flap was Michael Barbaro, "Where's the Petite Department? Going the Way of the Petticoat," *New York Times*, May 28, 2006, followed up by Michael Barbaro, "By Demand, Saks Revives Petite Department," *New York Times*, June 20, 2006.

Other key articles on this issue included Joy Sewing and Mary Vuong, "A Tall Order," *Houston Chronicle*, June 8, 2006; Jean Patteson, "For Petites, a Shrinking Debate Grows," *Orlando Sentinel*, June 23, 2006; Tanya Barrientos, "Petites Are Becoming the Odd-Woman-Out in Stores," *Philadelphia Inquirer*, June 26, 2006; and Anne Bratskeir, "No Small Fuss," *Newsday*, July 10, 2006.

Life expectancy data come from National Center for Health Statistics, United States, 2005, with Chartbook on Trends in the Health of Americans, Hyattsville, MD, 2005, Table 27, "Life Expectancy at Birth, at 65 Years of Age, and at 75 Years of Age, According to Race and Sex: United States, Selected Years 1900–2003," accessed October 2006, at http://www.cdc.gov/nchs/ data/hus/hus05.pdf#027.

For more on the state of America's sizes, see Leslie Earnest, "What's with Women's Clothing Sizes?," *Los Angeles Times*, May 1, 2005.

For more on the remeasuring of America, see Michael D. Sorkin, "Survey Sizes Up America for the Perfect Fit," *St. Louis Post-Dispatch*, March 7, 2004.

Survey data on the average American woman's discomfort with current styles and sizes come from a study done by Lifestyle Monitor, reported on the Web site of Cotton Incorporated and accessed January 2007, at http://www.cottoninc.com/lsmarticles/?articleID=356.

XII. Technology
Social Geeks

The data cited in this chapter come from a poll PSB did in conjunction with Microsoft's Market Research Group in September 2005. Thanks to Microsoft for their permission to use the study.

For more on Tila Tequila, see Lev Grossman, "Tila Tequila," *TIME*, December 16, 2006.

Data on degrees conferred by specific fields of study were taken from Table 252, "Bachelor's, Master's and Doctor's Degrees Conferred by Degree-Granting Institution, by Sex of Student and Field of Study: 2003–04," *Digest of Education Statistics: 2005*, National Center for Education Statistics, <http://nces.ed.gov/programs/digest/d05/tables/dt05_252.asp>, accessed March 2007.

New Luddites

The 2003 Pew Center study is Amanda Lenhart, "The Ever-Shifting Internet Population," Pew Internet and American Life Project, April 16, 2003. This study's description of Net Dropouts, pp. 21–23, was particularly useful.

Other articles useful to describing the attitudes of New Luddites include Kevin Cowherd, "Teen's Missionary Zeal for Technology Can't Convert Luddite Dad," *St. Paul Pioneer Press*, March 12, 2006; Ken Spencer Brown, "Wi-Fis, PDAs, Blogs, Smart Phones, PVRs, Hmm . . . Overload?," *Investor's Business Daily*, November 7, 2005; and Richard Seven, "Life Interrupted," *Seattle Times*, November 28, 2004.

For more on the faltering plan to allow cell phones on airplanes, see Paul Davidson, "Jet Passengers May Not Get to Chat on Cell Phones After All," *USA Today*, March 22, 2007.

Tech Fatales

The Consumer Electronics Association data on women outspending men on technology were cited in Yuki Noguchi, "On Cellphones, Girl Talk Comes with a Bling Tone," *Washington Post*, December 6, 2006. That article also describes the bejeweled phones having great success with young women purchasers.

The data on wholesale dollars influenced by women over time were provided by the Consumer Electronics Association (CEA).

The CEA market research on gadgets preferred by male and female teenagers was reported in Jack Schofield, "Toys for Boys and Girls: Technology Companies Must Come to Grips with the Fact That More Women than Men Now Buy Gadgets," *The Guardian* (London), February 10, 2006.

The Best Buy efforts are reported at Mindy Fetterman, "Best Buy Gets in Touch with Its Feminine Side," *USA Today*, December 20, 2006. Radio Shack's status was reported at "Study: Women Buy More Tech than Men," www.cnn.com, January 16, 2004.

The survey data of women's experiences shopping in technology stores were reported at May Wong, "Consumer Electronics Has Challenge: Wooing Women," *Ventura County Star*, January 14, 2004.

What women want in electronics comes from research done by Motorola, as reported in "On Cellphones, Girl Talk Comes with a Bling Tone," cited above.

Sharp's efforts were reported at "Shopping for Electronics: Isn't Just a Guy Thing," Associated Press, January 22, 2004.

Car-Buying Soccer Moms

To see the Superbowl commercials, check out http://www.ifilm.com/superbowl/2005.

The data on women's experience in automobile showrooms come from numerous sources, including "Survey Finds 77 Percent of Women Car Buyers Continue to Bring Man Along to Dealership," accessed June 2006, at http://www.theautochannel.com/news/2006/06/01/009311/html.

For more on La Femme, see Edmunds.com, "Winning Women Over in the Car-Buying Process," accessed June 2006, at http://www.autotrader.com/research/shared.article.jsp?article id=3883&refpage=buyingtip . . .

The Kelley Blue Book data on male versus female car-buyers were reported in Dan Lienert, "The Best-Selling Cars by Gender," *Forbes*, May 24, 2005.

For more on the Volvo Concept Car designed by women, see "Women Design Concept Car for Volvo," USA Today, March 2, 2004, accessed June 2006, at http://www.usatoday.com/money/autos/2004-03-02-ycc x.htm.

Data on male vs. female preferences for cars and brands come from Dan Lienart, "Most Popular Cars for Men and Women," Forbes, June 27, 2006; and the Auto Channel, accessed June 2006, at http://www.theautochannel.com/news/2005/07/11/137213.html.

The quotation by Marc Graham, president of Juffy Lube, was first reported at Leslie Toussaint, "No Longer an Afterthought: Women and the Aftermarket," Aftermarket Insider, Vol. 9, 2001; accessed June 2006, at http://4wheeldrive.about.com/gi/dynamic/offsite.htm?zi=1/XJ&sdn=4 wheeldrive&cdn=autos&tm=19&gps=406 984 1020 580&f=10&su=p284.7.420.ip p706.3.420 .ip &tt=2&bt=0&bts=1&zu=http%3A//www.aftermarket.org/Information/AftermarketInsider/women.asp.

XIII. Leisure and Entertainment
Archery Moms?

All of the sports participation data in this chapter come from the National Sporting Goods Association study, "2005 Youth Participation in Selected Sports with Comparisons to 1995," accessed January 2007, at http://www.nsga.org/public/pages/index.cfm?pageid=158. The data include, but are not limited to, youth participation.

Baseball data come from Joseph Carroll, "Football Reaches Historic Popularity Levels in Gallup Poll," January 19, 2007. Hockey data come from Tim Lemke, "Power Play," Washington Times, October 4, 2006.

For more on the rise of snowboarding, see Anne E. Wright, "It's All Downhill," Albuquerque Journal, February 15, 2004.

For more on teen viewing and playing habits, see David Wharton, "Generation Gap: Traditional Sports Don't Have Same Pull with Today's Teens," Los Angeles Times, May 7, 2002.

Lacrosse data come from Pete Thamel, "Lacrosse Is Coming into New Territory," New York Times, May 30, 2005. Fencing data come from Jacqueline L. Salmon, "Exploring New Fields: Other Sports Gain Popularity as Kids Discover Life Beyond Soccer," Washington Post, August 15, 2001. For more on USA Dance, see http://www.usabda.org/.

For more on Fantasy Fishing, see Kevin J. Delaney, "'Fantasy Fishing' Leagues Hook Interested Parties," Associated Press Financial Wire, July 20, 2006.

The data on the Olympic Games come from http://www.olympic.org/uk/games/past/index uk.asp?OLGT=2&OLGY=2006.

"Most Popular Male Athlete" is a Harris Interactive online poll, reported at, "Tiger Takes No. 1 Spot in Harris Poll of Fans," Associated Press, June 9, 2006, accessed January 2007, at http://sports.espn.go.com/espn/news/story?id=2476502.

XXX Men

The data on porn-watchers come from "Pornography Statistics 2007," accessed at http://internet-filter-review.toptenreviews.com/internet-pornography-statistics.html, and "Internet Pornography Statistics," accessed at http://www.mykidsbrowser.com/pornography stats.php.

As of spring 2007, an average Major League Baseball game had a Nielsen rating of about 2.4, which translates into fewer than 3 million households watching.

Articles useful for the data on porn consumption include Eric Retzlaff, "Pornography's Grip Tightened by Way of Internet," *National Catholic Register*, June 13, 2000; and Dennah Gresh, "A Decent Proposal: How to Take the High Road in a Low-Rise, Skin-Is-in-Society," *Today's Christian Woman*, May/June 2003.

The data on the size of the porn industry and its share in cyberspace come largely from the Pornography Statistics Web sites cited above.

The *Investor's Business Daily* article on porn and technology is Patrick Seitz, "High Def's Adult Situation Favors Toshiba," *Investor's Business Daily*, March 2, 2006. Thanks to Milo Jones, University of Kent, for steering us toward this insight.

Information on the declining age of Americans' first sex comes from Durex's *2004 Sex Survey*, accessed at http://www.durex.com/cm/GSS2004Results.asp. That survey was also used for global data regarding porn-watching.

For the International Picture on porn, useful articles included Michael Field, "The Pacific Porn Paradise," *Dominion Post* (Wellington, New Zealand), December 17, 2005; "Italy Probes Porn on a Mobile Network," *Global News Wire—Asia Africa Intelligence Wire*, May 6, 2006; Matt Richtel and Michael Marriott, "Ring Tones, Cameras, Now This: Sex Is Latest Cellphone Feature," *New York Times*, September 17, 2005; Phermsak Lilakul, "Survey: Youth Well Versed in Internet Porn, *The Nation* (Thailand), October 10, 2002; "Porn a Major Presence in Lives of Youth," UPI, February 26, 2007; and "African's 'Porn Centre' Seeks Cash," *BBC News*, December 14, 2004.

Video Game Grown-ups

Most of the data in this chapter come from Entertainment Software Association, "2006 Sales, Demographic and Usage Data: Essential Facts About the Computer and Video Game Industry."

Other useful resources included Mike Johansson, "Game On!," *Rochester Democrat and Chronicle*, May 21, 2004; Roy Rivenburg, "Plan Your Funeral or Play Nintendo," *Los Angeles Times*, October 26, 2006; and Mike Sneider, "These Mind Games Do You Good," *USA Today*, April 18, 2006; and Paige Craig.

For more on serious games, see Josh Schollmeyer, "Games Get Serious," *Bulletin of the Atomic Scientists*, Vol. 62, No. 4, July/August 2006.

Neo-Classicals

Useful articles for this trend, from which many of the cited statistics come, include Allan Kozinn, "Check the Numbers: Rumors of Classical Music's Demise Are Dead Wrong," *New York Times*, May 28, 2006; Ken Schwartz, "Classical Music Comes off Life Support," www. businesstoday.com, March 14, 2006; Barbara Jepson, "Classical, Now Without the 300-Year Delay," *New York Times*, March 26, 2006; Patrick Kavanaugh, "Rumors Greatly Exaggerated," *National Review*, June 30, 2003; and Robin Pogrebin, "Uncertain Times: Impulse Buyers Replace Ticket Subscriptions," *New York Times*, October 16, 2002.

Survey data on musical instruments at home come from the Gallup Organization, "American Attitudes Towards Music," conducted for the National Association of Music Merchants, March 2003, accessed January 2007, at http://www.amc-music.com/news/pressreleases/images/gallup/Gallup2003.ppt#281.6.

The older piano-player data come from Robin Schatz, "Your Inner Musician Is Just Waiting to Be Found," *BusinessWeek Lifestyle*, May 13, 2002, accessed January 2007, at http://www.businessweek.com/magazine/content/02 19/b3782107.htm.

The classicalarchives.com survey was accessed January 2007, at http://www.classical archives.com/demographics.html.

XIV. Education
Smart Child Left Behind

Articles useful to this chapter include Elissa Gootman, "Preschoolers Grow Older as Parents Seek an Edge," *New York Times*, October 19, 2006; "Parents Delay Kindergarten to Give Children an Edge" *New York Times*, April 27, 2004; "Postponing Kindergarten," *Chicago Tribune*, April 26, 2006; and Nara Schoenberg, "More Boys Finding They're Ahead of the Game When They're Held Behind," *Chicago Tribune*, April 25, 2006.

The term "Kindergarten Arms Race" was coined by Steve Sailer, "Redshirting: A Kindergarten Arms Race," UPI, July 25, 2002, accessed July 2006, at http://www.isteve.com/2002 Redshirting-A Kindergarten Arms Race.htm.

For doubts about the efficacy of red-shirting, see Michelle Keller, "'Academic Red-Shirting' Is Getting a Mixed Report Card," *Los Angeles Times*, July 5, 2006; Elaine Lapriore, "Delaying Kindergarten Has No Benefits," http://www.usc.edu/escnews/stories/12716.html, September 7, 2006; Hermine H. Marshall, "Opportunity Deferred or Opportunity Taken?: An Updated Look at Delaying Kindergarten Entry," *Beyond the Journal*, September 2003. But see also "Delaying Kindergarten: Effects on Test Scores and Child Care Costs," Pardee Rand Graduate School Research Brief, 2004.

For the data in the graph, we are indebted to Chris Chapman, program director, Early Childhood and Household Studies, National Center for Education Statistics, U.S. Department of Education, provided November 7, 2006.

America's Home-Schooled

The U.S. Department of Education study is D. Princiotta and S. Bielick, *Homeschooling in the United States: 2003* (NCES 2006-042), U.S. Department of Education. National Center for Education Statistics, Washington, D.C., 2006, accessible at http://nces.ed.gov/pubs2006/homeschool/. School-age population counts in 1999 and 2003 rely on http://www.census.gov/prod/2001pubs/p20-533.pdf and http://www.census.gov/prod/2005pubs/p20-554.pdf.

Data on students in charter schools come from U.S. Department of Education, National Center for Education Statistics, Schools and Staffing Survey (SASS), "Public School Questionnaire," 1999–2000, and "Charter School Questionnaire," 1999–2000, prepared December 2002.

Data on the size of the home-school industry come from "George Bush's Secret Army," *The Economist*, February 26, 2004.

The college policy information is taken from Tania Deluzuriaga, "Home School Phenomenon," *Orlando Sentinel*, June 12, 2005. The data on SAT's come from the Home School Legal Defense Association, accessible at http:www.hslda.org/docs/news/hslda/200105070.asp, and is based on information the HSLDA acquired from the College Board.

Spelling bee data come from the Web site of the National Spelling Bee, accessible at http://www.spellingbee.com/statistics.asp. Geography bee data come from the HSLDA Web site at http://www.hslda.org/docs/news/hslda/200305/200305300.asp.

Public opinion data on home-schooling come from Linda Lyons and Gary Gordon, "Homeschooling: Expanding Its Ranks and Reputation," reporting on a Phi Delta Kappa/ Gallup Poll study conducted May–June 2001.

All demographic data about home-schoolers come from the U.S. Department of Education study, cited above.

Data on home-school regulation come from the HSLDA Web site, at http://www.hslda .org/laws/.

Data on states proposing bills to let home-schooled students use public resources come from James Dao, "Schooled at Home, They Want to Play at School," *New York Times*, June 22, 2005.

International data come from the following sources: *The Home School Court Report*, a publication of Home School Legal Defense Association, Vol. 19, No. 5, September/October 2003; Tim Large, "Stay-at-Home Kids Shunning the System," *Daily Yomiuri* (Tokyo), September 2, 2000; Nechama Veeder, "Learning Without Lessons," *Jerusalem Post*, September 1, 2006; and Paul Belien, "2007 German Horror Tale; Nazi-Era Law Prosecutes Today's Home-Schoolers," *Washington Times*, February 28, 2007.

College Dropouts

All the celebrity college dropouts are reported at the Web site of the College Dropouts Alumni Association, accessed August 2006, at http://www.geocities.com/CollegePark/7734/ cdoaa.html; and/or http://www.answers.com/topic/college-dropout.

Trend data in college enrollment come from the Bureau of Labor Statistics, "College Enrollment and Work Activity of 2005 High School Graduates," released March 24, 2006, accessed July 2006, at http://www.bls.gov.news/release/hsgec.nr0.htm; and the National Center for Education Statistics, Digest of Education Statistics, 2005, accessed July 2006, at http://nces .ed.gov/programs/digest/d05/tables/dt05 182.asp.

College graduation data come from Laura Horn and Rachael Berger, "College Persistence on the Rise?," NCES 2005-156, U.S. Department of Education, cited in "Convergence: Trends Threatening to Narrow College Oppostunity in America," a project of the Institute for Higher Education Policy, April 2006 (hereafter "Convergence"), Figure 6, p. 11.

The *New York Times* article is David Leonhardt, "The College Dropout Boom," *New York Times*, May 24, 2005.

The rising number of college students failing to graduate was calculated by multiplying the rising college enrollment rates, reported by NCES at http://nces.ed.gov/programs/coe/2006/ section1/table.asp?tableID=443, by the steady nongraduation rate (34 percent), reported at Horn and Berger above.

Data on the costs of not graduating come from "Convergence," pp. i, 2.

The study on student debt was authored by Lawrence Gladieux and Laura Perna, "Borrowers Who Drop Out: A Neglected Aspect of the College Student Loan Trend," the National Center for Public Policy and Higher Education, May 2005. The cited *New York Post* article is Daphne Landau, "College Dropouts Costing the State $300 Million," *New York Post*, April 20, 2004.

Projections regarding undergraduate students come from "Convergence," p. 11–14.

Data on attitudes of college dropouts come from a PSB poll conducted October 5–6, 2006.

Numbers Junkies

Former Harvard president Larry Summers's speech was quoted in Peter Dizikes, "Civic Science," *Boston Globe*, April 30, 2006.

The Harvard and Yale data come from *Handbook for Students*, accessed at http://webdocs. registrar.fas.harvard.edu/ugrad handbook/current/ugrad handbook.pdf; and *Yale College Undergraduate Junior and Senior Majors, 1989–99 to 2005–06.*

STEM data come from the statement of Cornelia M. Ashby, director, education, workforce, and income security issues, on "Higher Education: Science, Technology, and Mathematics Trends and the Role of Federal Programs," published by the U.S. Government Accountability Office, May 3, 2006.

Key articles in the development of this chapter, from which some of the anecdotes are drawn, include Speed Weed, "POPSCI Goes to Hollywood," *Popular Science*, January 2007; and Jackie Burrell, "Number Mania TV Shows Go on Integer Alert," *Contra Costa Times* (CA), May 31, 2006.

The very wealthy math major is James Simons, former math major and math professor, and as of 2007 the head of his own hedge fund, Renaissance Technologies Corporation.

XV. International
Mini-Churched

The *New Yorker* cover was Saul Steinberg's *A View of New York from 9th Avenue*, and originally appeared on March 29, 1976.

The data on churchgoing in France and Germany come from Robert Manchin, "Religion in Europe: Trust Not Filling the Pews," the Gallup Poll for European Commission's Eurobarometer survey, September 21, 2004.

The first Peter Berger reference can be found in an article that was extremely helpful to this entire piece: Toby Lester, "Oh, Gods!," *Atlantic Monthly*, February 2002. The second comes from an excerpt from the Pew Forum's biennial Faith Angle Conference on Religion, Politics, and Public Life, "Religion in a Globalizing World," December 4, 2006, accessible at http://pewresearch.org/pubs/404/religion-in-a-globalizing-world.

David Barrett, George Kurian, and Todd Johnson, *World Christian Encyclopedia*, 2nd ed. (Oxford University Press, 2001), 2 vols. All references to it, including the descriptions of some of the religions, come from "Oh, Gods!," cited above.

Background on who joins NRMs comes largely from Vatican Sectarian for Promoting Christian Unity, "Sects or New Religious Movements: A Pastoral Challenge," *Vatican*, May 3, 1986, accessible at http://www.catholicculture.org/docs/doc view.cfm?recnum=1313.

For more on militant Islam as an example of rapid change, and the role of NRMs in law enforcement, see "Oh, Gods!," cited above.

International Home-Buyers

The Florida Realtor survey is National Association of Realtors, "The 2005 National Association of Realtors Profile of International Home Buyers in Florida," accessible at http:// www.realtor.org/Research.nsf/files/2005%20Profile%20of%of20International%20Buyers,pdf/ $FILE/2005%20Profile%20of%20International%20Buyers.pdf. This is also the source of the median home price figures and the buyer motivation data later in the chapter.

Helpful articles for data beyond Florida included Dick Hogan, "Euro, Low Airfares Boost Investments," *News-Press*, March 20, 2005; Ron Scherer, "House Not Home: Foreigners Buy

Up American Real Estate," *Christian Science Monitor*, July 15, 2005; and June Fletcher, "As US Buyer Pool Shrinks, US Sellers Look Abroad," *Wall Street Journal*, accessed April 2007, at http://www.realestatejournal.com/buysell/markettrends/20050407-fletcher.html.

Comparative currency data were reported in "Euro, Low Airfares Boost Investments," cited above.

For more on multi-currency mortgages, see Kelly Griffith, "Foreign Banks Can Choose Mortgages in Their Currencies, *Orlando Sentinel*, June 7, 2006.

The Middle Eastern and Latin American preferences for home design were suggested in Judy Stark, "Home Away from Home," *St. Petersburg Times*, February 19, 1994.

For more on the California bill, see "Stirring It Up: Doolittle Wants Loan Barriers for Foreigners," *Sacramento Bee*, March 6, 2007 (editorial).

Regarding the surveys on isolationism, see Andrew Kohut, "Tracking American Isolationism: Speak Softly and Carry a Smaller Stick," *New York Times*, March 25, 2006; and "America's Place in the World 2005: Opinion Leaders Turn Cautious, Public Looks Homeward," the Pew Research Center and the Council on Foreign Relations, released November 17, 2005.

LAT Couples (U.K.)

The data on British LATers come from a news release from National Statistics, "First Estimates of the Number of People 'Living Apart Together' in Britain, Population Trends 122 — Winter 2005," accessed December 2006, at http://www.statistics.gov.uk/pdfdir/poptrends1205 .pdf.

British marriage rate statistics come from Office for National Statistics FM2, Table 2.2, accessed December 2006, at http://www.statistics.gov.uk/downloads/theme population/Table 2a Marriage rates.xls.

Articles useful to this trend included Katy Guest, "The Love Issue," *Independent on Sunday* (London), February 12, 2006; Celia Brayfield, "One Heart, Two Homes," *The Times* (London), September 21, 2004; and Jasper Gerard, "Semi-Attached Couple," *The Sunday Times* (London) February 23, 1992.

Data on North American LATers come from Anne Milan and Alice Peters, "Couples Living Apart," *Canadian Social Trends*, Summer 2003, Statistics Canada, Catalogue No. 11-008.

The National Association of Home Builders Survey was cited in Tracie Rozhon, "To Have, Hold, and Cherish, Until Bedtime," *New York Times*, March 11, 2007.

Mammonis (Italy)

Data on Italian men living at home were taken largely from Marco Manacorda and Enrico Moretti, "Why Do Most Italian Young Men Live with Their Parents? Intergenerational Transfers and Household Structure," Centre for Economic Policy Research, June 2005, <http://www.cepr.org/pubs/dps/DP5116.asp>, accessed November 2006.

Other helpful articles included "Italian Parents Under Accusation," *La Repubblica*, February 3, 2006 (thanks to Enzo Caiazzo, CEO of Alenia, Inc., and Kristin Uzun, for help in translation); Gary Picariello, "In Italy—Living at Home Well into Your 30s Is Perfectly Normal," *Associated Content*, 2006; Donald MacLeod, "Italian Mammas Making Offers Their Sons Can't Refuse," *Guardian Unlimited*, February 3, 2006; and Deidre Van Dyke, "Parlez-Vous Twixter," *Time*, January 16, 2004.

Birth rate data come from "The World Factbook, Rank Order—Total Fertility Rate," March 15, 2007, <https://www.cia.gov/cia/publications/factbook/rankorder/2127rank.html>, accessed March 2007.

Eurostars

All data on total fertility rates come from United Nations Statistics Division, Social Indicators, Indicators on Child-Bearing, accessed January 2007, at http://unstats.un.org/unsd/demographic/products/socind/childbr.htm.

Useful articles for this chapter included Elisabeth Rosenthal, "European Union's Plunging Birthrates Spread Eastward," *New York Times*, September 4, 2006; Jeffrey Fleishman, "No Dearth of Births in This Town," *Los Angeles Times*, September 14, 2006; and Frank Bruni, "Persistent Drop in Fertility Reshapes Europe's Future," *New York Times*, December 26, 2002.

British marriage statistics, and all the British childbearing data cited below, come from Mike Dixon and Julia Margo, "Population Politics," Institute of Public Policy Research, February 19, 2006, pp. 80–85, accessed September 2006, at http://www.ippr.org.uk/publicationsandreports/publication.asp?id=341.

The figure on childbearing by educated German women comes from Lionel Shriver, "No Kids Please, We're Selfish," *The Guardian* (London), September 17, 2005.

The U.S. fertility rate analysis by 2004 red and blue states comes from Phillip Longman, "The Liberal Baby Bust," *USA Today*, March 13, 2006.

The generation gap analysis was cited in "Half a Billion Americans?," *The Economist*, August 22, 2002.

Data on the growth on Only Children come from "Female Population by Age and Total Number of Children Born Alive and Urban/Rural Residence, Each Census: 1948–1997," United Nations Demographic Yearbook, Historical Supplement, accessed January 2007, at http://unstats.un.org/unsd/demographic/sconcerns/natality/nat2.htm.

Helpful birth order articles included Kate Lorenz, "Oldest, Middle, Youngest: Who's More Successful?," accessed January 2007, at http://www.careerbuilder.ca/CA/JobSeeker/CarrerAdvice/ViewArticle.aspx?articleid=126&cb RecursionCnt=2&cbsid=41106e22d7764f2 d82054e70adfd763c-231267953-JJ-5; and "Birth Order," Child Development Institute, accessed October 2006, at http://www.childdevelopmentinfo.com/development/birth order.htm.

Vietnamese Entrepreneurs

Useful articles on this trend, from which some data are cited, include Keith Bradsher, "Vietnam's Roaring Economy Is Set for World Stage," *New York Times*, October 25, 2006; "The Middle Class Has Landed," *Vietnam Investment Review*, 2006, accessed at http://www.vir.com.vn/Client/VIR/index.asp?url-content.asp&doc=11907; "Good Morning at Last," *The Economist*, August 5, 2006; and "The Good Pupil: Vietnam's Economy," *The Economist*, May 8, 2004.

The Gallup data on optimism come from Gallup International Voice of the People Survey, press release, December 18, 2006.

French Teetotalers

International alcohol consumption data come from the Global Status Report on Alcohol 2004, World Health Organization, Department of Mental Health and Substance Abuse

(Geneva, 2004). French data in particular are accessible at http://www.who.int/substance abuse/publications/en/france.pdf.

Other data on the decrease in French wine consumption come from "Lawmakers Say French Youth Needs to Learn More About Wine Appreciation, Associated Press, December 6, 2006.

Information on French eating habits comes from "French Eating Habits," at www .EnjoyFrance.com, September 6, 2005, accessed April 2007.

Discussion of French and U.S. experience with crackdowns on drunk-driving was informed by Keith B. Richburg, "European Laws Place Emphasis on the Driving, Not the Drinking," *Washington Post*, December 30, 2004.

For more on classifying wine as a food, see Elaine Sciolino, "A Campaign to Drink Another Glass of Wine for France," *New York Times*, July 23, 2004.

The real book is Mireille Guiliano, *French Women Don't Get Fat*, (Alfred A Knopf, 2005).

The French smoking data come from Caroline Wyatt, "Bidding Goodbye to the Gauloises," *BBC News*, February 1, 2007, accessed April 2007.

The French wine industry's troubles are well documented in Peter Gumbel, "Too Much of a Good Thing," *TIME*, October 19, 2006.

Chinese Picassos

Key articles on Chinese art useful to this chapter included "Chinese Paintings Enjoy Increasing Popularity," www.china.org, June 30, 2005, accessed February 2007, at http:// www.china.org.cn/english/culture/133552.htm: "China Industry: Chinese Contemporary Art Catches On in a Big Way, *EIU Views Wire*, August 29, 2005; David Barboza, "China's Boom Industry?," *International Herald Tribune*, January 5, 2007; Julie Mehta, "Contemporary Chinese Art Finds a Place in Art History," *Art Business News*, November 1, 2003; Will Bennett, "China's New Millionaires See Capital Gain in Art," *Financial Times* (London), September 30, 2006; Will Bennett, "China Opens Up to Art Auctions," *The Telegraph* (London), January 1, 2005; and "Appreciating Oils: China's Art Market," *The Economist*, April 9, 2005.

The John Adams quotation is John Adams to Abigail Adams, [12 May 1780], *Adams Family Correspondence*, 3:342, accessed February 2007, at http://www.masshist.org/adams/quotes.cfm.

The Dafen story is told in "Painting by Numbers: China's Art Business," *The Economist*, June 10, 2006.

For more on Western museums' expansion plans, see Alan Riding, "France Frets as Louvre Looks Overseas," *New York Times*, January 1, 2007.

Information on other countries' growing GDPs comes from the International Monetary Fund, World Economic and Financial Surveys, World Economic Outlook Database, September 2006 edition, accessed March 2007, at http://www.imf.org/external/pubs/ft/weo/2006/02/data/index.aspx.

Russian Swings

The 1991 Pulse of Europe Survey, as well as all subsequent 2006 data on Russian views toward democracy, are reported at the Pew Global Attitudes Project, "Russia's Weakened Democratic Embrace," January 5, 2006, accessed February 2006, at http://pewglobal.org/reports/display.php?ReportID=250.

The Russian success story of the last decade is largely chronicled at Jason Bush, "Russia: How Long Can the Fun Last?," *BusinessWeek*, December 18, 2006, accessed February 2006, at http://www.businessweek.com/magazine/content/06 51/b4014056.htm.

Data on Russian safety and corruption come from Sergei Gradirovski and Neli Esipova, "Security in Russia: The Hoodlum Must Pay!", Gallup News Service, January 4, 2007; and Sergei Gradirovski and Neli Esipova, "Corruption in Russia: Is Bribery Always Wrong?", Gallup News Service, October 15, 2006.

Useful articles on Russian political developments in 2006 and 2007 include "Richer, Bolder—and Sliding Back—Russia," *The Economist*, July 15, 2006; Fred Hiatt, "Kasparov's Gambit," *Washington Post*, February 12, 2007; Steven Lee Myers, "Russians to Vote, but Some Parties Lose in Advance," *New York Times*, February 15, 2007; and Thom Shanker and Mark Landler, "Putin Says U.S. Is Undermining Global Stability," *New York Times*, February 11, 2007.

The 2006 survey reporting Russian wariness of President Putin's tactics is "The Putin Popularity Score: Increasingly Reviled in the West, Russia's Leader Enjoys Broad Support at Home," by Richard Morin, Pew Global Attitudes Project, and Nilanthi Samaranayake, Pew Research Center for the People and the Press, December 6, 2006.

Indian Women Rising

The Indian economic success story, combined with its challenges, is largely told at Haroon Siddiqui, "India: Misery and Magic," *Toronto Star*, February 8, 2007.

For more on Indian literacy, see O. P. Sharma, "2001 Census Results Mixed for India's Women and Girls," *Population Today*, May/June 2001; accessed March 2007, at http://www.prb.org/Articles/2001/2001CensusResultsMixedforIndiasWomenandGirls.aspx.

The urban employment growth figures come from the NSS Report No. 520: "Employment and Unemployment Situations in Cities and Towns in India, 2004–2005," National Sample Survey Organization, Ministry of Statistics and Programme Implementation, Government of India, March 2006. Helpful analysis can be found in C. P. Chandrasekhar and Jayati Ghosh, "Women Workers in Urban India," February 6, 2007, accessed March 2007, at. http://www.macroscan.org/fet/feb07/fet060207Women Workers.htm.

For more on high abortion rates of girl fetuses, see Scott Baldauf, "India's Girl Deficit Deepest Among Educated," *Christian Science Monitor*, January 13, 2006.

For more on parliamentary quotas for women, see P. Jayaram, "Bill to Reserve MP Seats for Indian Women in Limbo," *Straits Times*, December 9, 2006; and "MP Reserves 50% for Women in Local Bodies," *Indian Express Online Media Ltd Source: Financial Times*, March 31, 2007.

The research on the impact of female legislators was conducted by Irma Clots-Figueras, "Women in Politics: Evidence from the Indian States," January 24, 2005, accessed March 2007, at http://sticerd.lse.ac.uk/dps/pepp/PEPP%2014.pdf.

For more on Naina Lal Kidwai, see S. Prasannarajan "Power Pyramid," *India Today*, March 26, 2007. For more on Kiran Mazumdar Shaw, see Sudip Mazumdar, "First Lady," *Newsweek*, October 18, 2006. For more on Mira Nair, see http://www.mirabaifilms.com/home.html.

Data on Indian students in America come from "Open Doors 2006, Report on International Educational Exchange, Leading 20 Places of Origin 2004/5 and 2005/6," accessed April 2007, at http://opendoors.iienetwork.org/?p=89189.

For more on Indra Nooyi, see "Indra Nooyi Is India Abroad Person of the Year," Rediff India Abroad, March 24, 2007, accessed April 2007, at http://www.rediff.com/news/2007/mar/24iapoy.htm. For more on Kalpana Chawla, see NASA Web site at http://www.jsc.nasa.gov/Bios/htmlbios/chawla.html. For more on Swati Dandekar, see http://www.swatidandekar.com/. For more on Sania Mirza, see Randeep Ramesh, "Fatwa Orders Indian Tennis Star to Cover Up," *The Guardian* (London), September 10, 2005.

Educated Terrorists

The Terrorism Knowledge Base, accessible at http://www.tkb.org, is the self-described "one-stop resource for comprehensive research and analysis on global terrorist incidents, terrorism-related court cases, and terrorist groups and leaders." It integrates data from the RAND Terrorism Chronology and RAND-MIPT Terrorism Incident databases, the Terrorism Indictment database, and DFI International's research on terrorist organizations, and is funded through the U.S. Department of Homeland Security's Office of Grants and Training.

Key articles for this chapter include Bruce Hoffman, "We Can't Win if We Don't Know the Enemy," *Washington Post*, March 25, 2007; George Packer, "Knowing the Enemy," *New Yorker*, December 18, 2006; Daniel Pipes, "God and Mammon: Does Poverty Cause Militant Islam?," *National Interest*, Winter 2002; and Alan B. Krueger and Jitka Maleckova, "Seeking the Roots of Terrorism," *Chronicle of Higher Education*, June 6, 2003. In particular, the studies on terrorists in Egypt, Lebanon, and Israel are summarized in the latter piece.

Marc Sageman's book, *Understanding Terror Networks* (University of Pennsylvania Press, 2004), is helpfully excerpted in his Foreign Policy Research Institute e-note, November 1, 2004, accessed March 2007, at http://www.fpri.org/enotes/20041101.middleeast.sageman.understandingterrornetworks.html.

Index

Page numbers of charts and graphs appear in italics.

About Twelve

MISSION STATEMENT

TWELVE was established in August 2005 with the objective of publishing no more than one book per month. We strive to publish the singular book, by authors who have a unique perspective and compelling authority. Works that explain our culture; that illuminate, inspire, provoke, and entertain. We seek to establish communities of conversation surrounding our books. Talented authors deserve attention not only from publishers, but from readers as well. To sell the book is only the beginning of our mission. To build avid audiences of readers who are enriched by these works — that is our ultimate purpose.

For more information about forthcoming TWELVE books, you can visit us at www.twelvebooks.com.